READING
INSTRUCTION

READING INSTRUCTION

SECOND EDITION

Barbara D. Stoodt

University of North Carolina—Greensboro

HARPER & ROW, PUBLISHERS, New York
Cambridge, Philadelphia, St. Louis, San Francisco,
London, Singapore, Sydney, Tokyo

Sponsoring Editor: Alan McClare
Text Design Adaptation: North 7 Atelier Ltd.
Cover Design: CIRCA 86, Inc.
Cover Photo: Reading © Lew Merrium, Monkmeyer Press.
Text Art: Fineline Illustrations, Inc.
Photo Research: Mira Schachne
Production Manager: Jeanie Berke
Production Assistant: Beth Maglione
Compositor: ComCom Division of Haddon Craftsmen, Inc.
Printer and Binder: R. R. Donnelley & Sons Company

READING INSTRUCTION, Second Edition

Library of Congress Cataloging in Publication Data

Stoodt, Barbara D.
   Reading instruction.

   Includes bibliographies and index.
   1. Reading. 2. Reading—Language experience approach.
3. Reading comprehension. I. Title.
LB1050.S757 1989   372.4′1   88-24444
ISBN 0-06-046467-4

88 89 90 91 9 8 7 6 5 4 3 2 1

To Linda and Susan,
with Love, Mother

Contents

PART IV
THE INDIVIDUAL AND THE ELEMENTARY READING PROGRAM 337

Preface

Successful reading teachers are thinkers who constantly search for ways to guide children as they develop their love of reading. Their personal teaching styles grow out of reflection, knowledge, and experience. Through professional development (conferences, seminars, graduate courses, and the like), teachers are able to translate current research and educational thought into effective instructional strategies. This book helps teachers understand the importance of developing children's desire to read and identifies literature that excites them.

The second edition of *Reading Instruction* emphasizes whole language and combining whole language with other approaches. It has always been clear to me that children need to hear stories, write stories, and discuss stories to develop their reading ability. Children's trade books are introduced throughout the text as examples of literature to use in specific instances.

Reading Instruction also emphasizes thinking skills and higher-order thinking skills. Reading is a thinking process; reading fluency frees children to employ higher-order thinking skills to solve problems, make decisions, and think critically and creatively. Therefore, specific suggestions and models are included for teaching thinking skills.

This text is divided into four parts. Part I is the foundation for teaching reading, while Part II explores the skills of reading. Part III is concerned with the reading program and materials for teaching reading. Part IV addresses content reading and children's literature. Also included in Part IV is a chapter that explores the needs of special children who are mainstreamed in elementary school classrooms. Appendixes and a glossary are included at the end of the book. The appendixes include word and phrase lists, the Fry Readability Formula, and answers to the self-tests, included at the end of each chapter. The glossary defines key terms used in the book.

I wish to express my appreciation to my teachers, Dr. Robert Emans, Dr. Charlotte Huck, and Mrs. Avis Grace Dresbach, who have contributed enormously to my professional growth and development. I also wish to thank the reviewers whose suggestions and criticisms helped me think through and revise the several drafts of the manuscript:

Nancy S. Bailey, Metropolitan State College
Steve Hansell, Wright State University
Michael McKenna, Wichita State University
Don Pease, California State University—Fullerton
David Reinking, University of Georgia
Valerie M. Washington, Lehman College, CUNY
Donna Wiseman, Texas A&M University.

Thanks are also due to the staff at Harper & Row, Publishers, Inc.

Barbara D. Stoodt

PART

I

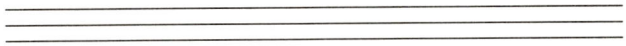

THE
FOUNDATIONS
OF READING

CHAPTER 1

Reading in Today's World

OVERVIEW This chapter creates a context for understanding elementary reading instruction in today's world. Understanding the nature of reading and the literacy requirements of our information-intensive society prepares teachers for their responsibility in helping children acquire this process. Readers process print to construct information, knowledge, and understanding in their minds; reading instructors need to address both process and product as they teach. Reading is a complex process, subject to influences like language, cognition, emotions, family and experiential background, and physical development. Understanding these factors helps teachers guide the elementary reading program.

Key Vocabulary

As you read this chapter, check your understanding of these terms

accountability	**job literacy gap**
competency testing	**literacy**
comprehension	**phonics**
context	**psycholinguistics**
critical reading	**schemata**
cultural literacy	**structural analysis**
decoding	**whole language**
interpretation	

Focusing Questions

As you read this chapter, think about these questions:

1. What is reading?
2. Why is reading important for contemporary youngsters?
3. How is cultural literacy related to the reading process?
4. What factors exert the greatest influence on reading skill?

READING SKILLS IN CONTEMPORARY LIFE

Reading is a basic life skill, the cornerstone of success in school and life. Contemporary life makes greater demands on our literacy skills than any other period of history. Naisbitt (1984) speaks of our society as literacy-intensive. Information is the primary product of our society; 90 percent of the new jobs created during the 1970s were information-, knowledge-, or service-related. Our literacy-intensive society generates massive amounts of information, exemplified in the following list:

- Between 6000 and 7000 scientific articles are written each day.
- Scientific and technical information now increases 13 percent each year, which means it doubles every 5.5 years.
- The rate of scientific information may soon jump to 40 percent per year; an increasing population of scientists will create new, more powerful information systems. This will mean a doubling of data every 20 months.
- By 1985 the volume of information grew between four and seven times what it was only a few years earlier (Naisbitt, 1984).

Clearly, the world has moved into a technological-information age requiring greater levels of literacy for full participation in education, science, business, industry, and the professions. As required reading levels have increased, the stigma associated with illiteracy has also increased. In the face of increased reading demands, high-school dropout rates are increasing and educational attainment has leveled off (Stedman and Kaestle, 1987). Functional literacy tests indicate that 20 percent of the adult population (30 million people) have serious difficulties with common reading tasks (Stedman and Kaestle, 1987). Furthermore, there is a growing discrepancy between the population's literacy level and the skills required to perform most of society's jobs (Mikulecky and Ehlinger, 1986; Mikulecky and Winchester, 1983). Stedman and Kaestle (1987) call this discrepancy the **job literacy gap**. Therefore, we must define literacy and the level of literacy needed to prevent the job literacy gap.

What Is Literacy?

Literacy is an elusive concept. The United States Census Bureau classifies **literacy** as the ability to read and to write a simple message in English or any other language (U.S. Bureau of the Census, 1971). Literacy is not a single skill, but a set of reading and writing skills that people have to varying degrees. Some individuals read well in one context but not in another. For example, they may read stories well, but may find it difficult to read content textbooks, or they may read the newspaper well, but may find it difficult to understand the printed directions for putting a lawn mower together.

Literacy skills, which are taught and measured in schools, are called reading and writing achievement. In the primary grades, children learn to read words in print they already know, and they learn to **decode** words that they do not recognize in print. Subsequently, they learn to acquire knowledge, information, and understanding from reading written language. During the high-school years, students learn to read content that involves more than one point of view. The highest level of reading is the ability to construct knowledge on a high level of abstraction, and to create one's own truth from the truths of others. This is achieved during the post high-school years (Chall 1983). Thus, acquiring literacy is a long-term process.

Literacy skills outside of schools are usually called "functional literacy." These skills are the reading and writing skills one needs to understand and use the printed material normally encountered in work, leisure, and citizenship (Stedman and Kaestle, 1987). The literacy demands of the workplace differ from those of schools (Mikulecky, 1982). Research indicates that adults need approximately twelfth-grade reading ability to read the ordinary written materials they encounter each day (Chall, 1983; Stoodt and Millhouser, 1979). These everyday reading materials include such materials as applications for credit, job applications, directions for constructing items purchased at discount stores, instructions for taking medication, ballots, directions for preparing TV dinners, and manuals that accompany automobiles and appliances.

In view of current data regarding the escalating reading demands of the workplace, some authorities recommend a renewed effort at literacy training. These efforts should include a monetary commitment as well as a close collaboration among educators, employers, community groups, and government agencies (Stedman and Kaestle, 1987; Kozol, 1985). Declining achievement and a high dropout rate led to efforts to make teachers and schools accountable (responsible) for teaching students to read.

Teacher Accountability for Literacy

The American public consistently blames teachers when reading achievement declines. However, the evidence indicates that reading achievement is not declining, but the reading demands of the workplace are increasing (Farr, Fay, and Negley, 1978; Eurich and Kraetsch, 1982). Thus, teachers must teach students to keep pace with the escalating reading demands of a literacy-intensive society. Competency testing of students and teachers establishes **accountability**. Increasing the requirements for licensing teachers and providing staff development for teachers helps them develop the skills to teach reading.

Competency testing is a means of monitoring students' reading achievement. Legislatures in many states have established minimum competency standards for high-school graduation, which include testing students' ability to read materials like driver's license applications, checks, television programming, insurance forms, and so forth (Pipho, 1978). To graduate from high school in most of the United States, students must pass examinations at a level established by state legislators. The majority of states also administer tests to elementary-grade students—in order to identify reading deficiencies before students reach high school; therefore, these problems can be remediated earlier in their educational career.

Competency testing is a controversial issue, very popular with some people as a reliable procedure that insures students will learn to read; however, various groups have objected to these tests. Some minority groups believe that competency testing discriminates against their members. Competency tests may influence curriculum because teachers may be encouraged to teach the skills and content that appear on the test. Some groups believe that the personnel who administer these tests and the atmosphere in which they are given could prevent students from successful completion of the tests. Many educators question whether a single test can, in fact, measure reading competency. Furthermore, such tests are not diagnostic; they do not identify the causes of reading failure.

Competency testing for teachers is a recent phenomenon. Some states administer a written examination, which teachers must pass at an acceptable level in order to retain their teaching positions. For example, the Texas Examination of Current Administrators and Teachers (TECAT) is a test of basic literacy (Shepard and Kreitzer, 1987). This test, like those used in some other states, was seen as a means of raising the public esteem for teachers and weeding out incompetents. Texas teachers prepared for the test with massive efforts; they reviewed basic skills and drilled on test format. After two tries, 99 percent of the 210,000 tested teachers passed (Shepard and Kreitzer, 1987).

Many teachers are self-motivated to increase their teaching competencies. These teachers refine their skills through participating in staff-development sessions sponsored by local school systems and professional organizations; some teachers may enroll in advanced graduate courses. Many teachers belong to such organizations as the International Reading Association (IRA), the National Council of Teachers of English (NCTE), the National Reading Conference (NRC), the Association for Supervision and Curriculum Development (ASCD), and the American Educational Research Association (AERA). Each of these organizations sponsors conferences and publishes professional materials that keep teaching professionals up-to-date on important issues and research in the field of education. The International Reading Association publishes three journals: *The Reading Teacher, Journal of Reading,* and *Reading Research Quarterly;* The National Reading Conference publishes the *Journal of Reading Improvement.*

The teacher-researcher movement represents still another approach to professionalization. Naturalistic research, which emphasizes observational data in classroom settings, has given momentum to this movement. Teacher-researchers, often in collaboration with other researchers, gather data that helps them understand teaching, learning, and the needs of individual students.

To seek information and research data, teachers may use professional journals as well as the Educational Resources Information Center (ERIC), which was established by the United States Office of Education, an agency of the federal government. The ERIC Center for Reading and Communication Skills is located at the headquarters of the National Council of Teachers of English in Urbana, Illinois. This center provides information related to the field of reading and computerized searches for information, which can be obtained through most college and university libraries.

An understanding of reading is one of teaching's basic needs. Subsequent sections of this chapter will develop your understanding of the reading process and the products of reading, which will enable teachers to extend literacy to their students.

WHAT IS READING?

Reading is the process of constructing meaning from written texts (Rumelhart, 1985). But what, in fact, are you doing when you read this page? This question has perplexed educators for a very long time. Reading is a covert activity, occurring in the brain, which makes it difficult to know precisely what happens during the process. We can see only such external manifestations as eye and lip movements. During reading, the eyes move across a line of print in jumps, stops, and regressions. The stops, which last for approximately a quarter of a second, are known as fixations. During fixations, the eyes send messages about the print to the brain. Regressions occur when the eyes move back to words previously seen. Regressions usually take place when the reader needs more information about a word, phrase, or sentence. Reading begins with the visual information sent to the brain.

You will find the discussion of reading more comprehensible if you understand the following key terms.

Comprehension is the ability to construct the author's message through experiential background, knowledge, language, and thinking skills.

Context refers to the use of word meaning and syntax as clues to an unknown word.

Critical reading is to evaluate those ideas that have been read.

Decoding is the ability to recognize words and associate meanings with them.

Interpretation is to infer meaning and to discover relationships among ideas. Readers use their experience and knowledge to infer. Interpretation is extremely important in reading because no text is completely self-explanatory, which means that readers must rely on existing knowledge to understand text.

Phonics is the relationship between spoken sounds and written symbols (letters), which is used to decode words.

Schemata is knowledge stored in memory, also known as abstract knowledge structure (Anderson and Pearson, 1984).

Structural analysis is the use of root words, prefixes, suffixes, inflectional endings, and contractions as units of meaning to aid word recognition.

The Reading Process

The brain coordinates a number of interrelated sources of information in order to read. These sources include linguistic data, prior knowledge (schemata), the conventions of print (punctuation, paragraphing, typography, spelling), decoding skills, story grammar, and expository grammar. Scientific research conducted over the past two decades has produced a more complex, unparalleled array of information about reading (Glaser, 1985). We now recognize that readers are more than decoders of the written word. Readers must constantly infer meanings that are not directly stated by the words of a text, but are, nonetheless, part of its essential content (Hirsch, 1987).

The following sentences illustrate the use of prior knowledge (Anderson et al. 1985):

1. The punter kicked the ball.
2. The baby kicked the ball.
3. The golfer kicked the ball.

Each sentence implies a different kind of ball. Readers must use prior knowledge to infer that the punter kicked a football, the baby kicked a different kind of ball, perhaps a plastic beach ball, and the golfer kicked a golf ball. Furthermore, readers should infer that each individual kicked in a different way. A punter is a trained kicker who is aiming for the goal line, while the baby may be irritated because he or she cannot throw the ball. A golfer presents still a different picture: he or she cannot legally kick a ball while it is in play.

Anderson et al. (1985) compare reading to the performance of a symphony orchestra. First, like performing a symphony, reading is a holistic act. Although reading can be segmented into subskills such as auditory discrimination and memorization of words, performing the subskills one at a time does not constitute reading. Reading occurs only when the separate parts are integrated. Second, success in both reading and playing a musical instrument comes from practice. Readers, like musicians, are involved in a lifelong endeavor. Third, as with a musical score, there may be more than one interpretation of a text. The interpretation depends on the background of the reader, the purpose for reading, and the context in which reading occurs.

Readers must also decode the majority of words in the text in order to associate related knowledge. Many readers automatically recognize most of the words in the text, but students who do not, must rely on the following strategies to help them identify unknown words. (See Chapters 3 and 4 for further discussion.)

1. looking at the **context**
2. using **structural analysis**
3. using **phonics** to approximate word pronunciation
4. looking for the word in a **dictionary**
5. asking another student or the teacher to pronounce the word

A *skills-based* explanation of the reading process, based on those *skills* associated with the reading process, is exemplified in the Gray-Robinson model. However, Gray (1960) concluded that the aspects of reading "are closely inter-related and form a psychologically coherent unit." Gray identified four major categories of skills, which include *word perception, comprehension, reaction, and assimilation.* Robinson (1966) added *rate* as a fifth major aspect of reading. Each skill component in the Gray-Robinson model is equally important.

Word perception is to identify and associate meaning with words in the text. Readers recognize words through memory (sight words), context clues, phonetic analysis, structural analysis, and dictionary usage. **Comprehension** skills are used to identify literal and implied ideas, as well as the significance of these ideas. Literal comprehension is to understand the ideas stated in the text. Inference skills are used to read between the lines in order to understand the author's meaning. To understand the significance of the author's ideas, the reader must identify the author's purpose, assumptions, generalizations, and conclusions. Readers read beyond the lines when they react to content. **Reaction** involves both critical and creative reading skills. **Critical reading** involves evaluating the text content and the author's qualifications; creative reading involves the readers' emotional response to the text. **Assimilation** is the ability to integrate written content with preexisting knowledge. The **rate** of reading should be adjusted to the type of content and the reader's purpose.

A **psycholinguistic** explanation of reading is based on the relationship among language, thought, and the learning process (Goodman, 1976). Psycho-linguists believe that language proficiency enables readers to anticipate (guess) the words on the page. For example, readers would anticipate a noun in the sentence " _____ ran down the street." Psycholinguists view reading as the ability to process meaning units, rather than decoding sounds in a one-to-one approach (as in a completely phonetic approach).

According to psycholinguists, readers' eyes move across the line of print, picking up minimal cues that enable them to "guess" the letters and words. These educated guesses are based on readers' knowledge of English and text meaning. When readers guess words incorrectly, their eyes regress along the line of print to obtain additional cues that will aid word recognition. Efficient readers use the following cues to identify words (Goodman, 1976).

1. cues within words (phonics, structural analysis, and sight words)
2. cues within the language of the text (syntax, repeated words and ideas, function words, and context)
3. internal cues (concept, experiential background, and language skills)
4. external cues (teacher, illustrations, charts, and dictionaries)

Goodman (1976) uses the term **miscues** to describe reading errors. He believes that miscues occur when a mismatch occurs between the reader's language and the book language; this mismatch causes the reader to anticipate words inaccurately. Miscues that do not change text meaning are not considered reading errors. A reader's miscues are illustrated with the insertions in the following sentence.

woods   *daddy*

The boy ran into the ~~forest~~ to find his ~~father~~.

The miscues in this example probably occurred because the words *woods* and *daddy* are commonly used in the reader's oral language and the expectation was created for reading these words. Note, however, that these miscues did not change the basic meaning of the content.

The psycholinguistic model of reading has led to the following commonly accepted understandings about the reading process and reading instruction:

1. Reading is not a precise, exact process.
2. Reading is a meaning-centered process. Efficient readers make intelligent guesses about content, which permit them to anticipate meaning. Beginning readers should be encouraged to read for overall meaning, not for word-by-word recognition.
3. Context is an important factor for reading. Readers may not know the meaning of an individual word until they read an entire sentence or paragraph. For example, the word *run* may refer to a run in a baseball game or a run in a stocking, depending on the context of the passage.
4. Reading skill is based on language competence.

Recently, Goodman (1985) has fine-tuned his psycholinguistic model to include more focus on the writing process, the characteristics of written language, and the process by which writers construct meaning. His new model is called **transactional psycholinguistics.**

Whole language explanations of the reading process are very similar to psycholinguistic theory. Whole language is based on the work of authorities like Platt (1984); Boutwell (1983); Taylor (1983); DeFord and Harste (1982); and Harste, Burke, and Woodward (1983). The whole-language theory maintains that children learn language processes by using their existing language knowledge. This helps them to understand discourse, which promotes language and learning. Whole-language reading instruction involves the simultaneous, integrated teaching of reading, writing, speaking, and listening. Reading activities include daily reading of trade books, magazines, newspapers, and books children have written (Smith-Burke, 1987). The following principles support the concept of whole-language instruction (see Chapter 2 for further discussion).

1. The four basic language skills—listening, speaking, reading, and writing are interrelated and reciprocal. Instruction in one of the language arts enhances the learning of the others.
2. There is a strong relationship between reading and writing, so reading and writing instruction should go hand in hand.
3. Children learn to read and write by hypothesizing and making predictions, confirming or disconfirming their predictions, or revising or modifying inaccurate predictions.

4. The goal of language use is to communicate meaning; therefore, instruction should focus on meaningful content.

The Reading Products

The products of reading are understanding, knowledge, appreciation, and pleasure. Each of these products contributes to further reading since they are incorporated into the reader's cognitive structure. New knowledge is incorporated with prior knowledge, which promotes further knowledge in subsequent reading experiences. The appreciation and pleasure derived from reading motivate the reader to read further, which develops reading fluency. The more we read, the more knowledge we gain for further reading.

Understanding the meaning of a written message is the essential skill in reading (Carroll, 1985). To construct the author's meaning, readers use informa-

Readers interact with what is being read; they contribute meaning to the book and take meaning from it. (*Courtesy Elizabeth Crews*)

tion from the text in conjunction with prior knowledge. This process is demon-strated in the following excerpt and discussion.

> Susan drove into the filling station and filled the automobile with gas. Then she went to the window and handed the attendant her credit card.

The first phrase in the preceding excerpt leads readers to expect that their existing knowledge of gasoline stations and automobiles will be relevant to the text. Words like *drove* and *filling station* stimulate readers to think about how much gas is in the tank, how to pump gas, taking the cap off the gas tank, the price per gallon, choosing leaded or unleaded gas, or deciding whether to take advantage of the free car wash that may accompany a fill-up. Existing knowl-edge about driving could lead readers to infer that Susan has a driver's license, that she owns the automobile, and that she has a credit rating that permitted her to obtain a gasoline credit card. These are just some examples that illustrate the potential chain of readers' knowledge related to a text. Notice, also, the complexity and interrelated nature of these ideas when compared to the origi-nal excerpt.

"World knowledge" is essential to the development of both reading and writing skills (Chall, 1983). World knowledge is also called **cultural literacy**, which is the network of information that all competent readers possess. It is the background information stored in their minds, which enables them to read a newspaper or a book with an adequate level of comprehension (Hirsch, 1987). No text is complete in itself; authors cannot write everything their audience will need to understand, so readers must have the knowledge that enables them to fill in gaps in the text. Therefore, the reading process cannot be separated from content.

Readers' knowledge (**schemata**) is activated when they see titles, subtitles, photographs, graphs, text segments, and text organization. Readers then use this information to form hypotheses or predictions about the meaning of the text and the author's intentions. The purpose for reading is to confirm or reject these hypotheses and predictions. Periodically, readers summarize or compare new data with existing schemata to determine whether the new information matches their hypotheses. They modify meaning and raise additional questions as they read the text. Throughout this process, readers use prior knowledge to make inferences about the text, as well as the relationship among the ideas in the text; this, in turn, may alter the reader's prior knowledge, as well as promote additional knowledge external to the text (Jones et al., 1987).

What items of "world information" are necessary for students to read successfully? Although many people decry students' lack of common informa-tion, there is little agreement regarding the precise pieces of information that students should have. E. D. Hirsch, Jr. (1987) researched and identified items like the following as "What Every American Needs to Know."

1066
Snow White

solar plexus

Spinoza

staccato

Hirsch believes that students should acquire the world knowledge (cultural literacy) needed to read early in their lives. He believes that fifth-grade students who lack this knowledge fall behind in reading; tenth graders who lack this knowledge become hopelessly discouraged. Thus, his data supports the importance of early education. Since Hirsch's research is recent, his findings will be examined and reexamined during the next few years. Eventually, we may have a core list of information that every elementary-school student should learn.

Recent research regarding memory and thinking skills provide us with guidance for teaching students the world knowledge that will enable them to read successfully.

Reading Process and Product

Each of the reading explanations presented in this chapter contributes to our overall understanding; however, no single explanation is sufficient. Reading differs, depending on the skill of the reader. Beginning readers are quite different from fluent readers. Beginning readers must concentrate on remembering and decoding words, while more fluent readers can recognize words. This automatically allows the more fluent readers to concentrate on understanding the passage as a whole; they are able to comprehend printed language so easily and quickly, that they can think critically and creatively about the content.

THE SIGNIFICANT INFLUENCES ON READING ABILITY

Many factors influence children's acquisition of reading skill. This section examines the factors that have a significant influence on students' ability to acquire reading fluency. These factors include: language; cognitive, emotional, and physical development; and experiential and familial background.

Language

Language is a basic tool for thinking, problem-solving, and other more complex symbolic activities. Reading is one of four language arts. Speaking and writing are called *expressive* language arts; listening and reading are called *receptive* language arts. The four language arts are complementary and interactive; each is based on experience and thinking skills (see Figure 1.1). Skill in one of the language arts enhances skill in each of the others. This fact suggests that reading instruction should be based on a total language arts program; that is, reading should not be taught as an isolated set of skills, but should grow out of the students' overall language competence.

<u>*Receptive*</u>   <u>*Expressive*</u>

Listening   Experience   **Speaking**

Reading   Thinking   **Writing**

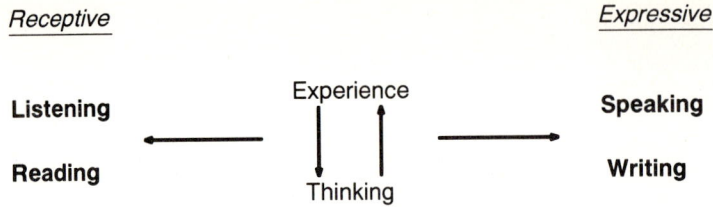

Figure 1.1   The four language arts.

Clearly, there is a close relationship between language and reading. Reading is an effort to understand an author's meaning from written content. Reading involves the interpretation of printed words, which, in turn, represent oral language (speech).

Language is a system of arbitrary vocal symbols used for human communication (Ellis, 1978). Word meanings are shared by people who speak a common language; this enables them to communicate by using that language. These shared-language meanings permit a speaker to make a statement such as *I am Linda* with the confidence that the listener (or reader) will understand. Language—the meanings of sounds, symbols (words), and grammar—varies from culture to culture. For example, the word *dog* in English represents a four-legged animal that barks; in German, the word *hund* stands for that same animal. A meaning in each instance has been assigned to the word, not to the sound of that word.

The field of language study is divided into several specialized areas, each of which contributes to our understanding of the reading process. *Linguistics* is the study of language as it is used by speakers of that language. *Psycholinguistics* is the study of the relationship between language, thought, and the learning process. *Sociolinguistics* is the study of language differences that are related to social contexts; these include regional differences, educational levels, and social-class differences. Sociolinguistics is also concerned with the social setting of language. *Semantics* is the study of word meanings. *Language development* is the study of language acquisition.

Three linguistic systems

Three linguistic systems comprise the English language: the sound system, *phonemics;* the word system, *morphology;* and the *syntactic* system, word order. The sound system includes phonemes—the smallest units of sound in the English language—as well as pitch, stress, and juncture. Morphology includes the words and word parts of English. Syntax is the system for organizing words to express ideas. Each of these linguistic systems contributes to our understanding of written language.

The English sound system

Phonemics

Phonemes comprise a sound system that is the basis for pronounciation in the English language. A written phoneme is a grapheme; for example, *g* is the grapheme for the phoneme /*g*/. A letter written between two slash marks represents a phoneme (for example, /*g*/). Opinions on the number of phonemes in the English language vary; however, approximately 44 phonemes are estimated in English. There are 21 consonants, 3 semivowels, 8 unglided vowels, 4 levels of stress, 4 levels of pitch, and 4 levels of juncture (Ruddell, 1974). The phonemic system of English will be discussed further in Chapter 4.

Components of the sound system

Pitch, stress, and juncture are also parts of the English sound system. *Pitch* refers to the height (high or low) of the voice when pronouncing certain words in a sentence. Pitch influences the meaning of words and sentences. An identical set of words may have two very different meanings if the pitch is varied. Notice how the pitch factor changes the meaning of the following sentences.

> Linda is coming. (The falling pitch is on coming, which is usually interpreted as a statement of fact.)
>
> Linda is coming? (The rising pitch is on coming, which is usually interpreted as a question.)

Stress is the volume associated with the pronunciation of a syllable or word. Variations in stress help convey meaning. Note how the meaning of the following sentences is changed as the stress is shifted. The italicized word in each sentence below is the stressed word.

> Is *Jane* going to eat that cake?
>
> Is Jane going to *eat* that cake?
>
> Is Jane going to eat *that* cake?
>
> Is Jane going to eat that *cake?*

Juncture is the length of the pause between one element of speech and the next. Variations in juncture within a sentence can change the meaning of that sentence. Note the meaning changes in the following sentences that are caused by juncture.

> Susan Helen's mother bought a house.
>
> Susan, Helen's mother, bought a house.
>
> What is in the street ahead?
>
> What is in the street, a head?

Punctuation aids the reader

Punctuation influences pitch, stress, and juncture in written language. A comma signifies a pause or juncture between two words. Punctuation at the end of a sentence affects the stress within that sentence. A question mark, for example, indicates different stress from a period notation. The meaning of a sentence also suggests to the reader the pitch, stress, and juncture. Thus the sound system is an important factor in comprehending written language in English.

Morphology

Morphology is the study of words and word parts. A *morpheme* is the smallest meaningful unit of language. There are two types of morphemes: free and bound. A free morpheme is used independently, such as *dog* or *girl.* A bound morpheme must be combined with a second morpheme to form a word; for example, *ante* is a bound morpheme meaning *before.* When *ante* is combined with the free morpheme, *room,* a new word, *anteroom,* is formed. An anteroom is a small room that one enters before a main or waiting room. Meaningful language is composed of both free and bound morphemes.

Syntax

The syntactic system in the English language refers to the arrangement of words into grammatical phrases and sentences. Order is very important in English because meaning is expressed through the particular order of words. For example, *the dog ran away* is a meaningful ordering of words, while *ran the away dog* is not meaningful.

Sociolinguistics

Variations in language, often referred to as *dialect,* are very important factors in the teaching of reading. A reader's language is the basis upon which learning to read occurs: thus variations in that language may affect the acquisition of reading skills. Sociolinguists are interested in describing variations in language that result from such factors as social class, regional differences, educational level, sex, race, and social setting.

Vocabulary, grammar, and phonology are greatly influenced by sociological factors. In the southern region of the United States, the short /i/ and the short /e/ are pronounced with the same sound; therefore, *sit* and *set,* and *pen* and *pin,* sound alike. *Greasy* is pronounced /*griy siy*/ in the northern states, but it is /*griy ziy*/ in the South. A paper sack is a *bag* or a *sack* in the North, but is a *poke* in certain parts of the South. A Southerner uses the word *carry* to mean *to take.* Imagine the confusion of the Northerner who was asked to "carry" his neighbor downtown and visualized carrying the neighbor on his back! Language differences, as illustrated in these examples, can clearly interfere with proper communication.

Sociolinguists also study the role of social context in language variation. They are interested in the ways in which language changes—particularly its relationship to the factors of *who, what, when, where,* and *why.* For example, we speak differently when conversing with a close friend than we do with a casual acquaintance. Similarly, there is a marked difference between the conversation at a cocktail party and that in a church.

Sociolinguists are interested as well in the attitudes, values, and beliefs of people and their language. They study listeners' reactions to various types of language. Intelligence and social-status impressions are often based on the language one uses. Student language may influence the orientation of a teacher's reading instruction program. Children who speak nonstandard dialects, however, should not be penalized in the classroom. Each individual's language should be respected. This important aspect of reading instruction will be discussed in greater detail in Chapter 11.

Language Concepts

The following is a list of basic language concepts for reading teachers to keep in mind:

1. Language is systematic.
2. Language is composed of phonological, morphological, and syntactical systems.
3. Language is arbitrary.
4. Language changes.
5. English is characterized by basic sentence patterns.
6. Language permits speakers to communicate; therefore, no language or dialect is better or worse than another.
7. Language variations result from sociological factors.

Children acquire language quickly

Language Acquisition

Language acquisition illustrates the unlimited potential of the human mind. The acquisition of language by children can be described as somewhat miraculous. Language development is an "unfolding" process in young children: they move from crying and babbling in infancy to word and sentence construction at three years of age.

Competency at five years of age

Although children have achieved a rather sophisticated stage of language development by four-and-one-half years of age, they continue to acquire syntactic structure through the age of ten. Strickland (1962) found that the average sentence length of first-graders was 11 words; this expanded to 14 words by the sixth grade. The stages of language acquisition are summarized in Table 1.1.

Cognitive Development

Reading is a thinking process. Readers must think in order to read; also, they must think about the content they read. Reading and thinking are interactive

Table 1.1 STAGES OF LANGUAGE ACQUISITION

Age	Language
Birth	Cooing
3–6 months	Babbling
9–18 months	Single words
18–24 months	Two words (telegraphic)
3–4½ years	Basic syntactic system
4 years	Phonological system complete
4½–10 years	Continues to acquire syntax

processes; readers bring meaning to the page and take meaning from the page. Thinking, reasoning, memory, problem-solving, and conceptual learning are cognitive skills that are basic to the reading process.

Intelligence

Intelligence is one aspect of cognitive development that may be defined as "the ability to learn and to apply what is learned" (Dechant and Smith, 1977). Reading is a learned skill and intelligence is a prerequisite for learning.

Intelligence tests measure those factors that are important in learning to read. Intelligence test scores are sometimes used to predict reading achievement levels; however, intelligence tests do have limitations. Children's intelligence is influenced by such factors as experiential background, personal attitudes, motivation, cultural background, and of course, the testing situation itself. These factors may cause inaccurate measurements of intelligence. Group intelligence tests are basically tests of reading; thus, a poor reader may score low on these tests due to weak reading skills, not because the reader has low intelligence. Intelligence quotients should be interpreted as ability ranges rather than specific scores.

Intelligence is a function of both environment and heredity. An individual's genetic inheritance provides the basis for intellectual potential; this must be further developed through experience in the environment. Children who have limited life experiences are likely to have limited intellectual development as well.

Conceptual Development

Conceptual development begins at birth. Infants encounter shapes, colors, sizes, textures, and sounds, which are stored in a memory bank; these provide a perceptual or sensory base for conceptual development. The thoughts of young children are characterized by crude concepts based on associating a variety of objects with a single word. Young children may call the physician, the mailman, and the television repairman, *daddy,* as *daddy* represents all men in their thinking. As children mature, their concepts are gradually refined and they achieve a more sophisticated level of conceptual development; they understand the generic concept of *man,* and realize that the physician, the mailman, and the repairman are simply individual members of a general classification.

Common properties

A **concept** is a generalized notion about a class of objects, ideas, or events. These elements are categorized into unique systems by children—systems that are related to personal experiences. In the process of developing concepts, the individual looks for common properties among objects, events, and ideas. Through comparison and contrast, the child begins to recognize and identify common properties—and these ideas are, in turn, the foundation upon which concepts are developed. Conceptual development, then, provides the groundwork for thinking and reading processes.

Perceptual Development

Perception provides sensory data for both cognitive development and reading achievement. Perceptual input is obtained through sensory channels: visual (seeing), auditory (hearing), olfactory (smelling), kinesthetic (touching), and taste. Perception is *developmental* because it changes significantly with the age and experience of the individual. It is also influenced by emotions, individual experiences, and physical development. Thus, each child's perceptual development is unique.

Aspects of perception

There are five aspects of perception: detection, discrimination, recognition, identification, and judgment (Ellis, 1978). *Detection* refers to the individual's awareness of a stimulus. Detection in reading refers to the reader's awareness of a word or idea. *Discrimination* is the ability to see both likenesses and differences. **Visual discrimination** refers to the ability to see likenesses and differences in printed symbols—a prerequisite for learning sight words. **Auditory discrimination** is the ability to hear likenesses and differences in sounds—a requirement for learning phonics. *Recognition* occurs when a reader recognizes a word as one previously known or unknown. *Identification* is the association of meaning with words. And, finally, *judgment* enters into the critical reading activity when the reader begins to evaluate the written content itself.

Stages of Cognitive Development

Piaget identified stages

Research by the Swiss psychologist Jean Piaget has contributed greatly to our current knowledge of intellectual development. Piaget promoted the idea that cognitive development occurs in orderly sequential stages. All children move through these stages in the same sequence, although the ages at which these levels of development are attained can vary widely.

The following section attempts to summarize some of the highlights of Piaget's stages of cognitive development. Particular attention is directed toward the relationship between these stages and the reading process.

The *sensorimotor period* extends from birth to approximately two years of age. During this period, children are engaged in active exploration and manipulation of their world.

The *preoperational period* is divided into two stages: the early preoperational and the later preoperational period. The *early preoperational period* occurs approximately between the ages of two and four. During this time,

Critical stage for reading

children learn that one thing can represent another. It is acknowledged, for example, that a picture of a dog represents a real dog itself. This stage of development is crucial in learning how to read since children must be able to recognize that written word meanings do, in fact, represent objects. The *later preoperational period* extends from approximately ages four to seven. During this stage, thinking is *centered* on a single striking feature of a situation. Children will tend to focus, for example, on the loudest, brightest, or biggest feature. Children also possess limited powers of concentration and are unable to reverse thinking in this period. Preoperational children are egocentric and can only understand a situation from their own points of view. They are unable to see relationships between parts as constituting a whole. This can cause difficulty in reading instruction if children are introduced to a reading program that requires identification of word parts. Many children can memorize word parts, but they may be unable to use them functionally until a higher level of cognitive development is achieved.

Concrete operational thought develops between the ages of seven to eleven. This is the period when children acquire the ability to reason deductively. During this stage, as well, children develop competence in dealing with cause and effect, classification, and seriation.

Formal operational thought is the final stage of cognitive development, beginning at about the age of eleven. Children in this phase are capable of logical, abstract thought. Learners are able to hypothesize about situations that are both concrete and abstract. This stage of development is important because reading comprehension requires the ability to abstract as well as hypothesize.

Emotional Development

Emotional development is a very significant factor in reading. Happy, secure children are more successful in learning to read than are insecure, anxious children. Children's emotions influence cognitive functioning. Athey (1976) identified six aspects of emotions that are related to reading achievement. These factors include self-concept, autonomy, environmental mastery, perception of reality, attitudes toward learning, and anxiety.

Self-concept is the set of attitudes and beliefs that one holds about oneself. It is the product of interactions with family, friends, teachers, and others. Children tend to adopt the attitudes of important people in their environment; therefore, children who have family and friends who treat them with respect, tend to develop stronger self-concepts. On the other hand, children who experience low esteem from others, tend to have poor self-concepts. The treatment children receive from those in their environment is the basis for their self-concept.

Successful learning builds self-confidence and self-esteem, while failure destroys self-confidence and self-esteem. Children with positive self-concepts usually achieve greater success in reading (Eldredge, 1981). Children who are competent readers feel that they have more control over their lives, while unsuccessful students feel that they have no control over what happens to them (Eldredge, 1981). Zimmerman and Allebrand (1965) report that good readers have feelings of personal worth, belonging, and self-reliance. Athey (1982) maintains that poor readers are immature, impulsive, and have negative feelings about themselves and the world around them. Students who believe that they are capable of reading, strive to read successfully, while those who lack confidence do not strive to read well. Self-concept is a facet of emotional development that significantly influences reading achievement; however, other emotional factors also contribute to readers' development.

Emotional factors have a powerful influence on learning to read. Some of the factors associated with reading success include autonomy, mastery of one's environment, accurate perception of reality, personal attitudes, and anxieties. *Autonomy* refers to children's ability to operate on their own. Independent students are often self-directed in their classwork responsibilities. *Mastery of the environment* makes children feel that they have some control over what happens to them. *Accurate perception of reality* includes a realistic perception of oneself, as well as one's relationship with the environment. *Personal attitudes* toward reading influence a student's ability to read. If students have unpleasurable reading experiences, they may develop an aversion to reading activities. The research on *anxiety* is inconclusive. Some degree of anxiety is undoubtedly useful in learning, but an extreme degree of anxiety appears to impede the learning process.

Experience

Successful reading often depends on the personal insights readers bring to printed language. Readers cannot fully comprehend a reading selection on animal life in zoos, for example, if they have never visited a zoo. Similarly, the child who reads "The breaking waves dashed against the reef," requires background experience to comprehend the sensory images of sight and sound, which are described in this sentence. Children's life experiences provide a storehouse of information and images for developing concepts. Photographs, television, movies, and reading materials add to students' world knowledge and develop their schemata. The breadth and richness of readers' direct and vicarious experiences determine the meaning that readers bring to and take from the printed page.

Familial Factors

The family that children are born into has a significant impact on their reading achievement. Parents contribute to children's language, as well as to their emotional and physical development. Parents who spend time talking with their children are encouraging language development. Love, patience, and understanding foster a sense of security that is the groundwork upon which successful learning can occur. In contrast, parents who neglect their children create feelings of rejection, insecurity, and anxiety—all of which interfere with the learning process. Parents who enjoy reading and promote it as an activity in the home, act as role models; this establishes an environment in which children will want to read. Parents build children's experiential background through walks, zoo and museum visits, and library outings.

Children whose parents are interested and involved with their school work are more successful students (Cattermole and Robinson, 1985; Rich, 1985; Walberg, 1984). Many parents welcome the opportunity to participate in their children's education; schools that offer parents opportunities for involvement enhance students' achievement.

Even before children can read by themselves, they can share in the rewards that reading has to offer. (*Courtesy Jean-Claude Lejeune*)

Children who are successful readers come from homes that exhibit the following characteristics:

1. stability
2. open communication between parents and children
3. parents who read regularly
4. the availability of books, magazines, and newspapers in the home
5. value the activity of reading
6. parents who involve their children in a variety of family and out-of-home experiences
7. children who are well-nourished and have adequate rest (physically developed)

Physical Development

One's experiences in the outside world are transmitted to the brain through the sense organs. Sensory experience is the channel through which thinking and learning occur. Thus, the healthy development of the sense organs is a prerequisite for reading success.

Vision

Reading essentially begins with seeing. The eyes move along the lines of print and, in doing so, send perceptual messages to the brain. Clear, accurate images are essential; otherwise, letters and words that have similar configurations (shapes) may be confused and the reading process will be impaired. Proper perception of letters, words, and sentences is necessary for reading to occur.

Teachers should be alert to the kinds of vision problems students may experience. The following are some common symptoms instructors should watch for:

Vision problems

1. inability to see the chalkboard
2. tilting of the head during reading
3. frequent rubbing of the eyes
4. frequent blinking and/or squinting
5. the closing or covering of one eye when reading
6. headaches
7. fatigue
8. holding written materials close to or far from the eyes
9. frequent skipping of lines or words when reading

Children who consistently display one or more of these symptoms should be referred to a specialist for further testing.

Hearing

Hearing is important for reading because readers associate oral language with printed words. If the reader cannot hear well, these associations are not made. Hearing is particularly important when a phonics approach to reading is used in classroom instruction. Students with poor hearing are unable to associate sounds with symbols (letters). The symptoms of poor hearing are:

Hearing problems

1. inattentiveness
2. frequent requests to repeat information
3. poor articulation
4. tilting of the head when listening
5. complaints of noises in the ears
6. frequent ear drainage
7. frequent colds

When one or more of these symptoms are observed, the child should be referred to a specialist for examination.

General Health

Good general health is important because reading is a complex and often arduous task. Good general health enables a reader to be alert, to concentrate, and to fully participate in classroom activities. Poor physical condition can create fatigue and decrease attentiveness. Poor health often interferes with school attendance and students who are absent when reading skills are taught fall farther and farther behind in their classes.

Factors that indicate poor general health include:

1. high absenteeism
2. frequent colds and respiratory infections
3. fatigue
4. headaches
5. irritability
6. an overweight or underweight condition

Children who exhibit these symptoms should be referred directly to a physician.

Screen for physical problems

Fortunately, most physical problems are correctable. Many schools have the services of a school nurse who can aid the teacher in identifying physical problems that may make reading difficult. Children at the elementary-school level should be screened regularly for physical problems. Insuring a student's physical comfort will make for a more successful instructional environment in the end.

SUMMARY

This chapter explored the complexity of the reading process and the major factors that have an impact on the reading process. Teachers who understand these interrelated factors are better prepared to teach elementary reading. The following list summarizes the key points of Chapter 1.

1. Literacy, a necessary skill in our society, is defined as the reading and writing skills needed to live comfortable lives.
2. Research reveals that many Americans do not have the literacy necessary to function comfortably in our society.
3. Reading is both process- and product-oriented. The reading process is concerned with understanding written language. To understand written language, readers must have world knowledge, which is also called cultural literacy. World knowledge is stored in cognitive structures called *schemata*. Readers use their schemata to read; as they read, they acquire more knowledge, which facilitates further reading.
4. The major factors that influence students' acquisition of reading ability include language, cognition, perception, emotions, experiential background, and family.
5. Language, phonemics, morphology, and syntax are important aspects of reading since reading is a process of understanding written language.
6. Conceptual, perceptual, and cognitive development are important to reading because it is a thinking process that involves using knowledge stored in the reader's memory to understand.
7. Emotional development has an impact on reading because emotions influence the cognitive processes. Positive self-concepts enable students to experience greater success in reading.
8. The family plays an important role in reading achievement because it contributes to experiential background, language development, think-

ing skills, perception, self-concept, emotional, and physical development.

SELF-TEST

Check your knowledge of the information presented in this chapter. The answer key is located in Appendix C.

1. Which of the following terms are synonyms for world knowledge?
   a. cultural literacy
   b. schemata
   c. both a and b
   d. neither a nor b

2. How do readers use schemata?
   a. to infer reading content
   b. to fill in gaps in the text
   c. both a and b
   d. neither a nor b

3. Why does the public have the false impression that students do not read as well as they did 25 years ago?
   a. because the reading tasks of today require a higher reading level
   b. because the research is incorrect
   c. this is not a false impression
   d. because many more people are illiterate today

4. What is the literacy gap?
   a. the number of illiterates in our society
   b. the number of people who are functionally literate
   c. the difference between the reader's skill and the level of reading required by the text
   d. none of the above

5. Why have many states initiated competency testing for students?
   a. to insure that high-school graduates can read
   b. to insure that all students who enter the public schools are competent
   c. to insure that all students are capable of learning to read
   d. all of the above.

6. How can teachers increase their own accountability?
   a. through belonging to professional organizations
   b. by participating in in-service education
   c. by taking graduate courses at a university
   d. all of the above

7. What does the acronym *ERIC* stand for?
   a. Educational Resources Information Center
   b. Educational Reading Information Center
   c. English Resources Information Center
   d. English Resources Information Conference

8. What does the acronym *NAEP* stand for?
   a. North American Education Program

b. New American Education Program
c. National Assessment of Educational Progress
d. none of the above

9. What evidence is often used to support the claim that reading achievement levels are declining in the United States?
a. declining SAT scores
b. the large number of people who prefer seeing movies to reading a book
c. both a and b
d. neither a nor b

10. It is impossible to observe the reading process because
a. it occurs in the brain
b. it is so complex
c. neither a nor b
d. both a and b

11. What kinds of eye movements occur in reading?
a. jumps
b. fixations
c. regressions
d. all of the above

12. What is decoding?
a. codification
b. the inability to recognize words
c. configuration
d. recognizing words and associating them with meaning

13. What does perception mean?
a. information derived from hearing only
b. associating meaning with information derived from the senses
c. information derived from vision only
d. associating colors with information derived from the senses

14. What components are included in the Gray-Robinson model of reading?
a. perception, comprehension, and rate
b. perception, comprehension, reaction, and assimilation
c. perception, comprehension, reaction, assimilation, and rate
d. perception and comprehension

15. Which of the following statements represent the basic psycholinguistic contributions to reading instruction?
a. Reading is not a precise process
b. Reading is a meaning-centered process
c. Reading skills are based on language competence
d. All of the above

16. What is an essential skill in reading?
a. getting meaning from a printed message
b. reading words with accuracy
c. reading very difficult books
d. recognition of Greek and Latin roots

17. What is linguistics?
a. a description of language as it is used by speakers of that language
b. the study of the history of language

    c. a description of English being spoken by peoples of other countries
    d. instruction in the grammar and usage of the English language

18. What is sociolinguistics?
    a. a description of language as it is used by speakers of that language
    b. the study of the history of language
    c. the study of language differences and their relation to social factors
    d. a test of language competence

19. What three systems comprise the English language?
    a. miscues, regressions, and fixations
    b. consonants, vowels, and schwa
    c. capital, lowercase, and cursive letters
    d. phonemic, morphological, and syntactic

20. What is the major focus of Piaget's research?
    a. finding the cure for reading problems
    b. cognitive development
    c. carpal development
    d. muscle development

21. What is the most important aspect of emotional development?
    a. self-concept
    b. attaining physical maturity
    c. having adequate nutrition
    d. none of the above

22. What are the family's contributions to children's reading achievement levels?
    a. language development
    b. cognitive stimulation
    c. experiential background
    d. all of the above

23. What physical factor is closely related to reading achievement?
    a. hearing
    b. vision
    c. general health
    d. all of the above

24. Why is experience important to the reading process?
    a. it enables the reader to understand written content
    b. because real experience limits one's potential
    c. both a and b
    d. neither a nor b

ENRICHMENT ACTIVITIES

1. Find out whether your state has established a competency testing program. If your state does have one, find out what skills are assessed. Try to obtain a copy of the competency test and take it yourself.

2. Keep a log of those situations requiring reading that you encounter for a week. Analyze your log to determine the amount of information that you actually obtain through reading.

3. Interview teachers to find out how demands for accountability have influenced their teaching approaches, lesson plans, record keeping, and methods of testing.

4. Develop a file of newspaper and magazine articles on reading and identify the main idea of each article. What is the press saying about reading today?

5. Read the Number 3 issue of *Reading Research Quarterly* for the current year. How many research studies on reading were reported? What types of studies were done? What was the most popular aspect of reading that the studies appeared to focus on?

6. Read a current issue of *The Reading Teacher, Language Arts, Reading World,* or *Journal of Reading Improvement.* Make a list of the suggestions for teaching that are discussed in the journal.

7. Visit a university library and find out how to contact ERIC for materials.

8. Observe children at various grade levels and compare their emotional, cognitive, and physical development.

9. Write your own definition of reading. (You may wish to modify your definition as you learn more about the subject of reading.) What are the instructional implications of your definition?

10. Listen to children of various grade levels read aloud. How many miscues can you identify in their reading? (You may wish to tape-record their reading for miscue analysis.)

11. Make a tape recording of young children talking with one another. Have your classmates listen to the tape and estimate the age of each child based on the language patterns.

RELATED READINGS

Carroll, J. B. (1985). "The Nature of the Reading Process," in *Theoretical Models and Processes of Reading,* 3d ed., H. Singer and R. Ruddell (Eds.), Newark, DE: International Reading Association, pp. 25–34.

Chall, J. (1983). *Stages of Reading Development,* New York: McGraw-Hill.

Cullinan, B. and D. Strickland (April 1986). "The Early Years: Language, Literature, and Literacy in Classroom Research," *The Reading Teacher,* Vol. 39, No. 8, pp. 798–806.

Ellis, H. (1978). *Fundamentals of Human Learning, Memory and Cognition,* 2d ed., Dubuque, IA: William C. Brown.

Goodman, K. (1985). "Unity in Reading," in *Theoretical Models and Processes of Reading,* 3d ed., H. Singer and R. Ruddell (Eds.), Newark, DE: International Reading Association, pp. 813–840.

Hirsch, E. D., Jr. (1987). *Cultural Literacy,* Boston: Houghton Mifflin.

Kozol, J. (1985). *Illiterate America,* New York: Doubleday.

Mavrogenes, N. (November 1986). "What Every Reading Teacher Should Know About Emergent Literacy," *The Reading Teacher,* Vol. 40, No. 2, pp. 174–179.

National Assessment of Educational Progress (1985). *The Reading Report Card,* Princeton, NJ: Educational Testing Service.

Platt, N. (Summer 1984). "How One Classroom Gives Access to Meaning," *Theory into Practice,* Vol. 23, No. 2, pp. 239–245.

Rich, S. (November 1985). "Restoring Power to Teachers: The Impact of 'Whole Language'," *Language Arts,* Vol. 62, No. 3, pp. 717–724.

Tway, E. (September 1986). "Language and Culture," *Language Arts,* Vol. 63, No. 5, pp. 495–501.

Vacca, J., R. Vacca, and M. Gove (1987). *Reading and Learning to Read,* Boston: Little Brown, Chapters 1 and 2.

REFERENCES

Anderson, R., E. Hiebert, J. Scott, and I. Wilkinson (1985). *Becoming a Nation of Readers,* Urbana, IL: The Center for the Study of Reading.

Anderson, R., and P. D. Pearson (1984). "A Schema-Theoretic View of Reading Comprehension," in *Handbook of Reading Research,* P. D. Pearson (Ed.), New York: David McKay, pp. 255–291.

Athey, I. (1982). "The Affective Domain Reconceptualized," *Advances in Reading/ Language Research,* Vol. 1, pp. 203–217.

Athey, I. (1976). "Reading Research in the Affective Domain," in *Theoretical Models and Processes of Reading,* 2nd ed., H. Singer and R. Ruddell (Eds.), Newark, DE: International Reading Association, pp. 352–380.

Boutwell, M. (1983). "Reading and Writing Process: A Reciprocal Agreement," *Language Arts,* Vol. 60, pp. 723–730.

Carroll, J. (1985). "The Nature of the Reading Process," in *Theoretical Models and Processes of Reading,* 3d ed., H. Singer and R. Ruddell (Eds.), Newark, DE: International Reading Association, pp. 25–34.

Cattermole, J. and N. Robinson (September 1985). "Effective Home/School/Communications—From the Parents' Perspective," *Phi Delta Kappan,* Vol. 67, No. 1, pp. 48–50.

Chall, J. (1983). *Stages of Reading Development,* New York: McGraw-Hill.

Dechant, E. and H. Smith (1977). *Psychology in Teaching Reading,* 2nd ed., Englewood Cliffs, NJ: Prentice-Hall.

DeFord, D. and J. Harste (1982). "Child Language Research and Curriculum," *Language Arts,* Vol. 59, pp. 590–600.

Eldredge, A. (October 1981). "An Investigation to Determine the Relationships Among Self-Concept, Locus of Control, and Reading Achievement," *Reading World,* Vol. 21, pp. 59–64.

Ellis, H. (1978). *Fundamentals of Human Learning, Memory and Cognition,* 2nd ed., Dubuque, IA: William C. Brown.

Erich, A. and G. Kraetsch (1980). "A 50-Year Comparison of University of Minnesota Freshman Reading Performance," *Journal of Educational Psychology,* Vol. 74, pp. 660–665.

Farr, R., L. Fay, and H. Negley (1978). *Then and Now: Reading Achievement in Indiana (1944–45 and 1976),* Bloomington: Indiana University Press (ERIC Document Reproduction Service No. ED 158 262).

Glaser, R. (1985). "Foreword," in *Becoming a Nation of Readers,* R. Anderson, E. Hiebert, J. Scott, and I. Wilkinson (Eds.), Urbana, IL: The Center for the Study of Reading.

Goodman, K. (1985). "Unity in Reading," in *Theoretical Models and Processes of Reading,* 3d ed., H. Singer and R. Ruddell (Eds.), Newark, DE: International Reading Association, pp. 813–840.

Goodman, K. (1976). "Reading: A Psycholinguistic Guessing Game," in *Theoretical Models and Processes of Reading*, 2nd ed., H. Singer and R. Ruddell (Eds.), Newark, DE: International Reading Association, pp. 497–508.

Gray, W. (1960). "The Major Aspects of Reading," in *Sequential Development of Reading Abilities*, H. Robinson (Ed.), Supplementary Educational Monographs, No. 90, Chicago: University of Chicago Press.

Harste, J., C. Burke, and V. Woodward (1981). "Children, Their Language and World: Initial Encounters with Print," NIE Final Report (NIE-G-79-0132), Bloomington, IN: Indiana University, Language Education Department.

Hirsch, E. D., Jr. (1987). *Cultural Literacy*, Boston: Houghton Mifflin.

Jones, B., A. Palincsar, D. Ogle, and E. Carr (1987). "Introduction," in *Strategic Teaching and Learning: Cognitive Instruction in the Content Areas*, B. Jones, A. Palincsar, D. Ogle, and E. Carr (Eds.), Alexandria VA: ASCD.

Kozol, J. (1985). *Illiterate America*, New York: Doubleday.

Kirkland, E. (February 1978). "A Piagetian Interpretation of Beginning Reading Instruction," *The Reading Teacher* Vol. 31, No. 5, p. 498.

Mikulecky, L. (1982). "Job Literacy: The Relationship Between School Training and Job Literacy Demands," *Reading Research Quarterly*, Vol. XVII, pp. 400–419.

Mikulecky, L. and J. Ehlinger (1986). "The Influence of Metacognitive Aspects of Literacy on Job Performance of Electronics Technicians," *Journal of Reading Behavior*, Vol. 18, pp. 41–62.

Mikulecky, L. and D. Winchester (1983). "Job Literacy and Job Performance Among Nurses at Varying Employment Levels," *Adult Education Quarterly*, Vol. 34, pp. 1–15.

Naisbitt, J. (1984). *Megatrends*, New York: Warner Books.

Piaget, J. (1966). *Judgment and Reasoning in the Child*, Totowa, NJ: Littlefield, Adams.

Pipho, C. (May 1978). "Minimum Competency Testing in 1978: A Look at State Standards," *Phi Delta Kappan* Vol. 60, pp. 585–588.

Platt, N. (1984). "How One Classroom Gives Access to Meaning," *Theory into Practice* Vol. 23, pp. 239–245.

Rich, D. (1985). *The Forgotten Factor in School Success—The Family*, Washington, DC: Home and School Institute.

Robinson, H. (1966). "The Major Aspects of Reading," in *Reading: Seventy-Five Years of Progress*, H. A. Robinson (Ed.), Chicago: University of Chicago Press.

Ruddell, R. (1974). *Reading-Language Instruction: Innovative Practices*, Englewood Cliffs, NJ: Prentice-Hall.

Shepard, L. and A. Kreitzer (August–September 1987). "The Texas Teacher Test," *Educational Researcher*, Vol. 16, pp. 22–31.

Smith-Burke, M. T. (1987). "Classroom Practices and Classroom Interaction During Reading Instruction: What's Going On?" in *The Dynamics of Language Learning*, J. Squire (Ed.), Urbana, IL: National Conference on Research in English.

Stedman, L. and C. Kaestle (Winter 1987). "Literacy and Reading Performance in the United States, from 1880 to the Present," *Reading Research Quarterly* Vol. XXII, No. 1, pp. 8–46.

Stoodt, B. and S. Millhouser (January 1979). *Reading to Work*, Greensboro, NC: The University of North Carolina Press.

Strickland, D. (1962). "The Language of Elementary School Children: Its Relationship to the Language of Reading Textbooks and the Quality of Reading of Selected Children," *Bulletin of the School of Education XXXVIII*, No. 4, Bloomington, IN: Indiana University Press.

Taylor, D. (1983). *Family Literacy: Young Children Learning to Read and Write,* Exeter, NH: Heinemann Educational Books.

U.S. Bureau of the Census (1980). "Educational Attainment in the United States: March 1978 and 1979," Current Population Reports, Series P-20, No. 356. Washington, DC: U.S. Government Printing Office.

Walberg, H. (February 1984). "Families as Partners in Educational Productivity," *Phi Delta Kappan,* Vol. 65, No. 16, pp. 397–400.

Waller, T. G. (1977). *Think First, Read Later: Piagetian Prerequisites for Reading,* Newark, DE: International Reading Association.

Zimmerman, E. and G. Allebrand (September 1965). "Personality Characteristics and Attitudes Toward Achievement of Good and Poor Readers," *Journal of Educational Research,* Vol. 59, pp. 28–31.

CHAPTER **2**

Teaching Children to Read

OVERVIEW Prior to entering school, children acquire skills, ability, and knowledge without formal instruction; however, upon entering elementary school, they experience planned instruction designed to develop reading ability. This planned set of reading experiences is the reading curriculum. Reading ability is acquired gradually, and with practice, the reading process becomes automatic. Competent teachers insure that students develop reading fluency through thoughtful, systematic interactions; they establish authentic reading situations, which incorporate both direct and indirect instruction. Instructional materials include carefully selected basal readers, trade books, magazines, and newspapers. This chapter addresses how to create effective reading lessons.

Key Vocabulary

As you read this chapter, check your understanding of these terms:

curriculum	learning
direct instruction	metacognition
indirect instruction	time on task

Focusing Questions:

As you read this chapter, think about these questions:

1. What tasks do teachers perform to create a sound reading program?
2. What traits characterize competent readers?
3. When is direct instruction appropriate for reading?
4. What are the components of a sound reading lesson?

THE ELEMENTARY READING PROGRAM

Sound reading programs are founded on learning experiences that lead students to build reading skills. The elementary reading curriculum involves more than teaching a series of subskills. Reading is not a linear process of decoding one word and adding each subsequent word to read sentences and paragraphs. In fact, readers do not move straight through sentences from left to right. For example, in the sentence "I made a run in the baseball game," the reader does not know the meaning of *run* until he or she reads *baseball*. To learn this complex process, students need reading skills, but they also need world knowledge or cultural literacy, as well as the desire to read. Cultural literacy gives them the knowledge necessary to infer. Authors cannot write everything that can be said about a topic, so they rely on readers to fill in those empty places (slots) with their experiential background. Students who have positive attitudes toward reading, read for pleasure; this enables them to become fluent readers.

Reading goals

The overarching goal of all elementary reading programs is to develop students who read well and often (Winograd and Greenlee, 1986). These students are strategic users of reading skills; they experience the satisfaction derived from reading. They automatically recognize words, which permits them to focus on understanding the text. Good readers know how to make sense out of the text; they monitor their own understanding of reading content. They have strategies to use when they realize that comprehension has gone awry (**metacognition**). A successful reading program develops students who like to read.

Children acquire reading fluency gradually. The most rapid growth occurs in the elementary-school years, although teachers at every level of education contribute to students' literacy. Extensive reading, effective instruction, and opportunities to experiment with language help students acquire reading fluency during the elementary grades.

Stages of reading

Students move through a series of discernible stages as they develop reading fluency. One view of the stages of reading development is presented by Chall (1983). She identified six stages of reading development, three in the primary grades and three in middle school, high school, and college. These stages are summarized in Table 2.1.

Developmental Reading in the Primary Grades

Primary-grade students exhibit varying degrees of reading readiness. Some young children have quite sophisticated readiness skills due to several years of preschool or nursery school education; other youngsters grow up in restricted environments that offer little intellectual stimulation. Some kindergartners have well-developed readiness skills; others may need extensive reading readiness development during the early stages of reading.

Word recognition and comprehension

The primary developmental reading program is designed to extend basic word recognition and comprehension skills, which permit the students to acquire the world knowledge (schemata) necessary for subsequent reading and

Table 2.1   STAGES OF READING DEVELOPMENT 0–5

Stage	Age	Characteristics
0	Birth–6 (Prereading)	Children learn language. Many children read signs, cereal boxes, and the like. This is the fastest period of reading growth. Children learn letters, they approximate writing, and often print their name. They enjoy being told and read stories. A literate environment is important. This is the fastest period of reading growth.
1	6–7 (Initial Reading Decoding)	Children learn letters and associate these with words and word parts. They are learning about print. Even at this early stage, children bring meaning to print. They read simple text. By the end of this stage, most children understand 4000 or more words at the listening level. They can read about 600 words.
2–3	7–8 (Confirmation Fluency)	Early in this stage, students read many stories to increase fluency. These stories include many high-frequency words. In this stage, students are confirming their ability to read and implement the reading skills they have acquired. They are not gaining new information. Much of this stage seems like review, but actually it gives children a chance to confirm and gain fluency.
3 (Reading for Learning the New)	4–14	Students read for new knowledge, information, thoughts, and experiences. Word meanings and prior knowledge become very important at this stage. The content that students read goes beyond common experiences. Content looks more bookish and includes abstract words. The sentences are longer and more complex.
4 (Multiple Viewpoints)	14–18	Readers at this stage are dealing with more than one point of view. Elementary materials deal with only one point of view. Content presents greater depth. Students need the basic knowledge acquired in stage 3 to read multiple viewpoints. Readers acquire new concepts and new points of view from reading.
5 (Construction and Reconstruction)	18–Above	The most mature stage. Readers know what to read and what not to read. They use printed material selectively to suit their purposes. Readers construct knowledge for themselves. Readers use process of analysis, synthesis, and judgment. Past knowledge about the subject and broad general knowledge are used for selecting, analyzing, and judging.

learning. Primary-grade students read uncomplicated books that reflect the experiences common to young children. These reading materials assist the transition from spoken to written language. The major reading goals of this period are:

1. To understand that spoken language can be written and that one can read and understand written language. (This concept is addressed in Chapter 3.)
2. To perceive letters, words, and sounds. (See Chapter 3.)
3. To understand letter-sound relationships. (See Chapters 3 and 4.)
4. To develop a sight vocabulary that includes instant recognition of high utility words. (See Chapters 3 and 4.)
5. To develop the skills necessary to decode unknown words using word-identification skills individually, and in combination (sight words, context clues, structural analysis, and phonics). (This subject is explained in Chapter 4.)
6. To add to their store of word meanings and concepts. (See Chapter 6.)
7. To expand world knowledge (cultural literacy, schemata). (See Chapters 6 and 7.)
8. To read thought units (phrases, sentences, and paragraphs). (See Chapter 6.)
9. To analyze written text. (See Chapters 6 through 8.)
10. To predict the author's ideas and words. (See Chapter 6.)
11. To summarize written content. (See Chapter 7.)
12. To develop the desire to read (discussed throughout this text).

Developmental Reading in the Middle Grades (Intermediate)

Fluent readers in the middle grades are independent students who use their literacy to learn. Average youngsters in the intermediate grades have sufficient control of the reading process to read widely for many different purposes. Their reading purposes and materials are quite different from primary grade students. For instance, intermediate-grade students read to prepare reports, summarize, develop hobbies, establish concepts, and for pleasure. They read trade books, reference materials, newspapers, magazines, and computer programs.

Middle-grade students exhibit considerable variation in reading achievement. In an intermediate classroom of 25 students, 11 or 12 students are usually assigned to a grade-level basal reader; four or five students, who read well beyond grade level, are assigned individualized reading programs for vertical enrichment. At the other end of the continuum, seven or eight students read well below grade placement. These youngsters need a slow-paced program with considerable reinforcement; they may spend part of the school day in remedial reading class. In addition, educable mentally handicapped students (EMH) students are often mainstreamed into reading groups in the middle grades. These widely varying needs make it necessary for intermediate teachers to diagnose students' reading strengths and weaknesses as they develop a reading program.

Content reading

The intermediate-grade reading curriculum should include the content reading instruction and study skills that are essential to independent learning. Intermediate-grade students read demanding social studies textbooks, science textbooks, and mathematics textbooks, requiring higher reading skills. Middle-grade reading instruction should prepare them for these reading tasks.

Recreational reading

Recreational reading is an important aspect of reading instruction in the intermediate grades. Recreational reading gives students opportunities to apply their reading and study skills to different types of content such as informational materials, textbooks, magazines, newspapers, and novels. Recreational reading develops reading fluency because students read materials they have chosen for their own purposes.

A sound intermediate- or middle-grade reading **curriculum** addresses the following learning experiences:

1. Systematic, planned reading instruction. Fluent intermediate-grade students need to develop additional reading skills in the following areas, which are addressed in greater depth in Chapters 4 and 5.

   word identification of polysyllabic words
   word meanings
   oral and silent reading
   reading many types of content
   reading for various purposes
   increasing fluency

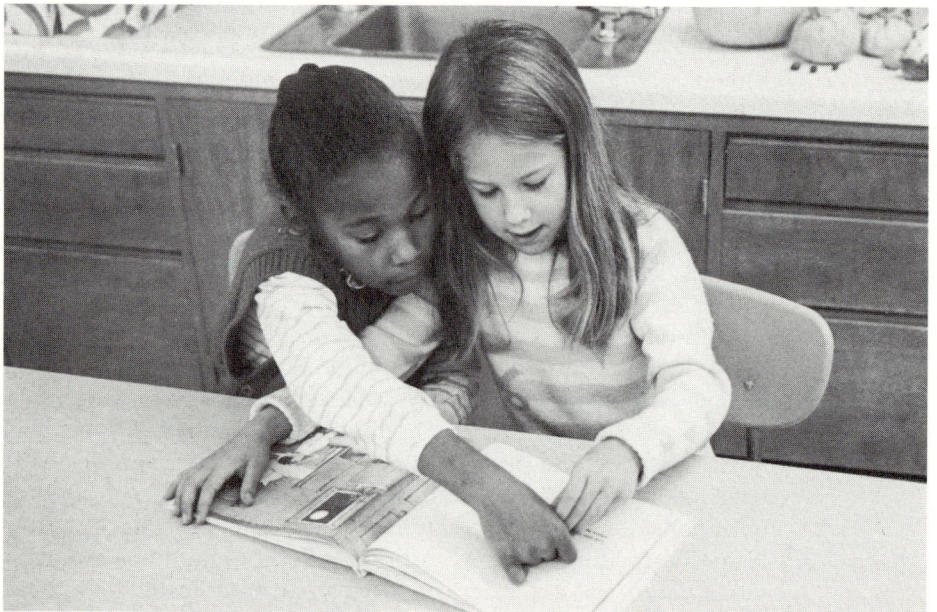

Reading for fun in the early grades can produce leisure-time readers of all ages. (*Courtesy Elizabeth Crews*)

2. Diagnosis of students' reading strengths and weaknesses. This topic is explored in diagnostic and prescriptive courses.
3. Vocabulary- and concept-building. Intermediate-grade students encounter many unfamiliar concepts in their content textbooks. **Direct instruction** will help students cope with new words and concepts. (For further discussion, see Chapters 4 and 5.)
4. Content reading and study skills instruction can help alleviate some of these difficulties. (See Chapter 7 for an in-depth discussion.)
5. Recreational reading. This contributes to reading fluency and motivation to read. (Recreational reading is addressed in Chapter 11.)
6. Teachers should read aloud to students each day. This helps to develop students' reading interests, writing models, and cultural literacy. (This subject is explored in Chapter 8.)
7. Literature is an important aspect of reading instruction. Intermediate-grade teachers use literature to create a foundation for lifelong reading interests. (This topic is addressed in Chapter 11.)
8. Reading instruction should develop fluency and speed. These aspects of reading are especially important for intermediate-grade students who must read a greater volume of content.
9. The students' ability to infer and read critically are increasingly important at this level. Authors cannot write everything that can be said about a topic; therefore, they rely on readers' ability to infer. Critical reading skills are important to intermediate-grade students as they evaluate content and ideas.
10. Cultural literacy (world knowledge, schemata) develops as a result of wide reading, as well as the reader's efforts to recall. The knowledge students acquire today becomes the prior knowledge they use to anticipate and infer as they read tomorrow. Cultural literacy or world knowledge is a significant determinant of comprehension.

The aspects of a sound reading curriculum are addressed in curriculum guides or courses of study; they specify the sequence of reading skills a school system should require.

An Elementary Reading Curriculum

The following curriculum guide is an example of the way that a reading curriculum might be organized. Individual school systems may sequence skills differently; also, they may alter grade placement of content.

I. Kindergarten
   A. Visual discrimination
      1. Left-to-right progression
      2. Identify alphabet letters: upper- and lowercase
      3. Recognize likenesses and differences in letters and words (visual)

B. Auditory discrimination
   1. Hear likenesses and differences in words
   2. Identify initial consonant sounds
C. Word recognition
   1. Students recognize their own names in print
   2. Recognize store names and brand names of products (Pepsi, Cheer)
   3. Recognize common sight words
D. Comprehension
   1. Follow oral directions
   2. Listen to stories that are read aloud and discuss
   3. Listen to stories and recall sequence of events
   4. Listen to stories and identify story grammar
   5. Compare stories, characters, and the like
   6. Discuss the differences between real and make-believe stories read aloud
   7. Students exhibit world knowledge (cultural literacy) necessary to comprehend

II. First Grade
   A. Word-recognition skills
      1. High-frequency sight words
      2. The use of context clues
         a. The ability to identify words in sentences containing context clues for unknown words
      3. Structural analysis (for example, *ing, s, es,* and *ed*)
      4. Phonics
         a. Extend knowledge of consonant sounds
         b. Long and short vowel sounds
   B. Comprehension
      1. Extend knowledge of word meanings
      2. Read and understand short stories
      3. Follow more complex oral directions
      4. Recall the sequence of events in a story
      5. Identify the main idea of a short story
      6. Describe the characters in a short story
      7. Understand common phrases used in a story
      8. Understand the meaning of sentences used in a story
      9. Use world knowledge (cultural literacy) to predict story events and infer as needed for understanding
      10. Use story structure (story grammar) to understand a story

III. Second Grade
   A. Word recognition
      1. Review and refine first-grade skills
      2. Extend knowledge of high-frequency sight words
      3. Structural analysis
         a. Inflected endings
      4. Phonics
         a. Consonant blends and digraphs
         b. Diphthongs
         c. Vowel digraphs

            d. Soft *c* and soft *g*

            e. R-controlled vowels

            f. Syllabication

     B. Comprehension

        1. Review and refine previously learned skills

        2. Understanding relationships

        3. Understanding cause and effect relationships between words and sentences

IV. Third Grade

     A. Word recognition

        1. Review and refine previously learned skills

        2. Structural analysis

            a. Possessive forms and adjective forms

            b. Common prefixes and suffixes

     B. Comprehension

        1. Review and refine previously learned skills

        2. Vocabulary development

            a. Homonyms

            b. Synonyms

            c. Multiple meanings

        3. Classification

     C. Study skills

        1. Map reading

        2. Skimming

        3. Using alphabetization to locate information

V. Fourth Grade

     A. Word recognition

        1. Review and refine previously learned skills

        2. Develop use of the pronunciation key in the dictionary

     B. Vocabulary

        a. Figures of speech

        b. Sensory images

     C. Comprehension

        1. Identify main ideas and details

        2. Outlining

        3. Summarize and organize

        4. Draw conclusions

        5. Critical reading skills

     D. Study skills

        a. Technical vocabulary

        b. Flexible rate

        c. Common writing patterns in the content areas

        d. Uses of the dictionary and encyclopedia

VI. Fifth Grade

     A. Word recognition

        1. Review and refine previously learned skills

     B. Vocabulary

        1. Continue to expand vocabulary ranges

     C. Comprehension

        1. Review and refine previously learned skills

        2. Literature skills
           a. Types of literature
           b. Style, characterization, theme, setting, plot considerations
        3. Appreciation of literature
    D. Study skills
        1. Review and refine previously learned skills
        2. Read with the aim of gathering information
        3. Organize information
VII. Sixth Grade
    A. Word recognition
        1. Review and refine previously learned skills
    B. Vocabulary
        1. Continue to expand vocabulary ranges
    C. Comprehension
        1. Review and refine previously learned skills
        2. Literature skills
           a. Review and refine previously learned skills
           b. Encourage students to use different types of literature as writing models
        3. Appreciation of literature
           a. Provide opportunities to explore and discuss different types of literature
    D. Study skills
        1. Review and refine previously learned skills
        2. Provide opportunities to apply study skills for various purposes (preparing for tests, report writing, etc.)

The preceding reading curriculum identifies the skills and knowledge that children need in order to read. However, the curriculum does not specify appropriate instructional approaches to teaching children to read. Subsequent sections of this chapter explore instructional approaches for teaching reading.

TEACHING READING

Teaching supports students' learning. It is a complex, multifaceted task; no specific teaching behavior will cause all students to learn in all situations (Rupley, Wise, and Logan, 1986). Effective teaching is difficult to analyze because it represents the interaction of complex factors. Nevertheless, researchers have shown that quality of teaching makes a significant difference in children's learning. Students learn more from effective teachers. Approximately 15 percent of the variation in children's reading achievement can be attributed to the teacher's skill and effectiveness (Rosenshine and Stevens, 1984).

Effective teaching

    In recent years, researchers have amassed considerable data regarding teaching. This data reveal a number of salient features that characterize effective teaching, which are summarized in the following list.

1. Effective teachers believe that all of their students can learn to read. They communicate these high expectations to the students who respond by living up to them (Bossert, 1985).
2. Teachers who are strong leaders produce achievement gains in their students. These teachers approach reading in a direct, businesslike manner (Rosenshine and Stevens, 1984).
3. Effective instruction has an academic focus. Students and teachers are goal-oriented (Rosenshine and Stevens, 1984).
4. Effective teachers are good managers. They minimize discipline problems, and quickly handle the ones that do arise. At the beginning of the school year, they establish classroom routines that save time. These routines include distributing supplies, obtaining help with assignments, turning in completed work, and so forth. The students in these classrooms know what is expected of them (Blair, 1984).
5. Successful teachers are explicit (concrete) in explaining reading processes. They explain and use clarifying examples; this makes instruction more concrete and understandable for students. Students in these classes know precisely what is expected of them (Rosenshine and Stevens, 1984; Emmer et al., 1982)
6. Effective teachers model thinking, questioning, and responding to make these abstractions more explicit. These topics are discussed later in this chapter.
7. Effective teachers instruct small groups, whole groups, and individuals (Kean, Summers and Raivetz, 1979). Interactions in various-sized groups facilitate learning. Reading groups are discussed later in this chapter.
8. Effective teachers realize that praise promotes greater achievement (Rosenshine and Stevens, 1985).
9. Effective teachers have clear, precise goal statements and well-developed, systematic lessons. They plan lessons in advance, break their lessons into small, concise parts for presentation, and use large group activities to monitor student progress (Blair, 1984). Lesson planning is discussed in subsequent sections of this chapter.
10. Effective teachers monitor their teaching success by watching, listening, and asking questions (Comber, 1987).

Effective teaching is important because learning requires the sustained, conscious attention of learners; it is not automatic. Teachers must create instruction that stimulates children to invest the effort necessary to learn. Effective reading instruction is developed in a literate environment, using interesting reading materials.

Teaching tasks

The teaching tasks involved in effective reading instruction include:

- planning and implementing reading instruction
- pacing instruction
- creating a warm, literate environment
- grouping children for instruction
- selecting reading materials
- evaluating instruction

Beginning with the task of planning and implementing reading instruction, each teaching task, except evaluation, is examined in the following section.

PLANNING AND IMPLEMENTING READING INSTRUCTION

Instruction is a complex concept. Educators agree about the importance of effective instruction and planning, but there is less agreement regarding how to create effective instruction. Effective teaching differs from situation to situation, and from student to student. For instance, effectively teaching word-recognition skills may not work effectively with comprehension skills. What works with Sarah Smith may not work with Dick Jones; these individuals have different world knowledge, varying motivation, and different abilities.

Among current instructional approaches, direct instruction is very popular; research shows that direct instruction produces good test results, particularly in basic reading skills. Direct instruction is systematic and focused on academics; it is active teaching that involves high pupil engagement, controlled practice, supervised seatwork, and corrective feedback (Lehr, 1986).

Direct and Indirect Instruction

Direct instruction refers to the deliberate teaching of something (such as vocabulary), as opposed to **indirect** instruction, which occurs when something is learned without deliberate teaching. During direct instruction, the teacher tells, shows, models, demonstrates, and teaches skills. To implement direct instruction, the teacher plans, guides, and leads instruction while interacting with the class. Indirect instructional activities include completing worksheets, kits, or workbooks independently.

Reading is more than skills

Direct instruction produces impressive reading test results; it enables students to perform well on reading achievement tests. By their nature, achievement tests assess specific, concrete skills, which direct instruction conveys to students. However, reading is more than a collection of skills (Lehr, 1986).

Direct instruction contributes to reading success, but indirect instruction also contributes to reading ability. For example, research has demonstrated that reading literature aloud to children develops reading comprehension skills. This is indirect reading instruction. Furthermore, reading is a skill; reading fluency is enhanced when students spend time reading silently on an individual basis (another indirect activity). Listening, speaking, and writing contribute to reading success; however, are not directly taught in reading classes. As we examine reading success, it becomes more and more apparent that both direct and indirect instruction play important roles in a sound reading program.

Well-designed lessons usually incorporate direct instruction of reading skills and skills practice; however, direct instruction is also used for reinforcement and independent skill practice. Students acquire much of the cultural literacy they need to comprehend from silent reading and class discussion, which are usually considered indirect instructional activities.

Academic engaged time or time on task is an important aspect of both direct and indirect instruction. This is explored in the next section.

Academic Engaged Time

When students are engaged in learning, they spend "**time on task.**" Research shows that students who are actively engaged in learning for a longer proportion of time have high achievement (Rosenshine and Stevens, 1984). In other words, the more time students spend reading, the higher their achievement. Of course, it is not surprising to learn that students' achievement is higher when they spend more time practicing a skill that has been taught. Students who spend more time reading become better readers; they are actively involved in acquiring reading fluency.

Time on task

Time on task is an important concept for teachers to remember; however, it is easy to overlook its importance in the daily flurry of activity in the average classroom. Many factors can be counterproductive to direct instruction and time on task. Students can spend more time passing out papers, lining up, waiting for the teacher to get materials for a lesson, and so forth. In some classrooms, time is wasted when the teacher does not properly plan the lesson, or when the teacher has to discipline students who are misbehaving (Leinhardt, Zigmond, and Cooley, 1981). Children who are completing seatwork while the teacher directly teaches a reading group, are not directly involved in learning. To make the most of instructional time, teachers need to plan seatwork carefully.

High-achieving reading groups are usually more actively engaged in the reading lesson than are low-level reading groups (Hiebert, 1983); therefore, high groups have more time on task than low groups, which contributes to the differences in achievement between groups. Careful planning of reading lessons can help teachers overcome these differences.

Questioning

Quality questions are a major means of implementing instruction. Teachers use questioning strategies to actively engage children in learning. Talking—asking and answering questions reveals our thoughts and feelings. This experience, in turn, clarifies our views and focuses our thinking (Christenbury and Kelly, 1983). Students exhibit their understanding of text when they respond to questions. Their answers give teachers the data that help them know whether they need to reteach a concept or clarify students' understanding. At times, answers reveal that students need more data to understand information or concepts. Far too often, we behave as if reading automatically results in understanding (King, 1984).

Hierarchies

During recent years, educators have explored hierarchies of questioning based on the theory that questions formulated to represent various levels of thinking stimulated students to think at the same levels (Redfield and Rousseau,

1981; Christenbury and Kelly, 1983). Earlier researchers suggested that teachers spent too much time asking lower-level questions, implying that questions at certain cognitive levels were of greater value than others (Christenbury and Kelly, 1983). Strict adherence to hierarchies does not necessarily increase learning. Refer to Chapter 5 for additional information regarding questions.

Following are example questions, based on a story appropriate for second graders, *The Winter Cat* by Howard Knotts

ANALYTICAL QUESTIONS:

Where does the cat live?
What is a wild cat?
How do the children help the cat?

INFERENTIAL QUESTIONS:

Why does the cat run away when the children approach him?
How does the author show us that the cat is cold?
How do the children feel when they see the cat shivering?
Why do you think the cat watches the children's house?

CRITICAL QUESTIONS:

What might the cat be thinking as he watches the snow?
What problems does the snow create for the cat?
What other animals have problems when winter comes?

CREATIVE QUESTIONS:

How can we help animals who have winter problems?
Compare wild animals with pet animals.

The following guidelines help teachers prepare thought-provoking questions.

1. Use questioning hierarchies as guidelines rather than strictly adhering to them. Write out questions in advance; this is particularly important for novice teachers.
2. Before creating questions, examine the content and identify the important ideas and concepts toward which you are guiding students. Then ask questions that will lead students to understand these ideas and concepts.

3. Be flexible—do not expect the discussion to go precisely as you planned. Listen carefully to students, making sure that you hear their entire response. Sometimes their incorrect response is better than the one you expected. At times, students' answers indicate their interests or problems, which the teacher may choose to explore with additional questions.

4. Ask questions that have more than one correct answer. Right- and wrong-answer questions do not stimulate much thinking. The really stimulating questions are the ones that have several appropriate responses; also, they give students more opportunities to experience success. Ask questions that require multiple-word answers; these questions tend to foster cognitive development. When students offer one-word answers, encourage them to expand their answers.

5. Encourage students to ask questions. Students should feel free to ask questions without fear of embarrassment; teachers should not be afraid of departing from lesson plans in order to answer students' questions. Questions also give teachers opportunities to tailor instruction to meet students' needs.

6. Allow sufficient "wait time." Hyman (1979) reports that teachers wait only 1 second for students to respond before asking another student to respond or restating the question. Insufficient "wait time" pressures students to answer incorrectly, even if they know the correct answer. Hyman (1979) notes that increasing the "wait time" from 3 to 5 seconds increases the quality of answers.

7. Avoid asking too many questions. Research shows that teachers who thought they were asking 12 to 20 questions every half-hour were actually asking 45 to 150. This appears to be more of an inquisition than a discussion. Such rapid-fire questioning discourages student participation.

8. Create an atmosphere that encourages students to discuss content with one another. Students should have opportunities to ask and answer each other's questions. Teachers have a tendency to dominate discussion; student interaction is more appropriate.

Think-Alouds

A think-aloud is a thinking-skills model. The teacher shares his or her thoughts, enabling students to understand what they should be doing as they read. When conducting a think-aloud, students should have copies of the text or it should be projected on an overhead screen. After the teacher (or other model) shares his or her thoughts, the teacher and students collaborate to identify the types of thinking that occurred. These types of thinking can be entered in a grid, which students use to identify the kinds of thinking they use in their own reading. Students may self-monitor, or one student can think aloud while another identifies the thinking activities.

Think-aloud script

A think-aloud script is shown in Box 2.1, which is based on the excerpt "In a Meadow, Two Hares Hide."

Box 2.1   Think-Aloud Script

Teacher: *In a meadow two hares hide.* Hmm, a meadow is like a pasture, it's a big field just like on the farm where I grew up. Two hares. Hares are rabbits, so there must be two rabbits in the story and they are in the meadow.

Teacher: The text says ". . . it was morning. The tall grass shone in the early sun." I can see the grass shining in my mind. The grass must be kind of tall or it would not reflect the sun. Of course the sun is shining or there would be no light to reflect on the grass.

Teacher: The rabbit's name is Mimo. That's an odd name.

Teacher: "She was hungry and thirsty." I never thought about rabbits drinking, but I have seen bowls of water in the cages of pet rabbits.

Teacher: She found "wild grapes, which were wet and sweet." Well, she found food and water at the same time. "Mimo chewed many of the grapes." She should not be hungry now since she ate many grapes.

Teacher: "She crouched in the darkness of the bushes and watched the meadow around her." Crouched sounds like she is afraid. I wonder why. Could it be hunting season?

Teacher: So far, I have only read about one rabbit. I wonder where the other rabbit is?

In a Meadow, Two Hares Hide

In a meadow, it was morning. The tall grass shone in the early sun. A young hare hopped about the field. Her name was Mimo. She was hungry and thirsty, and it was time to look for food.

Here, she found the last of the summer's wild grapes, which were wet and sweet. Mimo chewed many of the grapes. Then she crouched in the darkness of the bushes and watched the meadow around her.

Source: Leo Fay *et al., Front Row, The Riverside Reading Program,* Chicago: The Riverside Publishing Co., 1988. Reprinted by permission.

Did you notice that the teacher in this script used her own experiences to understand the text? She also extended her existing knowledge to include the fact that rabbits get thirsty. The thinking activities reflected in the preceding script are summarized in the following list:

Word meaning (meadow and hare)

Setting identification (morning in the meadow)

Visual imagery (shining grass)

Extended existing knowledge (regarding rabbit being thirsty)

Connotative meaning (crouched)

Questioned (why was the rabbit afraid)

Anticipated (second rabbit)

Used background experience (meadow and hunting season)

These thinking activities could be entered in a grid and used to guide subsequent thinking activities. Think-Alouds are also discussed in Chapter 5.

Lesson Planning

Thorough, careful planning is the key to effective teaching; it enables teachers to be systematic, yet flexible. Teachers can depart from the lesson plan if it becomes necessary to deal with interruptions or to make use of an unplanned "teachable moment:" Lesson plans help teachers achieve both yearly objectives and daily objectives. Without lesson plans, important skills, strategies, or content may be inadvertently omitted.

To plan lessons, teachers need to understand the nature of children's learning. This is why most teacher-education curricula include courses on educational psychology or the psychology of learning. The following list summarizes learning research as it relates to planning effective reading lessons. Research supports the following statements about learning (Jones, Palincsar, Ogle, and Carr, 1987).

1. Learning is goal-oriented.
2. Learning is influenced by development (students' level of development).
3. Learning occurs in phases, but it is not linear.
4. Learning is linking new information to prior knowledge.
5. Learning is organizing information.
6. Learning is acquiring a repertoire of cognitive and metacognitive structures.

Reading instruction and lesson plans should be built around these concepts.

Objectives
Lesson plans should include objectives that state exactly what and why students are to learn. In reading, for example, students should work actively to construct the meaning of what they read, and should monitor their understanding of the text (Brown, 1985; Pearson, 1985). Thus, the search for meaning is a global objective of the developmental reading program. Readers who recognize this objective can monitor their own understanding; this enables them to remedy their lapses in comprehension. Knowing the objective enables readers to focus on what is important (Mayer, 1984). Constructing meaning and self-monitoring (metacognition) are discussed in Chapters 6 and 7.

As you have learned in both child development and educational psychology courses, children's learning is influenced by their stage of development. Older children learn differently from younger children; therefore, they should be taught differently. Instructional intervention facilitates learning when the level of instruction is the same as the students' stage of development. Younger children benefit from explicit instruction because they have not developed abstract thinking skills. Teachers should remember that children exhibit individual differences in learning. Observation is usually a good source of information about children's learning, and should be a continuing aspect of planning and instructing. You might want to refer to a child development text or an educational psychology text to refresh your memory on learning and development.

Learning

Learning is not linear; it occurs in phases that are related to students' development. Learning, like reading, is a complex thinking process involving different skills and strategies at different phases of learning (Chall, 1983). Instruction must help young children move from spoken language to written language; some children do this best by learning whole words, while others learn through phonemes, which they blend to approximate words.

Link prior knowledge with new information

Learning is linking new information to prior knowledge (Jones et al., 1987). For example, existing knowledge structures about earthquakes enable learners to infer that an aftershock will follow an earthquake. Of course, the opposite is also true: learners who have little or no existing knowledge about a subject are unable to make predictions. Prior knowledge, also known as world knowledge or schemata, develops from learners' actual experiences. Sound reading instruction helps learners develop schemata. (See Chapter 5 for further discussion.) Lesson plans activate existing knowledge and connect it with new information.

Organize knowledge

Learning is organizing knowledge. Learning is facilitated when learners organize ideas or information into patterns. Authors help readers organize knowledge through the text structures they use. Fiction is structured by story grammar, while expository texts are commonly structured by comparison and contrast; cause and effect; description; problem and solution; sequence; and examples. Each of these structures has its own distinctive characteristics, which skilled readers and writers learn to recognize. Reading instruction should facilitate organization of knowledge. Instruction should help students organize knowledge. Identifying the causes and effects read in a social studies selection is an example of guiding students in structured learning. Structures for organizing knowledge are discussed in Chapters 6 through 8.

Learners develop a repertoire of cognitive and metacognitive skills; these enable them to develop reading skills and strategies. For instance, they learn to activate their existing schemata, which facilitates reading comprehension.

Successful learners are self-motivated. They stick to a task until it is done to their satisfaction; they attribute success to their own efforts. Successful learners know how to control their own learning, and they select appropriate strategies to use throughout the learning process (Jones et al., 1987). Thus, effective reading lessons develop both cognitive and metacognitive skills and strategies that students need for successful learning. For instance, learners know when to use context clues, structural analysis, or phonics to decode a word. Chapters 4 through 7 develop cognitive and metacognitive skills and strategies as they relate to reading.

Planning Reading Lessons

Research supports the *objective-demonstration-practice-feedback* model for reading lessons (Rosenshine and Stevens, 1984; Anderson et al., 1979; Good and Grouws, 1979). In the demonstration phase, new materials or skills are demonstrated or modeled. Then, teachers guide students as they practice using the material or skill, providing feedback, evaluating progress, and giving additional demonstrations, if necessary. Independent practice is the final stage of the reading lesson. In this phase, students practice without teacher guidance until their responses are rapid and confident. Independent practice may continue several days or weeks, depending on the skill or knowledge learned. Practice should continue until the skill or knowledge is *overlearned,* which assures automatic responses (Anderson, Evertson, and Brophy, 1982). Reading skills and knowledge should be regularly reviewed in order to maintain them.

Independent practice

Box 2.2, a second-grade lesson plan, based on the story *My Friend Jacob* by Lucille Clifton, demonstrates the objective-demonstration-practice-feedback model.

INSTRUCTIONAL PACE

The pace of instruction indicates students' growth in reading (Barr and Dreeben, 1983). Students exhibit higher reading achievement when teachers have lessons that move at a brisk pace. Brisk-paced lessons hold students' attention, while slow-paced lessons allow their attention to wander. Fast-paced lessons also expose students to more text and give them more opportunities to learn.

Ability groups

High-ability groups read more words of text each week than low-ability groups. One research study showed that low-ability first graders read 400 words a week, while high-ability students averaged 1100 words (Allington, 1984). Obviously, the more words students read, the more fluency they develop. The optimum pace depends on students' ability. Generally speaking, children should be able to accurately identify 95 percent of the words in the text they are reading, and they should be able to answer 80 percent of the teacher's questions correctly.

Careful planning and systematic instruction enable teachers to pace reading instruction; on the other hand, disorganized instruction allows wasted time in the classroom. Fast-paced lessons teach students key concepts before they have to apply them in follow-up assignments. Careful preparation of seatwork assignments avoids student confusion (Rosenshine and Stevens, 1984).

Efficient teachers should establish classroom routines early in the school year, so that children know where and how to obtain needed materials; thus, interruptions in instruction are avoided. Students also need to learn about appropriate behavior early in the school year, so teachers do not have to stop lessons to discipline students, which interferes with the pace of instruction.

Box 2.2   Instruction Cycle of a Lesson Plan

OBJECTIVE (GOALS):

Word recognition—introduce the final consonant cluster *ph*

Reteach (continued independent practice) short vowels

Comprehension—identify the ways that authors reveal character traits; compare and contrast characters

MATERIALS:

Multiple copies of the story

Chalkboard or flip chart

INTRODUCTION (DEMONSTRATION OR MODELING):

Review previously taught final consonant clusters to establish a basis for introducing *ph*. Have the students say the word *graph* aloud while listening carefully to the final sound, which introduces the *ph* sound. Explain that in the word, *graph*, the letters *ph* stand for the *f* sound. Write *graph* on the chalkboard, and underline the *ph*. Then pronounce a series of words that include both the final *ph* sound, and words that do not include the final *ph*. Examples of words with the final *ph* include: *autograph, paragraph, phonograph, photograph.* Students are to raise a hand each time they hear the *f* sound at the end of a word. Explain that they should listen for words with this sound in the story they are going to read.

Review the short vowel sounds with words from the story, for example, *Sam, best, sit, just, on.* Ask students to generate a list of words that contain short vowel sounds. Alert students to look for short vowel sounds as they read.

Teach the new story words in sentence context. Students should use a combination of phonics and context to decode the unknown words. Encourage children to identify short vowels as they study these words. As the students read the words, ascertain whether they can associate a meaning with each word. Following are examples of sentences with the new words underlined.

1. Sam played *basketball*.
2. We blew out the *candles* on the birthday cake.
3. It is fun to *celebrate* birthdays.
4. The *delivery* man brought a present.

5. When I am *seventeen*, I will drive a car.
6. My sister *suggested* that I play with her friends.
7. We took the little puppy *along*.
8. Take the puzzle *apart*.
9. This problem is *especially* difficult.

Introduce the story by explaining that they are going to read about an eight-year-old boy whose best friend is Jacob, a retarded teenager. Encourage students to discuss the kinds of things they do with their friends; this will activate schemata. (They may discuss playing games, riding bicycles, having meals together, working together, and the like.)

GUIDED PRACTICE:

Reading the story will provide students with guided practice.

1. Give students silent reading assignment. First, have them read to find out the things that Jacob and Sam did that showed they are good friends.
2. They should also read to find out what each character is like.

Following silent reading, discuss the silent reading purposes. Then discuss questions like these:

1. How are Jacob and Sam like other friends that you know?
2. How is their friendship different from other friendships?
3. Which of Jacob's traits make him different from other friends?
4. How is Jacob like other friends?

You may create a chart that compares and contrasts friendships.
Then discuss the ways that the author reveals character traits in this story. As the children identify these factors, write them on the chalkboard or chart. Make a list of words that describe the main characters in this story. Discuss ways that we can be good friends to people like Jacob.
Ask the students to identify words in the story that end with the *ph* cluster and ten words that contain short vowels.

INDEPENDENT PRACTICE:

Read and discuss the book *My Brother Steven Is Retarded* by Harriet S. Sobol. Children may write about ways that they can be friends with retarded individuals. The discussion can focus on identifying character traits and comparing characters.

CREATING WARM, LITERATE ENVIRONMENTS

A warm, literate environment stimulates language interchange and interaction. As children discuss books, plays, and shared experiences, they develop reading and thinking processes. Teachers stimulate children's thinking, encourage them to listen critically, and motivate them to read different types of literature for a variety of purposes. In a literate environment, children are encouraged to ask questions, to discuss, to investigate ideas, and report their findings to the class. Youngsters in these classes learn that literature is a model for writing and exploring ideas in writing.

Purposeful reading experiences

Reading ability is acquired when children have many reading experiences. For instance, children who have opportunities to record information about a pet hamster, as well as to read about hamster care, are engaging in purposeful reading. They can conduct research to learn why popcorn pops, or to learn how children lived on the American frontier. Aquariums, terrariums, classroom pets, group projects, experiments, and field trips stimulate reading and writing. Children should experience reading throughout the school day: in the classroom, on the playground, in the cafeteria, and in school corridors.

Students should have access to materials that stimulate language exploration. They should be able to select from trade books written at various reading levels, which address a wide variety of interests. Newspapers, magazines, brochures, almanacs, games, videocassette recorders, and computers should be available to students. Children who are limited to textbooks, workbooks, and worksheets do not achieve as well as those who have opportunities to explore many kinds of media (Leinhardt, Zigmond, and Cooley, 1981; Rosenshine and Stevens, 1984).

Classroom environment

The classroom environment encourages reading when children's work is displayed on the bulletin boards. Bright charts around the classroom, displays of trade books, interest centers, chalkboards, computers, and typewriters invite children to read and write. In addition, the classroom arrangement should give students easy access to the many resources in the classroom; for example, children should be able to obtain books, paper, and pencils without interrupting the teacher. The classroom arrangement should create places for children to work in various-sized groups.

GROUPING STUDENTS FOR READING INSTRUCTION

The major organizational plan for delivering reading instruction is ability grouping; however, ability grouping is an extremely controversial issue (Slavin, 1987). The issue is whether children learn better in ability groups or in groups formed on a basis other than ability or achievement. Recently, cooperative learning has provided another alternative to traditional grouping practices.

In ability grouping, children who have similar reading achievement are instructed together. The majority of contemporary primary teachers and many intermediate teachers form three ability groups in their classes for reading instruction. Grouping is considered necessary because most elementary classrooms include a span of five or more reading levels. Ability grouping allows students to keep pace with the reading instruction for that group. In addition, smaller groups of students are easier to actively engage in instruction than larger groups.

Unfortunately, ability grouping is not a perfect solution to pupil variability. When students are grouped on this basis, there is no assurance that other characteristics will be similar. For instance, individual students may decode words expertly, but fail to comprehend due to a lack of cultural literacy. Grouping such students on the basis of decoding skills does not necessarily mean that they are grouped appropriately for comprehension. Even when the skills of group members are very similar, some students simply process written language faster than others, so they are always finished before the other members of the group.

Three reading groups

The majority of elementary classrooms have three reading groups: a high-achieving group, an average-achieving group, and a low-achieving group. Students (and their parents) evaluate their own abilities on the basis of the group to which they are assigned. If they are in a high group, they consider themselves skilled readers, but if they are in a low group, they consider themselves poor readers. Research shows that children in high groups learn more than children in lower groups, thereby perpetuating the achievement levels of students (Allington, 1984).

Low-achieving groups

Teachers also have lower expectations for students who are in lower achieving groups (Cazden, 1979). Teachers instruct the various reading groups in different ways (Allington, 1984). Children in low groups read aloud more, and read silently less (Hiebert, 1983); however, research shows that silent reading is an important aspect of reading instruction. Low-achieving groups are introduced to vocabulary without context in lists or on word cards, even though the most effective way to introduce new words is in context. Teachers correct more of the oral reading errors in low groups; they correct mistakes through word pronunciation cues rather than meaning cues, which are reserved for students in high groups. Also, teachers tolerate more interruptions during instruction in low groups (McDermott, 1976).

Social maturity

Children in low groups tend to have lower "social maturity," which contributes to lower achievement. Lower social maturity is reflected in their reading group behavior. They do not attend to instruction, are frequently nonresponsive to questions, and are more impulsive (Stoodt and Costello, 1986). Children in lower achievement groups usually have lower ability; therefore, they make less progress than students in higher groups. They need more direct instruction to learn effectively; they do not learn well when working alone or in small unsupervised groups (Hiebert, 1983).

Slavin (1987) recently synthesized ability grouping research and made the following recommendations:

1. Students should be in heterogeneous groups at most times; they should be regrouped by ability only for subjects (reading, mathematics, and so forth).

2. Plan groups by the specific skill being taught, not simply by intelligence or overall achievement.
3. Groups should be frequently reassessed, and should be flexible enough for easy reassignment.
4. Teachers should vary the level and pace of instruction according to the needs and readiness of each group.
5. Group numbers should be small enough to allow direct instruction for each group.

Grouping   Reading groups are usually formed in the initial weeks of the school year. In order to group students, teachers should acquaint themselves with their achievement levels, interests, reading strengths, and weaknesses. This information can be obtained from standardized reading tests, informal tests, interest inventories, and observation (see Chapter 8). In order to assign students to reading groups, teachers should be aware of the following:

the speaking and listening ability of each student

the work habits of the individual student

the student's oral reading ability

the student's sight word knowledge

the student's ability to answer comprehension questions

the quality of the student's written work

the student's ability to follow directions

the student's reading rate

the student's participation in class discussion

informal reading inventories

No matter what type of data teachers use for grouping students, they cannot be neatly divided into three reading achievement groups. Some children always fall between groups. For example, the reading levels of a third-grade class, based on a standardized reading test, are listed here.

HIGH ACHIEVERS

5.3

5.0 (fifth grade)

4.8 (fourth grade, eighth month)

4.7

4.7

4.3

4.0

4.0

AVERAGE ACHIEVERS

3.5

3.4

3.3

3.2

3.2

3.1

3.1

3.1

3.0

3.0

3.0

LOW ACHIEVERS

2.9

2.3

2.3

2.1

2.1

1.9

1.8

When you examine these preceding test scores, realize that the test scores are only one piece of information; furthermore they are not static. Also, notice that the scores of the low group have a 13-month range, which means that the youngster at the top of this group is considerably more able than the lowest child in the group. Notice the 15-month range in the high-achieving group. It is obvious that grouping does not eliminate individual differences. It is also obvious that some students read better than the group below them, but not as well as the group above them. Therefore, even when a classroom is divided into reading groups, provision must be made for individual differences.

Flexibility

Flexibility

Flexibility is a key to addressing individual differences. Grouping practices should be flexible enough to allow teachers to reevaluate students, teaching techniques, and group placement on a regular basis. Some students start the year slowly, but their achievement surges as they become acclimated to school. When this occurs, they should be placed in a different group. On the other hand, some students start the year successfully, but illness or family problems interfere with learning. When this occurs, they should be assigned to a different group where they can experience success. Group placement should be a matter of identifying a group in which students can learn most successfully, not a matter for embarrassment or ridicule. Group placement should be neither a reward nor a punishment.

Teachers frequently name individual reading groups with names like, "blue birds," "red birds," or "buzzards" or they allow the students to name their own groups. This practice is not advisable because children frequently are categorized in their own minds—and in the teacher's mind. Rather than naming groups, it is best to ask children to come to a particular group by announcing the title of the book they are using.

Time allotment   The time allotted for reading instruction in the primary grades is usually a minimum of 1½ to 2 hours each day. In the intermediate grades, 1 hour a day is usually scheduled for reading. When the teacher directly teaches one reading group, the children in the remaining groups are usually engaged in independent work (seatwork)—which may include worksheets, workbooks, writing, reading games, silent reading, answering written questions, or completing enrichment activities related to basal reader stories.

One of the most difficult teaching tasks is making certain that the independent work period is a **learning** experience for children. A good independent activity must be difficult enough to hold students' interest, but easy enough for them to complete without a high proportion of errors. This balance is difficult to achieve. Worksheets, workbooks, and other independent activities are discussed in Chapter 7. Tables 2.2 and 2.3 illustrate how three individual reading groups might be managed. Table 2.2 focuses on a primary grade, and Table 2.3 shows an intermediate grade. As you examine Table 2.3, you will notice that intermediate groups are handled differently from primary groups due to time constraints.

The intermediate-grade teacher who has allotted only 1 hour for reading instruction daily, cannot provide adequate direction for all three groups. I recommend that the teacher assign independent work to one group, while providing direct instruction for the other two groups each day. By alternating among the groups each week, the direct instructional time is equalized.

Group size   Flexibility in grouping is also exhibited when teachers group students in a variety of group sizes. Students should have reading instruction in small groups, whole class groups, and individually; no one grouping is appropriate for all types of instruction. Teachers should choose the group size that is most appropriate for the instruction they plan, as well as the achievement level of the students they are instructing. Some students find it difficult, if not impossible, to work without direct teacher intervention.

Small-Group Instruction

Small-group instruction may be familiar; many of you experienced it in your own elementary-school experience. Small groups permit a higher level of in-

Table 2.2   PRIMARY GRADES (1–3): READING GROUP MANAGEMENT

Time allotted	Group I	Group II	Group III
10 minutes	Teacher explains the purpose of the independent work to the class.		
30 minutes	Silent reading (purposes assigned by teacher)	Phonics activity	Introduce story; read silently; purposeful oral reading
30 minutes	Discuss story; read silently; purposeful oral reading	Cut out pictures for consonant sounds	Visual discrimination activity
30 minutes	Read a book for pleasure	Directed silent reading; purposeful oral reading	Writing activity
15 minutes	Teacher reviews and checks independent work.		

Table 2.3   INTERMEDIATE GRADES (4–6): READING GROUP MANAGEMENT

Time allotted	Group I	Group II	Group III
5 minutes	Teacher explains the purpose of the independent work to the class.		
25 minutes	Individualized reading	Silent reading (purposes assigned by teacher)	Directed reading lesson
25 minutes	Teacher-pupil conferences	Basal activities	Worksheet
5 minutes	Follow-up independent activities.		

teraction; they create a good setting for teacher observation of students' progress. The greatest problem with small-group instruction is that students who are not in the group need to be actively engaged in learning; this is difficult to maintain when the teacher is engaged in direct instruction with another group. The greatest strength of small-group instruction is that it enables teachers to meet individual needs.

As stated earlier, small groups are most frequently formed on the basis of achievement or ability; however, several other possibilities exist. Students can be grouped on the basis of interests, friendships, skills, or peer tutoring.

Interests

Interest Groups

These are based on children's reading interests or their interests in hobbies, or a particular topic. Children who share common interests, can read and discuss materials that address their common interests. For example, children who became interested in "black holes," formed an interest group in one classroom. These children read and studied together for several weeks. In another classroom, a group of second graders became interested in monarch butterflies, and formed a separate interest group. These groups are short-term units that disband when the project is completed.

Social Reading Groups

These are comprised of children who are friends and who enjoy working together. Adults enjoy working with friends, and it follows that children would enjoy the same—thus, a social reading group affords them this opportunity. Furthermore, children learn more from their contact with a supportive group. These groups may carry out projects similar to those of interest groups. They also may organize and carry out literature-related activities, such as creative dramatics, art projects, puppet productions, research, creating bulletin-board displays, reader's theater, and playing reading games.

Skill groups

Flexible Skill Groups

These are formed for the purpose of teaching specific skills that students need. These groups are formed when several children need instruction in the same skill or ability, for example, learning vowel digraphs or context clues. Meetings are scheduled for as long as it takes the children to learn that skill or ability, and the group is disbanded thereafter. Additional flexible skill groups may be formed to meet other needs, as they arise. Since these groups focus solely on skill development, they should be short in duration—no longer than 15 minutes each day.

Peer tutoring

Peer Tutoring Groups

These may consist of pairs of students or small groups that work with a student who has already acquired the skill or ability. Students can usually communicate well with each other, and they can usually remember their own experiences in acquiring the skill or ability; this enables them to help another youngster. In peer tutoring groups, students coach and help one another. The student who is teaching or coaching learns from the experience: to teach a skill, one must have acquired it.

Cooperative Reading Instruction

Cooperative learning refers to a set of instructional methods in which students work in small, mixed-ability learning groups (Slavin, 1987). Slavin recommends that cooperative groups have four members—one high achiever, two average achievers, and one low achiever. The students in each group are responsible for learning the material being taught in class, and helping their groupmates learn. Often there is a group goal such as brainstorming, categorization, comparison and contrast, answering questions, activating background knowledge, and so forth (Uttero, 1988).

Cooperative learning

Cooperative groups probably work best above the second-grade level, since younger children lack both the reading skills and the independence to function well in such groups. Although third graders and above are more likely to have the maturity necessary for such groupings, they also need assistance in learning how to function within this particular organization.

Uttero (1988) offers the following guidelines for implementing cooperative work.

1. State the guidelines of working together cooperatively. Emphasize equal participation of group members.
2. Organize the groups. Determine group size. Assign students to groups heterogeneously, distributing group membership among boys and girls, high achievers and low achievers, enthusiastic and reluctant learners.
3. Describe the purpose of the cooperative work.
4. Model the strategies. Demonstrate each activity by completing it with a group.
5. Gradually turn over the responsibility for achieving group objectives to the students.
6. Observe the interaction between the students.

Whole-Class Instruction

Whole-class instruction is a valuable direct instructional approach, which also helps teachers overcome some of the problems inherent in ability grouping. Problems such as assigning students to ability groups, and differences in the instruction provided for different reading groups, are not as apparent during whole-class instruction. Whole-class instruction increases the amount of time students spend in teacher-directed instruction, which has proven effective in raising student achievement (Rosenshine and Stevens, 1984). In this organizational plan, students spend less time on seatwork and other forms of independent learning, which research indicates are not productive. Research shows that programs utilizing whole-class instruction have achieved good results (Engleman and Bruner, 1974; Hughes et al., 1982).

Whole-class instruction places different demands on teachers. Teachers must plan very carefully, to maintain a brisk pace and businesslike attitude. This is impossible without thorough planning, since the teacher would have to search for the next instructional step and the necessary teaching materials.

Teaching a whole class requires a high energy level. Teachers must move around the classroom while teaching, must maintain eye contact in order to hold students' attention, and also must see everything that is going on in the classroom. Moving around the classroom enables teachers to involve students in class activities. Teachers must be very observant; they must know when a student's interest is straying, and must be able to immediately draw the student(s) into class activity. Monitoring student progress and encouraging interaction with the lesson is more difficult in whole-class instruction. However, some teachers and administrators believe that whole-class instruction leads to greater achievement.

Combine groups   The recommended approach is a combination of whole-class instruction with flexible small groups. Students should have whole-class instruction whenever possible; there is no value in having teachers repeat the same material over and over to small groups of students. For instance, reading skills such as phonics skills, dictionary skills, locating information, and study skills can be developed in whole-class settings. However, students who do not grasp reading skills such as main ideas and supporting details, may need small-group instruction, since these are such important skills. Therefore, students who do not grasp a skill taught to the whole class, can be clustered in a small group to work on a specific skill. In some instances, this small group could be a cooperative group.

Individualized Instruction

There are times when teachers need to work individually with students to ensure their progress in learning to read. At times very able students are so advanced that it is difficult to challenge them within a reading group. When this occurs, a teacher may give them individual assignments that meet their particular needs, and may meet with them on an individual basis. Individualized instruction often takes the form of a conference to discuss a specific assignment or a book that the youngster has read.

Conferences   Less capable students also require individualized instruction. This instruction is also conducted in a conference. Students can be given individual assignments that address their particular needs. For example, a first-grade student who requires language development, may meet with the teacher for 10 minutes a day for individualized instruction. These conferences may involve teaching a skill, analyzing errors, completing an assignment, or discussing content the student has read. Individualized reading instruction is discussed in Chapter 8.

Oral and Silent Reading

Much reading group instruction is concerned with oral and silent reading of text. This section examines the nature of oral and silent reading programs in elementary reading instruction. Oral and silent reading are closely related, but they require somewhat different skills from students. The precise relationship between oral and silent reading is not clear. Research indicates that silent reading behavior cannot be predicted from oral reading behavior and vice versa (Rowell, 1978). Furthermore, students who spend too much time in oral reading during the primary grades have greater difficulty with silent reading (Bond, Tinker, and Wasson, 1979). The research reported here indicates that teachers should teach and test oral and silent reading as separate, but related skills.

Oral Reading

Elementary students should have frequent opportunities to participate in oral reading activities. Oral reading enables teachers to diagnose reading skills. Oral reading is challenging for some students because they must concentrate on word pronunciation and oral expression, in addition to text meaning. Five significant factors should be considered in oral reading instruction. First, teachers should focus students' attention on meaning and avoid "round robin reading." Second, teachers should be certain that students read the text silently before they read aloud. Third, students' oral reading errors must be handled tactfully, so that corrections do not inhibit future reading. Fourth, each student should have equal reading opportunities. Finally, students who are listening to oral reading, should not follow the text in their books; they should listen actively to the oral interpretation.

Oral reading
errors

Oral reading should focus on meaning. Every teacher knows of children who read aloud very well, but lack understanding. On the other hand, some children have poor oral reading skills, but can easily comprehend the text. In some cases, those who comprehend are penalized by teachers because they lack oral interpretation skills. Comprehension is the goal of oral reading; therefore, teachers should focus students' attention on meaning. They should make oral reading activities meaningful to enhance comprehension. For example, oral reading is more meaningful when students read to support points they are making in a discussion. Another avenue to meaningful oral reading is having students read their own compositions aloud; this activity integrates reading and writing activities.

"Round robin" or "barbershop style" reading are common approaches in elementary classrooms. When these approaches are used, each child in the reading group takes a turn reading a few sentences, a paragraph, or a page aloud. When teachers ask for volunteers, the more assertive students read, while quiet children do not. Each student in the reading group should have an opportunity to read during oral reading sessions. This is especially important in the primary grades. Oral reading should be purposeful and provide real audience situations. Strategies like these develop oral reading skill.

Specific Approaches for Purposeful Oral Reading

These approaches are based on careful selection and preparation of the content.

1. choral reading
2. plays (most basal readers include some plays)
3. student written plays, skits, and puppet shows
4. poetry and rhymes
5. student developed radio and/or television shows
6. school announcements
7. *brief* oral reports
8. riddles and jokes
9. sharing parts of favorite books read independently
10. reader's theater
11. students' own compositions (this should be a part of a sound writing program).

Oral Reading Strategies

These strategies are teacher directed and they follow silent reading. Notice that these strategies contribute to comprehension as well as purposeful oral reading. Ask students to read:

1. what a specific character said
2. the most exciting part of the story
3. the saddest part of the story
4. a descriptive passage
5. the most beautiful part
6. the funniest part
7. the part you liked best
8. the part you liked least
9. the most expressive part
10. the most pathetic part
11. the most incongruous part
12. the part that creates images (visual, auditory, kinesthetic, etc.)
13. the climax of the story
14. the turning point
15. the part where the action picks up
16. the denouement
17. an episode
18. the setting
19. the protagonist's problem
20. the most vivid part
21. the part that supports the answer to a question
22. the answer to a literal level question
23. a fact that is new to you
24. the part that proves a character was kind (cruel, understanding, intelligent, courteous, thoughtful, etc.)
25. the part that relates to a story or selection previously read
26. the part that foreshadows subsequent action
27. the action foreshadowed by a previous event or conversation
28. inaccurate information
29. problem solutions
30. the part of a poem that you liked best
31. a poem that relates to a reading selection

Correcting oral reading errors is something teachers should consider prior to encountering the problem. Many oral reading errors simply are "miscues," resulting from a mismatch between the text and the reader's own language. Many miscues reflect understanding. For example, the student who reads the sentence, "Father came home from the office," as "Dad came home from work," is not experiencing word recognition problems; he or she understands the text, but is reading the text in his own language. Miscues or errors that do not alter text meaning should be overlooked. *All* readers make minor deviations from the text when they read aloud. Reading is not an exact process. Furthermore, the goal of reading should not be to understand and read the

Miscues

words *exactly* as they are printed in the text. In fact, excessive concern for exactness in reading and word pronunciation can interfere with comprehension.

When a student reads an incorrect word, the teacher should wait to see whether the child self-corrects the error. If not, the teacher should direct the reader's attention to context clues to see whether the child can recognize the word without assistance. After the word is correctly identified, the *youngster should reread the entire sentence in which the word occurs.* This helps the youngster assimilate the word and the sentence meaning. Research shows that using this strategy makes the student more successful (Anderson et al., 1979). Teachers who routinely supply the correct word, or permit other children in the group to call out the correct word, get children in the habit of waiting passively for help (Anderson et al. 1985).

Silent Reading

This is an important part of the elementary reading program from the outset. Most of us spend more time reading silently than we do orally. We read newspapers, recipes, directions, books, magazines, and personal letters silently every day of our lives. Most of the thoughtful, meaningful reading done by adults— and children—is silent reading. The long-range goal of silent reading instruction is to develop the ability to read silently with good comprehension.

Focus on comprehension

Silent reading permits readers to focus on comprehension. In silent reading, readers may read words quickly or even skip over them because pronunciation is not required. Therefore, the silent reading rate is usually more rapid than the oral reading rate. Researchers have found that sixth-grade students who read silently at a rate of 210 words per minute, decreased to 170 words per minute when reading orally (Ransom and Mitchell, 1980). This is rather predictable because oral reading requires pronunciation, while silent reading involves processing language with the eyes and the mind.

Extended silent reading

Children at every stage of reading development should spend extended periods of time for silent reading. The amount of time spent reading silently is related to students' gains in reading achievement (Leinhardt et al., 1981). Silent reading instruction should begin when reading instruction begins in kindergarten or first grade. Students should learn to read with "their eyes" when they first start looking at print. They should develop a concept of silent reading at the same time they learn to read, which will enable them to gradually move from saying the words aloud to thinking them. Children who are not taught silent reading in the early stages of reading instruction have considerable difficulty acquiring this skill later.

Difficulty with silent reading interferes with comprehension. Reading for the higher thought processes should be silent, to permit readers to concentrate on text meaning without having to consider word pronunciation and expression. Students should *always* read silently before reading orally.

Purposeful silent reading

Silent reading should be purposeful. Teachers need to help students formulate purposes to guide their silent reading (see Chapter 6). In the primary grades, teachers can improve silent reading by teaching new vocabulary (in context) prior to the silent reading period. Many young children benefit from the Directed-Reading-Thinking-Activity (see Chapter 6) because they are not sufficiently independent to read silently. Uninterrupted, sustained silent reading is another useful strategy for developing silent reading skills (see Chapter 8).

SELECTING AND USING READING MATERIALS

A selection and use of reading materials is a complex topic. (Chapter 8 explores ways of choosing and using reading materials.) To develop effective instruction, teachers need both opportunities and time to reflect about the reading lessons they teach; this will enable them to analyze the strengths and weaknesses of these lessons (Wildman and Niles, 1987). Berliner (1985) has recommended that teachers spend at least several hundred hours across their careers studying and analyzing their teaching in field settings. Evaluation of reading growth requires background, which is developed in Chapters 3 through 7.

SUMMARY

The following list summarizes the key points of this chapter.

1. The reading curriculum is a planned set of experiences designed to develop students' reading ability. The reading curriculum developed in the primary grades is concerned with learning how to read familiar ideas, language, and stories. In the intermediate grades, the reading curriculum is concerned with teaching students to use reading as a means of learning.

2. Teaching is a complex activity designed to support students' learning. The quality of teaching makes a significant difference in students' learning. Approximately 15 percent of the variation in reading achievement is attributed to the teacher's skill and effectiveness. Effective teachers are strong leaders and good managers; they approach reading in a direct, businesslike manner. Their instruction is academically focused, with clear goal statements. Effective teachers explain and use examples to develop their students' understanding of the reading process, and to help students understand what is expected of them. Effective teachers model thinking, questioning, and responding. They teach small groups, whole groups, and individuals. They praise students when it is appropriate.

3. Teaching tasks include: planning and implementing instruction, pacing instruction, grouping students, creating a warm, literate environment, selecting materials, and evaluating assignments.

4. Both direct instruction and indirect instruction are involved in teaching students to read. Direct instruction is deliberate teaching, while indirect instruction occurs when a skill or fact is learned without deliberate teaching.

5. The more academic engaged time students spend on reading, the higher their achievement. Academic engaged time refers to the time spent on a particular task.
6. Questioning is an important teaching tool. Effective teachers use literal questions, inferential questions, evaluative questions, and creative questions.
7. Effective teachers model for students. A think-aloud is a form of modeling during which the teacher makes his or her thinking public; this helps students understand what they should be doing as they read.
8. Careful lesson planning is the key to effective teaching. Research supports the objective-demonstration-practice-feedback lesson plan model.
9. Grouping by ability is a debatable issue; however, other forms of grouping helps teachers meet students' needs.
10. In cooperative groups, students are responsible for their own learning, as well as the learning of other group members.
11. Both oral and silent reading are developed in the elementary reading program. However, oral reading and silent reading differ; children should be instructed in both types of reading.

SELF-TEST

Check your knowledge of the information presented in this chapter. The answer key is located in Appendix C.

1. What factors characterize direct instruction?
   a. academic focus
   b. systematic
   c. active teaching
   d. all of the above
2. What is direct instruction?
   a. unplanned teaching
   b. deliberate teaching
   c. independent teaching
   d. all of the above
3. What types of instruction are involved in teaching children to read?
   a. direct instruction
   b. indirect instruction
   c. both a and b
   d. neither a nor b
4. What is academic engaged time?
   a. time on task
   b. active engagement
   c. both a and b
   d. neither a nor b
5. Which reading groups achieve higher?
   a. those who spend less time reading silently
   b. those who spend more time reading

c. those who read with good oral expression
d. those who know the most phonetic rules

6. How can teachers improve the quality of students' answers to questions?
   a. by asking more questions
   b. by asking fewer questions
   c. by allowing for wait time
   d. by asking longer questions

7. What is the focus of inferential questions?
   a. information stated in the text
   b. unstated meanings
   c. judgments regarding text
   d. imaginative thinking

8. What is the focus of critical level questions?
   a. information stated in the text
   b. unstated meanings
   c. judgments regarding text
   d. imaginative thinking

9. How should teachers prepare to ask questions?
   a. by avoiding reading the text
   b. by writing many questions
   c. by identifying the important ideas and concepts in the text
   d. by asking questions as they occur to him or her

10. What happens when a teacher uses a think-aloud?
    a. students think aloud
    b. the teacher shares his or her thoughts
    c. a text is not used
    d. the teacher asks questions at the inferential level

11. Why is lesson planning important?
    a. it enables systematic teaching
    b. it permits flexibility
    c. it is not important
    d. both a and b

12. Which answers characterize successful learning?
    a. goal-oriented
    b. cognitive structure
    c. organizes information
    d. all of the above

13. How do learners relate new information to prior knowledge?
    a. by eliminating prior knowledge
    b. by memorizing new information
    c. by separating new information from prior knowledge
    d. none of the above

14. Which of the following are elements of lesson plans?
    a. objectives
    b. demonstration
    c. practice
    d. all of the above

15. Which type of practice occurs first in a reading lesson?
    a. guided practice
    b. independent practice
    c. both a and b
    d. neither a nor b

16. Why do fast-paced lessons contribute to reading growth?
    a. they hold students' attention
    b. they cover more content
    c. both a and b
    d. neither a nor b

17. How do classroom routines influence achievement?
    a. they help avoid wasted time
    b. they lower achievement
    c. they increase the amount of paper used in the classroom
    d. they make evaluation unnecessary

18. What is the value of a warm, literate environment?
    a. it stimulates language interchange and interaction
    b. it permits language to flourish and enhances reading development
    c. neither a nor b
    d. both a and b

19. What types of reading groups are used in elementary classrooms?
    a. large groups
    b. small groups
    c. pairs
    d. all of the above

20. What is the intent of grouping students?
    a. to mix the ability of students in a group
    b. to cluster students who are more alike
    c. to randomize student enrollment
    d. all of the above

21. What is a major value of small groups?
    a. students can listen better
    b. it is easier to actively engage students in instruction
    c. students do not have to read every day
    d. all of the above

22. What is a major value of whole group instruction?
    a. students do not have to pay attention
    b. students have opportunities to hear other students read
    c. students do not have to spend so much time on independent activities
    d. none of the above

23. How do lower achieving reading groups differ from higher achieving reading groups?
    a. teachers have lower expectations for lower groups
    b. teachers instruct the groups differently
    c. lower groups read aloud more and read silently less
    d. all of the above

24. Why is flexibility important in reading groups?
    a. it enables teachers to make students aware that they will be placed in a
       lower group if they do not read well
    b. it enables teachers to adjust group placement when achievement varies
    c. it interferes with learning
    d. it prevents moving students from group to group
25. Which of the following answers characterize whole-class instruction?
    a. brisk-paced
    b. teachers move around and maintain eye contact
    c. teachers observe students carefully
    d. all of the above
26. Why is oral reading challenging for some students?
    a. they do not like to read aloud
    b. they must pronounce words aloud and comprehend
    c. they cannot read loud enough
    d. they read too loud
27. When is "round robin" or "barbershop" reading appropriate?
    a. never
    b. every day
    c. when holding children's attention to the task
    d. all of the above
28. When should children read silently?
    a. never
    b. they should read everything silently before reading aloud
    c. they should read only the parts of a story that they will have to read aloud
    d. none of the above
29. What oral reading errors should be overlooked?
    a. none
    b. all of them
    c. those that do not alter text meaning
    d. those that alter text meaning
30. What proportion of readers make minor deviations from the text when they
    read aloud?
    a. all of them
    b. none of them
    c. one in five readers
    d. ten in 100 readers

THOUGHT QUESTIONS

1. Describe an effective reading teacher.
2. What kinds of information does a teacher need to form reading groups.
3. What kinds of reading groupings are used for reading instruction? Explain
   when each type of group is appropriate.
4. Compare oral and silent reading.
5. Identify the strengths and weaknesses of whole-class reading instruction.

6. How could a teacher overcome the weaknesses of ability-group reading instruction?

7. Why is ability grouping such a controversial issue?

8. How do cooperative groups function in the classroom? What are the values of cooperative groups? How could you use them in your classroom?

ENRICHMENT ACTIVITIES

1. Examine the reading curriculum for a local school system. Identify the skills, abilities, and interests that are developed in the recommended curriculum. Compare the primary curriculum with the intermediate curriculum.

2. Arrange to observe in an elementary classroom. Identify the components of the lesson that are discussed in this chapter.

3. Plan both a direct instruction lesson and an indirect instruction lesson for teaching the same skill.

4. Make a list of the factors that you consider important in creating a warm, literate classroom environment.

5. Make a file of cooperative learning activities that could be used in an elementary classroom.

6. Interview experienced teachers, elementary students, and parents regarding the characteristics they consider important for effective teachers.

7. Make a lesson plan for teaching a reading skill using the lesson plan guide suggested in this chapter.

8. Examine a basal reading series for one grade level, and select the skills and lessons that you consider most important at that grade level.

RELATED READINGS

Allington, R. (1983). "The Reading Instruction Provided Readers of Differing Ability," *Elementary School Journal,* Vol. 83, pp. 255–265.

Auten, A. (January 1985). "ERIC/RCS: Focus on Thinking Instruction," *The Reading Teacher,* Vol. 38, pp. 454–457.

Blair, T. (November 1984). "Teacher Effectiveness: The Know-how to Improve Student Learning," *The Reading Teacher,* Vol. 38, pp. 138–141.

Brown, A. (1985). "Teaching Students to Think as They Read: Implications for Curriculum Reform," Reading Education Report No. 58, Urbana, IL: University of Illinois, The Center for the Study of Reading.

Chall, J. (1983). *Stages of Reading Development,* New York: McGraw-Hill.

Christenbury, L. and P. Kelly (1983). *Questioning a Path to Critical Thinking,* Urbana, IL: National Council of Teachers of English.

Duffy, G. and L. Roehler (January 1987). "Teaching Reading Skills as Strategies," *The Reading Teacher,* Vol. 40, pp. 414–418.

Gersten, R. and T. Keating (March 1987). "Long-Term Benefits from Direct Instruction," *Educational Leadership,* Vol. 44, pp. 28–31.

Jones, B., A. Palincsar, D. Ogle, and E. Carr (1987). *Strategic Teaching and Learning: Cognitive Instruction in the Content Areas,* Alexandria, VA: ASCD.

Slavin, R. (Fall 1987). "Ability Grouping: A Best-Evidence Synthesis," *Review of Educational Research,* Vol. 57, pp. 293–336.

Slavin, R. (November 1987). "Cooperative Learning and the Cooperative School," *Educational Leadership,* Vol. 45, pp. 7–13.

Uttero, D. (January 1988). "Activating Comprehension Through Cooperative Learning," *The Reading Teacher,* Vol. 41, pp. 390–395.

REFERENCES

Allington, R. (1984). "Content Coverage and Contextual Reading in Reading Groups," *Journal of Reading Behavior,* Vol. 16, pp. 85–96.

Anderson, R., E. Hiebert, J. Scott, and I. Wilkinson (1985). *Becoming a Nation of Readers,* Urbana, IL: The Center for the Study of Reading.

Anderson, R., C. Evertson, and J. Brophy (1979). "An Experimental Study of Effective Teaching in First Grade Reading Groups," *Elementary School Journal,* Vol. 79, pp. 193–222.

Barr, R. and R. Dreeben (1983). *How Schools Work,* Chicago: University of Chicago Press.

Blair, T. (November 1984). "Teacher Effectiveness: The Know-how to Improve Student Learning," *The Reading Teacher,* Vol. 38, pp. 138–142.

Bossart, S. (May 1985). "Effective Elementary Schools," in *Reaching for Excellence: An Effective Schools Sourcebook,* R. Kyle (Ed.), Washington, DC: U.S. Government Printing Office, pp. 39–53.

Brophy, J. (1980). *Recent Research in Teaching,* East Lansing, MI: Institute for Research on Teaching, Michigan State University.

Brown, A. L. (1985). "Teaching Students to Think as They Read: Implications for Curriculum Reform," Reading Education Report No. 58. Urbana, IL: University of Illinois, The Center for the Study of Reading.

Cazden, C. (1979). "Learning to Read in Classroom Interaction," in *Theory and Practice of Early Reading,* L. Resnick and P. Weaver (Eds.), Hillsdale, NJ: Erlbaum, pp. 295–306.

Chall, J. (1983). *Stages of Reading Development,* New York: McGraw-Hill.

Christenbury, L. and P. Kelly (1983). *Questioning a Path to Critical Thinking,* Urbana, IL: National Council of Teachers of English.

Comber, B. (February 1987). "Celebrating and Analyzing Successful Teaching," *Language Arts,* Vol. 64, pp. 182–195.

Duffy, G. (1982). "Fighting Off the Alligators: What Research Has to Say About Reading Instruction," *Journal of Reading Behavior,* Vol. 14, pp. 357–372.

Emmer, E., C. Evertson, C. Sanford, B. Clements, and M. Worsham (1982). *Organizing and Managing the Junior High Classroom,* Austin, TX: Research and Development Center for Teacher Education, University of Texas.

Fisher, C., N. Filby, N. Marliave, R. Cahen, L. Dishaw, M. Moore, and D. Berliner (1978). "Teaching Behaviors, Academic Learning Time, and Student Achievement: Final Report of Phase III-B, Beginning Teacher Evaluation Study," San Francisco: Far West Educational Laboratory for Educational Research and Development.

Good, T. (February 1981). "Teacher Expectation and Student Perceptions: A Decade of Research," *Educational Leadership,* Vol. 38, pp. 415–422.

Hiebert, E. (1983). "An Examination of Ability Grouping for Reading Instruction," *Reading Research Quarterly,* Vol. 18, pp. 231–255.

Hyman, R. (1979). *Strategic Questioning,* Englewood Cliffs, NJ: Prentice-Hall.

Jones, B., A. Palincsar, D. Ogle, and E. Carr (1987). *Strategic Teaching and Learning: Cognitive Instruction in the Content Areas,* Alexandria, VA: ASCD.

Kean, M., A. Summers, M. Ravietz, and I. Farber (1979). *What Works in Reading,* Philadelphia: School District of Philadelphia.

King, M. (Summer 1984). "Language and School Success: Access to Meaning," *Theory into Practice,* pp. 173–182.

Lehr, F. (March 1986). "Direct Instruction in Reading," *Reading Teacher,* Vol. 39, pp. 706–713.

Leinhardt, G., N. Zigmond, and W. Cooley (1981). "Reading Instruction and Its Effects," *American Educational Research Journal,* Vol. 18, pp. 343–361.

Mayer, R. E. (1985). "Aids to Text Comprehension," *Educational Psychologist,* Vol. 19, pp. 30–42.

McDermott, R. (1976). "Kids Make Sense: An Ethnographic Account of the Interactional Management of Success and Failure in One First-Grade Classroom," Unpublished doctoral dissertation, Stanford University.

Pearson, P. D. (1985). "The Comprehension Revolution: A Twenty-Year History of Process and Practice Related to Reading Comprehension," Reading Education Report No. 57. Urbana, IL: University of Illinois, The Center for the Study of Reading.

Ransom P. and R. Mitchell (1980). "Curriculum and Objectives," in *Teaching Reading,* P. Lamb and R. Arnold (Eds.), Belmont, CA: Wadsworth, pp. 107–131.

Redfield, D. and E. Rousseau (1981). "A Meta-analysis of Experimental Research on Teacher Questioning Behavior," *Review of Educational Research,* Vol. 51, pp. 237–245.

Rosenshine, B. and R. Stevens (1985). "Teaching Functions," in *Handbook of Research on Teaching* 3d ed., M. Wittrock (Ed.), New York: Macmillan, pp. 376–391.

Rosenshine, B. and R. Stevens (1984). "Classroom Instruction in Reading," in *Handbook of Reading Research,* P. D. Pearson (Ed.), New York: Longman, pp. 745–798.

Slavin, R. (Fall 1987). "Ability Grouping and Student Achievement in Elementary Schools: A Best-Evidence Synthesis," *Review of Educational Research,* Vol. 57, pp. 293–336.

Slavin, R. (November 1987). "Cooperative Learning and the Cooperative School," *Educational Leadership,* Vol. 45, pp. 7–15.

Stoodt, B. and J. Costello (1986). "A Study of the Social Behavior of Disabled Readers," An unpublished research study, Greensboro, NC: University of North Carolina at Greensboro.

Winograd, P. and M. Greenlee (April 1986). "Students Need a Balanced Reading Program," *Educational Leadership,* pp. 16–21.

Uttero, D. (January 1988). "Activating Comprehension Through Cooperative Learning," *The Reading Teacher,* Vol. 41, pp. 390–395.

PART

II

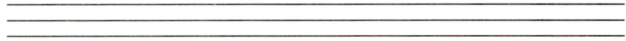

THE
SKILLS OF READING

CHAPTER 3

Reading Readiness and Beginning Reading

OVERVIEW   The early years of life are the most important in educating children. Parents are children's first and most influential teachers. What parents *do* to help their children learn is more important to academic success than is the family's financial success (U.S. Department of Education, 1986). Parents literally create a curriculum in the home. This curriculum includes daily conversations, household routines, attention to school matters, and affectionate concern for children's progress. Children come to kindergarten with varying degrees of readiness due to the differences in their home environment. Some children are already reading, while others have never seen anyone read or heard a story read.

What readiness skills and understandings should children acquire? When should reading instruction begin? What is the nature of appropriate initial reading experiences for young children? This chapter defines and describes reading readiness and beginning reading instruction.

Whole language and direct instruction   The instructional philosophy of this chapter (as in the entire text) combines whole language and direct instruction. Children need a whole-language background throughout the time they are learning to read, but direct instruction of specific skills is necessary to insure that all children are to achieve their full potential. Among the recommended instructional strategies for young readers are language experience, the shared book experience, kindergarten journals, and hearing stories read aloud.

Key Vocabulary

auditory discrimination	**shared book experience**
language experience	**visual discrimination**
readiness	

Focusing Questions

1. When is a youngster ready to read?
2. How are reading readiness and beginning reading instruction related?
3. What approaches to beginning reading instruction are most useful?
4. How is writing related to beginning reading?

INTRODUCTION TO READING READINESS

The traditional definition of reading readiness is preparedness for learning to read. Currently, reading readiness is viewed as an aspect of children's general language development associated with listening, speaking, reading, and writing. Educators recognize that children's experiences with oral language and world knowledge are important in learning to read. We now recognize that reading **readiness** is not a discrete set of skills that children must master before reading is introduced; it is the culmination of a series of learnings that begins at the time children start to speak, some four and one-half years before their entry into first grade (Frazier, 1968).

Reading Readiness and Parents

Parents must talk to their children about their experiences (Anderson et al., 1985), which extends children's concepts and associated vocabulary. Reflecting on experiences and describing events removed from the present, stimulates youngsters' language and thought development. Parents' responses and questions help children learn from their experiences; this helps them acquire the basic grammar of oral language (Olson, 1984).

Reading and discussing stories with children develops a critical aspect of reading readiness. "The single most important activity for building the knowledge required for eventual success in reading is reading aloud to children" (Anderson et al., 1985). Those fortunate youngsters who come from homes where language and reading are valued, enjoy the magic of books, and appreciate the function of books and the purpose of print. They look forward to reading stories for themselves and often pretend to read stories they have heard. They are motivated to learn to read.

Involve parents   Children learn more effectively when their parents are involved with their school work (Rich, 1985). Barr (1984) states that children who are given little or no help at home are unlikely to recognize printed words or letters, let alone letter sounds, and they need a year of instruction to reach the level of their more fortunate, parent-assisted peers.

Kindergarten children who know a lot about written language, usually have parents who believe that reading is important, and who read to their children (Heath, 1983). Parents and teachers should be partners in educating children; neither can do it alone. Teachers facilitate this partnership when they communicate with parents about goals, methods, and materials. They also can encourage parents' participation in educating their children and encourage them to enjoy the following activities with their children.

Read to them daily.

Listen to them talk about their school experiences.

Take them to the library regularly.

Read and discuss the papers and books children bring home.

Take them to interesting places and discuss the experiences.

Guide television viewing and discuss television programs.

Give children chalkboards and chalk as well as paper and pencil to encourage writing.

Have many printed materials in the home.

Readiness varies   At the outset of schooling, children's readiness varies markedly; they develop at different rates and have vastly different life experiences. In an average kindergarten class, some students exhibit quite sophisticated readiness for learning, while others have little or no readiness. Kindergarten classes commonly include children like Susan, who has been reading for nearly two years; she is capable of reading stories intended for third graders. Susan is a mature, independent youngster who has had many life experiences. However, the same class may include children like Janice, who is extremely immature. Janice is unable to hold a pencil, does not recognize the colors of her crayons, and speaks in "baby talk." The challenge of beginning reading instruction is meeting the needs of both the Susans and the Janices.

Researchers have identified the factors most frequently associated with success in beginning reading (Durrell and Murphy, 1963; Robinson, Strickland, and Cullinan, 1978).

1. Children who have broad experiential backgrounds are more successful in beginning reading than children from limited backgrounds.
2. Children who have a rich language background tend to fare better in initial reading instruction.
3. Children who are emotionally and socially mature are more ready to learn to read. Self-concept, an important aspect of emotional development, is a significant factor in reading readiness.
4. Intelligence (cognitive development) is a significant factor in learning to read. A high intelligence, however, does not insure reading success.
5. Physical development is correlated with success in reading. Girls physically mature more rapidly than boys and also experience greater success in beginning reading.
6. Motivation and the desire to learn to read are important to reading success.

7. Poor health and visual or hearing impairments are detrimental to learning how to read.

THE NATURE OF FIVE-YEAR-OLDS

Reading readiness and beginning reading instruction are important aspects of the curriculum for young children; therefore, it is important to understand the developmental status of five-year-olds. Traditionally, this is the age a child enters kindergarten.

Perpetual motion
Five-year-old children are in perpetual motion; they run, jump, hop, and climb. They often do not stop long enough to sustain a discussion; adults working with them should expect conversations that are punctuated with activity. Any instructional period of more than 15 minutes should include some form of physical exercise or movement to satisfy their need for activity (Robinson, Strickland, and Cullinan, 1978).

Language
Five-year-old children bring well-developed language to school. Research shows they can produce all of the basic sentence patterns of the English language (Hunt, 1965). Research by Templin (1957) and Menyuk (1971) indicates that most five-year-olds, in fact, have an extensive vocabulary; they use their language to express ideas and needs to both parents and teachers. This level of language development provides the foundation for reading readiness.

Sensory input
Research indicates that five-year-old children also have well-developed visual and auditory acuity. Eams (1962) found that vision in this age group is sufficiently developed to meet the demands of reading. Kindergarten teachers, however, should be alert to any symptoms of vision problems. Auditory acuity is also sufficiently developed for beginning reading instruction (Robinson, Strickland, and Cullinan, 1978). Visual and auditory acuity permit children to associate spoken words with printed words.

Five-year-old children are proud of their accomplishments and seek adult recognition. They demand their parents and teachers to "look at me" and "see what I did." They need recognition and reinforcement of their successes. Adults should freely offer appropriate compliments when children demonstrate their talents. Audiotapes of their discussions and songs and bulletin-board displays help draw appropriate attention to children's achievements.

CHILDREN'S READINESS FOR SYSTEMATIC READING INSTRUCTION

Readiness for systematic reading instruction is not a specific point in time. Children who are not ready to read on Thursday do not suddenly become ready the following Monday morning at 9 o'clock. Readiness is not an all-or-nothing proposition. Instead, readiness is a continuum beginning at birth and gradually unfolding as children grow into reading. Reading development is often uneven. Children may have excellent readiness in one area, but weaknesses in others. For instance, some children who have limited world experiences, may be fortunate enough to have adults who read to them regularly, thus developing their cultural literacy.

Age

Chronological age does not guarantee successful reading; however, children who are older when they enter school tend to have greater success than children who are younger at school entrance. Maturity interacts with experiences and instruction to enhance readiness.

Children entering kindergarten today know more about reading and writing than children did 10 or 20 years ago (Anderson et al., 1985). Readiness has been altered in recent decades by the many changes in our lives and culture. In general, children have more experiences than youngsters in earlier times. Many of these experiences result from increased family mobility.

Television

The universal availability of television brings an almost infinite number of experiences into our homes. For instance, "Sesame Street" is a very successful television program for developing reading readiness skills. Many preschool children are well acquainted with "Big Bird," "Burt," and "Ernie," the popular characters on this show. "Sesame Street" is a fast-paced program designed to hold young children's attention by introducing them to numbers, letters, sounds, concepts (such as *over* and *under*), and stories. Human relations and problem-solving activities are popular focal points of this program. Many parents report that their children are avid viewers. Research (Bogantz and Ball, 1971) shows that children who frequently watch "Sesame Street" learn the most from the program; furthermore, the children in this study learned the skills emphasized in the program.

Preschool programs

More children are participating in preschool education programs that enrich their experiential background. Many children of working mothers attend nursery school programs. In addition, more children are attending kindergarten than they did 20 years ago. Unfortunately, the curriculum developed in preschool education, kindergarten, and first-grade classes is often exactly the same; educators have not differentiated the curriculum at each of these levels. However, with the advent of widespread educational programs for four-year-olds, the duplication of curriculum may be eliminated.

Research indicates that kindergarten children can learn to read. Sutton (1969) found that children who were taught reading in kindergarten exhibited higher achievement than those who were not. Hillerich (1965) studied kindergartners to determine whether they could master and retain reading skills; he also investigated whether kindergarten reading made a difference in achievement at the end of first grade. He found that children mastered and retained the skills introduced in kindergarten.

Research

Durkin (1966; 1974–1975) has contributed valuable longitudinal research on the question of early reading in her studies of children who learned to read before first grade. Her subjects were characterized by a wide range of individual ability and socioeconomic status. She interviewed parents and guardians in an effort to identify the common characteristics of these early readers. Durkin found a number of common characteristics among early readers, which included persistence, competitiveness, self-reliance, and curiosity. The early readers in Durkin's studies had good memories and displayed early interests in both numbers and writing. Their environment included adults or older children who enjoyed spending time with them, answering their questions, and reading to them. However, early readers and early reading instruction is still a controversial issue for educators.

Kindergarten reading

Teaching kindergarten children to read seems to be less controversial than it once was. There is considerable evidence that preschool and kindergarten children benefit from reading instruction and language study (Taylor, 1983; Bissex, 1980; Durkin, 1974–1975; Soderbergh, 1977). In fact, Barr (1984) asserts that kindergarten reading is the rule rather than the exception. As readiness programs for four-year-old children become more commonplace, the real issue is *how* should five-year-olds learn to read, rather than whether they should learn to read. Kindergarten teachers need to be prepared to teach beginning reading.

READING READINESS AND BEGINNING READING

Reading readiness and beginning reading are based on common cognitive and motor tasks; therefore, they develop together (Mason, 1984). As children learn to recognize words, letters, and phonemes they are learning to read, and they are developing readiness for subsequent learning. Since reading and reading readiness develop at the same time and each enhances the other, there is no need to wait for readiness to develop before introducing reading.

Successful reading

The goal of both reading readiness instruction and beginning reading instruction is to develop successful readers. The instructional methods and materials for developing readiness and beginning reading are the same. For example, as students acquire **visual discrimination** skills through examining letters and words, they are developing the ability to recognize letters and words that are necessary in beginning reading. What skills and knowledge contribute the most to successful reading?

Current research indicates that the following skills and knowledge are most valuable to beginning readers.

Wide knowledge of the world (Hirsch, 1987; Wilson and Anderson, 1985). The more knowledge children acquire, the greater their chances for reading success. Wide knowledge enables children to understand the text they read. They also need to have opportunities to discuss their experiences.

A concept of reading and the functions of reading develop as children see people around them read (Clay, 1975; Weaver, 1988). Children who observe significant people around them reading, understand that reading is a pleasurable, worthwhile activity. For example, youngsters may read the instructions on a box of pudding mix as they help their mother or preschool teacher prepare it. Such activities develop their desire to read.

Many experiences with oral and written language (Weaver, 1988; Anderson et al., 1985). Children need to understand that print is talk that has been written. They must develop vocabulary, **auditory discrimination,** knowledge of letter names and letter sounds (phonemes). Experiences in speaking, listening, reading, and writing develop children's concepts about language and about print. All kindergarten and primary-grade children need many opportunities to explore oral and printed language, as well as an abundance of writing opportunities (Anderson et al. 1985).

Oral and written language experiences develop children's concepts of print, understanding of letters and words, and letter recognition. These experiences also develop concepts of print; they must learn that English is written from left to right and top to bottom. Along with these concepts, children learn to locate the front and back of books.

Successful reading is founded on a sense of story (story grammar) and a sense of expository structure (expository grammar). These are developed as children listen to stories and informative material and read well-structured text.

The ways and means to develop the preceding skills and knowledge are addressed in subsequent sections of this chapter.

Reading Readiness and Beginning Reading Instruction

Reading readiness and beginning reading develop as children have many opportunities to listen, speak, write, and read. Many of the early reading activities will involve **language-experience** stories that children dictate, along with enlarged stories and poems printed on posters that they can see easily. They need to manipulate language as well as books and pencils as they begin to make sense of printed language. To solve the puzzle of written language, children need both direct and indirect instruction.

Direct instruction

Direct instruction is important in the early stages of reading; we cannot assume that all children will acquire beginning reading skills in an informal, incidental approach (Mason, 1982). Certainly, current levels of illiteracy in the United States attest to this fact. Direct instruction is essential in developing word knowledge, letter names and letter sounds, auditory discrimination, and visual discrimination. A well-balanced reading program provides both formal and informal instruction.

Systematic instruction

Available data indicate that children learn to read best when initial reading instruction is systematic and organized (Darlington, 1981; Schweinhart and Weikart, 1980; Lazar et al., 1977). A sound beginning reading program includes both formal and informal experiences. The formal experiences (direct instruction) include activities such as introducing and reinforcing sight words, letter names, and letter sounds; informal experiences (indirect instruction) include such activities as writing in journals, discussions of classroom pets or incidents in the classroom, and storytelling. Many opportunities for informal language instruction arise during the school day. For instance, a student may find a cocoon on the way to school, which allows the teacher an opportunity to develop science concepts, as well as a language experience activity. Both direct and indirect instruction should occur within a meaningful setting.

Meaningful Setting

Children become literate when they are communicating about ideas and experiences that interest them. Reading, reading readiness skills, and knowledge should be introduced in meaningful settings. Sounds (consonants and vowels) should be introduced with words and pictures. Sight words should be introduced in sentences or phrases that help children associate meaning with print. A meaningful context builds interest and helps children remember words, concepts, letters, and sounds.

Young children must learn that print carries a message and that written language actually represents spoken words. In the early stages of reading, the teacher creates a bridge between spoken language and printed language. To accomplish this, children must learn about the relationships among speech, print, concepts, objects, and events. For instance, children should have opportunities to connect the spoken word *milk* with the printed word, along with the concept of milk as a beverage. *Milk* is a relatively easy concept to understand because it is within the experience of most children. This is why early reading materials concentrate on words, concepts, and experiences that are familiar to children; they learn to recognize words in print they already know. When children have opportunities to connect words and experiences, they learn that words are units of sound and meaning.

The following sections present both direct and indirect instructional strategies and activities for developing the knowledge and skills that are valuable for beginning readers.

World Knowledge or Cultural Literacy

World knowledge develops from many, varied life experiences. A rich background of experience is essential for children who are learning to read. In fact, poor and disabled readers may need remedial experience more than they need remedial reading. Readers use their world knowledge to construct or generate an understanding of text; therefore, children who have a wide knowledge of the world have a real advantage in learning to read. Note the world knowledge that is required to read the following:

Jane rode on the ferris wheel after watching the elephants. She later bought cotton candy and caramel corn to eat as a snack.

In order to grasp this passage, readers should be familiar with the words *elephant, ferris wheel, cotton candy,* and *caramel corn.*

*Experiential
foundation*

The knowledge children acquire before coming to school provides the foundation for reading. Children need to acquire concepts of understanding things, events, thoughts, and feelings, as well as the oral language vocabulary for expressing these concepts. Successful reading depends on a large store of world knowledge (cultural literacy, schemata) (Wilson and Anderson, 1985). Children who acquire a large store of knowledge before entering school have a better chance for success in initial reading instruction. Children who have been taken on trips and picnics, visited zoos, museums, and parks have knowledge to draw on when they read.

World knowledge is developed in the home, but schools also contribute through planned field trips, films, pictures, television programs, guest speakers, museums, plays, and concerts, reading aloud to children, models, and demonstrations. In the average community, there are many sites for student field trips; for example, a class may visit a grocery store to observe and identify the classifications of food. This reinforces the fact that many children can read product and store names before entering school. In many communities, there are individuals who garden, keep bees, train and groom pets, or build furniture; no doubt, they would enjoy sharing their special interests with children.

Discussion

Wide experience is not sufficient; children should integrate their experiences with their existing world knowledge through discussion and questions. This helps children understand and remember their experiences (Mason, 1984). When introducing a story, a film, a television show, or the like, teachers should encourage children to remember what they already know about the topic. For instance, when introducing a story about a kangaroo, ask children what they can tell you about kangaroos.

Concepts of Reading and the Functions of Reading

Children acquire concepts of reading by observing people reading for information, pleasure, or following directions. As they see how people rely on reading for information and entertainment, they develop a better sense of what reading can do for them, and in turn, are motivated to read. They recognize that print should make sense and that they can read what they and others have written.

*Reading is
communication*

Students should become aware of the communicative function of reading. They need to read many types of discourse for a variety of purposes. For example, they may read cereal boxes and billboards, stop signs and street names. Books like *The Jolly Postman or Other People's Letters* by Janet and Allan Ahlberg introduce children to Goldilocks's letter of apology to the three bears; a business letter from a firm of lawyers representing Red Riding Hood, who is suing the Wolf; and a postcard from Jack to the Giant. *The Z Was Zapped* by Chris Van Allsburg is an alphabet book, still another type of discourse. *The Popcorn Book* by Tomie de Paola is an informational book that includes directions for making popcorn. *What Do You Say, Dear?* by Sesyle Joslin is a book of manners for all occasions. Literature helps children understand the many functions that reading serves in our lives.

Developing Concepts of Language and Print

Children need many language experiences to acquire the data they need to solve the reading puzzle. They need to know that print represents talk, that one reads from left to right, that words represent ideas, and so forth. Listening, speaking, reading, and writing are interrelated; therefore, each enhances learning of the others. Listening, speaking, reading, and writing create a foundation for reading success. Activities like the following will contribute to this foundation.

1. Read and tell stories to children. Then discuss the stories with the children. This activity can be varied in many ways. For example, you may read part of a story and ask the children to think of a new ending. (See Chapter 10 for additional discussion ideas.)
2. Use wordless picture books and encourage children to think of the language that could be used with the story. Books like the following are useful in such an activity.

   Tomie de Paola, *The Hunter and the Animals*
   Ezra Jack Keats, *Clementina's Cactus*
   Sonia O. Lisker, *Lost*
   Mercer Mayer, *A Boy, A Dog, and A Frog*
   Mercer and Marianna Mayer, *A Boy, A Dog, A Frog and A Friend*
   Barney Saltzberg, *The Yawn*

   Wordless picturebooks for older children include:

   Corinne Ramage, *The Joneses*
   Renate Meyer, *Vicki*
   Lynd Ward *The Silver Pony*
   Holden Wetherbee, *The Wonder Ring*

3. Encourage children to tell their own stories. Puppets and flannel boards are useful for motivating storytelling. You may wish to tape record the children's stories, so they can listen by themselves.
4. Plan regular informal discussions, which permit the children to share their personal experiences.
5. Tape stories for children to listen to as they look at accompanying pictures.
6. Collect interesting photographs and illustrations for discussion. Ask children to describe what is happening in the pictures, who the characters are, what happened just before the picture, or what they think will happen immediately after the pictured incident.
7. Have children dictate stories or information and write their remarks on the chalkboard or on large charts. This material can be typed and bound into class books. Refer to subsequent sections of this chapter,

which address language experience activities. A simple language experience chart is shown in Figure 3.1.

8. Dramatize the children's favorite stories. You may collect props and cast-off clothing that will serve as costumes, although costumes are not necessary. Children may create puppets to use in their dramatizations.

9. Create learning stations for the children. A science learning station might contain books and displays of shells, plants, or bugs. Such learning stations encourage discussion, story dictation, and related reading.

10. Play games with children, such as a directions game that requires them to carry out various oral directions. For example, tell a child to stand up on the left side of the seat, walk to the chalkboard, and write the letter *b*. After the child has followed two directions accurately, the number of directions can be increased to three. This may also be conducted as a group activity.

11. Familiarize children with specific language concepts, such as *top, bottom, over, under, first, last, next, in, out, bigger, smaller, taller, shorter.* The concepts will aid cognitive development; also, it will help children understand directions in other activities. Illustrate these concepts with pictures of the objects. Ask children to identify whether the box is on the chair, or under the chair. After several of these exercises, have children begin to describe—on their own—the specific location of each object or person in a picture. Show children two objects and ask them to state which is bigger and which is smaller. Line up a group of objects and ask children to identify the first, last, and middle positions.

12. Develop vocabulary by introducing new words. Identify several interesting words in a story. Ask children to identify synonyms and an-

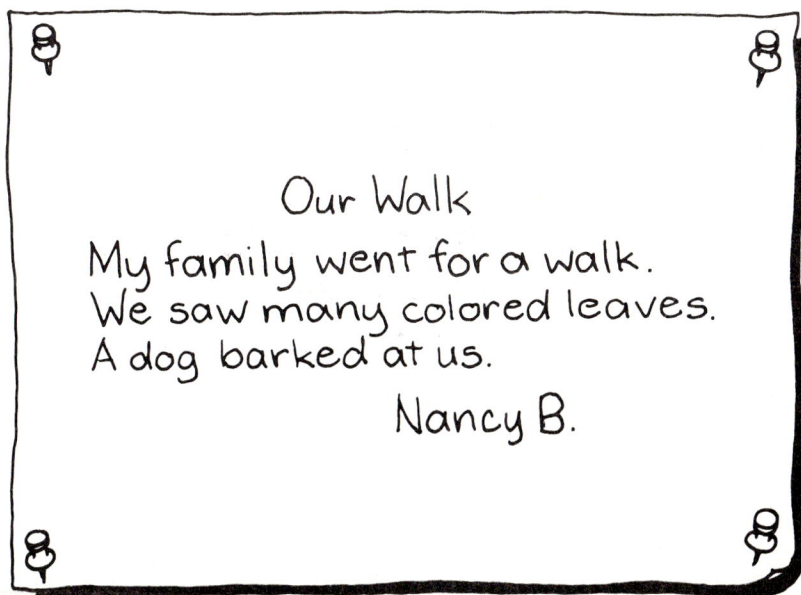

Our Walk
My family went for a walk.
We saw many colored leaves.
A dog barked at us.
                Nancy B.

Figure 3.1

tonyms for these words. They may also draw pictures or locate magazine photos that illustrate the new vocabulary terms.

Developing Children's Concepts of Print

Clay (1985) has identified the following concepts that children should develop
as preschoolers or during the early stages of reading.

1. The ability to identify books (as opposed to stories or magazines, and
   the like)
2. To know what one does with a book
3. To know where to begin reading a book and where to begin reading
   a page
4. To identify what a word is
5. To identify what a letter is
6. To locate the first letter in a word and the last letter in a word

Oral language

Beginning readers need to understand that utterances are comprised of
words and sounds. Children tend to hear sentences as unbroken streams of
sound like, "doyawantacookie?" instead of "do you want a cookie?" As children
listen to stories and begin to recognize words and letters in print, they develop
a sense of auditory segmentation, which is the ability to hear the separate
sounds and words in utterances. Along with the ability to separate sounds,
children need to develop the ability to perceive likenesses and differences
among sounds, which is called auditory discrimination.

Auditory discrimination

This is a language concept that is closely related to reading achievement (Robinson, 1972; Rosner and Simon, 1971). Gibson and Levin (1975) point out that
children must learn, at the outset, that words are composed of organized
sounds. Auditory discrimination enables children to relate spoken sounds with
the printed symbols (letters) that represent them. Thus, auditory discrimination
is the foundation upon which phonics skills develop.

Auditory discrimination

Many children have developed basic auditory discrimination skills before
coming to school, since they have been hearing and using language from birth.
To refine and develop auditory discrimination, teachers should encourage children to identify sounds that are alike as well as the sounds that are different.
For example, a teacher might ask if the words *come* and *came* are alike or
different. They can also ask students to identify words that begin alike, such as
words that begin like *boy*. Activities such as the following develop auditory
discrimination and segmentation.

1. The teacher pronounces a series of words and asks students to hold up
   their hands when the words sound the same (for example, *cat-cat,
   dog-cog, sat-sat*).

2. The teacher shows the class a series of pictures, and asks students to name each picture and to identify the ones beginning with the same sound.
3. The teacher shows the class another series of pictures, and asks students to identify each picture that begins like *dog* (or any key sound that they are studying).
4. Hillerich (1977) suggests playing word games with funny questions, such as *do you play ball or fall?* or *do you sit in a chair or a pair?*
5. Have children collect pictures of objects that begin with a sound that the teacher has already identified. These items can be used to create a bulletin board or a book of sounds. Figure 3.2 is an example. An auditory-discrimination activity that has been taken from a reading readiness workbook is shown on the top of p. 88. The child is asked to look at the first picture in the row, and then is asked to identify all of the pictures in the row that begin with the same sound.
6. Place colored cubes or beads in front of each child. Ask him or her to pick up a single bead and place it in a line each time he or she hears a specific word in a sentence that the teacher reads.

Visual Discrimination

Visual discrimination is the ability to see printed words and letters. Children need to learn that printed words are comprised of letters or groups of letters sequenced in predictable patterns, and that there are white spaces between words. Children whose parents have drawn their attention to print and have read to them, usually enter school with some visual discrimination skill. This skill is enhanced when children see their teachers writing language experience stories. Visual discrimination is a foundation skill for learning sight words and phonics.

Discriminate letters and words

Children learn to discriminate among letters and words by recognizing details that differentiate one letter or word from another. For example, *b* and *d* are essentially the same letter form, differing only in their direction. The visual differences between many letters and words are quite subtle; children must be able to discriminate these differences to become successful readers.

Many young children are not aware of the fine details that distinguish one printed form from another, since their previous experience has not required

Figure 3.2

Letter/Sound Relationship: Final Consonants _m, b, l, ll_   Help children identify the picture in each box. Then have them circle the letter or letters that stand for the sound they hear at the end of the name of the picture. Children should trace the circle to complete the first example.

Auditory discrimination: Help children identify the pictures. For each row, have them circle the pictures whose names begin with the same sound as the name of the first picture. (_Source:_ Leo Fay, _et. al., Get Set,_ The Riverside Reading Program, Chicago: The Riverside Publishing Company, 1989, p. 67. Reprinted by permission.)

them to be alert to such details. Prior to entering school, children were able to recognize that a toy truck was just that—a toy truck—whether it was upside down or right side up, but they did not know that a _b_ becomes a _d_ when it is turned around. Inexperience leads many young children to reverse letters and the sequence of letters in words. For instance, they may reverse _saw_ and _was._ These early reversals concern parents and teachers, but they are simply the result of inexperience, and most children overcome them in first or second grade.

In the past, visual discrimination exercises were based on pictures and shapes. For example, an exercise might require students to identify the flower that differed from another flower in a row of pictures. These exercises are useful only if one intends to read flowers; on the other hand, if students are to _read_ letters and words, they need to discriminate letters and words. The following activities are useful for developing visual discrimination.

ACTIVITIES FOR DEVELOPING VISUAL DISCRIMINATION

1. Encourage children to draw pictures and to "write" about what they have drawn.
2. Provide manipulative letters (wooden or plastic), magnetic letters, or link letters for children to use in creating messages.
3. a. Request that students make an X on all the letters in the row that are the same as the initial letter. (See Figure 3.3a.)
   b. Have children mark an X on each word that is the same as the initial word in the row. (See Figure 3.3b.)
4. Distribute word cards and have students match the words printed on the cards to words that appear on their experience charts. For example, a chart sentence that reads *My dog is big* would be associated with the individual word cards for *big, is, my,* and *dog.* The child who has the *dog* card would place it under the word *dog* that appears on the chart. Assist children in sharpening their discrimination ability by drawing their attention to the differences in letter forms (for example, descending letters such as *g,* ascending letters such as *l,* the crossbar on the *t,* and the dot on the *i*).
5. Teachers should point out the sequence of letters that are contained in particular words. As words are written on a chalkboard or chart, teachers should encourage children to observe their formation and sequence.
6. Students should have sets of plastic or wooden alphabet letters that they can manipulate to build their names—as well as words that are familiar to them.

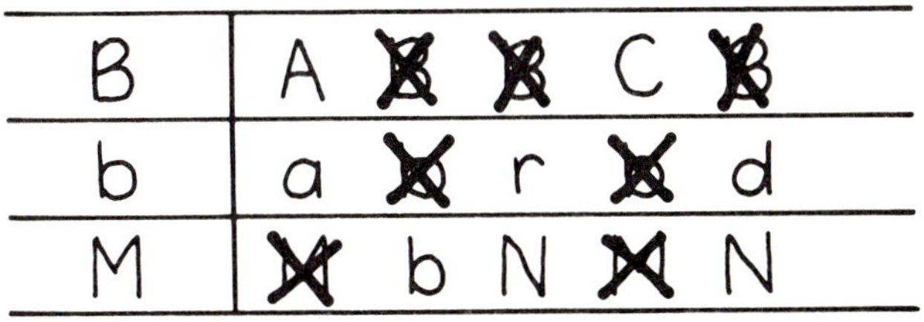

Figure 3.3a

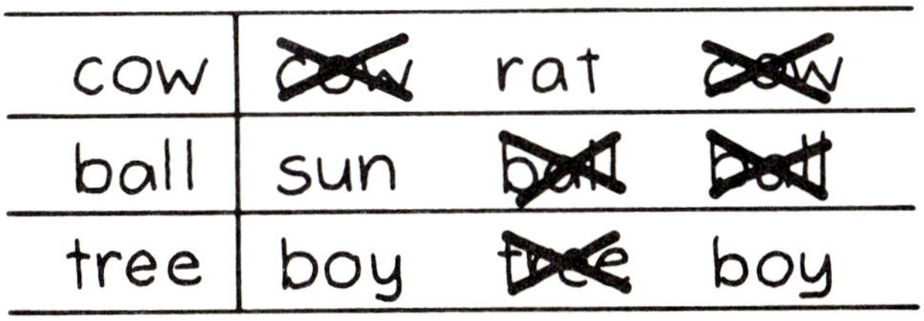

Figure 3.3b

7. Children should make use of letter wheels in which the outer wheel can be turned to match letters of the inner wheel. An example of a letter wheel is shown in Figure 3.4.

Knowledge of Letter Names and Sounds

Research indicates that knowledge of letter names correlates with reading success (Jenkins, Bausell, and Jenkins, 1972; Samuels, 1972). However, a correlation does not mean causation; it simply means that the two occur simultaneously. While the evidence does not prove that learning letter names increases reading achievement, logic suggests that knowing letter names is very useful to beginning readers; it indicates an awareness of language and print. Words are composed of letters and letter sequences, and knowledge of letter names permits students and teachers to discuss words and letters. For example, when the teacher states that a word begins with a *b*, students must be able to identify that letter in order to follow the discussion. Muehl and Kremenack (1966) found that children who knew letter names had a definite advantage in learning to read; thus, learning letter names is an appropriate part of the beginning reading program. Many beginning kindergarten children can name the letters of the alphabet when they enter school; however, we cannot assume that all children will have this knowledge (Hiebert and Sawyer, 1984).

Alphabet

Research also indicates that knowledge of letter sounds is even more useful than knowledge of letter names to beginning readers (Harste, Burke, and Woodward, 1982; Jenkins, Bausell, and Jenkins, 1972). Words are composed of sounds (phonemes), and sound recognition is important for learning phonics.

When teaching children phonemes (letter sounds), teachers frequently use pictures of objects that illustrate the sound. However, teachers must be certain to identify the picture for the students in order to avoid any confusion. For example, a cap might be called a stocking cap or a hat, while a coat may also be a jacket or a rain slicker. Children should repeat the picture name aloud—as a means of checking their comprehension as well as pronunciation practice. Hillerich (1977) suggests that teachers omit the article when they pronounce a word for a class, for instance, *a dog* should be, simply, *dog.* This prevents confusion in labeling pictures.

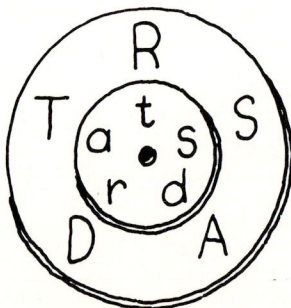

Figure 3.4

Sequencing letters

Developing a sequence for teaching letters and letter sounds can be a real challenge for teachers. Research studies do not suggest any one single approach to sequencing letters (Hillerich, 1977; Cohn, 1974; Groff, 1974). Logic suggests that consonants should be taught first; their sounds are more consistent and generally easier for children to hear. Letters that are similar should not be introduced at the same time (such as *b* and *d,* or *m* and *w*). Bryant (1969) recommends introducing only one of the letters likely to be confused at a time, and practicing until students have overlearned that letter before introducing the second easily confused letter. After overlearning both letters separately, children can be exposed to both letters at the same time. This approach prevents confusion.

Rhyming words

Many beginning reading programs emphasize rhyming words. Hillerich (1977), however, states that "There seems to be no reason to emphasize rhyming words as a skill in beginning reading." Rhyming words do not aid auditory discrimination development in young children and, furthermore, they cause confusion. Rhyming word drills encourage children to focus on word endings when they should be focusing on word beginnings—and examining them from left to right. Confusion can also occur when these children are asked to identify a word that begins like a new word the teacher pronounces. In this instance, children who have studied rhyming words tend to identify the previously learned rhyming words. A minilesson for teaching a letter sound is illustrated in the following example.

A Lesson Plan for Teaching a Letter Sound

1. *Objective:* The child will recognize the grapheme *t* and associate this with the phoneme /t/.
2. *Materials:* A chalkboard, pictures of objects that begin with the /t/ sound, and magazines.
3. *Procedure:* Write the uppercase *T* and the lowercase *t* on the chalkboard, followed by words beginning with this letter. Include the names of children in the class that begin with *T.*
   a. The teacher should pronounce the individual words aloud and students should listen to the beginning sound of each word.
   b. The children should pronounce the words themselves, at the same time listening to the beginning sound of the words.
   c. The teacher should place pictures on the chalk tray and identify each picture. Students should then select those pictures that begin with the sound of /t/.

4. *Practice:* Have children look through magazines for pictures beginning with the /t/ sound, and request that they paste these pictures on a class chart.
5. *Evaluation:* Hold up various sets of pictures for the class and ask them to sort out those pictures that begin with the /t/ sound.

The following activities are good for developing recognition of letters and knowledge of letter sounds.

1. Organize lotto games (similar to bingo boards). The teacher calls out letter names or letter sounds and children must place markers on the matching positions on cards. A winner is declared when a row on a student's card has been completed in any direction. A sample card that can easily be made is shown in Figure 3.5.
2. Each child in the class should have a set of plastic or wooden alphabet letters.
   a. The teacher should announce the name of a particular letter and have the children find that letter in their set.
   b. The teacher should say a letter sound and have students select the letter associated with that sound.

3. Have children locate letters named by the teacher in newspaper advertisements.
4. Each child could have a "magic slate" on which to practice writing letters.
5. Have children sort out objects or pictures based on their beginning sound. Use shoe boxes with the particular letter written on the front to hold the pictures or objects that are being sorted.
6. Have the class play "Go Fish." Attach paper clips to cards that have letters printed on them and place the cards in a plastic bucket or tub. Each student should have a fishing line with a magnet for the hook. Have each child drop the line in to catch a card and then say the name of the letter or the letter sound that was caught.
7. Play a match game. Have children find pictures or objects whose names begin with the same sound as their own personal names.
8. Have children draw pictures that begin with the same sound as a word pronounced by the teacher.

Children must learn left-to-right sequence since English is read from left to right. Unfortunately, children are not born knowing that English flows from left to right; in fact, it is quite natural for beginning readers to look at print from right to left, especially if they are right-handed. Young children must learn to look at words and sentences in an organized manner. Activities like the following help them develop this understanding.

1. The teacher should gently swing one hand under the line of print when reading aloud from language experience stories, big books, and the chalkboard.

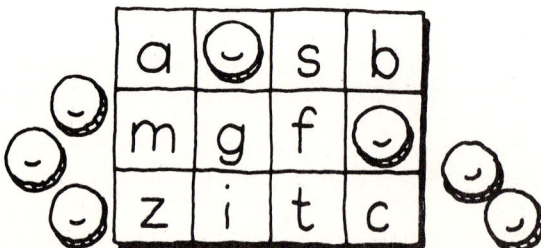

Figure 3.5

2. The teacher should draw students' attention to his or her writing when he or she writes on the chalkboard or on charts. The left-to-right sequence of letters and words should be pointed out as the writing proceeds.
3. Cut and paste letters and words in a left-to-right order.
4. Place a green arrow on charts and children's papers to show where reading and writing begin, and a red arrow to show where they stop.

CHILDREN'S LITERATURE IN THE BEGINNING READING PROGRAM

All of the knowledge and skills discussed in this chapter contribute to students' ability to construct the meaning of printed language. This section is directly concerned with developing children's knowledge and skills through exploration of children's literature.

Children's literature is an imaginative use of language. Children should be immersed in literature. It will contribute to their language development and language comprehension. Literature develops their sense of story, their concepts of print, and their understanding of the functions of reading. In addition, *Read aloud daily* literature provides a model for expressing their ideas when they write. Literature is the single most important aspect of the beginning reading program; therefore, teachers and parents need to read aloud to children daily.

We read literature to children for their delight and entertainment, but also to build knowledge. In planning story reading sessions, teachers should consider the literature selections, prereading discussions, reading the text, student participation, prediction, comprehension, and evaluation of the story (Heald-Taylor, 1987).

When choosing selections to read aloud, teachers should choose selections they enjoy; their enthusiasm will stimulate children's interests. They should also choose selections that are appropriate to the development of the class and their interests. Stories are usually chosen because they are interesting stories or because they are part of a theme being developed in the classroom. For example, the theme of friendship could be developed with stories like the following.

Arnold Lobel, *Frog and Toad Are Friends*

Else Minarik, *Little Bear's Friend*

Charlotte Zolotow, *My Friend John; Hold My Hand; The White Marble*

Before reading a book aloud, hold the book so that the students can see the cover. Ask them questions like:

What is the title of this book? Where is the title?

Who wrote this book?

What do you think this story will be about?

Why do you think that?

Sometimes, the teacher may choose to establish a listening purpose with students. For example, before reading *Bread and Jam for Frances* by the Hobans, the teacher could ask students to listen and find out "whether Frances liked bread and jam at the end of the story."

When reading aloud, hold the book so that children can see the print and the illustrations. Call children's attention to the print. After reading the story, the teacher may wish to look at the pictures again and discuss them with the students, since both the pictures and the words tell the story in a picture book.

Students may participate in the story. They may join in repeating predictable parts of the selection. Students may manipulate characters on a flannel board or with puppets, as a story is read or reread.

Encourage students to predict story events or character development. The teacher can do this by discussing pictures, reading the first paragraph or two aloud as a basis for predicting. Another approach involves reading part of the story and stopping at an appropriate point for students to think about what will happen next or various ways the story might end.

Comprehension is developed after reading the story. Teachers can ask questions like the following (Heald-Taylor, 1987):

What did you think about this story?

What did you like best about this story?

Was there a problem in this story?

What was the problem in this story?

How was the problem solved?

Can you think of other ways to solve the problem?

How did the author help us get to know the characters and the setting?

After reading the book *Bread and Jam for Frances* by the Hobans, teachers might ask these questions:

Why did Frances change her mind about the bread and jam?

How are you like Frances?

Do you think Frances was eating different foods at the end of the story? Why?

Why did Frances sing songs?

Children can evaluate stories that teachers read to them. Evaluation is an aspect of comprehension and of developing thinking skills. Heald-Taylor (1987) recommends asking children to rate a selection as *great* (everyone should read it), *very good* (most children would enjoy it), *good* (if they are interested in the topic, style, or genre), or *poor* (not recommended). Children should give reasons to support their rating. Teachers may keep a chart of the class evaluations.

Using Predictable Books for Initial Reading Instruction

Predictable stories have repeated patterns, rhythm, rhyme, logical sequence, and/or refrains. Books like *The Three Billy Goats Gruff, The Elves and the Shoemaker, Henny Penny,* and *The Little Red Hen* are examples of such books. These books are valuable for developing reading skills. The repeated words create a language pattern that children enjoy and they often chant these patterns. After hearing a pattern several times, many children will join in when the teacher reads the repeated patterns. Predictable books create a bridge between spoken and written language. The repetition of words in these stories help children subsequently learn them as sight words.

Repetition

Teachers should introduce the concept of pattern or repetition to children prior to introducing predictable books. In the initial introduction, have the students listen for the pattern or patterns in the book. After they have listened to a predictable story several times, it can be used for a **shared book experience**, which gives children opportunities to see the written pattern they heard.

Developing Students' Story Grammar

A story grammar is a structure that describes the parts of a well-structured story. The components of a story grammar are: the setting, which includes the time, place and main character; the story problem; the efforts to solve the story problem; and the resolution to the story problem. A simple story grammar is illustrated in Figure 3.6.

Comprehension

The importance of knowledge of text structure in reading comprehension has been widely researched (Rumelhart, 1975; Mandler and Johnson, 1977; Stein and Glenn, 1979). Researchers agree that students who have a sense of story grammar comprehend better than students who do not. Well-structured stories are easier to comprehend than stories that are poorly structured. Story grammar knowledge permits readers to anticipate the content and structure of stories and to remember the stories they hear and read. Writers use a story grammar to structure the stories they write.

Children acquire a story grammar from hearing and reading stories. In addition, story grammar can be taught. Teachers should follow these steps when teaching story grammar:

1. Write a well-structured story on a chart.
2. Explain to the students that stories have specific parts. Then show the students the chart and go through the story, identifying the story grammar.
3. Then have the children compose a story orally that has the story grammar components.

The Setting
Who, where, when
The Problem
The problem or conflict that the protagonist encounters and attempts to solve
Events
A series of attempts to solve the problem
The Resolution
The problem or conflict is solved and the story winds down. In an episodic story, each chapter has a story grammar. A novel may include a series of interlocking episodes, each with its own story grammar.

Figure 3.6   A story grammar.

4. Give the students a framework for writing stories. Spiegel (1985) suggests the following frames. This step may be done on the chalkboard or a chart with young children, while older children may write in the blanks provided by the frame.

_____(who)_____ lived ____(where)____ _____(when)_____ he had a terrible problem. His problem was _____ said, "____(about the problem)____. I want to ____(solve problem)____." So _____(who)_____ ____(attempted)____. And it (worked or did not work).

And __conclusion__.

5. Teachers should plan 15–20 minute lessons for several days. They may concentrate on one story part in each lesson and review the parts that students have already learned. Children need to practice identifying the story grammar in several stories over a period of one or two weeks in order to develop a sense of story. Story grammar is further discussed in Chapter 6.

Expository Grammar

Informational (expository) text is structured in characteristic ways. Although young children are not mature enough to understand expository structure, they should have many opportunities to hear teachers read information materials.

Many of their language-experience activities will result in expository text, which will expand their understanding of this structure.

Informs

Informational text is structured around main ideas and supporting details. This concept can be introduced to beginning readers with pictures. For example, show children a picture of a picnic and ask them to identify the main idea (picnic); then ask them to identify the details that support the main idea of a picnic. Students might identify food, the out-of-doors setting, and so forth. Main ideas are discussed more fully in Chapter 5.

Sequence

Sequencing is one form of structuring exposition that young children can understand. They can perceive the order of information in the books that are read to them, and they can consciously order the information they dictate or write. All of these experiences will prepare them for subsequent experiences with expository content.

APPROACHES TO BEGINNING READING

This section addresses approaches to reading instruction that incorporate components of initial reading programs. Each of the reading programs discussed offers children opportunities to use the language knowledge they bring to school, along with their experiential background, as they incorporate literature. Another factor these approaches have in common is that they depend on teaching skill. To implement these programs, teachers need to know how to develop experiential background, word and sentence knowledge, decoding skills, listening, speaking, and writing. The whole-language approach, which incorporates each of these factors, is introduced first.

The Whole-Language Approach

A whole-language approach to reading is based on the notion of giving children many opportunities to listen to, speak, read, and write language. Through listening, speaking, reading, and writing children refine their use and understanding of language. The following traits characterize whole-language classrooms (Weaver, 1988).

1. Teachers find out about students' interests, abilities, and needs. Then they use that information in planning curriculum.
2. They read or tell the students stories every day.
3. Students participate in authentic writing experiences every day.
4. Children read literature every day.
5. Students participate in discussions in which they consider the reading and writing processes.
6. Students help other students acquire literacy.

In addition to the traits discussed in the preceding list, teachers in whole-language classrooms often choose the language-experience approach to reading and the shared book experience. These approaches are discussed in the following sections.

The Language-Experience Approach

A language-experience approach is an excellent one for beginning reading instruction (Hall, 1976; Van Allen, 1976; Stauffer, 1979). As the term implies, language-experience stories are derived from language experiences. This approach incorporates listening, speaking, reading, writing, and thinking. When two children discuss a television show they enjoyed, they are sharing an experience that can spawn a language-experience activity. Reading materials are created from the stories, experiences, and ideas children dictate to the teacher. Language-experience stories are built on children's interests, and focus their attention on the reading-writing process.

Whole class or small group

The language-experience approach is quite flexible, allowing either an entire class to participate, or a small group, or an individual. Language experiences may be either oral or written—and they frequently are both. Language-experience activities provide many opportunities for students to develop reading skills. They begin to recognize words in print that they already have *heard* in conversation, as well as words they have *used* in their own oral language. Through language experiences, children's range of vocabulary and concepts are increased. Since language-experience stories are based on children's experi-

Translate experience

ences, they create a foundation for reading comprehension. During the composing process, children translate their experiences into language that contributes to comprehension.

Research substantiates the effectiveness of the language-experience approach to reading instruction. Researchers have compared the achievement of children who were taught to read in this manner with those participating in other instructional approaches. The evidence shows that language-experience instruction is associated with competent and superior readers (Hall, 1976; Van Allen, 1976; Stauffer, 1979). In addition, teachers who have used this approach believe that it is a practical and effective reading program (Hall, 1976).

Getting Started with Language Experience

Language-experience reading instruction is initiated best by showing children how their discussion of a first hand experience can be recorded and read. An activity like the following one could be used on the first or second day of school.

First, arrange to have an interesting object or animal in the classroom. An interesting object is one that children can touch, smell, listen to, and observe, such as a large seashell, a flower, an unusual toy, or an unusual fruit or vegetable.

Birds, hamsters, guinea pigs, turtles, dogs, cats, and fish are among the living things that often visit classrooms. The vignette in Box 3.1 illustrates how such an incident might occur.

What the Children Learned

Clearly, these children had a rich learning experience. The benefits of this experience are summarized in the following list.

1. They learned that reading is talk that is written down.
2. They saw the teacher read each sentence, as well as the entire story.
3. They saw the teacher point at words, which helped them develop concepts of print.
4. They experienced the fun of reading and saw their friends read.
5. They learned that print goes from left to right.
6. They saw how the teacher wrote letters and words.
7. Some of the children saw their names in print.
8. They saw their ideas in print.
9. They participated in a discussion that developed oral language.
10. They listened to one another and to the teacher.
11. They observed and asked questions.
12. They took turns and demonstrated respect for one another's ideas.
13. They had opportunities to draw a picture to illustrate the story.
14. Writing *Willard* on each drawing gave them additional opportunities to learn about words, letters, and meanings.
15. They observed the use of capital letters and punctuation.
16. The teacher was able to observe the language arts skills and knowledge of the children.

Respect language

When introducing language-experience activities to students, encourage them to respect written language and to take pride in their own ideas. In initial language-experience activities with young children (preschool, kindergarten, or early first grade), write exactly what they say until they develop the concept that reading is "talk written down"; then the dictated text should be edited. Edit to shorten sentences and to eliminate poor grammar. Initially, some children will only be able to dictate one word, but their language use will grow. However, children should be encouraged to sequence their ideas logically from the outset.

Children should have opportunities to watch the teacher writing language-experience stories; this helps them learn left-to-right progression, letter formation, spelling, writing down ideas, capitalization, and punctuation. After writing the dictated material, teachers should read it aloud and make comments like, "Is this what you said?" "I am writing exactly what you said, so we can read it." "I can write anything that you can say." "When we read, we are reading what an author has said."

Box 3.1

On the second day of school, Mary Bradley introduced Willard, a hamster, to her class. She placed Willard's cage on a table, and the children gathered around to observe. They noticed his whiskers, paws, color, and so forth. The teacher encouraged them to think about their experience and introduced the following questions:

What color are his eyes?

How does he look when he eats?

Why is he in a cage?

How long is he?

How much do you think he weighs?

What is his favorite toy? How do you know?

How many feet does Willard have?

Can you count his toes?

Does he have the same number of toes on his front and back feet?

What does he use his feet for?

What does he use his ears (whiskers) for?

How is Willard like a cat?

How is he different from a cat?

After the children discussed their experiences and observations, she covered Willard's cage. Then she wrote *Willard* on the chalkboard and explained this word was the hamster's name. Many of the children immediately wanted to try writing *Willard,* but Mary suggested that they wait until the story was completed.

Then Mary invited the children to give her ideas to write about Willard. As the children offered ideas, Mary printed them on newsprint, which was clipped to the easel. After each sentence was written, she read it aloud to the children while running her hand under the words, so they could see what she was reading. When the entire story was written, she read it aloud to the children; then the class read the story together several times. The teacher pointed to each word and said it with the children. Through the pointing and repeating, the children acquired a sense of reading written language. Mary established a rhythm as she read with the children, and she spoke clearly, so they could hear the words she was saying.

Then she had individual children come up to the chart and she read the story in unison with them. She found that many of the children recognized Willard's name, some of the children identified several words, and one child could read every word in the story. The children's story is shown below.

Willard

Shirley said, "Willard is a golden hamster." Chris said, "He has a short tail and he likes the wheel." Lauren said, "He has bright eyes and he likes to look at us." Tara said, "He crammed so much food in his cheeks that they looked very fat." Richard said, "We measured Willard, and he is 5 inches long."

Next, Mary gave each youngster a large piece of white newsprint and asked him or her to draw a picture of Willard. While the children drew, she went around the class printing the word, *Willard* on each paper. Several of the children said they would rather write for themselves, and she encouraged them to do so.

The next day, Mary gathered the children around the story and read it to them again, pointing to each word as she read it. Then the children read the story in unison. After that, Mary invited volunteers to read the story aloud. She assisted the children when they needed it.

Then she took out word cards that she had printed the night before, and held them up for the children to see. She held each word card under the word in the story that matched it, so the children could compare them visually. After that, she invited various children in the class to match words and to say them if they could.

As a follow-up to this language experience, Mary read a chapter from a story about a guinea pig, *Olga de Polga* by Michael Bond. Then she explained that Willard was going to live in the classroom; the children needed to learn how to care for him since it would be their responsibility. During the following week, the children looked at pictures and talked about hamster care. They also dictated many stories about the care and feeding of hamsters, which were bound into a class book.

1. The language-experience activity should be introduced to a class after a shared experience, story, or discussion. Children need content or knowledge on which to base their dictation or writing. Language-experience texts are based on children's own experiences; therefore, interesting and memorable experiences are important. The teacher can initiate discussions related to experiences as a basis for organizing ideas prior to dictation. Activities for developing language-experience activities may include field trips; class discussions about feelings; planning a party for parents; special events such as holiday celebrations; telling a story about a friend or family member; reviewing stories that have been read to the children; and sharing birthday or holiday greetings. Prepare reports on topics of class interest or ones that expand science or social studies topics. Develop thematic units such as things

we like, places we like to go, things we like to do, courage, and people we admire. *Language-experience activities should be purposeful.* Children should communicate ideas and thoughts that they want to share with others.

2. Ask the children to think about what they would like to say. Brainstorm words that could be used in talking about the experience. Write the brainstormed words on the chalkboard. This step is like the prewriting phase of the writing process or the preparation-to-read phase of reading.

3. The children should dictate their ideas to the teacher. If this is a group experience, each child dictates a sentence that is related to the preceding sentence. This is similar to composing in the writing process.

4. The teacher writes the ideas that are dictated on a chalkboard or chart. The teacher should feel free to cross out words, insert words, and check the spelling of words, because this models appropriate drafting and revising behavior.

5. The teacher reads a group story aloud, while running his or her hand under the sentences. If the language-experience activity is individual, the teacher and student may read in unison.

6. Children may volunteer to read a group story aloud, or an individual child may practice reading his or her story alone. Children should be encouraged to sweep their hand under the lines of print as they read. This reinforces the connection between oral and written language.

7. Rereading stories should be encouraged in order to develop fluency and a feeling of success. Hand the stories around the classroom at eye level. This encourages rereading. Children who work individually may exchange stories with one another for additional reading.

8. Group stories can be typed and copied for group distribution.

9. Individual and group stories can be bound together into books. They may also be placed in the library.

10. Language-experience materials are excellent for reading, writing, and language instruction, but students should have many opportunities to hear stories read aloud.

11. Students should have opportunities to read simple stories. In my experience, children who only read language-experience stories develop the attitude that they cannot read "real" books. This can be avoided by incorporating other materials and shared book experiences into the program. A balanced reading program introduces children to many forms of discourse. These reading materials introduce children to a variety of writing models, more elaborate language, story grammar, and they reinforce word recognition skills.

LANGUAGE-EXPERIENCE SUGGESTIONS AND IDEAS

1. Use colored pens to write the contributions of different students. For example, Richard's sentence is written in red, while Jenny's sentence is written in blue, and so forth.

2. Use the names of class members in stories.

3. Use interesting pictures from newspapers and magazines as story starters.

4. Write different organizational patterns such as cause and effect, sequential order, and problem-solution.

5. Use patterned stories like *Brown Bear, Brown Bear* as models. Read the story aloud and then have children compose a story in the same pattern.

6. Use a book like *The Jolly Postman,* which includes a letter from Goldilocks to the three bears. After reading the book, have children compose letters that Humpty Dumpty might write to the King about being put together again.

7. Shape stories: after a child dictates a story, the page can be cut into a shape that represents the story. As a variation, give the youngster the shape to begin the story and show how the story fits the shape.

8. The teacher may read a sentence aloud from a language-experience story. Have a youngster locate that sentence.

9. Choose one word in a language-experience story and ask children to think of a word that could be used in place of that word.

10. When teaching sounds, ask children to find words with a sound identified by the teacher.

11. Create a written conversation with a youngster thus creating dialogue. For example,

> Teacher writes: Do you have a pet?
> Student writes: Yes, I have a dog.
> Teacher writes: What is your dog's name?

12. Create cloze (a selection from which words are deleted) language experience by covering words in a language-experience chart; have the children think of a word that would fit in the blank.

Language-experience stories offer many teaching opportunities. The following is a list of extensions that can be used to develop reading skills.

1. Oral reading reinforces reading and language skills. In addition to children reading text orally, the teacher may read the text aloud, while a student tracks, by running a hand under the line of print being read. A student may read while the teacher tracks.

2. Word study is an excellent language-experience extension. The following activities are examples.
    a. Hand the child a word card on which a word is printed; ask him or her to locate the word in the story.
    b. Ask children to locate a color word, a name, or a word that is something they like to eat, and so forth.
    c. Have children find all of the words in a story that begin with an initial consonant sound the teacher identifies—for example, "find all of the words that begin with a *B.*" This activity can be varied by having students find all of the words that have the same beginning sound as a word the teacher identifies.
    d. Have children find all of the long words in a story, or all of the short words, or ascending letters; for example, t, l, b, d, h, k.

   e. Identify all of the common sight words used in a language-experience story, and place them in a word bank for future reinforcement.
   f. Focus on words that children will encounter in the first-grade basal readers. Some teachers teach all of the words that youngsters will read in a book prior to introducing that book. This works particularly well with first-grade preprimers.

3. Make copies of the story for the children in the class to read and illustrate. Then they can take these stories home to read to their parents.
4. Read stories that are similar to the language-experience stories. The similarity may be in theme, characters, plot, language patterns, and so forth.
5. Children can read language-experience stories to the students in other classes.
6. First-grade teachers often combine language experience with the basal reader. The basal reader provides stories that provide content and/or structure to guide the development of language-experience activities. The basal reader can reinforce skills, words, and content that are introduced in language-experience activities. One way to combine instruction is to use the basal reader on Monday, Wednesday, and Friday and language experience on Tuesday and Thursday, or the reverse schedule. Another approach is to use both the basal and language experience every day, but the language experience is used for only 10–15 minutes. Students' seatwork also can be related to language experience by using the activities listed previously and having students complete them independently.

Examples of language-experience stories are shown in Figure 3.7.

Language Experience in the Content Areas

Language-experience activities are also useful in the content areas. The following is an example of language experience as applied to science content.

Key-Word Approach

The language-experience approach can be initiated through the *key-word approach* (Veatch, 1973), which Ashton-Warner (1964) calls "organic words." Key or organic words are ones that have emotional impact for the student. The steps for learning key words are:

1. *Each child selects a word that has emotional impact.* This word may be the child's favorite word or a word that is considered either happy or sad. The teacher should ask the children why they like the particular word that has been selected.
2. *The word is printed on a word card.* After the child whispers the word to the teacher, he or she prints it on a card using a colored pen or crayon.

Our Walk

Our class went for a walk today.
We saw a blue jay, a sparrow, and a robin.
The robin took a bath in a mud puddle.
We visited Mr. Wilson's garden.
He gave us flowers for our classroom.

The First Grade

Muffin

I have a little black dog.
My dog's name is Muffin.
Muffin likes to play.
She likes to run fast.
Muffin also likes to eat from her dish.
I love my dog.

Susan G.

Figure 3.7 Language-experience stories.

3. *The children trace their words with their fingers.*
4. *Each child has an activity that is associated with the word.* The activity may be forming the word with movable letters, writing the word on the chalkboard, drawing a picture to represent it, or finding a magazine photograph that illustrates the word.
5. *Review key words regularly.* In the early stages of learning to read, children should practice identifying their words each day. Eventually, they may review their words every other day.
6. *Store key words.* Each child should have a personal file box or shower curtain ring in which to store word cards.

Word Banks

Constructing a word bank is an activity that is often associated with the language-experience approach but is, in fact, an outgrowth of the key-word method. A word bank is simply a file of key words and other words used in individual language-experience stories. These words are written on cards and are stored in personal file boxes, so that children possess their own banks. These cards record the number of words that are learned, and they can also be the source of reading activities. The following exercises may be done utilizing student word banks.

1. The words can be categorized into a nearly limitless number of classifications, such as people, animals, foods, words having long vowels, or words beginning with *c*.
2. Students can be asked to think of their own categories for words in their files. For example, they might select the words, *elephant, monkey, kangaroo, lion,* and *zebra* and invent the classification zoo animals.
3. Scatter the children's word bank cards on the floor, face down. Have the children identify their own words by holding up each card and telling the class what the word is. Thus children must recall their words in order to retrieve their cards.
4. Ask students to act out one or more of their words.
5. Have the class compose sentences using words from their banks.
6. Have children select words from their banks that express emotions, such as words that suggest happiness, sadness, fear, or excitement.
7. Provide pictures for the class and have students select words that relate to these pictures.

SHARED BOOK EXPERIENCE

Many young children enjoy hearing stories read aloud, and they pretend to read their favorite stories to younger children. Holdaway (1979) builds "big books" from these interests in the shared book experience. After the teacher shares books with children through reading them aloud, he or she creates an enlarged version of the stories that children particularly enjoy. A "big book" is an enlarged version of a favorite story. The big book is placed on an easel where all

Big books

of the students can see it, and the teacher shares the book with the class. Then the shared book becomes the basis for beginning reading instruction. The big book helps children see a clear association between the words on the page and the illustration. With repeated readings, the children, aware of the meaning of the story, will be able to anticipate many of the words. As the children learn which words are coming next, they will join in and read along with the teacher (Slaughter 1983). Big books are the basis for many classroom activities as children learn to comprehend, to identify words, letters, and sounds.

Holdaway recommends 30 minutes for initiating the big book experience. In his method, the teacher reads a regular-sized story to the children before presenting the previously prepared big book on the easel for sharing. After the children have experienced big books, Holdaway suggests that the teacher vary the activity by reading up to the last word of a particular sentence, and pausing for the children to supply the missing word. As children associate more and more printed words with spoken words and become more confident, they are invited to read the big book by themselves.

Choosing stories

Some teachers vary this approach by choosing stories for big books that the children have heard and enjoyed a number of times, writing the text on charts, and having the children draw the illustrations. This activity reinforces the relationship between text and illustrations, which enhances comprehension. When children create illustrations they are encouraged to interpret the story.

Any book the children will enjoy can be enlarged into a big book; however, books should be chosen that are worthy of repetition and are likely to become class favorites. Holdaway believes that we need not be concerned with simplicity or progression of materials as in a basal program (Park, 1982). I find that teachers who use big books recommend using predictable books with simple, familiar language at the outset. The use of predictable materials allows beginning readers to apply their language to the reading task. You may refer to Rhodes (1981) for a list of suggested predictable books to make into big books. In addition, nursery rhymes, songs, and so forth are interesting text for big books.

To enlarge books into big books, you may use large chart paper. This paper may be bound between two stiff covers, or the teacher may bind the pages together. Big books can be made more durable by laminating them. Slaughter (1983) notes that children learn sequence by putting the pages in order.

Follow-up   Follow-up activities for big books help children acquire reading skills and knowledge. One of the most valuable aspects of big books is that they motivate children to read and reread stories, which helps them develop reading skills.

All of the activities listed for language experience will function with big books. Children enjoy dramatizing many of the stories that they read in big books. They may use these stories as models for writing their own stories.

Holdaway recommends preparing audiotapes to accompany big books so the children can listen to the book independently. Key words can be printed inside the big book cover to help teacher and children, and word banks can be created to accompany them. Some teachers create pupil-sized books of the stories included in the big book. Then the children can illustrate them and practice reading their own copies.

WRITING AND BEGINNING READING

Writing is a significant aspect of reading readiness (Bissex, 1980). Preschoolers should have chalkboards, pencils, crayons, and paper. Magnetic boards and letters that children can manipulate also develop their concepts of letters and words, just as scribbling and coloring develops concepts of written language. They begin to understand how to write messages for others to read and to read messages written by others; such activities develop children's concepts of written language. They learn that print represents spoken language in order to learn to read.

Natural writing   During the early stages of learning to read, children learn about writing through language-experience dictation and through scribble-writing their own stories. As they learn to form letters and words, they replace scribble-writing with actual letters and words. Thus reading and writing are interacting in the early stages of literacy. Writing reinforces word and letter knowledge, and reading words and letters helps children learn to write them.

Journals   As early as kindergarten, children can keep their own journals. In the early stages, these journals include pictures and scribble-writing, but these are replaced with words as children learn words.

The stories that teachers read to children and the stories they read in language-experience charts, big books, trade books, and basal readers are models for the children's own writing. The written texts children are exposed to provide them with ideas; basal readers are models for the children's own writing. The written texts children are exposed to provide them with ideas, motivation, and schemata for writing. Furthermore, children learn how to express their ideas in written language and they learn to observe the conventions of print from writing. As they write their own ideas, children develop an understanding of how authors express their ideas in writing, which enhances comprehension. Young children should have many opportunities to read their own writing to other children in the class.

In addition to programs like language experience, whole language, and the shared book experience, there are a variety of published workbooks, kindergarten kits, and so forth. These materials are discussed in the next section, but the discussion does not include basal readers, which are examined later in this book.

READING READINESS WORKBOOKS AND PACKAGED PROGRAMS

Many basal reading programs include reading readiness workbooks and/or packaged programs, such as instructional kits. Frequently, basal reading programs include two readiness level workbooks; teachers may have the option of using these materials in kindergarten or first grade. There is great variation in the use of these materials. For instance, some schools have students complete both books in kindergarten, some use one workbook in kindergarten and one in first grade; other schools choose to rely on teacher-designed curriculum, and do not use any readiness materials.

Basal   Reading readiness workbooks reflect a structured prereading program
workbooks that leads into the adopted basal reading series. The workbooks provide colorful pictures; language-development activities like storytelling, concept, and vocabulary development; visual and auditory discrimination; left-to-right sequence; letter names and sounds; and comprehension readiness. The teachers' editions accompanying these workbooks include teaching suggestions.

Reading readiness workbooks have been subject to considerable criticism. A valid criticism is the fact that many teachers regard the workbooks as a total program; such an attitude restricts children's development, since these teachers tend to overlook the importance of including literature, language experience, and developing children's experiential background. Viewing a workbook or kit as a total program is particularly dangerous; published materials tend to concentrate on concrete measurable skills like auditory and visual discrimination and knowledge of letters, which represent a very narrow perspective on readiness. Teachers need to recognize that reading readiness workbooks and similar packaged programs are only one aspect of a total readiness program.

Weaknesses   Another weakness of workbooks and packaged programs is that many children may have already acquired the skills included in the materials, which means that they could be completing exercises that have little value for them. On the other hand, published materials rarely have enough exercises to teach and reinforce skills that students lack. Thus, teachers may use these materials to reinforce skills, but they need to use their own knowledge and experience to provide for the richness needed in a reading readiness program.

When readiness workbooks are used judiciously, they can contribute to students' development. Teachers should see readiness workbooks as only one component of the entire reading program. They are most effective when used to reinforce skills and knowledge that are being developed in the reading readiness curriculum. Teachers should assess students' readiness and choose the workbook exercises that students need rather than working straight through the workbook. Workbooks are discussed in greater detail in Chapter 8.

When deciding whether to use a workbook or how much of the workbook to use, you may use the following guidelines.

1. Is this skill or knowledge important in the reading curriculum? (You may consult the local or state reading curriculum.)
2. Is this skill appropriate for the students I am teaching?
3. Have the students learned this skill or knowledge previously?
4. Will this exercise teach/reinforce the appropriate skill or knowledge?
5. What other things should I do to help students acquire this skill or knowledge?
6. What teacher's edition suggestions will be most useful for my students?

ASSESSING READING READINESS

Reading readiness tests examine the skills and knowledge that research indicates are related to further reading success. Typically, the following factors are tested: auditory discrimination, visual discrimination, concept development (word meaning), understanding spoken language, visual-motor skills, letter names, and letter sounds. In addition, a few tests like the *Murphy-Durrell Reading Readiness Analysis* sample students' ability to learn whole words.

Assessment of reading readiness is included in many schoolwide testing programs. Reading readiness is assessed for the following reasons:

1. As a basis for predicting reading success. Harris and Sipay (1985) state that there is a positive relationship between reading readiness test scores and school achievement. This means that a child who has a low reading-readiness test score will tend to have low reading achievement at the end of first grade.
2. To group children for beginning reading instruction. Test data enable teachers to group children together who have similar levels of skill development.

3. To identify specific strengths and weaknesses. Reading readiness tests are not designed to be diagnostic, since they do not sufficiently sample reading readiness skills and knowledge.

Durkin (1974) believes that reading readiness is not a single skill. Therefore, reading readiness tests should measure some of the more complex aspects of readiness such as attention span, cognitive style, and experiential background. Although readiness tests do not yet measure these aspects of readiness, the currently available tests help teachers identify some potential problems. Reading readiness is assessed through standardized tests and informal tests.

Standardized Reading Readiness Tests

A standardized test is one "that has been given to various samples or groups under standardized conditions and for which norms have been established" (Farr and Carey, 1986). Norms are "values that describe the performance of various groups on a test or inventory. Norms are only descriptive of existing types of performance and are not to be regarded as standards or as desirable levels of attainment" (Farr and Carey, 1986). Standardized reading readiness tests are composed of subtests that are designed to assess those factors that are significantly related to reading readiness. Subtests are "subgroups of items that are developed to supposedly measure specific subareas of a more general ability" (Farr and Carey, 1986).

Subtests

Some of the more popular standardized reading readiness tests and subtests are:

Analysis of Readiness Skills: Reading and Mathematics (1972), The Riverside Publishing Company. **Subtests:** visual perception of letters, letter identification, mathematics. Directions and norms for both English- and Spanish-speaking children.

Clymer-Barrett Readiness Test (1983), Chapman Publishing. **Subtests:** recognizing letters, matching words, auditory discrimination of beginning and ending sounds, completing shapes, and copy-a-sentence.

Lee-Clark Reading Readiness Test (1962), California Test Bureau. **Subtests:** visual discrimination of letter forms, concepts, and visual discrimination of word forms.

Metropolitan Readiness Tests (1976), Psychological Corporation. **Subtests:** auditory memory, rhyming, letter recognition, visual matching, school language, listening, and quantatitive language, and an optional copying test.

Murphy-Durrell Reading Readiness Analysis (1965), Psychological Corporation. **Subtests:** sound recognition, letter names, and learning rate.

When selecting standardized reading readiness tests, the following factors should be considered. Additional information regarding test selection is included in Chapter 9.

1. Define the objective of the testing. What do you as teacher, need to know to make instructional decisions?
2. Does the test assess skills that are relevant to the reading program? For example, a school that uses explicit phonics, should use a test that assesses auditory discrimination and phoneme knowledge.
3. Can young children follow the directions given in the test without confusion? If directions are unclear, the teacher cannot determine whether the child lacks skills or is simply unable to make sense of the instructions.
4. Teachers should score their own tests in order to diagnose students' strengths and weaknesses.

Informal assessment also contributes to our understanding of students' strengths and weaknesses.

Informal Assessment

Informal assessment of reading readiness refers to observing students' performance as guided by checklists, informal inventories, and anecdotal records. Farr and Carey (1986) point out that informal approaches to assessment can be more reliable than standardized reading tests. Informal measures offer individual evaluations of strengths and weaknesses; they are not designed to compare students. Informal assessment of reading readiness can provide the information necessary to plan effective classroom instruction. This data is frequently more helpful to classroom teachers than test scores.

Checklists are designed to guide and record teacher observations. A suggested checklist of reading readiness skills and abilities is included in the Appendix. In using this checklist as a guide, teachers can make up a sheet for each student and mark an S for *satisfactory* and a U for *unsatisfactory* alongside each question.

SUMMARY

The following list summarizes the key points of this chapter.

1. Reading readiness is achieved when the individual's skills and the instructional strategies employed make it possible for the student to successfully acquire reading skills. Reading readiness is related to many factors; however, research has shown that the factors that are most important include a rich experiential and language background, emotional and social maturity, intelligence, normal physical development,

motivation, and the desire to learn to read. Poor health, as well as visual and hearing impairments, are detrimental to beginning reading.

2. Children usually enter school at the age of five; therefore, the nature of five-year-old children should be considered in planning a reading readiness program. Five-year-olds are very active and have a well-developed language ability. They are characterized by visual and auditory acuity, and they seek adult approval. Research suggests that many kindergarten children are ready to learn to read and that reading does not harm these children. This early start in reading is a maintained advantage throughout the elementary years.

3. The objectives of a recommended reading readiness program are the development of the desire to learn to read, the understanding of oral and written language, auditory discrimination, visual discrimination of letters and words, knowledge of letter names and sounds, left-to-right sequence, a broad background of experience, and thinking strategies.

4. Reading readiness is assessed through both standardized and informal testing. A number of standardized reading readiness tests are available. Informal assessment includes checklists, informal inventories, and anecdotal records of observations.

5. A beginning reading program should be informal, both child- and language-centered, and should offer opportunities for children to read interesting material. The objectives of a beginning reading program are to learn that reading is written language, that reading is an enjoyable activity, that the reader should think about reading content, that common nouns, verbs, and commonly used words can be identified, and that children will learn consonant sounds.

6. The beginning reading program should include the language-experience approach, the shared book experience with big books, and many opportunities for children to write. The language-experience approach is based on reading materials that children compose and dictate to the teacher. In this program, children can see their spoken words turned into print. Both comprehension and word recognition skills can be developed with language-experience stories. Shared book experiences, which are similar to language-experience activities, involve reading literature to children and enlarging the stories into charts; this allows children to join in reading them and eventually reading them independently. Writing and reading develop concurrently; therefore, young children should have opportunities to write every day.

SELF-TEST

Check your knowledge of the information presented in this chapter. The answer key is located in Appendix C.

1. What is reading readiness?
   a. preparedness for learning how to read
   b. prereading skills
   c. a composite of skills and attitudes
   d. all of the above

2. When does reading readiness occur?
   a. at the age of six
   b. it is a continuum rather than a point in time
   c. when the child physically matures
   d. none of the above

3. What factors are related to reading readiness?
   a. instruction is the only factor related to reading readiness
   b. all of the factors that influence the reading process
   c. both a and b
   d. neither a nor b

4. What are the characteristics of five-year-old children?
   a. they are in perpetual motion
   b. they desire attention and approval from adults
   c. they have a well-developed language ability
   d. all of the above

5. What is the point of view expressed in this chapter regarding the development of reading readiness?
   a. reading instruction should be delayed until readiness has developed
   b. reading readiness should be developed simultaneously with beginning reading
   c. neither a nor b
   d. both a and b

6. Why should teachers demonstrate the importance of reading in children's lives?
   a. to develop the child's desire to learn to read
   b. because reading is unimportant in today's world
   c. because children expect teachers to do this
   d. all of the above

7. What reading skill is based on listening?
   a. visual discrimination
   b. configuration
   c. comprehension
   d. none of the above

8. Which language concepts should be developed in young children?
   a. diacritical markings
   b. Latin roots
   c. concepts such as *top, bottom, on, over, first,* and *last*
   d. none of the above

9. What is the role of auditory discrimination in beginning reading?
   a. it is unimportant
   b. it is the foundation for developing phonics skills
   c. it is the basis of visual discrimination
   d. both a and b

10. How is visual discrimination related to learning to read?
    a. it is the basis for learning sight words
    b. it is the ability to differentiate between letters and words
    c. it is the basis of auditory discrimination
    d. both a and b

11. Why do many young children reverse letters and words?
    a. to trick the teacher
    b. because of inexperience
    c. due to weakened brain cells
    d. due to poor instruction

12. When do most children overcome reversals?
    a. when they become teenagers
    b. at the age of 10
    c. during first and second grades
    d. during fifth and sixth grades

13. Which of the following should be developed during the reading readiness period?
    a. letter names, letter sounds, auditory discrimination, visual discrimination, left-to-right sequence, and the desire to read
    b. syllabication, letter names, and visual acuity
    c. letter sounds, visual acuity, and matching geometric shapes
    d. matching colors, stress rules, diacritical markings, and visual discrimination

14. What are the advantages of learning letter names?
    a. it helps children to focus on individual letters and words
    b. it helps children to remember individual letters and words
    c. it helps children to more successfully follow the teacher's directions
    d. all of the above

15. How is reading readiness assessed?
    a. by standardized tests
    b. by informal tests
    c. by checklists
    d. all of the above

16. Which of the following are standardized reading readiness tests?
    a. Murphy-Durrell
    b. Bond-Balow-Hoyt
    c. Gray-Oral
    d. Roswell-Chall

17. How has the character of children's reading readiness changed in recent years?
    a. it hasn't changed at all
    b. children have greater opportunities for experiences today due to television and other factors
    c. children today take many more vitamins
    d. children eat junk food at an earlier age

18. Whose research studies focused on children who read before enrolling in school?
    a. Helen K. Smith
    b. Dolores Durkin
    c. Linda Gambrell
    d. Donald Edwards

19. Which statement describes children who learned to read at an early age?
    a. they enjoyed reading and maintained an advantage in being able to read during the elementary grades

      b. reading was injurious to them
      c. early reading damages the eyes
      d. these children avoided reading in the end

20. Which of the following characteristics describe an effective kindergarten reading program?
      a. fast-paced
      b. interesting, child-centered, and language-centered
      c. formally structured
      d. all of the above

THOUGHT QUESTIONS

1. Discuss the relationship between reading readiness and beginning reading.
2. Why is the language-experience approach such an ideal one when one considers reading readiness skills and beginning reading?
3. Discuss the role of visual discrimination and auditory discrimination in developing word recognition skills.
4. How is reading comprehension developed during the readiness period?
5. How important is experiential background in beginning reading?
6. Discuss the use of the shared book experience in reading readiness and beginning reading.

ENRICHMENT ACTIVITIES

1. Observe a kindergarten child using the readiness checklist that is presented in this chapter. Write a brief summary of the child's overall level of readiness.
2. Obtain a standardized reading readiness test and administer it to a kindergarten child. Score the test and analyze the child's readiness. Does the child have any special strengths or weaknesses? What instructional strategies could you use to overcome these weaknesses? How could you use the strengths to help the child learn to read?
3. Interview kindergarten teachers from different school systems and ask them what type of readiness program they use in their classes.
4. Use the minilesson plan in this chapter as a model for making a lesson plan to teach consonant sounds. If possible, teach the lesson to a child or a group of children. If this is not possible, teach the lesson to a peer group and ask for comments afterward.
5. Visit a kindergarten class and conduct your own language-experience lesson with the members of that class.
6. Obtain reading readiness workbooks from several reading series and compare them. Determine which skills are the objectives in each book. How do the skills introduced in the workbooks compare with the skills discussed in this chapter?
7. Plan a lesson for a kindergarten or first-grade class using the chart teaching approach presented in this chapter. Visit a class and teach your lesson.

RELATED READINGS

Buckley, R. (November 1987). "A Funny Thing Happened on the Way to 'Reading Readiness.' A Teacher Learns from the Learners," *Language Arts,* Vol. 64, pp. 743–747.

Gentile, L. and J. Hoot (January 1983). "Kindergarten Play: The Foundation of Reading," *The Reading Teacher,* Vol. 36, pp. 436–439.

Fields, M. and D. Lee (1987). *Let's Begin Reading Right,* Columbus, OH: Charles Merrill.

Gunderson, L. and J. Shapiro (January 1988). "Whole Language Instruction: Writing in 1st Grade," *The Reading Teacher,* Vol. 41, pp. 430–439.

Hall, M. (1977). *The Language Experience Approach to Reading,* 2nd ed., Newark, DE: International Reading Association.

Heald-Taylor, G. (March 1987). "How to Use Predictable Books for K–2 Language Arts Instruction," *The Reading Teacher,* Vol. 40, pp. 656–664.

Kaisen, J. (February 1987). "SSR/Booktime: Kindergarten and 1st Grade Sustained Silent Reading," *The Reading Teacher,* Vol. 40, pp. 532–537.

Kostelny, S. (November 1987). "Development of Beginning Writing Skills Through a Total School Program," *The Reading Teacher,* Vol. 40, pp. 156–159.

Mallon, B. and R. Berglund (May 1984). "The Language Experience Approach to Reading: Recurring Questions and Their Answers," *The Reading Teacher,* Vol. 37, pp. 867–873.

Ollila, L., Ed. (1978). *The Kindergarten Child and Reading,* Newark, DE: International Reading Association.

Reiner, B. (January 1983). "Recipes for Language Experience Stories," *The Reading Teacher,* Vol. 36, pp. 396–401.

Seaver, J. and M. Botel (March 1983). "A First Grade Teacher Teaches Reading, Writing, and Oral Communication Across The Curriculum," *The Reading Teacher,* Vol. 36, pp. 656–665.

Templeton, S. (January 1986). "Literacy, Readiness, and Basals," *The Reading Teacher,* Vol. 39, pp. 403–409.

REFERENCES

Anderson, R., E. Hiebert, J. Scott, and I. Wilkinson (1985). *Becoming a Nation of Readers,* Urbana, IL: The Center for the Study of Reading.

Ashton-Warner, S. (1964). *Teacher,* New York: Simon and Schuster.

Barr, R. (1984). "Beginning Reading Instruction: From Debate to Reformation," in *Handbook of Reading Research,* P. D. Pearson et al. (Eds.), New York: Longman.

Bissex, G. (1980). *Gnys at Wrk: A Child Learns to Read and Write,* Cambridge, MA: Harvard University Press.

Bogantz, G. and S. Ball (November 1971). "A Summary of the Major Findings," in *The Second Year of Sesame Street: A Continuing Education,* Princeton, NJ: Educational Testing Service.

Bryant, N. D. (1969). "Some Principles of Remedial Instruction for Dyslexia," in *Remedial Teaching,* W. Otto and K. Koenke (Eds.), Boston: Houghton Mifflin.

Calkins, L. (1986). *The Art of Teaching Writing,* Portsmouth, NH: Heinemann.

Clay, M. (1985). *The Early Detection of Reading Difficulties,* 3d ed., Portsmouth, NH: Heinemann.

Clay, M. (1975). *What Did I Write?*, Portsmouth, NH: Heinemann.

Cohn, M. (May 1974). "Letter Recognition Difficulties: Their Real Nature," a Paper presented at the annual meeting of the International Reading Association.

Darlington, R. (1981). "The Consortium for Longitudinal Studies," *Educational Evaluation and Policy Analysis,* Vol. 3, pp. 37–45.

Durkin, D. (1974–1975). "A Six Year Study of Children Who Learned to Read in School at the Age of Four," *Reading Research Quarterly,* Vol. 10, pp. 9–61.

Durkin, D. (1966). *Children Who Read Early,* New York: Teachers College Press, Columbia University.

Durrell, D. and H. Murphy (December 1963). "Reading Readiness—Research in Elementary Reading: 1933–1963," *Journal of Education,* Vol. 46, pp. 3–10.

Dyson, A. (October 1984). "N Spell My Grandmama": Fostering Early Thinking About Print," *The Reading Teacher,* Vol. 38, pp. 262–271.

Eams, T. (May 1962). "Physical Factors in Reading," *The Reading Teacher,* Vol. 15, pp. 427–432.

Farr, R. and R. Carey (1986). *Reading: What Can Be Measured?* 2nd ed., Newark, DE: International Reading Association.

Gibson, E. and H. Levin (1975). *The Psychology of Reading,* Cambridge, MA: MIT Press.

Graves, D. (1983). *Writing: Teachers and Children at Work,* Portsmouth, NH: Heinemann.

Groff, P. (1974). "Sight Words and the Disabled Reader," *Academic Therapy,* Vol. 10, pp. 101–108.

Hall, M. (1981). *The Language Experience Approach for Teaching Reading: A Research Perspective,* 3d ed., Newark, DE: ERIC Clearinghouse on Reading and Communication Skills and the International Reading Association.

Harste, J., C. Burke, and V. Woodward (1982). "Children's Language and World: Initial Encounters with Print," in *Reader Meets Author/Bridging the Gap,* J. Langer and M. Smith-Burke (Eds.), Newark, DE: International Reading Association, pp. 105–131.

Heald-Taylor, G. (March 1987). "How to Use Predictable Books for K–2 Language Arts Instruction," *The Reading Teacher,* Vol. 40, pp. 656–663.

Heath, S. (1983). *Ways with Words: Language, Life, and Work in Communities and Classrooms,* New York: Cambridge University Press.

Hiebert, E. and C. Sawyer (April, 1984). "Young Children's Concurrent Abilities in Reading and Spelling," a paper presented to the annual meeting of the American Educational Research Association, New Orleans, LA.

Hillerich, R. (1977). *Reading Fundamentals for Preschool and Primary Children,* Columbus, OH: Charles Merrill.

Hipple, M. (March 1985). "Journal Writing in Kindergarten," *Language Arts,* Vol. 62, pp. 255–261.

Hirsch, E. (1987). *Cultural Literacy,* Boston: Houghton Mifflin.

Holdaway, D. (1979). *Foundations of Literacy,* New York: Scholastic.

Hunt, K. (1965). *Grammatical Structures Written at Three Grade Levels,* Champaign, IL: National Council of Teachers of English.

Jenkins, J., R. Bausell, and L. Jenkins (Winter 1972). "Comparisons of Letter Name and Letter Sound Training as Transfer Variables," *American Educational Research Association Journal,* Vol. 9, pp. 75–86.

Lazar, I., V. Hubbel, H. Murray, M. Rosche, and J. Royce (1977). *The Persistence of Preschool Effects,* Washington, DC: Department of Health, Education and Welfare.

Mandler, J. and N. Johnson (1977). "Remembrance of Things Passed: Story Structure and Recall," *Cognitive Psychologist,* pp. 111–151.

Mason, J. (1984). "Early Reading from a Developmental Perspective," in *Handbook of Reading Research,* P. D. Pearson et al. (Ed.), New York: Longman, pp. 505–543.

Mason, J. (1982). "Acquisition of Knowledge About Reading," paper presented at the Annual Meeting of the American Educational Research Association, New York, NY.

Menyuk, P. (1971). *The Acquisition and Development of Language,* Englewood Cliffs, NJ: Prentice-Hall.

Muehl, S. and S. Kremenack (1966). "Ability to Match Information Within and Between Auditory and Visual Sense Modality and Subsequent Reading Achievement," *Journal of Educational Psychology,* Vol. 57, pp. 230–239.

Olson, D. (1984). "See! Jumping! Some Oral Language Antecedents of Literacy," in *Awakening to Literacy,* H. Goelman, A. Oberg, and F. Smith (Eds.), Exeter, NH: Heinemann, pp. 185–192.

Rich, D. (1985). *The Forgotten Factor in School Success—The Family,* Washington, DC: Home and School Institute.

Robinson, H. (1972). "Visual and Auditory Modalities Related to Methods of Beginning Reading," *Reading Research Quarterly,* Vol. 8, No. 3, pp. 7–39.

Robinson, V., D. Strickland, and B. Cullinan (1978). "The Child Ready or Not?" in *The Kindergarten Child and Reading,* L. Ollila (Ed.), Newark, DE: International Reading Association.

Rosner, J. and D. Simon (1971). "The Auditory Analysis Test: An Initial Report," *Journal of Learning Disabilities,* Vol. 4, No. 7, pp. 384–392.

Rumelhart, D. (1975). "Notes on a Schema for Stories," in *Representation and Understanding,* D. Bobrow and A. Collins (Eds.), New York: Academic Press.

Samuels, A. (1972). "The Effect of Letter-Name Knowledge on Learning to Read," *American Educational Research Journal,* Vol. 9, pp. 65–74.

Schweinhart, L. and D. Weikart (1980), *Young Children Grow Up: The Effects of The Perry Preschool Program on Youths Through Age 15,* Ypsilanti, MI: High Scope Educational Research Foundation.

Slaughter, J. (April 1983). "Big Books for Little Kids: Another Fad or a New Approach for Teaching Beginning Reading?" *The Reading Teacher,* Vol. 36, pp. 758–761.

Sulzby, E. (Summer 1985). "Children's Emergent Reading of Favorite Storybooks: A Developmental Study," *Reading Research Quarterly,* Vol. 20, pp. 458–481.

Soderbergh, R. (1977). *Reading in Early Childhood: A Linguistic Study of a Preschool Child's Gradual Acquisition of Reading Ability,* Washington, DC: Georgetown University Press.

Spiegel, D. (1985). "A Story Grammar Approach to Reading and Writing," *Reading Today,* Vol. 3, p. 13.

Stauffer, R. (1970). *The Language-Experience Approach to the Teaching of Reading,* New York: Harper & Row.

Stein, N. and G. Glenn (1979). "An Analysis of Story Comprehension in Elementary School Children," in *New Directions in Discourse Processing,* R. Freedle (Ed.), Norwood, NJ: Ablex.

Sutton, M. (April 1969). "Children Who Learned to Read in Kindergarten: A Longitudinal Study," *The Reading Teacher,* Vol. 22, pp. 595–602.

Taylor, D. (1983). *Family Literacy: Young Children Learning to Read and Write,* Exeter, NH: Heinemann.

Templin, M. (1957). *Certain Language Skills in Children: Their Development and Inter-relationships,* Minneapolis: University of Minnesota Press.

U.S. Department of Education (1986). *What Works: Research About Teaching and Learning,* Washington, DC: U.S. Department of Education.

Van Allen, R. (1976). *Language Experiences in Communication,* Boston: Houghton Mifflin.

Veatch, J., F. Sawicki, G. Elliott, E. Barnette, and J. Blakey (1973). *Key Words to Reading,* Columbus, OH: Charles Merrill.

Weaver, C. (1988). *Reading Process and Practice from Sociopsycholinguistics to Whole Language,* Portsmouth, NH: Heinemann.

Wilson, P. and R. Anderson (1985). "Reading Comprehension and School Learning," in *Reading Education: Foundations for a Literate America,* J. Osborn, P. Wilson, and R. Anderson (Eds.), Lexington, MA: Lexington Books, pp. 319–328.

CHAPTER 4

Teaching Children to Recognize Words

OVERVIEW Readers recognize words when they associate pronunciation and meaning with printed words. Three broad goals guide word-recognition instruction. First, children need to associate meanings with printed and spoken words. Second, they need to develop automatic recognition of words that occur frequently in written text. These words are sight words (memorized words). Finally, they must develop the strategies that will enable them to decode words they do not recognize automatically, and subsequently, add these decoded words to their sight vocabulary. Achieving these goals gives students the reading independence needed to understand written text. Independence in word recognition means that readers can understand text without assistance. Children who lack independence must interrupt the reading process to obtain assistance in identifying problem words.

This chapter introduces ways of teaching sight words, as well as context clues, structural analysis, and phonics skills. The chapter theme is introducing words in meaningful settings, since students are more likely to remember words that have meaning for them. In addition, a balanced approach to word recognition is advocated, which means that sight words, context clues, structural analysis, and phonics are included in a sound decoding program, and they are combined to figure out unknown words.

Key Vocabulary

As you read this chapter, check your understanding of these terms:

analogy decoding	**decoding**
automaticity	**phonics skills**
blending	**sight words**
context clues	**structural analysis**

Focusing Questions

As you read this chapter, try to answer these questions:

1. What happens when readers identify words?
2. What are the four basic methods of recognizing words?
3. How do fluent readers recognize most words?
4. How do the word-recognition skills interact in a balanced reading program?

INTRODUCTION TO WORD RECOGNITION

Readers extract visual information from printed words. They send this information to their brains where it is used in conjunction with their experiential background and cultural literacy to construct the meaning of written text. Fast, accurate word identification is one of the cornerstones of skilled reading (Perfetti and Lesgold, 1979). In fact, decoding efficiency is one of the major factors separating skilled readers from poor readers (Adams and Huggins, 1985; Biemiller, 1977–1978; Perfetti and Lesgold, 1979). Fluent readers process words quickly and accurately; this enables them to concentrate on the author's meaning rather than on his or her words. However, even fluent readers have to interrupt their smooth, rapid comprehension when they encounter unknown words. When **decoding** becomes necessary, both fluent readers and novice readers use *memory* (**sight words**), **context clues, structural analysis,** and **phonics**. Recent research recognizes a *combination or analogy* approach to decoding (Cunningham, 1975–1976). These skills are explained later in the chapter.

Decoding Skills

Sight words are words readers have memorized through seeing them repeatedly in meaningful text. Memorization of words enables students to recognize them automatically. Frequently occurring words should be memorized; thus, readers do not have to decode them every time they encounter these words. A sight-word vocabulary enables students to use **context clues**. These are word-recognition clues inferred from the meaning of the words in the phrase or sentence in which the unknown word occurs (Gough, 1983). For example, in the sentence *The boy ran through the door of the white _____* , the reader would most likely insert *house* in the blank; the sentence meaning suggests this word. Students who know a core of sight words and can use context clues, have access to **structural** clues, which they can use to decode words. In structural analysis, words are decoded through *morphemes* (meaning units), which include prefixes, suffixes, root words, compound words, inflected endings, and

Independent readers understand text without assistance. (*Courtesy Elizabeth Crews*)

contractions. For example, students who recognize the word *go,* will usually recognize the word *going,* if they note the structural change that occurs when the inflected ending *ing* is added.

Sounds

Phonics skills are also decoding skills. Phonics skills involve analyzing whole words into smaller spelling units (syllables) and relating these units to speech sounds. Then the sounds are blended together to approximate word pronunciation. Readers must understand that printed words represent spoken words, if they are to use phonics analysis most effectively. Students also use phonics skills most effectively when they are decoding words that are already in their listening or speaking vocabulary. In the following example, phonic analysis is applied to the word *moment.*

Blending

mo | ment (divided into syllables)

mō | mĕnt (associating speech sounds with spelling units)

mo ment (blending speech sounds to approximate pronunciation)

An **analogy** approach, which is also called *mediated word identification* or the *compare/contrast* strategy (Cunningham, 1979), is a process of searching through a store of known words to compare the unknown to the known. In some instances, readers find it necessary to segment unfamiliar words into manageable units; then they compare these units to units in known words. Finally, the units are recombined to identify the word or words. This process is illustrated in the following example. While reading, Steve came across the word *employ*, which he did not recognize in print. However, he knew *embarrass* and *empire*, which he used to recognize the beginning of *employ*; and he knew *boy*, *joy*, and *toy*, which he used to decode *ploy*. Then he recombined the word parts and pronounced it to determine whether he had heard the word before, and realized that he had indeed heard the word *employ*.

Although you probably have learned some of the strategies described in the preceding paragraphs, you may have forgotten the specific word-recognition skills, since the process becomes so automatic; that is, you recognize words without conscious effort. Many people learn to read without acquiring a set of rules for decoding words; therefore, they read but cannot state the rules that enable them to do so. Whether they learned the rules and forgot them, or never learned any formal set of rules, most adults underestimate the difficulty children experience when trying to recognize the marks on paper that we call *words*. They have to learn to attend to words and to convert these random marks on paper to meaning. If you turn this book upside down and try to read it, you will begin to understand how print looks to children when they first attempt to read. However, these children already know many words that they can learn to recognize in printed form.

Sound and meaning

"A child who is ready to read knows the sound and meaning of hundreds of words, and he knows how these words are put together in phrases to convey ideas" (Gray, 1960). In the early stages of word-recognition instruction, students are learning to identify—in print—words that are in their listening and speaking vocabularies. In the intermediate grades, the focus shifts from recognizing the printed form of known words to expanding the student's knowledge of word meanings. The intermediate-grade student recognizes most of the words in his or her existing listening and speaking vocabulary; therefore, he or she can extend vocabulary knowledge through learning the meaning of formerly unknown words.

How Children Perceive Words

The reading process occurs in the brain rather than the eyes. Our eyes send information to the brain for interpretation. This information is derived from print, but the interpretation is based on past experiences (schemata) and cultural literacy (world knowledge). The brain is relatively independent of the eyes; for example, our eyes send an upside-down image to the brain, which turns it right side up.

Fixations

In reading, our eyes move across the page in jerks and stops. The stops are called fixations that are approximately ¼ of a second in duration. The number of words seen in one fixation depends on the reader's fluency, his or her interest in the topic, and knowledge about the topic. Average readers read about 240 to 300 words per minute, although it is possible to read 960 to 1200 words per minute (Weaver, 1988).

Our eyes do not process all words from left to right, as the word *gate* illustrates. An average reader decoding this word would look at the *ga*, but would not know the sound of *a* until looking at the *e*, which indicates that the *a* is long. Thus, the decoder's eyes might move in this manner.

Furthermore, the majority of readers do not consciously see individual letters in a word, nor do they consciously look at every word in a sentence. Readers look for ideas, thoughts, and information rather than letters and words. Fluent readers only become aware of letters and words when they are unable to make sense of the text they are reading. Then they look at letters and words as a means of decoding what the author said.

Fluency

After readers acquire some fluency, the reading process becomes automatic, which means that it occurs with little or no conscious effort. During this process, the brain directs the visual perception of words. Some word features are more important than others; for instance, readers rely on consonants more than vowels. This will become apparent as you read the first of the following passages, from which the vowels have been deleted, and the second passage, from which the consonants have been deleted. You may wish to have a friend time you as you read these passages. Which passage took longer to read? The complete passages are located at the end of this chapter on p. 174.

Passage 1

Th_r_ _s n_w s_bst_nt__l _v_d_nc_ th_t st_d_nts w_rk_ng t_g_th_r _n sm_ll c__p _r_t_v_ gr__ps c_n m_st_r m_t_r__l pr_s_nt_d b_ th_ t__ch_r b_tt_r th_n c_n st_ d_nts w_rk_ng _n th__r _wn.

Passage 2

_oo_e_a_i_e _ea_i_ _e_e_ _o a _e_ o_ i__u__io_a _e_o_ i_ _i_ _u_e__ _o_i__a_, _i_e-a_i_y_ea_i_ _ou_. _e _ou_ u_ua_y _a_e _ou_ _e_e_ _o_e _i_ a_ie_e_, _wo a_e_a_e a_ie_e_, a_ o_e _ow a_ie_e_.

Readers use the top half of lines of print more than they use the bottom half of lines of print. This is illustrated in Passage 3 and Passage 4. You may wish to have a classmate time your reading of these passages to determine which of the two passages is easier to read.

Passage 3

Teachers can use several activities to help students attach meanings to learning experiences. Writing logs/diaries can document students' reactions to events and are particularly useful if the entries interpret what has happened.

Passage 4

Writing a precis, a concise abridgment, asks students to identify the gist of an experience, reading, or observation. It requires students to prioritize their own impressions and become more articulate about the meanings they have attributed to experiences

When identifying words, readers tend to use the beginnings of words more than they use the middles and endings of words. This principle is illustrated in Passage 5 and Passage 6.

Passage 5

Th_ stud____ i_ ea_ gro__ ar_ respon_____ no_ on__ fo_ lear____ th_ mate____
be___ tau___ i_ cla__, bu_ al_ f_ help___ th__ group_____ lea__.

Passage 6

___ply ___ting ___ents __to __xed ___lity ___ups __d _____aging ___em _o __rk
____ther __e __t ___ugh _o ___duce ___ning __ins: ____ents __st __ve a __son _o
__ke _ne ____her's _____ement ____ously.

A mystery

The preceding passages help us understand how children perceive words, but how they identify words remains essentially a mystery, even after a century of research (Gough, 1984). When we teach sight words, context clues, structural analysis, and phonics we are, in fact, teaching children how to attend to words. For example, when memorizing sight words, students learn to scan the visual image of words repeatedly so they are committed to memory. On the other hand, teaching context clues encourages children to attend to the meaning clues provided by the known words in the sentence; structural analysis directs readers' attention to word structure, and phonics instruction directs their attention to the phonemes comprising the word.

No best way

There is no one best way to decode unknown words. Ideally, children use five means of learning words (memory, context clues, structural analysis, phonics, and a combination or analogy approach). Some words like the word *come* are best memorized because they occur frequently and are phonetically irregular; this means readers would have to know many exceptions to the usual phonetic rules to decode them. Context clues are useful tools for decoding, but they do not always reveal the exact identification of an unknown word. For instance, in the sentence "The boy ran into the _____", readers might predict words like *house, cave, door,* or *car.* Therefore, readers who combine knowledge of consonant sounds with context clues, can use their knowledge of the consonant *c* with the context. This will allow them to accurately identify the unknown word in this sentence, "The boy ran into the c_____."

A Balanced Decoding Approach

The approach to decoding, a balanced word-recognition program that includes instruction in *each* approach to identifying words, insures success for more children (Winograd and Greenlee, 1986). Programs that overemphasize one approach to decoding words, while neglecting the others, can cause difficulty for students. For instance, overemphasizing sight words and context clues creates readers who are dependent on teachers for assistance. Overemphasis on phonics, on the other hand, creates slow and overly analytic readers. A balanced decoding program gives children opportunities to acquire and use each decoding skill, which gives them the necessary foundation for successful reading. Figure 4.1 illustrates a model of word recognition.

Teaching Children to Identify Words

For several decades the major issue in word recognition was whether children should learn sight words or phonics. However, that issue has been resolved; educators have developed a more complete understanding of the reading process. Today, the majority of educators believe that phonics instruction is one of the essential ingredients in a sound reading program.

Phonics and sight words

Phonics and sight-word approaches to reading have prevailed in a cyclic fashion throughout the history of American reading instruction. During the 1930s and 1940s, sight-word instruction prevailed. In 1955, Flesch published the book *Why Johnny Can't Read,* which criticized sight-word instruction and advocated a phonics approach as the solution to reading problems. This book was instrumental in turning the focus of word identification instruction to phonics. Chall's book *Learning to Read: The Great Debate* added impetus to this movement. This book details the findings of a Carnegie Foundation research study, which identified the *code emphasis approach* (decoding words through phonic analysis) as most effective in beginning reading. Chall does not state that a *code emphasis approach* is a "cure-all" for reading problems; rather, she points out that this approach generally produces the best readers. She notes that children learn in different ways. Chall also points out that a creative teacher is a very important factor in successful reading instruction.

Research

In an effort to identify the best approach to teaching reading, the United States Office of Education sponsored a series of studies involving 30,000 children and 1000 teachers. These studies took into account such approaches as language experience, basal readers, phonics, linguistics, modified alphabets, and individualized reading. The researchers found that phonics was a valuable part of the reading program (Bond and Dykstra, 1967). They further concluded that combination approaches to word recognition were more effective than a single approach, and no single method was better than any other for teaching students to recognize words. These researchers agreed with Chall regarding the teacher's importance in children's reading achievement.

Teachers are important to reading success because they interpret and

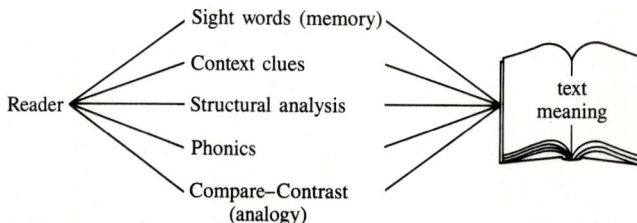

Sight words (memory)

Context clues

Reader   Structural analysis   text meaning

Phonics

Compare–Contrast (analogy)

Figure 4.1

implement the curriculum. They choose the materials that students read and the activities that provide skills practice. Teachers can alter the sequence of skills and program focus. Teachers who believe that children must decode every word accurately in order to read well, will emphasize phonics and exact reading of every word in the text. On the other hand, teachers who believe that readers can grasp the text without reading every single word, tend to focus on combination approaches (memory, context, structural analysis, and phonics). No matter what method or materials are used in teaching children to identify words, the teacher is the most powerful determinant of reading success.

Sound-symbol relationships

Current research shows that on the average, children who are taught phonics get a better start in reading than children who are not taught phonics (Williams, 1985; Johnson and Bauman, 1984; Chall, 1983; Pflaum et al., 1980). This finding is because English is an alphabetic language based on consistent relationships between letters and sounds. Unfortunately, these relationships are not entirely consistent and predictable; the English alphabet has 26 letters, but 44 sounds (phonemes) are necessary for pronouncing words. Therefore, some letters (graphemes) represent more than one sound in English, which creates confusion for the beginning reader. This confusion is illustrated by the varying sounds of the letter *a* in the following words.

*a*way: the *a* is an unstressed vowel sound (schwa) producing the /ŭ/ sound.

aw*ay:* the *ay* in the same word produces the /ā/ sound.

s*a*t: the *a* in this word produces the /ă/ sound.

f*a*ther: the *a* in this word produces the /ä/ sound, which is described as a broad *a* sound.

Additional confusion arises from the historical development of English, which led to silent letters and words that are pronounced differently from their spelling, as in the example, *bough* and *bow.* Furthermore, *bow* can be a *bow tie* or the *bow of a boat,* or a *bow by an actor.* Of course, in these examples, readers must use sentence meaning (context clues) to determine pronunciation and word meaning.

Intensive phonics

While research shows there is little doubt that early, reasonably intensive phonics instruction results in superior word-identification skills, these studies do not show improved comprehension ability (Johnson and Bauman, 1984; Resnick, 1977). In fact, some research had reverse outcomes; in other words, the phonics groups were superior in word identification, while the meaning groups excelled in comprehension (Johnson and Bauman, 1984; Norton and Hubert, 1977).

What does this data mean for teachers? It means that phonics instruction is an essential component in the elementary reading program. In fact, Anderson and his colleagues (1985) recommend an early introduction to phonics. However, comprehension should be the focal point of reading instruction from the

outset. Children must realize that reading is always directed toward comprehending.

Meaningful text   Children should have many experiences reading meaningful text. They
should read many types of written language (newspapers, magazines, poetry,
expository text, stories, and so forth). They should spend time reading interesting material each day in order to advance their word identification and comprehension skills. This helps them retain the words and ideas they read. When
readers process meaningless text, they are engaging in a rote memorization
task. Therefore, beginning reading materials should have interesting stories
and informational articles. The language-experience materials and shared book
experiences, discussed in Chapter 3, provide interesting, meaningful content
for beginning readers.

Automaticity

Word recognition is the process of associating meaning with the printed word
or words. Most teachers have encountered students who read words accurately,
but slowly; thus, they frequently experience difficulty in comprehending content. These readers spend more time trying to remember words or rules for
decoding words, which distracts them from dealing with the content of the
selection. Mackworth (1977) states that children who have difficulty processing
a printed word, show prolonged eye fixations, indicative of an inner cognitive
struggle with the material.

Without   According to **automaticity** theory, a fluent reader decodes text automati-
conscious effort cally—that is, without conscious effort (Laberge and Samuels, 1974). Accurate
word recognition is only one aspect of the process, since automaticity theory
also suggests that word recognition should occur quickly and without conscious
thought. Thus, readers' attention is freed for understanding content. Cunningham (1978) states that the following factors are associated with automatic word
recognition during fluent reading:

1. The ability to immediately recognize frequently occurring words.
2. The ability to use one's knowledge of sound-symbol relationships (phonics).
3. The ability to use semantic cues to predict the meaning of words.
4. The ability to use syntactic cues (word order) to predict the use of a
   word.
5. The ability to use context and phonics clues to identify upcoming words
   in a sentence, without having to "process" the unfamiliar word in
   question. In other words, the reader could use both the context and the
   initial sound of the word for word identification—without having to
   think of the sound associated with each letter of the word.

Beginning readers are not automatic decoders; therefore, they must concentrate on word recognition. This makes the process of reading all the more
difficult and slow. Thus, one of the goals of reading instruction should be the

automaticity of word recognition—so that readers can proceed to concentrate on meaning (Cunningham, 1978). Practice in reading content and in recognizing an increasing number of words helps children achieve automaticity.

Teaching Word-Recognition Skills

Automaticity of word recognition is important to reading success. Children who automatically recognize words can focus their attention on understanding the text. To achieve automaticity, students need many opportunities for meaningful, interesting reading. Teachers should avoid practice that lacks meaning, since students will be unable to make the associations necessary to identify, remember, and understand the author's words. Content is meaningful when students have the world knowledge (experience, cultural literacy) to understand it. When students lack the background to associate meaning with text, teachers must build the necessary background.

Interesting materials

Although interesting reading material is the best source of skills practice, games and other practice activities are useful for introducing words, phrases, and sounds. Practice activities help teachers prepare for the three stages of development necessary for developing word-recognition skills: *knowledge, habit,* and *skill. Knowledge* refers to students' ability to identify a word or sound—such as the diphthong spelling pattern *oi* in *coin* or the *aw* in *saw.*

Practice

Through practice, students learn to *habitually* use specific word-recognition methods. *Skill* is achieved when readers recognize words with both speed and precision. They are then able to identify words without consciously working out decoding rules. These readers are like adults who drive their cars on the same route each day. These drivers do not consciously think about each turn they make; likewise, readers who have achieved automaticity, no longer need to concentrate on decoding individual words.

Schell (1978) recommends that teachers use five stages of instruction in teaching word-recognition skills. These stages are present, practice, apply, review, and *re*review. The teacher introduces (presents) word-recognition skills to the class in a meaningful setting, and then provides opportunities (activities and worksheets) to practice the skill. The next stage calls for skill application through reading interesting content. The teacher provides review instruction and exercises, and, as children progress, opportunities to *re*review skills are also scheduled. Many beginning teachers underestimate the amount of review and reteaching that is necessary for children to develop word-recognition skills. Providing for repeated experiences with a new task, helps prevent "Monday morning amnesia" in students.

Strategic Decoding

Strategic readers control the way they read. They know when they have identified words accurately because the text makes sense. They know when they have failed to decode a word accurately because the text does not make sense, and they know a series of steps or strategies that will help them identify the word or words. Readers cannot always identify words accurately, but strategic readers know what to do about it.

Flexible

Strategic readers are flexible; they use appropriate strategies to identify words. "The child with few strategies or the child using one scheme predominantly may experience limited success" (Frenzel, 1978). No single approach to word recognition is adequate. Competent readers employ all four word-identification methods in a balanced approach. They also apply the most appropriate method in the particular instance.

The following steps will guide readers' use of word-identification strategies.

1. The reader looks at the word to determine whether he or she has memorized it (sight word).
2. When the word is not a sight word, the reader should determine whether context provides clues for identifying it.
3. If context clues do not work, determine whether the word has structural parts (such as prefixes, suffixes, or root words) to use in identifying it.
4. If structural analysis does not help solve the word, the reader uses phonics clues to identify the word.
5. After identifying a word, the reader checks the accuracy of his or her identification by reading the word in context to determine whether it makes sense.

Table 4.1 shows the uses and limitations of the various word-identification approaches. This information helps students decode words strategically.

SIGHT WORDS

Sight words are words readers recognize automatically. Young readers have to decode unknown words, but eventually they come to recognize most words at sight. The average adult, in fact, reads almost entirely by sight words. Sight words must be so well known that they are identified immediately and without conscious effort when they appear in the text. Readers who have to decode every word in a reading selection face a slow, laborious task and often experience comprehension difficulties.

Expedite reading

A sight-word vocabulary expedites the reading process because it enables readers to focus on comprehension. Many reading experts (Ehri and Wilce, 1985; Searfoss and Readence, 1985; Dechant, 1982) agree that beginning readers should learn a core vocabulary of 30 to 50 words, which helps them understand that print and meaning are related. These sight words also give readers a basis for remembering the letter patterns in words. Sight words illustrate letter-sound relationships (phonics) and facilitate children's acquisition of phonics skills. Furthermore, readers must have sight words at their disposal to utilize context clues and to analyze word structure. Thus, sight-word knowledge facilitates all of the word-recognition skills.

Table 4.1   FOUR WORD-RECOGNITION APPROACHES: THEIR DEPENDENCIES, USES, AND LIMITATIONS

Approaches	Dependent on	Uses in word recognition	Limitations
Sight Words	Visual memory of words and shapes Configuration skills Using high utility words Discrimination skills Associating words and images	Needed to build initial vocabulary Foundation for other attack skills Provides cues in concert with other strategies Bank of sight words is individual thing	Impossible to learn thousands of words by sight Similar configurations are confusing Detached from meaning Visual memory inefficient in learning large numbers of words Pronouncing isolated words is not true reading Some may not learn well from visual approach
Phonics	Knowledge of sight words Ability to associate certain sounds with certain symbols Synthesizing skills Analyzing skills Following a sequential development of decoding skills Ability to use visual and auditory discrimination skills Good speaking and listening vocabularies	Used systematically to attack words with general commonalities Used in blending, patterning, and substituting skills Used to manipulate sounds to obtain acceptable results Used best in conjunction with other attack options Operates in reading, spelling, and writing Applied best to familiar words	Generalizations may have low utility value English is inconsistent: irregularities cause problems Sounding letters in isolation is unrealistic and confusing Laborious letter-by-letter sounding is slow; child can become overly analytical Some may not learn well from auditory approach Piecemeal identification tends to lose bigger meaning

(continues on p. 132)

Source: Norman J. Frenzel. "Children Need a Multipronged Attack in Word Recognition." *The Reading Teacher*, Vol. 31 (March 1978): pp. 628–629. Reprinted with permission of the author and The International Reading Association.

The Sight Words Students Should Learn

Initial sight words include interesting words, meaningful words, high utility words, and concrete words. Children find interesting words that have meaning for them easier to remember. Concrete words are also easier to learn (Levin, 1981). However, high utility words are used in beginning reading instruction, because they appear often, so they are useful for readers to know.

Table 4.1 (*Continued*)

Approaches	Dependent on	Uses in word recognition	Limitations
Structural analysis	Knowledge of sight words Synthesizing skills Analyzing skills Visual cues to word parts Good speaking and listening vocabularies Knowledge of semantic effects of word parts Following a structure-meaning sequence	Used along with context phonics, and sight words Used in getting meaning through word parts Aids in building words from known words Operates in reading, spelling, and writing Uses structure to determine root, inflection, or derivative Applied best to familiar bases	Generalizations may be erroneous or inapplicable May get meaning without pronunciation Not all words can be analyzed structurally Cannot memorize lists of affixes Some may not transfer structural analysis skills Overanalysis tends to make each syllable a word Cannot look for little words in big words
Context clues	Speaking and listening vocabularies Awareness and use of syntactical and semantic signals Prediction and anticipation skills Intuitive knowledge of language and its patterns Comprehension skills Visualization skills	Used along with phonics and structural analysis skills Identifies words in a realisitic and meaningful setting Some words must be in context to obtain proper pronunciation and meaning Might be first consideration in attacking an unfamiliar word Forces thinking while reading; aids understanding	Unknown words must be familiar Guessing may produce incorrect words Material may not have sufficient or strong context clues Reliance on one type of signal may produce problems

Associate experience

Meaningful words are ones with which children can associate experiences. Meaningful words are usually in children's listening and/or speaking vocabulary. Words like *mother* (or *mom*), *dad, grandmother, cat, dog, toys, cars,* and *doll* are examples of words that have meaning for many children. Of course, city students rarely see cows, while rural students may never have seen fire hydrants. Thus, life experiences have an impact on the meaning vocabulary of students. Teachers can find out what words are meaningful for students by listening and observing. They can consult language-experience stories, children's journals, students' drawings, and writing, which will reveal the words they find meaningful.

Meaningful words are often the words that are most interesting to a child.

They have particular value for a student. A child must be "hooked" by his or her own excitement and confidence to understand the black squiggles in *The Billy Goats Gruff* or *Charlotte's Web*. If the words represent a child's own important images, he or she will be able to understand and remember. Johnson (1987) includes lists of interesting words selected for reading by different students. The following words were identified by a kindergarten youngster named Sally.

> Duchess, Mama, Dad, Ronnie, Emily, Mommy, Gwennie, Silver, Mrs. Eldridge, hunting, light bulb, ghost, witch, Santa Claus, Santa's helper, snow angel.

When youngsters read their own words, their curiosity is aroused about all words: they are hooked. This technique is also called the "key-word" approach, which was discussed in Chapter 3.

High utility words

In addition to introducing interesting words, sight-word instruction almost always includes high utility words. High utility words like *a, an, the, in,* and *on* occur frequently in printed language; they comprise as much as 75 percent of all primary reading and 50 percent of all adult reading. Therefore, they are very helpful to beginning readers. These high utility words are often abstract words that do not represent real objects and ideas, which makes them more difficult for children to learn. The Fry list of instant words given in the Appendix is a good example of a high utility word list. The following list is another type of high utility list. The author (Dechant, 1982) states that ten words, *a, and, be, I, in, of, the, to, we,* and *you,* make up 25 percent of all words in ordinary writing. The following words make up nearly 50 percent of all words in ordinary writing:

a	have	so
all	he	that
and	I	the
are	if	this
as	in	time
at	is	to
be	it	very
been	letter	was
but	me	we
can	my	when
do	not	will
for	of	with
from	on	would
get	one	you
go	our	your
good	put	yours
had	she	

Source: Emerald V. Dechant, *Improving the Teaching of Reading,* 3rd ed. © 1982, p. 155. Reprinted by permission of Prentice-Hall, Inc., Englewood Cliffs, N.J.

Concrete words   Concrete words that represent real objects and actions are good words to begin sight-word instruction. Children commonly find that nouns and verbs are usually easier to learn because they are accustomed to naming objects and actions. Wolpert (1972) investigated imagery and word learning and found that "high" imagery words are learned more readily than "low" imagery ones—and are better retained in memory. High imagery words, such as *tree, house,* and *child,* are words that the learner can associate with a concrete visual image. *Low imagery words,* like *air, place,* and *way,* are much more difficult to associate with a specific visual image. The Appendix includes the Dolch list of the 95 most common nouns, which are high imagery words.

Phrases   Sight phrases are useful for beginning readers. Sight phrases are comprised of structure words (articles, conjunctions, prepositions, and adverbs) that derive their meaning from sentence context and common nouns. Aside from the Dolch list, teachers can make up phrases from high utility words, common nouns, and verbs for students to practice. Sight-phrase practice helps children learn words, and teaches children to group or cluster words together, which facilitates reading fluency and comprehension. Hood (1974) recommends checking word knowledge before using phrase cards, so that children are not forced to work with too many unknown or half-known words.

Bookwords are valuable sight words for children. Since students should read trade books, as well as basal readers, they need to learn words that are frequently used in trade books. Eeds (1985) researched the words commonly found in books for beginning readers and identified 227 high frequency words for beginning reading. Table 4.2 identifies these words.

How Children Learn Sight Words

Children must be able to see the differences in words. For instance, they must be able to see the difference between *cat* and *car* (visual discrimination). Distinctive features enable children to differentiate among letters and words. The *t* in *cat* is distinctive because it is an ascending letter that is crossed. Word length is another helpful feature. For example, *grandmother* is considerably longer than *dog.* Teachers should be sure to call attention to such distinctive features as length, ascending letters (like *t* and *l*), descending letters (like *g* and *y*), and double letters (like the *tt* in *little*). Perceiving the similarities and differences in words helps children learn words, but learning words also sharpens their discrimination.

Context   A number of reading authorities emphasize the importance of having children understand the word (to be learned) in oral context (Cunningham, 1980; McNinch, 1981; Merlin and Rogers, 1981). After they understand the word in oral context, it should be presented in written context and in isolation. Presenting the word in both context and isolation enables children to visually perceive it.

Application   Following this introduction, children should have many opportunities for meaningful application of word knowledge. Children learn sight words from

Table 4.2 BOOKWORDS: FINAL CORE 227 WORD LIST BASED ON 400 STORYBOOKS FOR BEGINNING READERS

the	1334	good	90	think	47	next	28
and	985	this	90	new	46	only	28
a	831	don't	89	know	46	am*	27
I	757	little	89	help	46	began	27
to	746	if	87	grand	46	head	27
said	688	just	87	boy	46	keep	27
you	638	baby*	86	take	45	teacher*	27
he	488	way	85	eat	44	sure*	27
it	345	there	83	body*	43	says*	27
in	311	every	83	school	43	ride*	27
was	294	went	82	house	42	pet*	27
she	250	father	80	morning	42	hurry*	26
for	235	had	79	yes*	41	hand	26
that	232	see	79	after	41	hard	26
is	230	dog	78	never	41	push*	26
his	226	home	77	or	40	our	26
but	224	down	76	self*	40	their	26
they	218	got	73	try	40	watch*	26
my	214	would	73	has	38	because*	25
of	204	time	71	always*	38	door	25
on	192	love*	70	over	38	us	25
me	187	walk	70	again	37	should*	25
all	179	came	69	side	37	room*	25
be	176	were	68	thank*	37	pull*	25
go	171	ask	67	why	37	great*	24
can	162	back	67	who	36	gave	24
with	158	now	66	saw	36	does*	24
one	157	friend	65	mom*	35	car*	24
her	156	cry	64	kid*	35	ball*	24
what	152	oh	64	give	35	sat*	24
we	151	Mr.	63	around	34	stay*	24
him	144	bed*	63	by	34	each*	23
no	143	an	62	Mrs.	34	ever*	23
so	141	very	62	off	33	until*	23
out	140	where	60	sister*	33	shout*	23
up	137	play	59	find	32	mama*	22
are	133	let	59	fun*	32	use*	22
will	127	long	58	more	32	turn	22
look	126	here	58	while	32	thought	22
some	123	how	57	tell	32	papa*	22
day	123	make	57	sleep*	32	lot*	21
at	122	big	56	made	31	blue*	21
have	121	from	55	first	31	bath*	21
your	121	put	55	say	31	mean*	21
mother	119	read*	55	took	31	sit*	21
come	118	them	55	dad*	30	together*	21
not	115	as	54	found	30	best*	20
like	112	Miss*	53	lady*	30	brother*	20

*Indicates words *not* on Durr list.

Source: M. Eeds. "Bookwords: Using a Beginning Word List of High Frequency Words from Children's Literature," *The Reading Teacher* (January 1985) vol. 38, pp. 418–423. Reprinted with permission of the author and the International Reading Association.

Table 4.2 (*Continued*)

then	108	any	52	soon	30	feel*	20
get	103	right	52	ran	30	floor*	20
when	101	nice*	50	dear*	29	wait	20
thing	100	other	50	man	29	tomorrow*	20
do	99	well	48	better*	29	surprise*	20
too	91	old	48	through*	29	shop*	20
want	91	night*	48	stop	29	run	20
did	91	may	48	still	29	own*	20
could	90	about	47	fast*	28		

repeated exposures; therefore, teachers should select materials and activities that provide meaningful repetition. They must plan instruction for children who learn a word after seeing it once; average children need 38 repetitions (Singer, 1971) to learn a word, and less able students may need hundreds of repetitions. Students who learn words easily should spend their time reading rather than in direct sight-word instruction; however, many students in an average class need direct instruction to learn words.

How many sight words should be taught at one time? A good rule of thumb is to introduce five words in a single lesson. If students experience difficulty learning five words, then reduce the number to three. If five words are learned easily, the number can be increased to seven. Practice periods, however, should be short—approximately 10 minutes in duration. Guidelines like the following should direct sight-word instruction.

1. Present an unknown word in context. Sentences may be written on the chalkboard or on chart paper, and the word should be underlined. Some basal readers include a page of "new" words in context at the beginning of each story. If the basal reader you are using does this, it is unnecessary to create a chart. A sentence for introducing the word, *flower* follows.

    She picked the red *flower.*

2. Encourage children to examine the new word carefully. The teacher should pronounce the word aloud.
3. Students should pronounce the word aloud.
4. Have the students read sentences in which the word appears. All of the words in the sentences should be familiar to the students except for the new word.
5. Games and activities should be used to reinforce the new word.
6. Do not introduce words that are easily confused at the same time.
7. Encourage students to write the words.

Difficult Sight Words

Certain types of words present greater difficulty for students than others (Wiesendanger and Bader, 1987). Abstract words are more difficult to learn because they do not have a referent. Words like *a, an,* and *the* do not represent real objects and ideas. This is one reason sight phrases help students learn words; the abstract words are attached to concrete words in the phrases.

Some words are easily confused, like *there* and *where, was* and *saw,* and *this* and *that.* Easily confused words should not be introduced at the same time. One of the easily confused words should be taught and practiced to the point of overlearning before introducing the other one. Both overlearning and creating a distance between the easily confused words helps prevent problems.

Many children learn to recognize pronouns that occur frequently in early reading materials. However, pronouns are problematic for many primary-grade students because the referent is not always clear to beginning readers. For instance, in the sentence, *Jim went to the baseball game where he caught a fly ball,* most young readers would fail to recognize that the pronoun *he* refers to *Jim.* Teachers should use instructional strategies that will help students learn difficult or easily confused sight words.

Activities

Sight-word activities can be used with individual students, small groups, and in some instances, with a whole class. Many of the activities are useful for pairs of children in the same grade; they work together cooperatively to help one another learn. The children may take turns reading to one another, or they may work together to complete activities. Children benefit from pairing for reading activities.

The single most important word-learning activity is reading interesting, meaningful text daily. Reading predictable books and the shared book experience, described in Chapter 3, help students learn words. Rereading familiar books also provides valuable practice and should be encouraged.

"Picture Nouns," which are words that represent easily pictured common objects like dog or ball, can be taught with picture word cards (Fry, 1987). Picture word cards can be made with the printed word on one side and a picture of the object on the other side. The pictures can be drawn or cut from magazines and pasted on the cards. A picture word card is shown in Figure 4.2.

An easy practice activity for students is to have them look at the word, try to say the word, then turn the card over and look at the picture. If the student identified the word correctly, he or she is reinforced; if not, he or she learns the correct word from the picture.

Pictures

Picture word cards can be used as rebuses. In this instance, the picture is used in a sentence in place of a word. For example:

The _____ played with the _____ . (The boy played with the dog.)

Figure 4.2

Picture word cards can also be used for semantic mapping. A common type of semantic map uses four categories of description or function related to the word under study (Fry, 1987). Figure 4.3 illustrates a simple semantic map. In developing this activity, the teacher and students discuss and develop categories and elements that belong in each category. Examples of categories are: functions, description, and needs of dogs. Dogs can also be classified as pet animals and/or work animals.

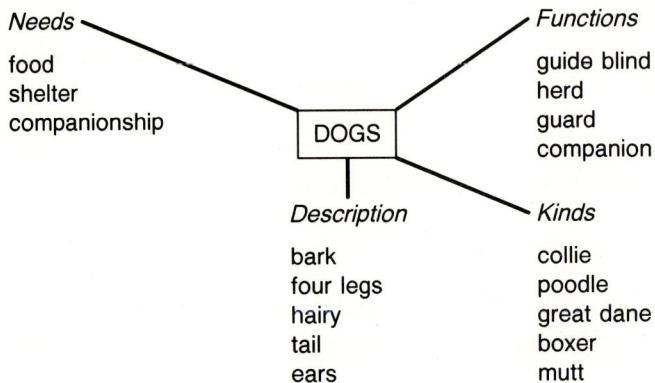

```
Needs                                    Functions
food                                     guide blind
shelter                                  herd
companionship                            guard
                    ┌────────┐           companion
                    │  DOGS  │
                    └────────┘
         Description                      Kinds
         bark                             collie
         four legs                        poodle
         hairy                            great dane
         tail                             boxer
         ears                             mutt
```

Figure 4.3   Semantic map.

Sorting and matching words helps students learn sight words. Students can sort picture word cards, sets of pictures, or cards that have words printed on them. For example, they can find three cards that have the word *can* printed on them, and two cards that contain the word *boy*. The teacher can hold up a word card and pronounce the word, then students locate cards in their own stacks that have the same word printed on them. Students can sort their cards into various categories, such as people, which might include words or pictures like the following, *boy, girl, mother, father,* and *grandmother.*

Games

Lotto games, which are variations of bingo, help students learn sight words. Sight words are written on the game cards; the teacher or another student calls out a word, and the students place a marker on the word if it appears on their card. When students complete a row in any direction, they win. A variation of lotto is developed when the teacher calls out a word, and a student makes up a sentence using the word. After the youngster composes a sentence, a marker is placed on the word square on the lotto card.

Students need to perceive the features that differentiate words; looking for likenesses and differences helps them identify these features. You may give the students cards with sets of words printed in columns and have the students count the words that are alike and those that are different. Everyone earns one point for matching words and two for each word pair that is dissimilar.

The following activities give students opportunities to see words over and over, which helps them acquire a sight-word vocabulary.

1. *Illustrating words.* Students can draw pictures to illustrate particular words, or cut out photographs from magazines.

2. *Dramatize words.* The teacher holds up a word or phrase card, and the students act out the word (good words to use are *walk, skip, jump*).
3. *Writing activities.* Children can write sight words and sentences using sight words. A class contest can be planned to identify the youngster who made up the most sentences using a single sight word identified by the teacher.
4. *Spinner games.* Have the student pronounce the word that the spinner lands on. Paper places or cardboard circles can be used to make spinner games.
5. *Game boards.* The child must recognize a word in order to move a marker along the word game board that the teacher has made. The players use different colored markers. A variation of this game would be to have the players make up a sentence that include the word in order to move the marker. A game board is illustrated in Figure 4.4.
6. *Sight-word or sight-phrase games.*
   a. "Go Fish." Make word cards and attach a paper clip to each card. Put the cards into a large plastic bucket. Make fishing poles with a magnet tied to a piece of string. Have each child drop the fishing line into the bucket to catch a word card. Each word that is caught must be pronounced by the child.
   b. Put the spots on the dog. Cut out spots and write a word on each one. Cut out the outline of a large dog from a piece of cardboard. Have each child take a spot card and pronounce the word on that card before placing the spot on the dog.
   c. Feed Oscar. Write words on cards. Draw a face on a plastic bucket and cut out a mouth. Have the children say the word on their cards before putting them into the mouth (feeding Oscar).

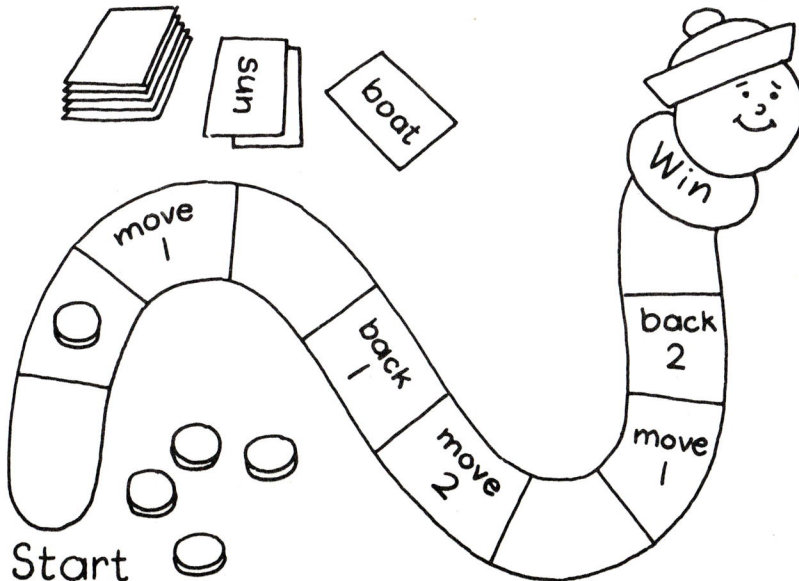

Figure 4.4

7. *This author has had much success with kinesthetic approach,* which involves tracing a word and saying it aloud. This approach is primarily designed for students who have difficulty learning sight words, and it should not be imposed on children who learn easily. Some teachers tend to avoid this approach because it is time-consuming—and this is unfortunate because it may prove to be very helpful for some children. This method should be used for approximately six or eight weeks out of the school year. The following suggested activities are based on the kinesthetic approach:

a. Put cornmeal or grits in a shallow baking pan. The teacher writes a word in the material and the child traces over the teacher's writing, while saying (not spelling) the word aloud. The child should trace the word and say it five times. Then the eyes should be closed and the child should attempt to recall the word from memory. Finally, the child should try to write the word—this time, without a model.

b. Have children write words on the chalkboard (children often enjoy writing on this surface because it provides a strong tactile sensation). They should trace the teacher's model, saying the word at the same time. The model should then be erased and children should attempt to write the word without actually seeing it in front of them.

c. Encourage children to keep, for review purposes, a file of words that they learn through this approach.

Once children have acquired a basic word vocabulary of 30 to 50 words, they have the foundation for using context clues to decode unrecognized words. The following section explores the use of meaning or context clues to identify words.

CONTEXT CLUES

When readers do not recognize a word instantly, the next step is to look for meaning (context) clues in the text. Authors frequently provide aids to help readers understand the words used in the selection. These clues may occur in the same sentence as the word in question, or they may occur in either the preceding sentence, the succeeding sentence, or anywhere else in the paragraph in which the unidentified word appears. Note the italicized word and clues that are circled in the following examples.

"*Purr,* purr, purr," said the (kitten) She was (happy)

People searched for better ways to get rid of (trash) and (garbage.) One (way) that was discovered is called *landfill.*

The use of context clues is one of the most popular word-recognition methods employed by mature readers. Mature readers are able to use these clues extensively because they have the experiential background, language development, and exposure to literature that allows them to easily make use of clues. Most adults identify the majority of unknown words they encounter in a given context. Research indicates that context clues account for a substantial proportion of the vocabulary growth that occurs in the elementary school (Nagy, Herman, and Anderson, 1985).

Context clues may be semantic clues; that is, a clue derived from the meaning of the remaining words in the sentence. For example, in the sentence *We watched the football game from the bleachers,* the words *watched, from, football,* and *game* help the reader identify the word *bleachers.*

Context clues are also suggested from syntax. Syntactic clues are derived from the grammar of a phrase, sentence, or paragraph, and they suggest a particular part of speech to insert in the sentence. For example, in *John* _____ *a touchdown,* a reader can deduce that the unknown word must be a verb.

McCullough (1945) identified six types of context clues:

1. *Definition:* the unknown word is defined in the content. (Example: I eat *breakfast* in the morning.)
2. *Comparison:* contrasting words in the sentence help the reader identify a word that might be unfamiliar. (Example: A mouse is tiny, but an elephant is *enormous.*)
3. *Summary:* The unfamiliar word is a summary of the ideas that precede it. (Example: Cookies, cakes, pies, and ice cream are all *desserts.*)
4. *Familiar expression:* knowledge of familiar expressions can often help the reader to identify a new word. (Example: Mice *nibble* on cheese.)
5. *Experience:* the reader's background experience may aid in identifying an unknown word. (Example: The Chinese eat with *chopsticks.*)
6. *Synonym:* recognizing a synonym in a sentence containing an unknown word may prove to be helpful. (Example: A *computer* is a mechanical brain.)

When the context is altered, the meaning of a particular word changes as well. Therefore, children must be alert when they read in order to detect shifts in the meaning of the context. The following sentences illustrate a case in which a shift in meaning has occurred.

Place the plate on the *table.*

Read the *table* of contents.

In addition to the meaning clues provided by the text, pictures, charts, graphs, diagrams, and typographical clues (quotation marks, parentheses, definitional footnotes) provide readers with context. Beginning readers rely on context clues provided by pictures. Many of the teaching activities suggested in the following section can be used with pictures, as well as words.

Teaching Context Clues

Children in the primary grades should learn to use the meaning of context as a means of recognizing words. Children in the intermediate grades can also benefit from learning to use each of the basic types of context clues. Students are able to use these context clues most effectively when the reading content is characterized by the following:

The reader knows most of the words in the selection.

The reader understands the content.

The author's language and the reader's language are similar.

Listening strategies

A good way to prepare children to use context clues is through the use of listening strategies. Read selections—sentences or short paragraphs—aloud to children. Omit a word (or several words) and have the children suggest what they think the missing word should be. In the example, *Albert felt tired again. The things on his back were getting* _____ , the missing word would be *heavier*. Context clue activities are very useful for kindergarten and first-grade levels, as well as for older children who continue to have difficulty in reading.

Attend to meaning

Many children identify words incorrectly because they are not paying the proper amount of attention to the meaning of the content. Children should understand that the content presented to them in class will always "make sense." Teach children to use the following strategy when they come to an unknown word: Read the entire sentence and substitute any word (such as *candy* or *moonbeam*) for the unknown word. Then go back and think of a word that would make sense in the context of that sentence. For example, in reading the sentence *The dragon breathed fire and smoke,* the child might not recognize the word *dragon* and might insert the word *moonbeam* for the unknown word. The child should reread this sentence and determine if this word actually makes sense in the sentence.

ACTIVITIES FOR TEACHING CONTEXT CLUES

1. Fill in the blanks.

    Example: The boy rode a _____ . (bicycle, house, balloon)

    a. Provide the initial letter of the missing word and have the child complete that word based on the context.

    Example: The dog b_____ at the cat. (bounced, barked, backed)

2. Circle the clues for the unknown italicized word in the sentence.

    Example: During the first (quarter) of the (football game,) the (quarterback) made a *touchdown.*

3. Give students a group of sentences in which the meaning of the new word is revealed through the context of the sentence. Have students synthesize this information and write the meaning of the underlined word as they now understand it.

> Example: A *landfill* site is constructed in a location that does not have water running underground. A pit is dug, trash is thrown into it, and the trash is then covered with dirt.

> Possible answer: *Landfill* is trash covered with dirt.

4. Match pictures to sentences or paragraphs, as in Figure 4.5.
5. Riddle workbooks are available commercially. Teachers may write riddles for the class or may have the children attempt to write their own riddles for each other.

> Example: I am an animal. I am small. I purr when I am happy. I meow and I like milk. What am I? (More complex riddles could be composed about familiar persons and places.)

6. Explain to the class why the meaning of the underlined word changes in the following sentences.

> I *object* to the changes you are making.
> What is that strange *object?*

> I hit a *run* in the baseball game.
> My mother has a *run* in her stocking.

7. Have children cross out the words in the paragraph that do not make sense.

> Example: I am a dog. I like to chew on bones. ~~I purr when I am happy.~~ I bark at intruders.

8. Readance, Bean, and Baldwin (1982) suggest a five-step instructional procedure that teaches students to recognize words and to associate meaning with the words in question. This procedure is most appropriate for middle or intermediate grade students.
   a. Identify words that are likely to be problematic. These words should be central to comprehension.

Figure 4.5

b. The teacher writes a sentence for the word that includes context clues to word meaning. The sentence may be selected from the text in which the word appears.

c. Present the word or words to students in isolation and ask them to think of the meanings. The meanings are written on the chalkboard as students generate them.

d. Ask students to select the best meanings according to the context in step b, from those written on the chalkboard. Students may vote to determine the best meanings.

e. Students may check the meaning in a dictionary or thesaurus.

Context clues are quite valuable to readers who have a core sight-word vocabulary and who have good listening and speaking vocabulary. However, students in the middle grades (intermediate) encounter many words that have two or more syllables, which are composed of root words, prefixes, and suffixes. Readers find structural analysis very helpful in decoding these words. This approach to word identification is examined in the following section.

STRUCTURAL ANALYSIS

Structural analysis involves examining the meaningful parts or structural elements of unknown words to determine their meaning and pronunciation. The word parts used in structural analysis are *morphemes,* so it is also called morphemic analysis. Word parts are also known as *morphemes,* which are the smallest units of meaning in the English language. Morphemes can be either free or bound. *Free morphemes* occur alone as an independent word like *cat.* *Bound morphemes* must be attached to other morphemes. The *s* in *cats* is a bound morpheme. The word *forewarned* has three morphemes: fore/warn/ed. When using the structural elements of words to identify them, children can usually identify the word once they recognize the morphemes that compose that word.

The structural elements included in structural analysis of words are prefixes, suffixes, root words, compound words, inflected endings, and contractions. The following operational definitions of words will help you understand this decoding strategy.

Prefixes are a letter or letters that precede a root word and that change the meaning of the word. (Example: *un*tie means to release from being tied; *re*call means to call again.)

Suffixes are a letter or letters added to the end of a root word that change the meaning of the root word. (Example: care*less* means without care; joy*ful* means full of joy.)

A *root word* is a part of the word that conveys the majority of the word's meaning. Adding prefixes, suffixes, or combining a root with another word will alter the meaning of the root itself. (Example: pre*view* means view before; *color*ful means full of color.)

Compound words are two words joined together to make a new word. (Example: *baseball, grandmother, rainfall.*)

Inflected endings (suffixes) consist of a letter or letters that are added to the end of a root word to indicate case, gender, mood, number, person, or tense. Table 4.3 shows how various parts of speech may be inflected. Inflected endings are commonly used in children's oral language, and thus, they should be easily understood in the process of reading. Children who are most likely to have difficulty with inflected endings are those who speak nonstandard dialects. (See Chapter 11.)

Contractions are a combination of two words written in a shortened form. The deleted letter (or letters) is indicated by an apostrophe. (Example: *can not* is the equivalent of *can't; was not* is the equivalent of *wasn't.*)

Structural analysis is a useful approach to word recognition, but it is most useful when combined with the other word-recognition methods. Most children can benefit from a study of the common prefixes, suffixes, inflected endings, common contractions, and compound words; however, memorizing lists of these elements has a somewhat limited value. Many morphemes also have multiple meanings that can confuse children; thus, only commonly occurring morphemes with dependable meanings should be discussed.

Children in the primary grades study inflected endings, compound words, and contractions. They also study some simple prefixes, suffixes, and root words but, aside from this, instruction in structural analysis is usually reserved for the intermediate-grade levels.

Table 4.3 INFLECTED ENDINGS

Parts of speech	Meaning *(example)*	Inflected words
Nouns	Number *(boy)*	*boys*
	Gender *(actor)*	*actress*
	Possession *(Susan)*	*Susan's*
Verbs	Tense *(work)*	*works, worked, working*
Adjectives	Comparison *(big)*	*big, bigger, biggest*
Adverbs	Comparison *(fast)*	*faster*

The following prefixes, suffixes, and root words are useful because they occur frequently in elementary reading selections.

PREFIXES

ab: away from (absent)

ad: to (admit)

anti: against (antifreeze)

bi: two, twice (biweekly)

co, com, con: with, together (coordinator)
de: away from (depart)
dis: apart from (disembark)
ex: out (exit)
extra: more than (extraordinary)
in: not (incorrect)
mid: middle (midtown)
post: after (postgame)
pre: before (pregame)
pro: in favor of (pro-Asian)
re: again (rewrite)
sub: under (submarine)
tri: three (triangle)
un: not (untie)
uni: one (unicycle)

SUFFIXES

able: capable of being (readable)
er: a person who (helper)
ful: full of (beautiful)
less: without (helpless)
ly: characteristic of (fatherly)
ment: action or process, state of (amazement)
ness: state of (goodness)
ous: full of (joyous)

ROOT WORDS

circ: ring (circus)
color: color (colorful)
cycl: circle (bicycle)
dent: tooth (trident)
div: separate (divisor)
form: shape (uniform)
geo: earth (geography)
gram: letter (telegram)
graph: write (graphic)
min: small (minute)

mov: move (remove)

phon: sound (earphone)

tele: distant (telephone)

vis: see (television)

ACTIVITIES FOR STRUCTURAL ANALYSIS

1. What does the underlined word in each sentence mean?
   a. Jane will *retell* the story.
   b. Please *unlock* the door.
   c. He is a *farmer.*
   d. I had a *sleepless* night.

2. Write sentences using the following words.
   a. redo, precook, untied, unhappy, dislike
   b. readable, helpless, miner, motherly

3. Identify the prefix or suffix in each of the following words.
   a. repaint, dislike, untied, reopen, unhappy
   b. fearless, reporter, newest, slowly

4. Add a prefix from the list below to each root word to make a new word. Tell what each new word now means.

   Example: _____tied _____read _____open _____happy
   Prefixes: pre, re, un, dis

5. Add a suffix to each root word from the list below to make a new word. Tell what each new word now means.

   Example: help_____ good_____ read_____ care_____
   Suffixes: able, er, ness, ful

6. Circle the root word in each of the following: unfriendly, colorless, intersection, incredible.

7. How many words can you think of that belong to a specific root word family? You must be able to tell what each word means.

   Example: marine (sea)—submarine, mariner, maritime, aquamarine, marina.

8. Combine the words in the two lists below to make compound words. Tell what each new word now means.

fire	fast
grand	ball
ice	man
foot	cream
every	father
break	where

9. Make compound words in each of the following sentences by filling a word in each blank.

      a. Jerry built a large snow_____ .
      b. My grand_____ is coming for a visit.
      c. The fire_____ rode on the fire engine.

10. Circle the compound word in each sentence below.
      a. My father made a doghouse for my dog.
      b. My brother is on the baseball team.
      c. Susan went downtown to shop.

11. A morpheme concentration exercise (Burmeister, 1976). Prepare pairs of cards that can be combined to form words. Shuffle the cards so that they are in random order. Write numbers on the backs. Arrange them in numerical order with the numbers face up. A player gives two numbers and these cards are turned up to see if they form a word. If they do, the child gets one point; if not, they are turned back down. The game continues until all of the cards have been matched. The player with the largest number of points wins the game.

12. A morpheme tree or mobile (Burmeister, 1976). Words based on one root can be used to make a display. Words with the same prefix or suffix can also be used.

          Example: *color, discolor, colorful, Colorado, coloration.*

13. Each sentence defines a compound word. Write the correct compound word response in the blanks provided.
      a. We fill it with water to take a bath. _____
      b. A house for a dog. _____

14. Read each sentence and insert the inflected ending that makes sense in the blank that is provided.
      a. I went walk_____ yesterday.
      b. Jane want_____ a new dress for the party.
      c. Muffin is Susan_____ dog.

15. Change each of the following nouns to a possessive: *girls, driver, children.*

16. Change each of the following adjectives and adverbs to a form that indicates a comparison: *big, smaller, fast, slow, busy, happy, dry.* Write a sentence using these new words correctly.

17. Select a contraction that correctly completes each sentence.
      a. Jerry _____ going to play.
      b. _____ a very happy person.
      c. _____ a candy bar.

          Contractions: isn't, she's, they're, here's

18. Make a list of the contractions that you find on the front page of a newspaper.

Teaching Structural Analysis

Structural analysis instruction focuses on teaching students how to use the structural elements of unknown words to decode them. Structural elements help students pronounce words and associate meaning with them. Research shows that students who have the most experience with the structural elements of words use them most successfully for decoding (Wysocki and Jenkins, 1987).

Structural analysis is introduced in the primary grades with inflected endings and contractions; however, it becomes especially important in the middle grades. The vocabulary of middle-grade students increases dramatically; they encounter many unknown words that they must identify (Wysocki and Jenkins, 1987).

Structural analysis instruction often begins with contractions, since children frequently use contractions in their oral language; therefore, they understand their meanings. In teaching contractions, the emphasis is on teaching students to recognize written contractions that they use in speech.

Contractions

Many of the traditional exercises involving contractions require students to match the contracted forms with the words they represent. This is usually unnecessary because students recognize—and understand—the meanings of contractions without specifying the words they represent. Durkin (1974) suggests that the only time a detailed discussion of contractions is warranted is when the concept of contraction is taught.

Phonics Skills

When readers are unable to recognize a word as a sight word, they must analyze it through context, structural analysis, or phonics. Phonic clues are related to the spelling and sound systems of language. Durkin (1974) states, "If children are to learn how to identify words not recognized in their printed form, they have to be taught to use spellings along with other types of cues to help identifications. And that is what phonics is all about." Phonic skills enable readers to use visual clues to figure out words they do not recognize in their written form. The major objective of phonics instruction—as in the case of other word-recognition instruction—is to develop reading fluency and comprehension. According to Anderson et al. (1985), The goal of phonics is not that children be able to state the "rules" governing letter-sound relationships. Rather, the purpose is to get across the alphabetic principle—that there are systematic relationships between letters and sounds.

Alphabetic principle

Phonics skills have been at issue throughout educational history; however, current research has laid these issues to rest, and all major published reading programs include instructional material for phonics. The Commission on Reading (Anderson et al., 1985) recommends teaching phonics early, keeping it simple, and except in cases of diagnosed individual need, phonics instruction should be completed by the end of second grade.

To understand the discussion of phonics instruction, teachers should be familiar with these terms:

Phonetics is the study and classification of sounds made in speech.

Phonics is the method of teaching children to read and pronounce words by learning the phonetic value of letters and letter groups.

A **phoneme** is the smallest unit of sound that is associated with speech.

A **grapheme** is a letter unit that is associated with a writing system. The *b* in the word *ball* is a grapheme that corresponds to the phoneme /*b*/. The word *boat* has four graphemes—*b, o, a,* and *t*—and three phonemes—/*b*/, /*o*/, and /*t*/.

A **phoneme-grapheme correspondence** refers to a letter-sound relationship.

Irregular spelling patterns

Although phonics skills can be a valuable aid to readers, there is a flaw in this approach—word spellings in English are often irregular and pronunciation is not always based on spelling. Irregularity is a result of two factors. The first is that language changes. For example, the *k* in *know* was once pronounced, but now it is a silent letter. The second factor is that the English language utilizes an alphabet of 26 letters to spell approximately 44 phonemes (sounds); therefore, irregular spelling patterns are inevitable. For example, the letter *a* is associated with a variety of sounds, each based on the particular word in which it appears:

ă as in *hat*

ā as in *cape*

ǝ̆ as in *about*

ä as in *father*

This irregularity presents a major problem for children who are learning to decode English. Since there is not a one-to-one match in English between phonemes and graphemes, it is difficult—if not impossible—to sound out various words precisely. Readers attempt to approximate words through phonics. "If their approximations are similar enough to words in their vocabulary they will succeed in identifying the word at that point" (Ives et al., 1979). Students need to be flexible in applying phonics skills; they must "try out" words to see if they make sense in the context of the text they are reading. When sounding out a word, children should try a logical phoneme-grapheme correspondence. If the word does not sound familiar, the child should reanalyze it by using alternate grapheme-phoneme correspondences or syllabic divisions. For example, a reader who comes across the word *island* would probably divide it into syllables and sound it out as *is/land,* which would produce a recognizable word. In reanalyzing the word, the reader could use a long *i* in the first syllable, and arrive at a closer approximation of the word pronounced. Durkin (1974) points out that "it is only when flexible application is stressed and taught that the potential of phonic learnings can be realized."

Systematic
instruction

Phonics instruction should systematically incorporate many concrete examples of words illustrating the letter-sound relationship under study. When children compare unknown words to similar known words, they are using an analogy approach, which Cunningham (1975–1976) has researched widely. An analogy approach might compare an unknown word like *silver* with the words *silk* and *river* to arrive at a pronunciation. Providing students with many examples helps them use word analogies to decode unknown words.

The Utility of Phonics Generalizations

The goal of teaching phonics is to convey the letter-sound correspondences that will help children achieve reading fluency and comprehension. However, some sounding principles have greater utility than others. Determining the specific sounding principles and sequencing these principles, have been controversial matters in reading instruction. As Anderson and his colleagues (1985) learned, a number of reading programs try to teach too many letter-sound relationships, which causes phonics instruction to drag out over too many years. Heilman (1985) suggests, "In the final analysis, the optimum amount of phonics instruction for every child is the minimum he needs to become an independent reader."

Useful and
functional

Children should be taught phonic generalizations that are useful and functional. Clymer (1963) studied the utility of commonly taught phonic generalizations. He examined 45 generalizations found in primary reading materials and found that 33 of these generalizations characterized more than 60 percent of the words in primary materials. However, when he used a 75 percent criterion, he found that only 18 generalizations were worth teaching. Research by Emans (1967) also focused on the utility of phonic generalizations in materials above the primary level and concluded that 18 are useful. These generalizations differed somewhat from those identified by Clymer due to differences in content at the upper-grade levels. These studies suggest that many of the phonics generalizations presently taught to children have limited value.

Explicit and Implicit Phonics Programs

Letter sounds are taught first in an *explicit (synthetic)* phonics program; children are taught how to blend these sounds together in order to build words. Phonemes (sounds) are introduced in isolation and children learn to associate a specific sound or sounds with a grapheme. Initially, explicit phonics programs emphasize words that exhibit sound-symbol relationships, and the reading content is largely comprised of these regular words. Children in an explicit program could be taught the phonemes /n/, /a/, and /t/; then they would be able to build such words as *at, tan, an,* and *ant.*

In an *implicit (analytic)* program, children are introduced to letter sounds through whole words that are familiar rather than isolated sounds. In teaching the word *bat,* the teacher would point out that the word begins like *boy* and ends like *cat.* Children would then use this knowledge to analyze the unfamiliar word.

Teaching Phonics

The phonics program should be based on a core of known sight words, which can be used to explain and illustrate phonics generalizations. For example, the consonant phoneme /*b*/ could be introduced through the sight words *boy, ball,* and *bird.* The correspondences between phonemes and graphemes should be illustrated using the context of known sight words. A difficulty with explicit or synthetic phonics is the possibility that a child may sound out the word *bat,* by saying *buh-ah-tuh-a*—a response that clearly distorts the word beyond recognition. However, there is value in isolating the sounds associated with most letters; this teaches children to blend the sounds together to approximate word pronunciation (Anderson, 1985). A combination of explicit and implicit phonics instruction seems to produce the most able readers.

Identifying unknown words

Teachers should avoid teaching phonics generalizations that require the reader to pronounce the word before sounding it out. For example, some phonics programs encourage children to divide a word immediately after a long vowel sound for syllabication—as in the word *lo/cal.* This assumes that the reader is able to identify the long vowel and finally divide the word into syllables. There is no need to divide a word into syllables and sound it out if the reader already knows how to pronounce that word. The objective of phonics instruction is to help readers identify *unknown* words. Therefore, phonics generalizations should be based on the visual features of words.

Teaching children about the application of phonics generalizations is probably the most important aspect of phonics instruction. Many children who are able to use phonics generalizations to recognize words cannot, in fact, verbalize these generalizations. On the other hand, I have taught many disabled readers who were familiar with the details of phonics generalizations, but who simply could not apply them in the actual process of reading. The objective of word-recognition instruction is to achieve reading competence, but this appears to be unrelated to the memorization of phonics generalizations.

Errors in published materials

Durkin (1974) points out that published phonics materials contain many errors. Teachers must become competent themselves in this area of instruction so that they can recognize these mistakes in the materials they may read. Teachers should, in effect, feel secure enough in their own knowledge that they can comfortably identify errors, even though they are in published form. Teachers should never be totally dependent on commercial materials for direction in teaching phonics. They must be able to both select and develop their own instructional materials.

Phonics Generalizations

These rules are the principles that govern the application of phonics for decoding unknown words. The English alphabet contains 26 letters (graphemes) that are divided into consonants and vowels—resulting in a total of 44 sounds (phonemes). There are 21 consonants and 5 vowels *(a, e, i, o,* and *u). W* and *y* are **semivowels;** that is, they may function as either a consonant or a vowel. A **consonant** is a flow of air through the mouth that is completely or partially broken by the lips, teeth, and tongue to produce variations in sound. **Vowels** are produced by an unbroken flow of air through the mouth, with variations in sound produced by the vocal cords and changing the shape of the mouth cavity. Readers can test this definition by saying the long vowel sounds aloud while concentrating on the shape of the mouth.

Phoneme-grapheme correspondence essentially comprises four basic steps:

1. Recognizing graphemes, such as *f, e,* and *r.*
2. Dividing the word into parts or syllables.
3. Recalling the phoneme associated with a grapheme.
4. Blending (synthesizing) phonemes to approximate a word.

Scope and sequence

At the present time, there is no information available on the ideal scope and sequence of phonics instruction. This is the case because children learn in very different manners; thus, some programs teach short vowels first, others teach long vowels first, and still others introduce consonants at the outset. Any one of these programs can be successful for individual children. There are also some children who will fail in each program as well.

A Suggested Scope and Sequence for Teaching Phonics Generalizations

The phonics program described in the following list includes those generalizations that research appears to confirm are the most valuable in teaching children. This program simply suggests a particular order for introducing phonics generalizations. Instructors, however, should be flexible in their teaching plans, since there is no single preferred approach to sequencing phonics instruction.

1. **Consonant** sounds should be introduced because they are more consistent phoneme-grapheme correspondences than are vowel sounds. In addition, children who know consonant sounds can use them in combination with context clues to identify new words. Confusion between letters such as *b* and *d* can be avoided by introducing the phoneme and grapheme of *b* early in the phonics program; present the *d* only when the *b* has been overlearned. See Chapter 3 for a sample lesson plan on teaching a consonant sound (Bryant, 1967).
2. **Blends,** also called *consonant clusters,* are two or three dissimilar consonants that appear together but retain the same sound as when they occur separately. Consonant sounds are pushed together when they occur as blends. Some blends occur at the beginning of words, while others occur at the end—as illustrated in the example that follows.

Examples of initial blends:
*gr*een
*scr*eam
*fl*ood

Examples of final blends:
si*nk*
ju*mp*
so*ld*

Many children can decode blends without direct instruction because they can use their knowledge of consonants to do this. Therefore, it is wise to observe children decoding words that contain blends to determine whether they need this instruction. In any case, there is no point in having students memorize lists of blends.

3. Introduce the soft *c* (*s* sound). *C* has a soft sound when it is followed by *e, i,* and *y*—as in *c*ent, *c*ity, and *c*ycle.
4. Introduce the soft *g* (*j* sound). *G* has a soft sound when followed by *e, i,* and *y*—as in *g*entle, *g*iant, and *g*ym.
5. The regular consonant digraphs should be presented. A **digraph** is a combination of two letters that represents a single sound. Some examples are *sh* (shoe), *th* (voiceless, as in thing), *th* (voiced, as in them), *wh* (when), *ch* (choose), *gh* (laugh), *ng* (song), and *ph* (phone). The following is a suggested lesson plan for teaching consonant diagraphs.

LESSON PLAN FOR TEACHING CONSONANT DIGRAPHS

I. *Objective:* The student should associate the phoneme /*ch*/ with the grapheme *ch.*
II. *Introduction:* Write words beginning with *ch* on the chalkboard. The list of words could include *choose, chip, cherry, chair, child,* and *chance.*
  A. The teacher should pronounce each word while the class listens closely to the *ch* sound.
  B. Underline the *ch* in each word on the chalkboard.
  C. Have students pronounce the words, this time on their own.
  D. Ask students to suggest additional words that begin with the /*ch*/ phoneme.
III. *Guided Practice:* Ask students to construct sentences using words beginning with this phoneme.
IV. *Independent Practice:* Have students make a list of those words beginning with the /*ch*/ phoneme that they can locate on newspaper pages.
V. *Evaluation:* Observe students' application.

6. Introduce long vowel sounds that are represented by the *macron* (-), such as the *a* in *bāke,* the *e* in *bēat,* the *i* in *kīte,* the *o* in *bōat,* the *u* in *cūte,* and the *y* in *crȳ.*

7. Introduce short vowel sounds that are represented by the *breve* (ˇ), such as the *a* in *căt,* the *e* in *sět,* the *i* in *rĭd,* the *o* in *hŏt,* and the *u* in *cŭp.*
8. *Vowel digraphs* are two vowel graphemes that represent one sound. In vowel digraphs, both letters lose their individual sound and produce a new sound by being together. This generalization can be summarized as "When two vowels go walking, the first one does the talking." The use of vowel digraphs in decoding words was not supported by Clymer's (1963) research; however, additional research suggests that this generalization does have some value, especially when the reader is flexible in its application. Some examples of vowel digraphs are *ai* (sail), *ea* (each), *oa* (coat), *ee* (beet), *ay* (may), *oo* (food), and *oo* (look).
9. *Vowel diphthongs* are sounds that consist of a blend of two vowels. Some examples are *ou* (out), *oi* (oil), *oy* (toy), and *ow* (low).
10. Introduce the concept of *r-controlled vowels* to the class. When vowels are followed by an *r,* they do not have a long or short sound, but a so-called *r*-controlled sound. Some examples are *ar* (far), *er* (her), *ir* (fir), *ur* (turn), and *or* (for).
11. Have the class sound out one-syllable words. A **syllable,** the basic unit for sounding words, is a vowel sound to which one or more consonant sounds have been added.
    a. In a one-syllable word with one vowel, the vowel is usually short. (Example: *cat, sit,* and *set*)
    b. In a one-syllable word with two vowels, the vowels usually produce the long sound of the first vowel. The second vowel is not sounded. (Example: *cāpe, sēat,* and *cōat*)
12. Discuss the syllabication of words with two or more syllables. Point out that each word has as many syllables as there are vowel sounds. Some considerations for syllabication are listed below.
    a. Prefixes, suffixes, root words, and inflected endings are usually a separate syllable.
    b. Words that contain consonant digraphs, vowel digraphs, blends, diphthongs, and *r*-controlled vowels must be divided into syllables without separating these sound units.
    c. Divide words into syllables by vowel and consonant patterns. Some examples are listed below.

    v/cv   spī/der
    vc/cv   căn/dȳ
    vc/ccv   ĕn/trȳ

    Also note that consonant *le* endings form a separate syllable. (Example: no/ble, bot/tle, and an/kle.)
13. Keep in mind the following vowel sound considerations that may appear in each syllable.
    a. A single vowel followed by a consonant is usually short. (Example: sŭm/mer)
    b. A single vowel at the end of a syllable usually has a long sound. (Example: lō/cō/mō/tĭve)

c. Vowel digraphs, diphthongs, and *r*-controlled vowels have the sounds indicated in the generalizations related to them.

14. *Practice activity.* The words listed below have been divided into syllables, and the vowel sounds are marked according to the generalizations discussed in this chapter. Study these examples to make certain you understand syllabic divisions, sounding units, and vowel sounds.

> *Mas/cot: Mascot* is divided by the *vccv* pattern. The *a* is short because it is followed by a consonant; the *o* is short because it, too, is followed by a consonant.
>
> *P(er)/fect: Perfect* is divided by the *vccv* pattern. The *e* is *r*-controlled; the second *e* is followed by a consonant so that it has a short sound.
>
> *Ti /g(er): Tiger* is divided by the *vcv* pattern. The *i* is the last sound in the first syllable, and thus is long. The *e* is followed by an *r*, and therefore it is an *r*-controlled vowel.

The Schwa

In words that are composed of more than one syllable, there is often less stress on one of the syllables. Vowels in unstressed syllables have a *softened* vowel sound that is called a **schwa**; it sounds like a short *u* (Heilman, 1985). A schwa sound can be represented by any vowel sound and it is symbolized by ə. Note the schwa sounds that are italicized in the following examples: *a*lone, beaut*i*ful, for*e*st, lem*on,* and circu*s*. The *le* word ending is also an unstressed syllable and thus contains a schwa sound; for example: *pur/ple* (pəl) and *trou/ble* (bəl).

Accent

The syllables in words containing more than one syllable are pronounced with varying degrees of stress (force). These variations in stress are called **accent**. *Primary accent* refers to the syllable that receives the greatest stress. For example, in the word *pret/ty,* the primary accent is on the first syllable. *Secondary accent* refers to the syllable that receives less stress; for example, in *in'vi ta'tion,* the secondary accent is on the first syllable. Syllables may also be unaccented, as in *cor ǎl.* A dictionary is a useful tool for checking where accents fall in any particular word.

The following are some suggestions to keep in mind for teaching the concept of *accent.*

Teach children to sound out familiar words, experimenting with stress on different syllables until the word sounds familiar.

Point out to the class that when in doubt about primary or secondary accent marks, the word should be looked up in the dictionary.

General accent rules do not have much application to English because our language is essentially comprised of words from many languages. The accent of words has been influenced by a variety of factors, which have been associated with the development of the English language.

Blending

Blending is the ability to combine sounds in order to pronounce a word. Research has confirmed that blending is an important aspect of phonics instruction (Jeffrey and Samuels, 1973). Children must be able to blend sounds in order to identify words. Sounds should be said softly when blending to avoid distortion. Instruction in blending should begin with short words. Children should be taught to blend the first two letters and then to add the final letter. Note the following examples:

ca t   (cat)

ba t   (bat)

si t   (sit)

ra n   (ran)

Only after children have become proficient with short word blends should instruction with longer words proceed. Some examples of long word blends are:

ch   choo se   choose

sh   shee t   sheet

ACTIVITIES FOR BLENDING

1. Construct word wheels in which the beginning syllable of a word is on the outer wheel and the ending syllables are on the inner wheel. The child turns the wheel to form words.
2. Demonstrate the blending sounds to the class. Children should listen and be able to identify the words that are blended by the teacher.

Activities for Teaching Phonics

The activities suggested in this section can be adapted for teaching the phonics skills discussed in this chapter.

1. The most important activity for learning phonics is reading interesting, meaningful discourse.
2. Spinner games can be constructed from paper plates or cardboard circles, as in Figure 4.6. The child should identify the particular sound that the spinner lands on.

Figure 4.6

3. Have children look through magazines and newspapers to locate pictures of objects that begin with or include a sound identified by the teacher. The class could then put together a sound book containing these pages.
4. Have students sort out pictures or objects that begin with a sound identified by the teacher. Shoe boxes and egg cartons are good containers for sorting activities. For example, children could sort out items that begin with a /d/ sound and put them into a box with a dog drawing on the top.
5. Bean bag toss. Paint large letters or words on an oilcloth sheet (see Figure 4.7) and have a child toss a bean bag onto this game board. The child must then say the sound or word that the bean bag lands on. Each child receives one point for each correct response.
6. A baseball field game board, as in Figure 4.8, can be used to teach word-recognition skills. One variation could be to make a stack of word cards and have each child draw a card and tell how many syllables are in that word. The child starts at the batter's plate and moves one base for each correct response. The child who has the greatest number of runs at the end is declared the winner.
7. Fill in the blank.
   a. Have children insert a consonant in the blank space in front of each syllable in the examples provided and pronounce the words that are made.

   Example: _____and _____et _____end
   (Possible words: *band* or *sand*, *set* or *bet*, and *send* or *bend*.)

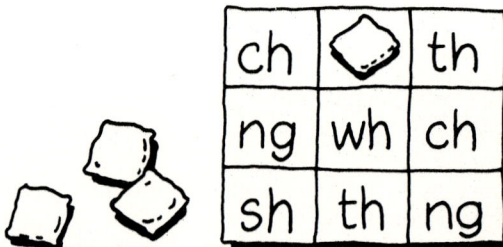

Figure 4.7

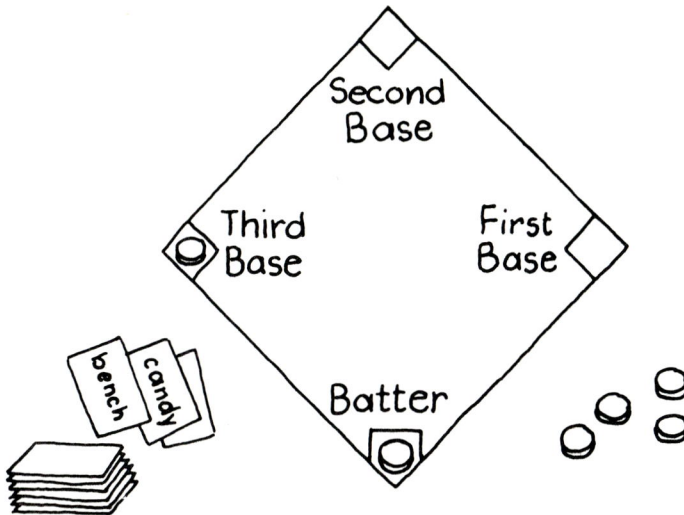

Figure 4.8

> **b.** Fill in each blank with a blend to make a new word. Pronounce the words that are made.
>
> Example: _____ile _____ue _____ed
> (Possible blends: *sm, bl,* and *sl.*)

8. Game boards can be easily constructed and used to teach phonics skills. Write words or sounds on individual cards and have members of the class draw from a stack of these cards to play the game. Each child moves a marker one space and follows any directions that are given on the square on which the marker lands. Teachers can buy old game boards at garage sales or make their own out of cardboard. Toy cars may also be used as markers. Figure 4.9 is an example of a game board.

9. Have children insert a vowel in each blank that is provided to make a word. When the sentences are completed, have students read them aloud.

> Example: Muffin _s _ L_ttl_ bl_ck d_g. Sh_ b_rks _nd b_rks.

10. Have the class find as many words as possible in their reading lessons (or on the front page of the newspaper) that have long vowel sounds. Variations on this theme can include any other sound or even words containing a particular number of syllables.

11. Make up exercises in which a line must be drawn through the word that does not belong in the word group provided. Have the child explain why this word was chosen.

> Example: *coin, soil, boy*
> Explanation: *oi* and *oy* are diphthongs; *or* is an *r*-controlled vowel

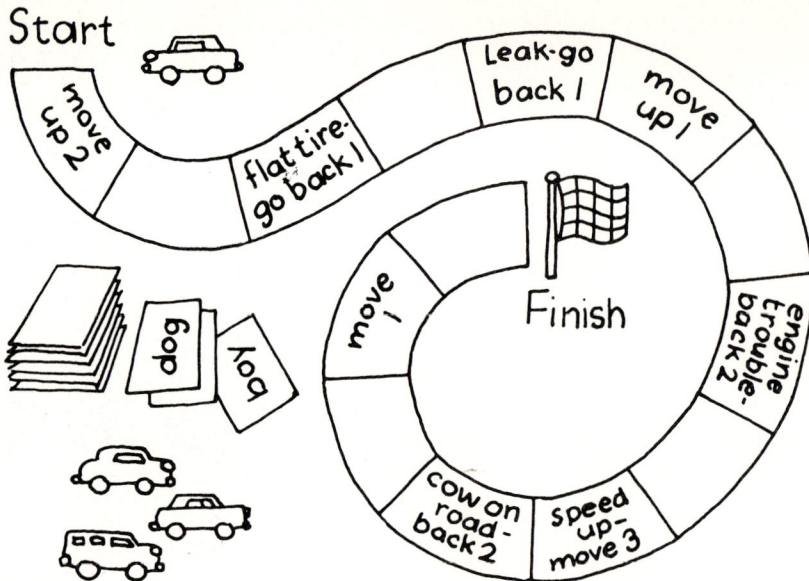

Figure 4.9

12. Have students add an *e* to make a new word in the examples provided. Each new word should also be pronounced.

   Example: cap   cap_
            cut   cut_
            hop   hop_
            fir   fir_
            pin   pin_

13. Write one-, two-, and three-syllable words on cards and have children sort out the cards according to the number of syllables in each word. Review the words in each of the three stacks of cards once they have been sorted by the class.

14. Make up exercises in which a circle must be drawn around the words that contain a diphthong.

   Example:

   boy   bone   eat

   beg   mouse   rain

   coin   owl   own

15. Ask students to list words that have similar controlled vowel sounds under the key word provided in each column.

          1   2   3
   fur, her, bird   car   corn

   Answers: fern, barn, mark, fork, shirt, turtle

16. **a.** The teacher should say several words to the class, and children should be asked to circle the letter that represents the long vowel sound they heard in each word.

Possible words: (1) make, (2) coat, (3) shine.

(1)   (ā)   ē   ī

(2)   ū   ā   (ō)

(3)   ū   ē   (ī)

b. Circle the letter that represents the short vowel sound heard in each word.

Possible words: (1) bat, (2) top, (3) up.

(1)   (ă)   ŭ   ĕ

(2)   ă   ĭ   (ŏ)

(3)   (ŭ)   ĕ   ŏ

TEACHING CHILDREN TO USE COMBINATION, COMPARE-CONTRAST, OR ANALOGY DECODING SKILLS

Combination, compare-contrast, and **analogy decoding** skills are used as synonymous terms in this book. Such an approach is probably most useful in identifying words containing two or more syllables. To use this approach, children need a basic sight-word vocabulary and an understanding of context clues. Basic phonics skills and structural analysis are also helpful to students using this decoding strategy.

Cunningham (1979) recommends a specific set of steps for students who are learning to use the compare-contrast strategy.

1. Have students begin a tangible word store by writing five words on separate index cards:

   he   went   her   can   car

2. Explain to students that you will show them a two-syllable word, the parts of which are similar to some of the words on their index cards. Their job is to find two index cards that will help them decode each two-syllable word. Students should write the two matching words for each word by the word. Then have students pronounce the two matching words and the word decoded. Words that might be used and their matching words are:

meter (he-her)	cancer (can-her)	serpent (her-went)
garter (car-her)	merger (her-her)	recent (he-went)
barber (car-her)	percent (her-went)	farther (car-her)

3. Have students make additional index cards for:

   in   at   then   it   is

Using these cards, and the cards prepared in the preceding lesson, present students with words like the following. Have them match the words that will help them to decode; then, have them pronounce the decoded words along with the words that helped them solve the words.

bitter (it-her)
scatter (at-her)
center (then-her)
winter (in-her)
batter (at-her)
margin (car-in)
matter (at-her)

4. Add the following five words to index cards:

let   fish   sun   big

The students have a total of 15 cards to use when decoding. Proceed as in step 3.

5. Then add the following words to the store of words on index cards:

and	up	ate	top
on	face	am	but
Bob	up	rose	them
dance	us	fish	go
care	side	Tom	boy
found	rain	or	

Then use this larger list as a basis for decoding unknown words, following the pattern established in the earlier steps.

Many mature readers develop analogy decoding skills without direct instruction. However, the majority of elementary school children need specific instruction in using this strategy. In addition to specific instruction, like that suggested in the preceding list, children need considerable guided practice in decoding unknown words with the compare-contrast strategy.

Word-Recognition Strategies to Avoid

There are several word-recognition strategies for decoding words that may mislead children; thus, they should be avoided. Some of these misleading practices are described in the following list.

1. Avoid having children find short words in longer words. This exercise does not aid children in word recognition. Note the distortion that occurs in the following words when this strategy is attempted:

bo(at)

co(at)

(not)(ice)

he̲lp

sa̲me

2. A second erroneous practice is that of using *configuration clues*—clues that are based on the shape of the word. For example,

hall

This can be confusing because many words actually have the same shape, as in

hall   and   ball

To become competent in reading, children must learn to look at the *details* within the words themselves.

Writing and Word Recognition

One of the strategies that helps children see details within words is writing. Translating one's ideas into words teaches children to encode words, which helps them see details within words. Reading and writing are closely related; thus, learning to write enhances reading development. When children write they use a trial-and-error approach to make sense of written language. They construct a set of encoding rules for writing words, which helps them decode unknown words.

Furthermore, the word spellings that children invent before they learn conventional spelling and the spelling errors they make as they mature, give us insight into their understanding and use of letter-sound relationships. For instance, if a youngster consistently substitutes a *w* for an *r* in the word *rabbit*, it would suggest a mispronunciation of a specific sound, which influences the letter this reader will associate with the letter *r*. Writing develops the word-recognition skills of both primary and intermediate readers.

Writing activities also afford children good opportunities to reinforce and apply their letter-sound knowledge. Even before they are able to use pencils, children can manipulate plastic or metal letters on magnetic boards to form words. Flannel or cardboard letters on a flannel board offers a similar experience. As children think of the letters to represent sounds, and sequence them to form words on a typewriter or computer, they are advancing their word-recognition skills.

Computers and Word Identification

Word-identification instruction is the most popular domain for computer-based reading programs. Programs are available to instruct children in the areas of sight words, context clues, structural analysis, and phonics. Unfortunately, current commercial offerings are dominated by programs that overemphasize phonic and spelling cues, without comparable concern for the role of word meaning (Geoffrion and Geoffrion, 1983). Many of the current programs are merely electronic workbooks. Most popular school microcomputers do not possess the sophisticated voice synthesis capability necessary for creating sophisticated decoding materials. Some computer programs coordinate cassette tapes with the computer to overcome this problem (Rude, 1986).

As small computers grow more sophisticated, we can hope that the software will also become more sophisticated. Computers do have the advantage of providing novel, motivating reinforcement of word-identification skills with immediate reinforcement. They enable teachers to meet the individual needs of students. For instance, students who need extra practice can have it by computer, while children who do not require so much reinforcement can move ahead.

Since computer software is of mixed value, teachers must choose carefully. The review form shown in Figure 4.10 is helpful in critiquing computer materials; however, you may wish to tailor it to your specific needs.

Title of Materials:

Source:

Copyright Date:

Time (needed to run program):

Grade Level:

Objective/s:
1. Does the material focus on meaning?
2. Are decoding skills taught within the context of words?
3. Are students encouraged to combine word recognition skills?
4. Does the material emphasize word meanings?
5. Does the material encourage application of skills?
6. Is the material based on extrinsic phonics or intrinsic phonics or a combination of the two?
7. What is the difficulty level of the material? (high, low, average)
8. Does the student receive appropriate, understandable feedback?
9. Does the student have opportunities to transfer what he or she has learned to other situations?
10. Do you recommend acceptance or rejection of the material? Why? _____

Reviewer: _____

Figure 4.10 Computer Materials Review Form for Word Identification

SUMMARY

The key points of this chapter are listed in the following.

1. Word-recognition skills are based on the ability of a reader to associate a particular meaning and pronunciation with a printed word. Four basic word

recognition approaches were discussed in this chapter: sight words, context clues, structural analysis, and phonics skills. Sight words are words that the reader has memorized. Context clues are aids for word recognition that are inferred directly from the content that is being read. Structural analysis refers to the recognition of words through morphemes, along with prefixes, suffixes, root words, inflected endings, and contractions. Phonics skills are concerned with phoneme-grapheme correspondences that help the reader to recognize unknown words.

2. Automaticity in word recognition allows readers to focus attention on the meaning of the content as they read. A systematic approach to recognizing words helps readers become more effective. Readers should be flexible and open to using various word-recognition approaches in their attempt to identify an unknown word.

3. Basic principles of word-recognition instruction are:
   a. A child's speaking and listening vocabulary is the basis on which new words are identified. Children are unable to recognize words with which they have no association.
   b. Teachers should explain the value of learning word-recognition skills to their class. Children should understand how a knowledge of letter sounds can aid in identifying words.
   c. Word-recognition instruction should stress the meaning of words in specific contexts.
   d. Children should be able to comfortably make use of the following approaches to word identification (listed in order of preference): sight words, context clues, structural analysis, and phonics skills.
   e. Word-recognition approaches should be combined to facilitate word identification. In other words, all four methods discussed in this chapter should be introduced in a balanced program.

4. Current research establishes the importance of introducing phonics early in the reading program, through a combination of extrinsic and intrinsic phonics. Except in unusual cases, phonics instruction should be completed by the end of second grade.

5. An analogy or compare-contrast approach to decoding encourages students to combine their knowledge of sight words, context clues, structural analysis, and phonics. In using this strategy, readers compare known words with unknown words as they search for clues to help them identify the word.

6. Writing helps children understand written language, how to encode words, and how to decode words.

7. Computers can provide students with word identification practice, although computerized materials must be carefully chosen to avoid the pitfalls of computerized workbooks.

SELF-TEST

Check your knowledge of the information presented in this chapter. The answer key is located in Appendix C.

1. What is word identification?
   a. the ability to say words
   b. the ability to associate a particular meaning and pronunciation with a printed word
   c. the ability to associate diacritical markings with a printed word
   d. the ability to associate language and punctuation with one another

2. What are sight words?
   a. words a reader is able to see without glasses
   b. words that are identified within a given context
   c. words the reader has memorized
   d. words the reader cannot identify

3. What skill would a reader probably use to identify the word that belongs in the blank space provided in the following sentence: *We packed sandwiches in a basket and drove to the country for a* _____
   a. structural analysis
   b. dictionary usage
   c. memorization
   d. context clues

4. What word identification approach should a reader use to decode the word *circumnavigate?*
   a. structural analysis
   b. context clues
   c. vowels
   d. graphemes

5. Which of the following methods would a reader use to identify words by the sound of individual letters and syllables?
   a. sight words
   b. phonics
   c. phrases
   d. ideographs

6. What happens in the early stages of reading instruction?
   a. children read diagrams
   b. children learn to identify print words that are already in their listening and speaking vocabularies
   c. children read basal readers only
   d. children use the look-say approach

7. How many basal readers on the market today use only the look-say approach to reading instruction?
   a. ten
   b. five
   c. none
   d. all of the readers on the market

8. Which of the following books initiated the movement to phonics in the 1950s?
   a. *Why Johnny Can't Read*
   b. *What Ivan Knows that Johnny Doesn't*
   c. *Phonics is the Answer*
   d. *Everything You Always Wanted to Know About Phonics*

9. What were the results of the studies undertaken by the United States Office of Education?
   a. they indicated that the phonics approach was the solution to all reading problems
   b. they found that a combination of approaches to word identification was most effective
   c. they concluded that linguistics was the best way to teach reading
   d. they showed that materials are more important than the figure of the teacher in reading instruction

10. How can a teacher plan a balanced word-identification program?
    a. by having an emphasis on phonics only
    b. by having an emphasis on comprehension only
    c. by emphasizing all four word-identification approaches
    d. this kind of program cannot, in fact, be organized

11. What is automaticity?
    a. the application of a word recognition approach without conscious thought
    b. the inability to identify words
    c. word blindness
    d. reading instruction that makes use of machinery

12. Why is automaticity important in reading?
    a. because it utilizes modalities
    b. because it makes research possible
    c. because it frees the reader's attention for understanding the content that is being read
    d. none of the above

13. How is automaticity achieved?
    a. through practice
    b. through working slowly
    c. through training on machines
    d. through auditory discrimination

14. What is *flexibility* in word identification?
    a. eye movements
    b. using all four word-identification approaches
    c. using phonics skills only
    d. using sight words only

15. How are sight words learned?
    a. through practice with pictures to develop visual discrimination skills
    b. through dyslexia
    c. through meaningful repetition
    d. all of the above

16. What are context clues?
    a. meaning clues
    b. phonics clues
    c. structural analysis
    d. auditory discrimination

17. What kinds of information provide context clues?
    a. syntactic information
    b. semantic information

    c. both a and b
    d. neither a nor b
18. What is another term for structural analysis?
    a. morphemic analysis
    b. strephosymbolia
    c. syntax
    d. all of the above
19. Why are contractions relatively easy for children to learn?
    a. because they are easy to spell
    b. because children use them in their oral language
    c. because they are not commonly used in English
    d. because they do not occur in foreign languages
20. What is phonics based on?
    a. attaching phonemes to graphemes
    b. blending sounds together
    c. both a and b
    d. neither a nor b
21. What is a limitation of the approach to word recognition?
    a. there are no limitations
    b. there is not a one-to-one match between letters and sounds
    c. phonics does not enable children to identify words independently
    d. phonics is too flexible an approach
22. What should a child do when sounding out a word that is not familiar?
    a. stop trying to sound it out
    b. do nothing
    c. try to change the vowel sounds
    d. all of the above
23. What is the ideal amount of phonics instruction?
    a. the minimum needed for independence in word identification
    b. the child must learn all of the rules and the exceptions to the rules needed to sound out English
    c. consonant and vowel sounds only
    d. phonemes
24. How do semivowels function?
    a. as vowels
    b. as vowels or consonants
    c. as consonants
    d. as graphemes
25. How many vowel sounds are in each syllable?
    a. one
    b. two
    c. three
    d. four
26. Which of the following are consonant digraphs?
    a. *bl*
    b. *wh*
    c. *oi*
    d. *cy*

27. Which of the following are diphthongs?
    a. *ch*
    b. *sc*
    c. *oi*
    d. *eo*
28. Which of the following words contain a schwa?
    a. *coin*
    b. *away*
    c. *mascot*
    d. *tiger*
29. What is *stress?*
    a. the amount of force that the speaker uses to pronounce a syllable
    b. the syllable in which a schwa occurs
    c. the pattern for dividing words into syllables
    d. a new method for teaching word identification
30. What is *blending?*
    a. attaching the correct sound to the correct letter
    b. the skill of writing sounds
    c. combining sounds to pronounce words
    d. a research method
31. When should phonics be introduced?
    a. in fourth grade
    b. in second grade
    c. in kindergarten
    d. only when other methods have failed

THOUGHT QUESTIONS

1. What are the differences between intrinsic phonics and extrinsic phonics?
2. How can the four approaches to word identification be combined?
3. What is the relationship between word identification and comprehension?
4. How are fluency and word identification related?
5. What is strategic reading?

ENRICHMENT ACTIVITIES

1. Obtain a teacher's manual for a basal reading series. Make a list of the word-identification approaches introduced in the series. Indicate the levels at which these approaches are introduced. Make lists for different reading series and compare them.
2. Obtain a child's edition of a basal reading series and do a task analysis of the word-identification approaches required in a single story. A task analysis is done by looking at each word in the story, deciding whether it can be considered a sight word, or whether the word can be decided through context clues, structural analysis, or phonics skills.

3. Observe a child during several class reading lessons and keep a diary of the ways in which the child identifies words. Note those methods that the child feels comfortable using and those that appear to cause problems.

4. Use the phonics generalizations discussed in this chapter to decode the following nonsense words: *rete, poih, tiras, jerty, ceint,* and *oricle.*

5. Administer a standardized test to a child and analyze the word-identification skills of the student.

6. Prepare a minilesson plan for one of the word-recognition approaches. If possible, teach the lesson to a child. If this is not possible, teach it to a peer group.

7. Use the form provided in Figure 4.10 to analyze a computerized word-identification program.

RELATED READINGS

Anderson, R., E. Hiebert, J. Scott, and I. Wilkinson (1985). *Becoming a Nation of Readers: The Report of The Commission on Reading,* Urbana, IL: The Center for the Study of Reading.

Casteel, C. (December 1984). "Computer Skill Banks for Classroom and Clinic," *The Reading Teacher,* Vol. 38, pp. 294–297.

Cunningham, P. (November 1980). "Teaching *Were, With, What,* and Other Four Letter Words," *The Reading Teacher,* Vol. 34, pp. 160–163.

Dechant, E. (1982). *Improving the Teaching of Reading,* 3d ed., Englewood Cliffs, NJ: Prentice-Hall, Chapters 8–9.

Duffy, G. and L. Roehler (January 1987). "Teaching Reading Skills as Strategies," *The Reading Teacher,* Vol. 40, pp. 414–427.

Eeds, M. (January 1985). "Bookwords: Using a Beginning Word List of High Frequency Words from Children's Literature K–3," *The Reading Teacher,* Vol. 38, pp. 418–423.

Fry, E. and E. Sakiey (January 1986). "Common Words Not Taught in Basal Reading Series," *The Reading Teacher,* Vol. 39, pp. 395–402.

Geoffrion, L. and O. Geoffrion (1983). *Computers and Reading Instruction,* Reading, MA: Addison-Wesley.

Groff, P. (May 1986). "The Maturing of Phonics Instruction," *The Reading Teacher,* Vol. 39, pp. 919–923.

Heilman, A. (1985). *Phonics in Proper Perspective,* 5th ed., Columbus, OH: Merrill.

Johnson, K. (1987). *Doing Words,* Boston: Houghton Mifflin.

McNinch, G. (December 1981). "A Method for Teaching Sight Words," *The Reading Teacher,* Vol. 35, 269–272.

Rude, R. (1986). *Teaching Reading Using Microcomputers,* Englewood Cliffs, NJ: Prentice-Hall.

Searfoss, L. and J. Readence (1985). *Helping Children Learn to Read,* Englewood Cliffs, NJ: Prentice-Hall, Chapter 5.

Silvers, P. (March 1986). "Process Writing and the Connection to Reading," *The Reading Teacher,* Vol. 39, pp. 679–684.

Weaver, C. (1988). *Reading Process and Practice,* Portsmouth, NH: Heinemann.

REFERENCES

Adams, M. and A. Huggins (Spring 1985). "The Growth of Children's Sight Vocabulary: A Quick Test with Educational and Theoretical Implications," *Reading Research Quarterly,* Vol. 20, pp. 262–281.

Anderson, R., E. Hiebert, J. Scott, and I. Wilkinson (1985). *Becoming a Nation of Readers: The Report of the Commission on Reading,* Urbana, IL: The Center for the Study of Reading.

Askov, E. and K. Kamm (1976). "Should We Teach Children to Use a Classification System in Reading?" *Journal of Educational Research,* Vol. 69, pp. 341–354.

Bond, G. and R. Dykstra (1967). Final Report, Project No. X001, Washington, DC.: Bureau of Research, U.S. Department of Health, Education, and Welfare.

Bryant, N. D. (1969). "Some Principles of Remedial Instruction for Dyslexia," in *Remedial Teaching Research and Comment,* W. Otto and K. Koenke (Eds.), Boston: Houghton Mifflin, pp. 210–215.

Burmeister, L. (March 1976). "Vocabulary Development in Content Areas Through the Use of Morphemes," *Journal of Reading,* Vol. 19, pp. 481–487.

Chall, J. (1983). *Learning to Read: The Great Debate,* 2nd ed., New York: McGraw-Hill.

Clymer, T. (January 1963). "The Utility of Phonic Generalizations in the Primary Grades," *The Reading Teacher,* Vol. 16, pp. 252–258.

Cunningham, J. (January 1979). "An Automatic Pilot for Decoding," *The Reading Teacher,* Vol. 32, pp. 420–424.

Cunningham, P. (November 1980). "Teaching *Were, With, What* and Other Four Letter Words," *The Reading Teacher,* Vol. 34, pp. 160–163.

Cunningham, P. (1975–1976). "Investigating a Synthesized Theory of Mediated Word Identification," *Reading Research Quarterly,* Vol. 11, pp. 127–143.

Dechant, E. (1982). *Improving the Teaching of Reading,* 3d ed., Englewood Cliffs, NJ: Prentice-Hall.

Dolch, E. (1951). *The Teaching of Sounding,* Champaign, IL: Garrard.

Durkin, D. (November 1974). "Phonics Instruction that Needs to be Improved," *The Reading Teacher,* Vol. 28, pp. 152–156.

Durkin, D. (October 1974). "Some Questions About Questionable Instructional Materials," *The Reading Teacher,* Vol. 28, pp. 13–17.

Ehri, L. and L. Wilce (1985). "Movement Into Reading: Is the First Stage of Printed Word Learning Visual or Phonetic?" *Reading Research Quarterly,* Vol. 20, pp. 163–179.

Emans, R. (January 1967). "The Usefulness of Phonic Generalizations Above the Primary Grades," *The Reading Teacher,* Vol. 20, pp. 419–425.

Flesch, R. (1966). *Why Johnny Can't Read,* New York: Harper & Row.

Frenzel, N. (March 1978). "Children Need a Multipronged Attack in Word Recognition," *The Reading Teacher,* Vol. 31, pp. 627–631.

Fry, E. and E. Sakiey (January 1986). "Common Words Not Taught in Basal Reading Series," *The Reading Teacher,* Vol. 39, pp. 395–402.

Geoffrion, L. and O. Geoffrion (1983). *Computers and Reading Instruction,* Reading, MA: Addison Wesley.

Gough, P. (1984). "Word Recognition," in *Handbook of Reading Research,* P. D. Pearson, et al. (Ed.), New York: Longman, pp. 225–254.

Gough, P. (1983). "Context, Form, and Interaction," in *Eye Movements in Reading: Perceptual and Language Processes,* New York: Academic Press.

Gray, W. (1960). *On Their Own in Reading,* rev. ed., Glenview, IL: Scott, Foresman.

Heilman, A. (1985). *Phonics in Proper Perspective,* 5th ed., Columbus, OH: Charles Merrill.

Hood, J. (March 1974). "Why We Burned Our Basic Sight Vocabulary Cards," *The Reading Teacher,* Vol. 27, pp. 579–582.

Ives, J., L. Bursuk, and S. Ives (1979). *Word Identification Techniques,* Chicago: Rand McNally.

Jeffrey, W. and J. Samuels (1973). "The Effect of Method of Reading Training on Initial Learning and Transfer," *Journal of Verbal Learning and Verbal Behavior,* Vol. 6, pp. 354–358.

Johnson, D. and J. Baumann (1984). "Word Identification," in *Handbook of Reading Research,* P. D. Pearson, et al. (Ed.), New York: Longman, pp. 583–608.

Johnson, K. (1987). *Doing Words,* Boston: Houghton Mifflin.

Karlin, R. (1975). *Teaching Elementary Reading,* 2nd ed., New York: Harcourt Brace Jovanovich.

LaBerge, D. and S. Samuels (1974). "Toward a Theory of Automatic Information Processing in Reading," *Cognitive Psychology,* Vol. 6, pp. 293–323.

Mackworth, N. (1977). "The Line of Sight Approach," in *Language and Reading Comprehension,* S. Wanat (Ed.), Arlington, VA: Center for Applied Linguistics.

McNinch, G. (December 1981). "A Method for Teaching Sight Words," *The Reading Teacher,* Vol. 35, pp. 269–272.

McCullough, C. (January 1945). "Recognition of Context Clues in Reading," *Elementary English Review,* Vol. 22, pp. 1–5.

Merlin, S. and S. Rogers (December 1981). "Direct Teaching Strategies," *The Reading Teacher,* Vol. 35, pp. 292–297.

Muller, D. (1973). "Phonic Blending and Transfer of Letter Training to Word Reading in Children," *Journal of Reading Behavior,* Vol. 5, No. 3, pp. 13–15.

Nagy, W., P. Herman, and R. Anderson (Winter 1985). "Learning Words from Context," *Reading Research Quarterly,* Vol. 20, pp. 233–253.

Norton, D. and P. Hubert (1977). "A Comparison of the Oral Reading Patterns Developed by High, Average, and Low Ability First Grade Students Taught by Two Approaches—Phonic Emphasis and Eclectic Basal," College Station, TX: Texas A & M University, ERIC Document Reproduction Service No. ED 145 393.

Perfetti, A. and A. Lesgold (1979). "Coding and Comprehension in Skilled Reading and Implications for Reading Instruction," *Theory and Practice of Early Reading,* Vol. 1, L. Resnick and P. Weaver (Eds.), pp. 57–84.

Pflaum, S., H. Walberg, H. M. Karegianes, and S. Rasher (1980). "Reading Instruction: A Quantitative Analysis," *Educational Researcher,* Vol. 9, pp. 12–18.

Rash, J., T. Johnson, and N. Gleadow (Summer 1984). "Acquisition and Retention of Written Words by Kindergarten Children Under Varying Learning Conditions," *Reading Research Quarterly,* Vol. 19, pp. 452–460.

Readence, J., T. Bean, and R. Baldwin (1982). *Content Area Reading: An Integrated Approach,* Dubuque, IA: Kendall/Hunt.

Resnick, L. (1977). "Theory and Practice in Beginning Reading Instruction," Pittsburgh: University of Pittsburgh, ERIC Document Reproduction Service No. ED 149 292.

Rude, R. (1986). *Teaching Reading Using Microcomputers,* Englewood Cliffs, NJ: Prentice-Hall.

Schell, L. (May 1978). "Teaching Decoding to Remedial Readers," *The Reading Teacher,* Vol. 31, pp. 281–287.

Searfoss, L. and J. Readence (1985). *Helping Children Learn to Read,* Englewood Cliffs, NJ: Prentice-Hall.

Singer, H. (1971). "Teaching Word Recognition Skills," in *Teaching Word Recognition Skills,* M. Dawson (Ed.), Newark, DE: International Reading Association, pp. 2–14.

Weaver, C. (1988). *Reading Process and Practice,* Portsmouth, NH: Heinemann.

Williams, J. (1985). "The Case for Explicit Decoding Instruction," in *Reading Education: Foundations for a Literate America,* Lexington, MA: Lexington Books.

Winograd, P. and M. Greenlee (December 1986). "Students Need a Balanced Reading Program," *Educational Leadership,* Vol. 43, pp. 16–21.

Wisendanger, K. and L. Bader (December 1987). "Teaching Easily Confused Words: Timing Makes the Difference," *The Reading Teacher,* Vol. 41, pp. 328–332.

Wolpert, E. (November 1972). "Length, Imagery Values and Word Recognition," *The Reading Teacher,* Vol. 26, pp. 579–582.

Wysocki, K. and J. Jenkins (Winter 1987). "Deriving Word Meanings Through Morphological Generalization," *Reading Research Quarterly,* Vol. 22, pp. 66–81.

The following paragraphs are the intact text of the paragraphs on pages 124 and 125 of the text.

Passage 1

There is now substantial evidence that students working together in small cooperative groups can master material presented by the teacher better than can students working on their own.

Passage 2

Cooperative learning refers to a set of instructional methods in which students work in small, mixed-ability learning groups. The groups usually have four members—one high achiever, two average achievers, and one low achiever.

Passage 3

Teachers can use several activities to help students attach meanings to learning experiences. Writing logs/diaries can document students' reactions to events and are particularly useful if the entries interpret what has happened.

Passage 4

Writing a precis, a concise abridgment, asks students to identify the gist of an experience, reading, or observation. It requires students to prioritize their own impressions and become more articulate about meanings they have attributed to experiences.

Passage 5

The students in each group are responsible not only for learning the material being taught in class, but also for helping their groupmates learn.

Passage 6

Simply putting students into mixed ability groups and encouraging them to work together are not enough to produce learning gains: students must have a reason to take one another's achievement seriously.

CHAPTER 5

The Comprehension Process Before Reading

OVERVIEW   This is one of two chapters addressing the reading comprehension process and teaching students to comprehend. In this chapter, we examine the reading comprehension process and teaching strategies employed prior to reading that insure understanding. Chapter 6 scrutinizes strategies employed during and following actual reading, along with several strategies such as the directed reading and thinking activity and writing (composing); these strategies address the overall comprehension process.

Comprehension is a constructive process. Readers construct text meaning using information they gather from printed text, their language comprehension, their world knowledge, their thinking skills, interests, and visualizing ability. They bring meaning to the page and take meaning from the page. This chapter examines these aspects of the comprehension process as a basis for facilitating comprehension prior to reading.

Key Vocabulary

As you read this chapter, check your understanding of these terms:

activating schemata	literal thinking
creative thinking	reading comprehension
evaluative (critical) thinking	schema theory
interpretive (inferential) thinking	

Focusing Questions

As you read this chapter, try to answer these questions:

1. What is *reading comprehension?*
2. How are word recognition and reading comprehension related?
3. What are the levels of comprehension?
4. What instructional strategies used prior to reading facilitate comprehension?
5. What strategies can readers use prior to reading?

THE COMPREHENSION PROCESS

Reading comprehension is the heart of the reading process. Students who understand written text are successful readers, but those who fail to understand, fail to read. Smith (1975) asserts that comprehension and learning are one and the same process; this process is one in which new experiences are associated with readers' prior knowledge. The "already known" refers to readers' previous experiences and knowledge, which are the *schemata* they use to create meaning. In order to understand, readers need to "make sense" of written language (Smith, 1978; McNeil, 1987). "A discussion of reading comprehension really has to be a discussion about language comprehension" (Carroll, 1985). Reading is one aspect of language, just as listening, speaking, and writing are language skills.

Bring meaning to print

Reading is less a matter of extracting sound from print than of bringing meaning to print (Smith, 1978). Readers' background experiences and knowledge enable them to comprehend. They create meaning using the knowledge (schemata) they have acquired from television, movies, personal experiences, and stories. Children reading a story about a pet gerbil, for example, use their experiences with pets to comprehend. Youngsters who do not have experiences with pets have greater difficulty understanding such a story.

Blueprint for meaning

The text is a type of blueprint for meaning, a set of clues that readers use as they build a model of what the text means (Collins, Brown, and Larkin, 1980). Readers are not expected to memorize or produce an exact duplicate of text, rather they construct text meaning based on their knowledge of the subject and their purposes for reading. For instance, in this sentence from a fourth-grade text, "Slowly the tugboat moved past the harbor docks into the open sea," the author does not explain or describe the harbor docks, so readers must fill in those details from their experiential background. The following example illustrates the comprehension process.

An Example of the Reading Comprehension Process

Jan, a fourth-grade student, decided to write a story about a baby elephant, because the local zoo had a new baby elephant that fascinated her. She thought about elephants and realized that she already had some information about them. For instance, she knew that there were Asian elephants and African elephants, and she remembered that one kind of elephant was difficult to train. She knew they were large, ate a lot of food, that they were used to move heavy things; however, she did not know exactly how much they weighed, how much food they ate, or how long it took a baby elephant to grow into adulthood, or how they were trained. These questions provided her with reading purposes. Her sketchy knowledge provided schemata to which she could relate information acquired from reading.

At this point, she decided to consult *World Book Encyclopedia.* Her location skills enabled her to select the E volume, and her alphabet knowledge enabled her to locate elephant within that volume. Then she read the information about elephants. She read that Asian elephants were often trained and that this training occurred when they were 15 to 20 years of age. She learned that well-trained elephants can learn 30 spoken orders. In addition, she learned that wild elephants eat 500 to 600 pounds of food a day, but elephants in captivity eat only 150 pounds of food a day.

Compare information

Comparing this new information to Jan's prior knowledge explains how she used language to elaborate on her existing knowledge. She also acquired new information regarding how they live in the wild. She elaborated on existing knowledge regarding the amount of food elephants eat as well as the trainability of elephants. She was able to answer the purpose questions established prior to reading.

Early in the comprehension process, Jan visualized elephants she had seen at the zoo and in books as as a basis for creating her story. Notice that Jan was especially interested in the topic, that she used specific skills to locate information, she analyzed information, and compared her prior knowledge to what she learned during reading. She used thinking skills to determine that she had found the accurate information needed to write a story.

Comprehension is complex

This example helps us realize that comprehension is not a single skill nor is it a specific set of identifiable skills (Rosenshine, 1980). Unfortunately, reading comprehension is an abstract, invisible process that cannot be directly observed because it is a covert activity occurring in the brain. However, extensive research (Durkin, 1978–1979; Rosenshine, 1980; Anderson and Pearson, 1984; Duffy, Roehler, and Mason, 1984; Anderson et al., 1985) has shed more light on the nature of the reading comprehension process. Reading comprehension is a constructive, holistic process involving skills, knowledge, and processes including schemata (world knowledge, cultural literacy), language, thinking skills, readers' interests, visualizing ability, and the structure of written texts. These facets of comprehension are discussed in subsequent sections.

Schemata

Schemata and language are closely aligned. Students use language to attach meaning to their experiences, which they store in the form of schemata. Associating words with experiences and knowledge helps students organize and remember new and previous experiences. Thus, word meanings and syntax are important to schemata.

Experiences are sources of schemata

The primary source of schemata is readers' experiences (Anderson and Pearson, 1984). Schemata are readers' concepts, beliefs, expectations, and processes; they comprise virtually everything from past experiences used to make sense of things and actions. In reading, schemata are used in making sense of text; the printed word evokes readers' associated experiences, as well as past and potential relationships (McNeil, 1987). Schemata are frameworks that readers impose on text. In the scenario described earlier, Jan used her existing knowledge about elephants as a structure to help her comprehend. A schema is an abstraction of reality (Tuinman, 1980). For example, if teachers have a well-developed schema of a classroom in an elementary school, they would be familiar with the general layout of a classroom and the basic equipment found in that environment. They would have acquired this schema from their previous experience in classrooms. When entering a new classroom, they would use this general schema to acquaint themselves with the specifics of this classroom such as the location of the chalkboard, the teacher's desk, and the students' desks.

Types of
schemata
According to McNeil (1987) there are three kinds of schemata. First are the *domain* schemata, which represent specific knowledge needed to understand particular subject matter like math, science, and social studies. Content instruction and textbooks develop much of this knowledge; however, students may need to use reference materials like encyclopedias when there is a void in their schemata.

Second are the *general world knowledge* schemata, which help us understand social relationships, causes, and activities. "Cultural literacy" fits into this category; many of the items that E. D. Hirsch (1987) identifies as important to reading comprehension are general world knowledge. For example, the statement, "he smiled a Cheshire Cat grin," has special significance to those who have read *Through the Looking Glass.* Individuals who cannot read or do not read widely often lack the general world knowledge necessary to understand content. Hirsch (1987) identified the information he believes literate individuals need to comprehend; he recommends that students learn this information. Arriving at consensus regarding necessary world knowledge is difficult if not impossible and many people disagree with the specific information Hirsch identified. Nevertheless, it is clear that readers who have a large store of world knowledge have a clear advantage in understanding written language.

The third type of schemata is the *knowledge of rhetorical structures.* These schemata are concerned with the conventions used in organizing text. A story grammar is a schemata for a story, a sense of the ways that stories are structured, which enables readers to understand stories. Of course, the structure of poetry and exposition differ from that of stories. Students who recognize the use of main ideas and details in structuring exposition are better able to process text.

Schemata serve a variety of functions in comprehension (McNeil, 1987). They are the slots for integrating additional information—using a schema for *dessert,* it is easy to assimilate a new dessert called "pudding cake." This is why it is important to expand and enrich students' schemata; students who develop more schemata have the basis for increasing their understanding.

Schemata also help readers sort important ideas from unimportant ideas. Readers who have schemata for story structure (story grammar) identify the problem or conflict in a story as more important than a character's name. A schema for reading directions helps us realize the importance of attending to the sequence of steps in directions. Thus, readers need many schemata in order to sort out the important ideas in different types of text.

Schemata and
inferencing
Schemata permit inferencing. They give us a framework in which to organize existing information and fill in the information that authors have not

included. No text ever specifies all of the relationships among characters, events, and nuances of style that authors hope readers will infer about the text. Authors must rely on our ability to use schemata to understand. For example, schemata about sports which involve balls enables us to differentiate between a ball used in a golf game and one used in a basketball game. The author does not have to include specific information about this equipment. We would probably be bored if authors tried to tell us everything.

Schemata help us remember what we have read. While we read, our interpretation of the text is stored in memory rather than a word-by-word replica of the actual text. Schemata provide readers with a structure for associating and remembering their interpretation of the text.

Elaborate
knowledge

Schemata also enable readers to construct text meaning; however, the text meaning is often new knowledge that alters or elaborates on existing knowledge. For example, youngsters reading about Australia use their prior knowledge about the seasons to understand Australian weather. However, reading reveals that it is winter in Australia when it is summer in the United States, so this data must be incorporated into their existing schemata. The next time these students read about Australia or climate, this new knowledge regarding Australian weather becomes prior knowledge which may be altered or added to. Today's knowledge becomes tomorrow's prior knowledge. Figure 5.1 illustrates the interrelationship of prior knowledge and new knowledge.

Thinking Skills and Higher-Order Thinking Skills

Thinking skills play an important role in reading because comprehension is largely a matter of reasoning about the text one will read, has read, or is reading. *Thinking* covers a range of thought processes. In this text, deBono's (1983) definition of thinking as "the operating skill with which intelligence acts upon experience" is used. Researchers (Presseisen, 1985; Sternberg, 1985; and Beyer, 1985) have identified essential cognitive processes which readers use in comprehending text. These processes include: predicting, inferring, classifying, analyzing, comparing, contrasting, cause and effect, and sequencing. These thinking skills are interdependent; for example, prediction depends on readers' ability to infer. Among the many inferences readers make is identifying the schemata (prior knowledge) that are most appropriate in understanding a specific text (Langer, 1984).

Cognitive
processes

In some instances thinking is described by the cognitive levels of questions that students are asked, because, theoretically, readers think at the level de-

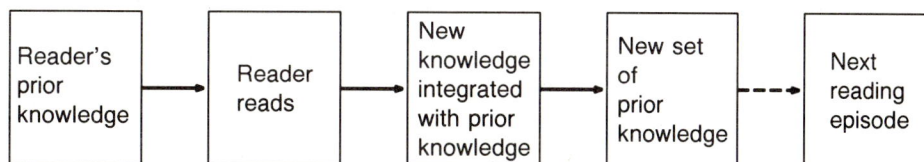

Figure 5.1 Prior knowledge cycle.

manded by the question. Literal, inferential, critical, and creative levels of questioning are most frequently used in basal readers, lesson plans, and published materials to guide students' thinking. These levels of questioning can be used to encourage students to predict, infer, classify, analyze, compare, and so on. For example, when a teacher asks "What do you think will happen next?" he or she is asking students to predict through inferencing. Such inferential predictions are based on students' schemata and their use of these schemata along with the data acquired from reading the text, which enables them to predict story action. Critical thinking occurs when a teacher asks students to evaluate a character's actions in a story they are reading. Questions are a powerful tool for developing students' thinking. You will find additional information regarding levels of questioning in Chapter 2.

Interact with environment

Children acquire thinking skills as they interact with the environment (Feuerstein and Hoffman, 1985). However, children also need adults to model and mediate thinking processes. Researchers have found that children's thinking snowballs as a result of acquiring thinking strategies and adult mediation (Feuerstein and Hoffman, 1985; Vygotsky, 1962). Instruction enhances students' thinking.

Savell, Twohig, and Rachford (1986) summarized the research related to teaching thinking skills, and their summary indicates that teaching strategies and methods appear to be more important than the materials and worksheets used. For example, learning alternative ways to solve problems is more important than filling in worksheet blanks as problem solving practice.

Mediated learning

Feuerstein and Hoffman (1985) discuss thinking instruction in terms of a "mediated learning experience," which occurs when a youngster is shown or taught cognitive methods for interpreting information, for solving problems, or for learning something. For example, a teacher might illustrate the usefulness of categorizing information and then demonstrate a technique for categorizing. Teachers are mediating thinking skills when they do a "think-aloud" like the one shown later in this chapter in Box 5.3. Box 5.1 illustrates a mediated learning experience for problem solving.

When applying thinking strategies and skills to text, readers must learn to concentrate completely, so they avoid mind wandering. Readers also need an attitude of demanding meaning from the content; they should expect text to make sense. Students who read words without thinking about the ideas behind them will not comprehend. Instruction should focus students' attention on the text and develop the attitude that content is supposed to make sense.

Higher-order thinking skills

Among educators, it is commonly agreed that higher-order thinking skills are important for successful reading. However, they are much less agreeable in identifying and defining higher-order thinking skills. Resnick (1985) suggests that higher-order thinking skills are difficult to identify and define, because they are more complex processes, they involve nonroutinized thinking in which right and wrong answers cannot always be specified, and in which complex reasoning and nuanced judgment may produce responses not previously en-

Box 5.1   Mediating Problem Solving*

1. Identify the problem and state it in your own words.

   Warton must escape from the owl who is going to eat him on Tuesday.

2. Brainstorm: generate possibilities, alternatives.

   run (hop) away
   convince the owl not to eat him
   get help
   jump out a window
   kill the owl
   convince the owl that he won't taste good
   get something else for the owl to eat

3. Examine possibilities generated and eliminate those that cannot work.

   Warton has an injured foot, so he will not be able to run away.

4. Think aloud, ask yourself questions.
5. Compare this problem to other problems that are similar (analogy). Is it like another problem that you know about?

   Compare to television plots
   Jumanji by Van Allsburg
   My Robot Buddy by Slote
   Amos and Boris by Steig

6. Discuss the problem with another person; talking helps thinking.
7. Collect relevant information. How have other people solved similar problems?
8. Break down the problem into parts—"slice it." What are the subproblems?

   Being eaten on Tuesday
   Being eaten at all
   Hurt foot
   No one knows where he is
   What other things do owls eat?

9. Restate the problem (say it in another way)

   Warton does not want to die
   Warton wants to go home
   The owl needs a meal

10. Write it out. Writing out how to do a math problem, often helps us solve it.

*based on *A Toad for Tuesday* by R. Erickson

countered by an instructor. In this text the higher-order thinking skills are defined as problem solving, decision making, critical thinking, and creative thinking (Presseisen, 1986).

- *Problem solving* includes using thinking to resolve a difficulty. Problem solving usually includes defining the difficulty, assembling facts, inferring possible solutions, testing the appropriateness of solutions, reducing the problem to simpler terms, and evaluating the value of solutions.
- *Decision making* involves choosing the best response from several options. Thinkers must compare advantages and disadvantages to determine whether additional information is needed. They judge the options and justify the choice.
- *Critical thinking* uses thinking to analyze arguments which generate insights regarding meaning and interpretations. Critical thinking identifies bias and/or point of view, as well as logical reasoning patterns.
- *Creative thinking* uses thinking to develop or invent novel, aesthetic, and constructive ideas or products. Emphasis is on using known information or material to predict, as well as to elaborate on the thinker's original perspective. Creative thinking equally emphasizes the intuitive, affective, and rational aspects of thinking.

The following story serves as a basis for sample questions that address the various types of thinking presented in this section.

Tarheels

People who live in North Carolina are called *Tarheels*. The name *Tarheel* originated when North Carolina was an English colony. Many pine trees grew in North Carolina. The early farmers tapped the pine trees for raw turpentine, which they processed into rosin, tar, and pitch as a source of income. Lacking shoes, the farmers went barefoot, and the soles of their feet became covered with tar. When other people observed the tar on the farmers' feet, they called them *Tarheels*.

During the Civil War, the North Carolina farmers who became soldiers still were too poor to wear shoes, and they still had tar on their feet. Therefore, soldiers from other states continued to call them *Tarheels*. In those days, the North Carolinians were ashamed of the name, but this changed when Governor Vance, the popular Civil War governor, took the name as well. From that time on, *Tarheel* has been a cherished name.

Questions like the following might be generated for this story:

- Why did the farmers have tar on their feet? (analysis)
- What caused North Carolinians to be called *Tarheels?* (cause and effect)
- Compare the North Carolinians' attitudes toward the name *Tarheels* before and after the Civil War. (comparison)
- How did the North Carolinians' attitudes about the name *Tarheels* change? (inference)
- How could one person change the feelings of so many other people? (critical)

- Can you think of other meanings for the name *Tarheel?* (For example, being persistent, as one who sticks with a task) (creative)
- Do you think *Tarheels* is a good name for people who live in North Carolina? Why or why not? (evaluative)
- Why has the name *Tarheels* existed so long? (critical)
- Can you think of a different nickname for North Carolinians? (creative)
- What symbol could be used to represent *Tarheels?* (creative)

TEACHING COMPREHENSION

Teachers must assume a central, active role in teaching reading comprehension. Current research and knowledge show that teachers help children understand when they model (thinking, reading, and so on), guide practice, and provide feedback to students. Teachers who define reading comprehension as an active, constructive process, view themselves as facilitators of comprehension. They can facilitate comprehension by designing instruction to emphasize individual students' knowledge and to support language processing skills. To teach reading comprehension, teachers must consider the reader, the text, and the instruction that leads to understanding.

Develop schemata

When it becomes apparent that students lack the knowledge and experiences needed to comprehend, teachers must make instructional provisions; comprehension activities and strategies cannot succeed unless students have adequately developed schemata. When teaching comprehension as a process, teachers must take the responsibility for helping students develop schemata that are missing or limited. When schemata exist, instructors activate them, so students have a means of understanding. Cooperative activities offer another avenue for helping students who lack schemata. Teachers can initiate activities that stimulate youngsters to work together and share their background experiences, since some youngsters may have schemata that others lack.

Environment

Teachers must create an environment in which thinking can flourish, so students learn to comprehend. When they accept students' answers that differ from their own, and when they tolerate and encourage different points of view, they are establishing such an environment. Students' thinking should be respected and valued. Teachers should ask questions such as "What do you think will happen?" and "Why do you think that?" These types of questions clarify and widen students' thinking. They should allow adequate time for students to think about the answers to questions.

In this text, teachers are encouraged to take an active role in providing reading comprehension instruction. Instruction is organized around prereading, during reading, and postreading.

TEACHING THINKING AND QUESTIONING

Thinking and questioning pervade the comprehension process; therefore, they are discussed at this point. Teachers use questions to stimulate thinking, facilitate comprehension, and to encourage active reading; questions are a fact of life in elementary classrooms. Furthermore, the ability to answer questions determines whether students are competent or incompetent readers. Purposing questions are posed prior to reading; they activate students' schemata and encourage them to predict meaning. During reading, students should ask themselves questions (metacognition). These self-questions are concerned with "What is the author saying?" and "Do I understand the text?" Following reading, comprehension is reinforced and expanded through discussion of the text.

Can we teach students to answer questions effectively? Research shows that instruction does improve elementary school children's ability to answer questions (Hansen, 1981; Hansen and Pearson, 1983; Gordon and Pearson, 1983).

Effective Questioning

Instructional questions are teachers' major tool for developing thinking skills. Effective questions activate students' schemata and encourage active involvement with the text. They are clear and precise; they address important ideas and concepts in the text. Teachers should preplan their questions in order to ask effective questions.

When preparing questions, teachers should ask themselves the following questions:

- What are the most important ideas (or facts) in this selection?
- What ideas (or facts) should the students remember from this selection?
- What thinking skills have the students already developed?
- What thinking skills do the students need to develop?
- What questions will prompt students to support and explain their answers?

How to Encourage Students to Ask Their Own Questions

Poorly chosen questions and answers that emphasize insignificant details are detrimental to the growth of thinking skills. If we ask questions about trivial details students will focus their attention on these details, rather than on the important ideas. For example, children who are asked questions like "What color was Mary's dress?" "Who picked up the newspaper?" or "Which seat in the automobile was Kathy sitting in?" soon learn to focus on low-level details, which are not central to the text. Readers who focus solely on details do not grasp the "big picture," and they experience difficulty inferencing and remembering.

Integrated line of questions   Skillful teachers establish a coherent, integrated line of questions, which leads to greater understanding of the entire reading selection. Questions should form a structure that facilitates understanding; otherwise, questions can lead students to focus on discrete pieces of the text which fragments their understanding. Beck et al. (1979) suggest that teachers' questions should be developed from a "story map," which is a graphic representation of a story grammar. Story-map questions help teachers develop a line of questioning that enhances understanding. Box 5.2 illustrates the use of a story map for generating questions. This story map is based on the book *My Robot Buddy* by Alfred Slote. It is the story about Jack, who receives a robot named Danny One for his birthday. The only observable difference between Jack and Danny One is the stiff way that the robot walks, but Jack has practiced walking like a robot, so the robotnappers confuse the real boy with the robot.

The following questions might be generated from this story:

1. What is the problem in this story? (inference)
2. How are Danny and Jack alike and how are they different? (comparison/contrast)
3. What caused the problem in this story? (cause/effect)
4. How did Danny help solve the problem? (problem solving)
5. What do you think would have happened if Danny had not been able to call the police? (critical)
6. Why did Jack receive a robot as a present? (analysis)
7. Do you think that Jack anticipated Danny's help? Why or why not? (inference)

Box 5.2   Story Map

The Setting

Characters: Jack Jameson, Danny One

Place: The future, robot factory, isolated country home

The Problem

Jack is robotnapped.

Efforts to Solve Problem-Story Events

Jack tells the robotnappers that he is a real boy, but they do not believe him.

Danny tells the robotnappers that he is the actual robot, but they do not believe him.

Danny One uses his radio button to call the robot factory and they call the police.

Resolution

The police rescue Jack and Danny

Teachers who use questions as instructional instruments use techniques that enhance the learning that questions stimulate. They ask students to answer questions in their own words rather than promoting memorization of the text or choosing among multiple-choice answers. When students generate answers and state them in their own words, they are exhibiting more understanding than when they quote the text exactly. Students who explain and support their answers engage in thinking, rather than in random guessing. At times, they may cite sentences or paragraphs from the text to document their answers, but they can also use their own experiences and prior knowledge to answer questions.

Wait time

Teachers should allow adequate "wait time" for students who are answering questions. "Wait time" is the time students have to think about their answer to a question. Students who have more time to think about their answers give better answers to questions; they have more time to utilize their prior knowledge and to infer from the text.

Inferencing

Inferential thinking is a basic aspect of reading comprehension. Inferential thinking is concerned with meanings that are not directly stated in the text. The author suggests and hints at ideas, rather than stating them directly, and the reader must interpret the author's words to understand the intended meaning. Readers use their experiences and knowledge to fill in information the author has not stated. In the sentence, "Socks, you are getting to be a big fat nuisance," the reader infers that Socks (a cat) is irritating his owner because of the words *big fat nuisance.* Authors cannot tell readers everything; stories would be too long and the detail would make them boring. Authors must rely on their audience to fill in the empty spaces.

Instruction improves inferencing ability (Dewitz, Carrs and Patberg, 1987; Allen, 1985, Hansen, 1981). To infer, readers relate experience, knowledge, and values to the text. Inferring may involve comparison, application, cause and effect, drawing conclusions, forming generalizations, predicting outcomes, and understanding figurative language. These processes can be taught through activities like these:

Activities to Develop Inferencing Skills

I. Implied meanings.
   A. Give several students pieces of paper describing a situation. Have these students make statements to the rest of the class that hint at the particular situation described on their papers. For example, a student who receives a piece of paper with the note *Today is my birthday,* could say *My mother is baking a cake for me today.*
   B. Select newspaper stories that are accompanied by photographs. Separate the stories from the pictures. Have students read the stories and match them with the appropriate picture.
   C. Put the following items in a paper bag: a child's note that reads, "Dear

Mom, may I take Mary along?"; a handwritten list that reads, "Things We Have to Take: hot dogs, catsup, mustard, sleeping bags, ice chest, charcoal, and tent"; a paper plate; and marshmallows. Ask children to examine the objects in the bag and make up a story about what they are going to do and where they are going.

    D. Provide students with pictures and objects from which they can make inferences. (Example: snapshots, song lyrics, bus schedule with under-lined items, a key ring and keys. Possible answer: Taking a vacation trip on a bus to visit friends.)

  II. Cause and effect.

    A. Provide students with a list of causes and have them supply the appropriate effects. For example:

      Cause: It is raining very hard.
      Effect: (possible answer): I need to wear my raincoat.
      Cause: Tom mowed Mrs. Smith's lawn.
      Effect: Mrs. Smith paid Tom for his work.

    B. Cause-and-effect match. Write "cause" sentences on file cards and "effect" sentences on another set of cards. Have students match these cards to make correct responses. This is shown in Figure 5.2.

    C. Provide students with a list of sentences and ask them to identify causes and effects.

      Example: Susan cried when she lost her favorite doll.
      Cause: Susan lost her favorite doll.
      Effect: Susan cried.

  III. Comparisons.

    A. Collect sets of pictures that children can contrast. For example, show the class a picture of a dog and one of a cat. Have them make a list of the ways in which these animals are alike and different. For example:

Dog	*Cat*
barks	meows
four legs	four legs
hair	hair

    (Children can also compare breakfast cereals.)

Figure 5.2

    B. Have children read paragraphs and have them determine what details can be contrasted with one another in these paragraphs. (For example: *Linda has a red ten-speed bicycle. She can ride very fast on her bicycle. Susan has a blue tricycle. She rides it very slowly.*)

IV. *Making generalizations.* A *generalization* is a statement of a broad relationship between two concepts. *All living things need water to survive* is an example of a generalization. Listing ideas that lead to a generalization helps students to arrive at a conclusion.

    A. After reading stories, ask children questions that lead to generalizations.

Sequence may be implied or stated. These activities help students learn both.

    A. Provide students with comic strips that have been cut apart and ask them to put the frames back together in sequential order.

    B. Ask students to list the things they do each morning when they get up. These activities should be arranged in sequential order. Students can also list the sequence of television programs that they watch in an evening.

    C. Have children draw pictures to illustrate the sequence of events in a story. (This can be done in comic strip fashion.)

    D. Provide the class with a group of pictures that represent events in a story that has just been read. Have students arrange the pictures in the same sequence as the events that were described in the story.

    E. Cut apart the sentences in a language-experience chart. Ask children to put the sentences back in the correct sequence.

    F. Have students follow a set of written directions for an activity—such as yarn painting. You will need a piece of yarn as well as some paint and paper for this exercise. The directions should tell students to dip the piece of yarn into the paint and then pull the yarn across the paper to make designs. (A variation on this activity is to make thumbprint art. You will need a piece of paper and a stamp pad. The directions should tell children to press their thumbs on the stamp pad and then slowly on the paper. Ask students to use magic markers to draw faces with such features as hair, eyes, and smiles.)

    G. Have a group of students prepare a class "treat" by following a set of cooking directions on a food mix box (for example, cookies, cake, or pudding).

    H. Give students oral directions for drawing a figure. Tell them to draw a vertical line 1 inch in length in the middle of a piece of paper. Then have them draw a horizontal line 1 inch in width through the middle of the vertical line.

V. *Predicting outcomes.* Predicting an outcome requires the reader to analyze the given data and anticipate what the outcome will be. The reader must look for facts and make comparisons before making inferences from the selection.

    A. Give children a picture and ask them to predict what they think will happen next. They should explain the basis for their prediction.

    B. Read part of a story and ask children to predict what will happen next. Again, they should explain the reason for their answer.

    C. Have children write endings for various stories.

D. Put short stories on file cards and put the endings for these stories on another set of cards. Students are to match the stories with the correct endings.

VI. *Cloze procedures.* These passages with systematically deleted words are excellent instructional activities for inferencing skills (Dewitz, Carr and Patberg, 1987). They are discussed on pages 254–255.

Thinking

Evaluative or **critical thinking** requires that the reader make judgments about the quality, value, and validity of the content being read. Evaluative thinking is very much dependent on the ability to read well at the literal and interpretive levels. The reader must evaluate the accuracy of the material, synthesize information, make comparisons and inferences, and suspend judgment to avoid jumping to conclusions. Critical readers must be able to recognize the author's purpose, point of view, and use of language. They must be able to distinguish fact from opinion. Critical readers should test the author's assertions against their own observations, information, and logic. Research confirms that critical reading skills can be taught to elementary school children.

Words influence Semantic skills in critical reading are primarily concerned with the ways in which words are used to influence readers. Semantic skills include the understanding of denotative and connotative uses of words, the use of vague and precise words, and the use of words in a persuasive manner. For example, have students think about the differences between the following two statements:

My grandmother is coming for a visit.

That crabby old lady is coming for a visit.

Suspend judgment Critical reading is based on logical and objective thoughts about the content. The reader must suspend judgment while gathering the necessary data on which to base the eventual subjective evaluation. Suspending judgment means that the reader must avoid jumping to conclusions. The reader's background experience provides the information for making judgments. Critical reading should be approached with an open-minded, problem-solving sensibility.

ACTIVITIES FOR DEVELOPING CRITICAL READING SKILLS

I. Semantics.
   A. Ask students to find examples of the use of "loaded" words in newspapers, magazines, and textbooks. *Loaded words* are those that cause readers to have pleasant or unpleasant associations. For example, many readers have unpleasant associations with the words *unAmerican, communist,* and *radical.* Many readers react favorably to such words as *freedom, peace,* and *human rights.*
   B. Identify examples of the vague use of words. (Example: *Most* is a vague word.)

II. Logic.
   A. Have students create syllogisms that state an author's premises and conclusions. (A syllogism contains two premises and a conclusion.) For example:

   Premise 1: *All third-graders study reading.*
   Premise 2: *Jane is a third grader.*
   Conclusion: *Therefore, Jane studies reading.*

   B. Authors frequently do not specify whether their details are actually facts or opinions. The reader must look for such qualifying words as *think, probably, maybe, appear, seem, believe,* and *could,* which indicate statements of opinion. Have students examine various reading materials to locate opinion words. (Examples: I *believe* this is the best pie I have ever eaten. Susan will *probably* come home from college. A headache *could* mean that you are getting a cold.)

   C. The identification of **propaganda** is one of the skills required by critical readers. The following is a discussion of propaganda devices and techniques for analyzing this material (Smith, 1978).
      1. *Bad names.* Disagreeable words are used to arouse distaste for a person or a thing. One example of "bad names" propaganda would be an advertisement for dishwasher detergent that states, *Don't have spots on your glasses. Use brand X.*
      2. *Glad names.* This is the opposite of the bad names strategy. Pleasant words are used to create good feelings about a person or a thing. One example would be a coffee advertisement that says *Fantastic, fresh perked flavor.*
      3. *Plain folks.* This kind of propaganda makes an effort to avoid artificiality and sophistication. Political candidates use this technique when they shake hands, kiss babies, and play with dogs. They are, in effect, trying to appear like the "man next door."
      4. *Transfer.* This type of propaganda attempts to transfer the reader's respect for the flag, the cross, or some universal symbol to a person or thing. One example would be a flag that is pictured in the background of an automobile advertisement.
      5. *Testimonial.* This technique is similar to transfer except that, in this case, a famous person gives a testimonial for a product or another individual. Positive feelings for the well-known figure are assumed to be transferred to the product or the other person. For example, an actor may appear on television on behalf of a political candidate, or an athlete may claim to use a particular after-shave.
      6. *Bandwagon.* This type of propaganda is an attempt to convince the readers that they should accept an idea or purchase an item because "everyone is doing it." It is the kind of thinking behind a slogan such as *20 million people can't be wrong.*
      7. *Card stacking.* This technique utilizes accurate information, but generally omits pieces of that information so that only one side of a story is told. For example, a cigarette may be advertised as smooth-tasting and mellow, but the negative effects of smoking will not be mentioned (Smith, 1963).

Propaganda devices rarely occur by themselves, but are often used in combination with one another in an advertisement.

After learning to identify propaganda devices, the reader should analyze the selection, keeping the following questions in mind:

Which propaganda device is used here?

Who composed this material?

Why was this piece of propaganda written?

To what reader interests, emotions, and prejudices does the propaganda appeal?

Will I allow myself to be influenced by this material?

III. Authenticity.
  A. Have students verify the facts found in local newspaper stories and basal reader stories.
  B. Assign students a topic and ask them to compare the information related to that topic that they find in several sources. They should identify those points of similarity and points of difference that they come across in their investigation.
  C. Provide students with books and magazine articles and ask them to evaluate the authors' qualifications after researching their background or writing their own story on the topic.
IV. Literary forms.
  A. Read various types of literature to children and ask them to identify whether it is fantasy, realistic fiction, historical fiction, biography, poetry, or nonfiction. Ask them to explain how they arrived at their response.
  B. Have children read various forms of literature on the same topic. For example, they could read a poem and biography about Abraham Lincoln. Ask the class to discuss how the poem and the biography are both alike and different.

Creative Thinking

Creative thinking is imaginative, original thinking that requires the reader to think beyond the lines of print. Creative reading is an effort to use the information and ideas read as a basis for arriving at new ways in which to view the world. Elementary school children should be exposed to ideas that are new to them. Creative thinking occurs after the child has read and understood a selection; it may take the form of a new idea, a new story, a design, a painting, an improved method, or an invention.

Flexible and open-minded Creative thinkers are flexible and open-minded in their thinking. Creative children may be able to come up with several ways of solving a math problem or several approaches to an experiment in science class. Creative thinkers may be able to turn a situation from a basal reader story into a puppet show, a skit, a painting, or even a piece of sculpture. They may be able to invent a new toy or a new machine. Creative thinkers must be able to synthesize previous knowledge into a new form. Such creativity is threatened when teachers demand that activities be completed in accordance with precise specifications—and do not permit any deviation from the prescribed format. Inventiveness should be rewarded rather than "punished" because such support will encourage further creativity.

Activities for Developing Creative Thinking Skills

Creative thinking can be encouraged through the use of stimulating content materials and instructional questions.

1. Schedule brainstorming sessions. During this activity, children should be encouraged to voice any thoughts that arise *before* they analyze the ideas. These thoughts can be examined after the brainstorming session. Follow-up activities may be related to the following areas: writing, debate, artwork, and drama.
2. Encourage children to select music pieces that reflect the mood of a story that has been read.
3. Look for books that encourage creative thinking, such as *Swimmy* by Leo Lionni and *Conrad's Castle* by Ben Shecter.

Modeling as a Means of Teaching Thinking

Thinking skills are developed through modeling. One modeling approach is the "think-aloud" strategy; teachers verbalize their own thoughts while displaying text on an overhead screen or with individual copies of the text for each student. While the teacher makes his or her thinking public, the students follow the text. A think-aloud strategy is illustrated in Box 5.3.

A natural extension of the think-aloud activity is to have students verbalize their own thought processes while reading. This makes them conscious of their thinking processes, and gives teachers the data they need to identify aspects of students' thinking that need to be refined. Thinking aloud is a natural activity for young children. They often hypothesize and anticipate story events aloud when they read and listen to stories.

Another extension of think-alouds is to list the types of thinking used. For instance, the teacher in Box 5.3 used the following types of thinking:

inferential

predictive

analytical

comparative

cause and effect

Box 5.3   A Think-Aloud Script

Teacher: Jumanji. The title has no meaning for me. I can't predict anything about the story from the title. The first illustration shows a boy and girl in a park, so I anticipate they are in the story.

Teacher: In the first sentence, Mother says "keep the house neat." I expect that means that the house is going to get messy before the story is completed. Then the author mentions that Judy and Peter giggled? Apparently they giggled because they took all of their toys out and made a terrible mess. The plot thickens. Peter and Judy are bored, so they go to the park. It must be the park I saw in the picture.

Teacher: They find a box labeled *JUMANJI, JUNGLE ADVENTURE GAME.* The label is written in capital letters, so this is an important event. The title of the game is the same as the title of the story. Also, there is a notation on the box to "read instructions carefully." The game description states that the game is designed for the "bored and restless," which suggests they may be in for some excitement.

Teacher: The directions state that "Once the Game of Jumanji is Started, it Will not be Over Until One Player Reaches the Golden City." I wouldn't like to play a game that I couldn't stop when I wanted to. I wonder why the illustrations are black and white instead of colored?

Students may identify the types of thinking they use, and they may work in pairs to identify the types of thinking that one another uses in a think-aloud.

Literature and Thinking

Children's literature provides thinking models as well as stimulating thinking. In books like *Come Sing, Jimmy Jo* by Katherine Paterson, *Alexandra The Great* by Constance Greene, and *A Wrinkle in Time* by Madeline L'Engle, students read about children who solve problems and make difficult decisions. Picture books like Wanda Gag's *Millions of Cats, Make Way for Ducklings* by Robert McCloskey, and *Jumanji* by Chris Van Allsburg, show characters in situations that require thinking. Reading stories aloud to children and discussing the thinking and problem situations, helps children to acquire and refine thinking skills. Thinking skills play an important role in prereading comprehension instruction.

PREREADING COMPREHENSION INSTRUCTION

Prereading instruction is concerned with creating a bridge between the reader and the text. The reader's prior knowledge interacts with the text to build understanding. Prereading instruction is largely directed toward preparing students to understand the text; it builds background knowledge, activates schemata, anticipates text content, preteaches vocabulary, and focuses attention on the important aspects of the text.

Predictions

Readers' schemata are the basis of expectations (predictions) in reading comprehension. Schemata enable readers to predict the author's ideas, concepts, language, and organization. Then they read to confirm or discount these predictions. Readers who are able to anticipate, comprehend better than students who lack the schemata to predict.

When readers lack the prior knowledge necessary to comprehend, teachers must intervene with instruction to help readers comprehend. Three suggestions appear often in instructional literature: teach vocabulary as a prereading step; provide experiences, vicarious or otherwise, which fill in and expand on students' existing knowledge; or introduce a conceptual framework analogous to that of the text, which will enable students to build appropriate background for themselves (Tierney and Cunningham, 1984).

Teaching Word Meanings

Knowledge of word meanings is integral to comprehension. The importance of word meanings to comprehension cannot be overestimated; readers' knowledge about a topic, particularly key vocabulary, is a better predictor of comprehension than any other measure of reading ability or achievement (Johnston and Pearson, 1982; Johnston, 1984; Freebody and Anderson, 1983; Stall and Fairbanks, 1986). Generally speaking, the more word meanings known, the better the comprehension. Knowing the meanings of words included in the text does not guarantee comprehension, but it gives readers a better chance to understand. Therefore, teachers need to teach the new words in a story before reading the story.

Denotative and connotative

To teach word meanings, teachers need to understand some aspects of word meanings. Words have different kinds of meanings. Words have denotative meanings and connotative meanings. Denotative meanings are formal meanings like those found in a dictionary. The denotative meaning of *farm* is a "tract of land along with the buildings, animals, personnel, and equipment necessary to operate it." On the other hand, the connotative meaning, the emotional response to a word or concept, differs from individual to individual depending on his or her experiences. I grew up on a farm; therefore, I have certain responses to the word *farm.* I think of space, "Old Gold," a milk cow, Gypsy, the dog who herded cows, sunshine, chickens clucking, and pigs grunting. When individuals read, they use both denotative and connotative meanings to understand. Many words have both connotative and denotative meanings for the individual reader.

Multiple meanings

Many English words have multiple meanings, which are difficult for children to understand. For example, among the meanings of the word *hard* are *firm, strong-minded,* or *difficult.* This means that words are not learned one at a time, but children usually learn *one* meaning of a word at a time; they need a variety of experiences and opportunities to elaborate word meanings. Conceptual and categorization activities are effective ways to help students elaborate their word knowledge. One approach is illustrated in Figure 5.3.

This figure shows a word map; it helps students explore the dimensions of words. It is based on a concept presented by Schwartz and Raphael (1985).

Abstract meanings Some words are harder to learn than others (Sorenson, 1985). Words with abstract meanings are more difficult to learn than words that have concrete meanings. *Elephant* is easier to learn than is *courage.* Concrete words are easier to explain and conceputalize through actual experience; on the other hand, abstract words cannot be illustrated and explained so easily. This means that teachers must provide more experiences and activities to help children learn abstract words.

Concept labels Words are essentially labels for concepts; therefore, students need to learn something about the concepts (Green, 1984). Anderson and Freebody (1981) suggest that the child who knows the word *mast* is likely to have knowledge about sailing. This means that the child knows *mast* as part of a conceptual framework, rather than as a separate entity. Trying to teach children a single *sailing* concept, separate from related concepts, is inefficient. Therefore, it makes ultimate sense to teach vocabulary as a network of ideas.

Mentioning words is not sufficient for learning (Sorenson, 1985). Fluent readers learn some words from context, as they read, but students do not acquire an adequate, meaningful vocabulary from incidental experiences with words. Pronouncing a word correctly does not prove that children have a network of meanings to associate with it. Memorizing dictionary definitions does not solve the problem of learning words either. Children need to fit a word with a concept, they need to relate it to a network of ideas, and this is not facilitated by dictionary definitions. Children need direct instruction to learn words, as well as many opportunities to implement their understandings as they read.

Prior to teaching a reading lesson, teachers need to directly teach the words that will be covered. This is a means of making sure that children have

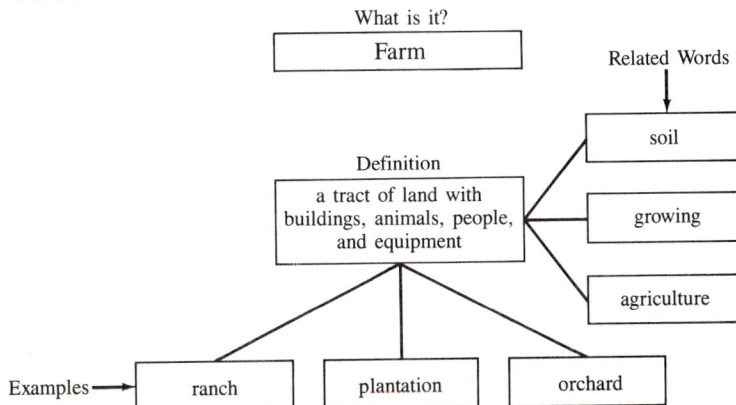

Figure 5.3 Word map.

the necessary foundation to read and understand text. We cannot assume that children can learn these words incidentally, or that mentioning the correct pronunciation of a word constitutes teaching it. The direct vocabulary instruction program should provide for the following factors.

- Words should be taught as part of a conceptual network.
- Teachers should build children's interest in words.
- Provide many direct and vicarious experiences with words.
- Preteach difficult words. Teach students to focus on words that are frequently repeated in a selection, since they are usually important to comprehension.
- Teach student connectives (conjunctions, prepositions, and articles) as well as substantive words (nouns, verbs, and adjectives). Connectives show relationships.
- Help students develop their own systems for learning words.
- Encourage children to use context clues as aids to learning the meaning of unknown words.
- Teach commonly occurring prefixes and suffixes that have invariant meanings. This aids learning new words.
- Encourage children to read widely.
- Encourage students to utilize the dictionary and thesaurus.

The following sections address these components of a vocabulary program.

Concepts

A filing system

Concepts are like a mental filing system; they aid the reader in sorting out and organizing information. Such categories help us make order and sense out of a vast amount of information. Concepts also enable children to both distinguish between and make associations with a variety of objects, events, and ideas. A student can know quite a bit about an object before knowing how to classify that object. For example, a child may recognize an object as a flower but be unable to specify the type of flower.

Teachers should closely examine student reading assignments to identify those concepts that the author presumes students to have learned. Frequently, authors assume concepts that students, in fact, lack. Attention should be paid to those particular concepts that are essential for comprehension of a selection. If students lack these basic concepts, the teacher must make provision for developing them before reading actually takes place. For example, if the class is to read a story about a skunk and they are not familiar with what a skunk looks, acts, and smells like, teachers should provide pictures and other discussion materials to illustrate the concept of *skunk*.

Related concepts

Teachers can facilitate the learning of concepts by selecting materials that will cause students to recognize patterns in these classroom activities. Students should be encouraged to identify likenesses and differences among their own experiences, as well as the content of their reading selections. This provides a basis for categorizing information and forming concepts. Common factors in form, function, and color should all be used for categorization. Sense perceptions can aid size, shape, touch, taste, sound, and smell categorizations. Students can begin to become familiar with such labels as *sour, red, square,* and *sweet-smelling.*

Creating *semantic maps* is an excellent comprehension activity which functions to develop concepts and word meanings, as well as to activate schemata because it builds a connection between known and new information. Figure 5.4 illustrates a semantic map for *bird.* This figure does not represent a complete semantic network because this would vary from individual to individual. Furthermore, it is literally impossible to include all of the related concepts and relationships in a map because the possibilities are almost endless.

The steps for constructing a semantic map are as follows:

1. Ask children to think of words that are related to the key word (the focus of the semantic map). Write the words students generate on the chalkboard.

2. When all of the words they can think of are listed, categorize them. For instance, responses to *government* included the following: democratic, communist, socialist, senate, house, President, congress, Vice President, supreme court and so forth. These words are then categorized as forms of government, branches of government, and government officials. Students who have difficulty generating words and categorizing them will probably need opportunities to develop schemata before reading the text.

3. Students read the selection, and review the categories established to determine whether they should be revised to include information acquired from the text. The original map can be augmented and corrected to incorporate the new information. Thus the semantic map connects existing knowledge with new knowledge.

ACTIVITIES FOR CATEGORIZATION

1. Have students collect pictures from catalogs and magazines and sort these into such categories as clothing, furniture, tools, and appliances.

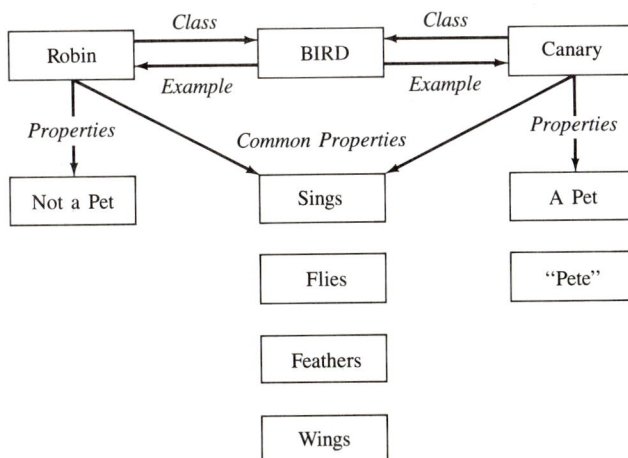

Figure 5.4 Semantic map for the concept of bird.

2. Divide the class into groups and provide each group with a variety of objects. (These objects may be obtained from a variety store and may include toys as well as functional items.) Students should categorize the objects on the basis of such common characteristics as form, function, color, and texture. Some examples are:

a. Objects: ball, balloon, top.
   Common characteristics: round (shape), blue (color), smooth (texture), and play (function).

b. Objects: a pickle and a lemon.
   Common characteristics: sour (taste), eat (function), small (size), and rough (texture).

3. Specify a category and ask students to supply the concepts that would relate to this. For example, the category of *school* might suggest such words as *chalkboard, chalk, teachers, pupils, books, school buses, cafeteria,* and *recess.*

4. Provide students with a worksheet that divides items into categories and that includes one item that does not belong in each category. The student must mark those items and tell why they should not be associated with the other entries of the list.

Example: petunia   cow
            zinnia   horse
            ~~onion~~   ~~lion~~
            daisy   sheep

5. Provide students with a categorizing worksheet and ask them to suggest words that could be included in these categories.

Example: *fruit*   *birthday*
            apple   party
            banana   presents
            pear   cake
            grapes   candles

6. A sort-out-the-word game. Make a game board by dividing a piece of cardboard into nine equal sections. Place one word card in each section. Children should receive eight word cards and markers. Players take turns trying to create a category by matching one of their cards in their hand with one of the cards on the board. A marker should be placed on each card that is successfully matched to form a category. The player who has three markers lined up in a row is the winner. For example, if the word *father* were on the board and a child held the word card for *sister,* the category of *people* would be created. If the word *house* were on the board and the word *store* was a card in someone's hand, a category of *places* or *buildings* could be suggested.

7. Present the class with a group of objects. Ask pupils to identify one object that represents the general category and have them explain how the remaining objects relate to this. For example, one group might include a single page from a book—a dust jacket, a bookmark, a book cover, or an entire book—intact.

8. Present a group of objects and ask children to find the one that does not belong. For example, a peach, an apple, a banana, and an onion.

The Vocabulary Program

Sensitivity to words and the motivation to learn new word meanings are the cornerstones of the vocabulary development program. A sense of excitement—and even wonder—about words are essential ingredients in expanding students' vocabulary. This interest in words must be maintained in children; it serves as a most powerful motivator. This sensitivity also leads to an alertness of new words that continue to appear in one's environment. Resource books are useful for developing student interest in words. The following books contain interesting information about words and suggest creative approaches to words.

Alexander, Arthur. *The Magic of Words,* Englewood Cliffs, NJ: Prentice-Hall, 1962.

Asimov, Isaac. *Words of Science,* Boston: Houghton Mifflin, 1959.

———. *Words on the Map,* Boston: Houghton Mifflin, 1962.

Ferguson, Charles W. *The Abecedarian Book,* Boston: Little, Brown, 1964.

Funk, Charles Earle. *Thereby Hangs a Tale,* New York: Warner Paperback, 1950.

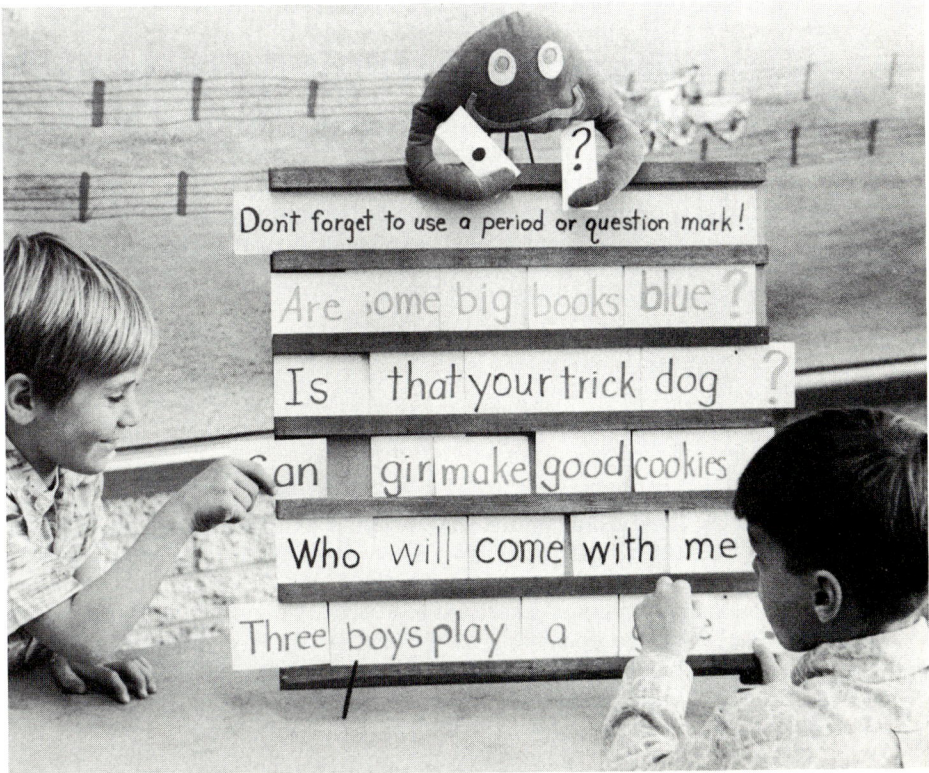

Games and activities can serve as aids in developing word-recognition. (*Courtesy Strickler, Monkmeyer Press Photo*)

————. *Heavens to Betsy*, New York: Warner Paperback, 1955.

Gwynne, Fred. *The King Who Rained*, New York: Young Readers, 1970.

————. *A Chocolate Moose for Dinner*, New York: Windmill Books, 1976.

————. *The Sixteen Hand Horse* Englewood Cliffs, NJ: Prentice Hall, 1980.

Heller, Ruth *A Cache of Jewels and Other Collective Nouns*, New York: Grosset and Dunlap, 1987.

Merriam, Eve, and Paul Galdone. *A Gaggle of Geese*, New York: Alfred A. Knopf, 1960.

O'Neill, Mary. *Words, Words, Words*, New York: Doubleday, 1966.

Rand, Ann and Paul. *Sparkle and Spin*, New York: Harcourt, Brace & World, 1957.

Reid, Alastair. *Ounce, Dice, Trice*, Boston: Little, Brown, 1958.

Shipley, Joseph T. *Playing with Words*, Englewood Cliffs, NJ: Prentice-Hall, 1960.

ACTIVITIES FOR DEVELOPING WORD SENSITIVITY

1. Listen to a television or radio program and have children make a list of new words.
2. Draw pictures to illustrate some new words.
3. Make a list of words that various members of the class like to use. Make a list of words that children dislike.
4. Provide children with a magazine picture and have them make a list of all the words that they associate with that picture. For example, an advertisement showing a kitchen could prompt the following list of related words:

sink	salt and pepper
stove	cook
forks	garbage
spoons	bake
knives	food
cups	

5. Television game shows—such as "Password" and the "Wheel of Fortune" can be adapted for vocabulary activities. Commercial games, such as "Scrabble," are also useful in building vocabulary. Crossword puzzles and hidden word puzzles may be obtained in published materials, or constructed by teachers (and students) themselves. The crossword puzzle example, shown in Figure 5.5, contains key words from a basal reader story at the third-grade level. The hidden word puzzle example, shown in Figure 5.6, contains key words from a basal reader story at the second-grade level.
   In addition to learning various ways in which a word can be

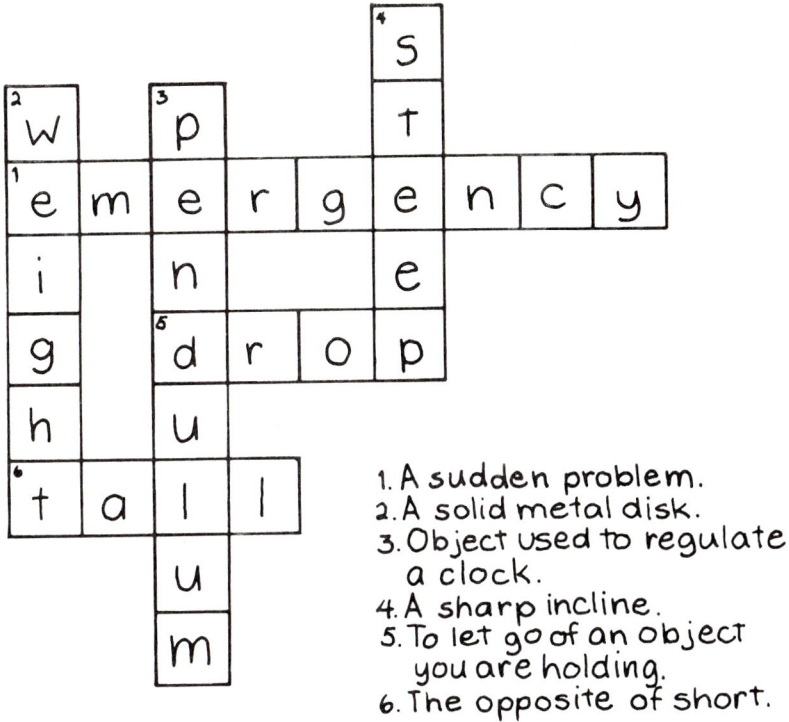

1. A sudden problem.
2. A solid metal disk.
3. Object used to regulate a clock.
4. A sharp incline.
5. To let go of an object you are holding.
6. The opposite of short.

Figure 5.5

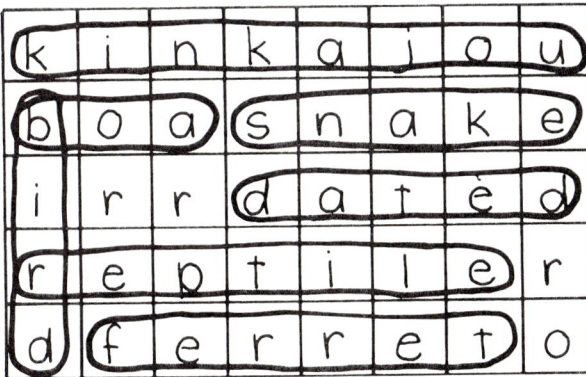

Hidden word puzzle answers:
kinkajou, bird, boa, snake,
dated, reptile, ferret

Figure 5.6

defined, children should learn the attributes of words. Some of these are listed:

1. Words name people, places, and things. (Example: *Linda* is a word name for a girl.)
2. Words can describe action. (Example: Linda *skipped* down the street.)
3. Words can describe. Describing words are usually adjectives and adverbs. (Example: Linda is a *pretty* girl; Bill skipped *happily* down the street.)
4. One word may have multiple meanings. (Example: John will *court* Mary; Tennis is played on a *court;* The lawyer will go to *court* tomorrow.)
5. Many words in English have almost the same meaning. (Example: scarlet and crimson.)
6. Words may have denotative or connotative meanings. **Denotation** refers to the type of definition of a word that is given in the dictionary. **Connotation** refers to the meaning—that is sometimes emotional—that we tend to associate with a word—and this may often differ from the dictionary definition. For example *mother* denotes a person who gives birth to a child, but the word connotes an individual who provides warmth, love, and care for that child. Some activities to practice word meanings are:
   a. Have class members discuss their emotional reactions to television commercials. Make a list of the words they use to describe their emotions.
   b. Ask children to list words that connote happiness or sadness. Locate these words in the dictionary and see if these suggested meanings agree with the dictionary definitions.

Preteach vocabulary

   Words that are important to children's comprehension should be taught prior to assigning a reading selection. This vocabulary should be introduced in a context that students will understand. Teachers may use worksheets, study guides, crossword puzzles, and game boards to introduce new vocabulary words. The following is a sample vocabulary study sheet for a basal reader selection that could be utilized as an in-class exercise.

Vocabulary Study Sheet for a Basal Reader Story

Children should match each word in the left-hand column with the correct definition in the column on the right. The letter of the correct definition can be inserted in the blank space that is provided.

draft horse _____   a. pulls light carts and carriages
quarter horse _____   b. is a work horse
Arabian horse _____   c. is trained to work with cattle
Morgan _____   d. runs long distances without food or water

Teach connectives

Although the emphasis in vocabulary instruction is on substantive words—such as nouns, adjectives, and verbs—connective words are also important. Comprehension is improved when children understand the meaning of connectives (Robertson, 1968; Stoodt, 1972). Thought connectors include prepositions, conjunctions, relative pronouns, and some adverbs. Connective words connect thoughts and suggest relationships between these thoughts. Some examples of connective words follow:

Words that indicate time and positional relationships:

about	beneath	of
across	between	outside
after	beyond	through
against	by	to
along	from	until
among	in	up
around	inside	upon
at	like	with
before	near	without

Words that signal that an important idea will follow:

thus	in conclusion	without question
therefore	in summation (in	significantly
consequently	summary)	unquestionably
finally	in brief	absolutely
hence	as a result	

Words that indicate contrasting ideas:

but	meanwhile	otherwise
yet	however	although
nevertheless	on the other hand	despite

Words that indicate cause and effect:

because	since	when
if	though	while
now	where	unless

ACTIVITIES FOR TEACHING CONNECTIVES

1. Read a selection aloud, omitting the connectives, and ask students to supply appropriate words. For example:

   "I pledge allegiance _____ the flag _____ the United States _____

   America, _____ _____ the Republic _____ _____ it stands, one nation

   _____ God, indivisible, _____ liberty _____ justice _____ all."

2. Omit connectives from written exercises and ask students to select the correct connective from the multiple choice answers.

   Example: Mary _____ Jane went to the store.

        but, and, to

   A good vocabulary program helps students to acquire new words on their own. Students should develop a system for learning these new words. Such a system should include the following steps:

Look at the word.

Pronounce the word aloud and say it several times.

Write down the word and think of a synonym or brief definition for it.

Use the word in a conversation during the course of the day.

Pronouncing and thinking about the meaning of a new word may require assistance from the teacher, teacher's aide, or even a classmate. A dictionary or thesaurus may also be useful in learning the meaning of a word. In any case, a systematic approach to learning vocabulary is crucial for developing independent readers.

The Vocabulary File

A vocabulary file is a very effective tool for increasing children's vocabulary. Teachers should create—and maintain—student interest in this activity by varying the exercises that are related to it. The file should include only those words encountered in reading and listening activities. Students could maintain their own word files as well. Figure 5.7 is an example of a word card from a vocabulary file that is kept by a teacher.

Evaluate
Teachers should continually evaluate the status of words in the file if vocabulary instruction is to be effective. Evaluation is a serious matter that must be planned carefully. Students may test each other in pairs or they may construct crossword puzzles from their own word files for other classmates to

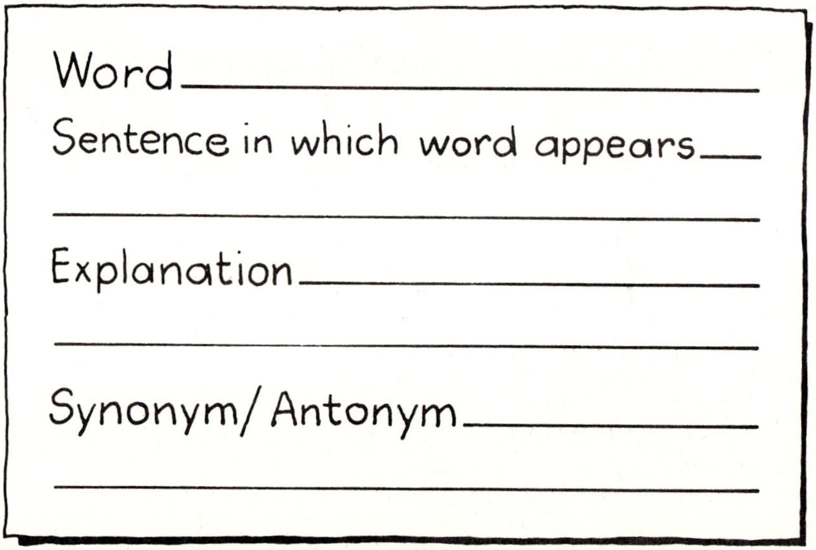

Word_____

Sentence in which word appears____

_____

Explanation_____

_____

Synonym/Antonym_____

_____

Figure 5.7   A sample word card for a vocabulary file.

complete. The teacher may evaluate the file by asking students to build sentences using these words, or by asking students to place their words in general categories that are specified. Words may also be taken from the files and used for vocabulary games. Teachers should be creative in devising activities that evaluate the status of words in vocabulary files.

Extensive reading does not necessarily expand vocabulary, but it does have the potential for aiding vocabulary development because new words are continually encountered. Thus teachers should encourage reading—both in class and at home. Students may be motivated to do outside reading that is related to their personal interests.

Real and vicarious experience

The importance of both real and vicarious experience in developing student understanding of words cannot be underestimated. Games, exercises, worksheets, and reading assignments are important ways to develop vocabulary, but they are not as valuable as field trips to such places as museums, concerts, farms, stores, and special exhibits. For example, a field trip to a local historical or science museum may be more instructive to students than a particular assignment in a history or science textbook.

Media

Teachers should also make use of television, films, photographs, radio programs, charts, maps, models, dramatizations, and resource speakers. These media provide vicarious experiences in the classroom; they provide invaluable opportunities for introducing and expanding vocabulary.

Children should be familiar with a variety of word definitions because this will increase comprehension. Johnson and Pearson (1978) suggest the following seven ways in which words can be defined.

> *Usage.* Ask a student to define a word by using it in a sentence. (Example: *steep*—Mary had a difficult time climbing the steep hill.)
>
> *Synonym.* Have the student define a word by identifying another word that has a similar meaning. Example: red—crimson.)
>
> *Antonym.* Identify a word whose meaning is the opposite of the given word. (Example: hard—soft.)
>
> *Classification.* Suggest a general category that includes the given word. (Example: *brunch*—Brunch is a meal.)
>
> *A visual match.* Provide a picture to illustrate the word. (Example: *lake*—A photograph of sailboats on Lake Erie.)
>
> *Comparison.* Compare the word to another word that is close in meaning but is not a synonym. (Example: *mountain*—A mountain is a very large hill.)

Enriching Background Knowledge (Schemata)

Researchers have found that presenting background information related to the text topic prior to reading helps readers learn from the text (Hayes and Tierney, 1982). The following teaching strategies help children develop schemata.

1. Read frequently to students; encourage them to develop schemata that will help them comprehend the material. The selections read in class should represent a wide variety of literature and nonfiction.
2. Encourage children to anticipate ideas and to predict the incidents they expect to find in a selection.
3. Encourage children to develop a purpose or purposes for reading.
4. Analogy is helpful in enriching background. Analogy is a method of comparing sets of information that are similar enough to transfer attributes from one set of information to another (Tierney and Cunningham, 1984). For instance, children who know about horses can use this information to help them learn about zebras when they compare horses and zebras. This approach is particularly useful when expanding background knowledge in the content areas.
5. "Advance organizers" or "previews" are helpful in building the prior knowledge necessary for comprehension (Graves, Cooks, and LaBerge, 1983; Lawton and Wanska, 1979; Ausubel and Fitzgerald, 1962). Previews or advance organizers prepare readers to gain information from reading that they could not have otherwise gained (Bransford, 1979). Advance organizers should identify the key ideas in a reading selection, and should be structured to bridge the gap between existing knowledge and new knowledge. For example, a preview for *Goldilocks and the Three Bears* might look like the following:

Goldilocks has a misadventure that involves Mother Bear, Father Bear, and Baby Bear. She invades their home and inspects their chairs, food, and beds. The bears find her asleep in their home and awaken her; then Goldilocks flees.

Activating Schemata

If readers have the necessary background knowledge to comprehend, teachers should activate that knowledge, which will expedite comprehension. **Activating schemata** involves recalling existing schemata that are related to a specific subject, and relating these schemata to the content being read. When the appropriate schemata are activated, students are better able to anticipate the author's ideas and information. Readers do not automatically use schemata to increase understanding; therefore, teachers must use a variety of activities to encourage students to activate appropriate schemata (Rowe and Raeford, 1987).

Focus attention

Schemata can be activated and attention focused through semantic maps and advance organizers, as well as through the following activities.

Brainstorming (free association) of words and phrases related to the topic.

Preview guides. These are statements or questions related to the major concepts that the teachers wishes students to understand and remember after reading the selection. The students' responses show what information they already know about the topic, which enables them to comprehend new information in the reading selection. After reading the selection, students check the accuracy of their responses to the preview guide questions.

Table 5.1 shows a preview guide that is based on a social studies textbook chapter addressing the Mediterranean countries.

Purpose questions can be used to build readers' anticipation of the author's ideas, focus their attention, and lead them to read actively. Purpose questions indicate the important ideas in a selection; they give students a structure for organizing content during reading. They can relate the important ideas indicated by the purpose questions to the message of a selection.

Initially, purpose questions are generated by the teacher; however, as students mature into reading, they should learn to generate questions to guide their own comprehension. Student generation of questions is discussed more fully in Chapter 6.

Broad questions   Purpose questions should be broad enough to guide readers through an entire selection. If the questions are too specific, students might read only until they have found ideas to answer the questions. Teachers may formulate two or three purpose questions for a selection.

A good source of purpose questions is the list of questions that many textbooks provide at the end of each chapter. Reading these questions before reading the selection gives students a sense of the important ideas. Another source of purpose questions is a textbook's chapter titles and subheadings. These headings point out the important ideas in a chapter; students can turn these ideas into questions, thus generating purpose questions to answer as they read. Finally, students may read the first paragraph of a selection and then formulate questions that are based on the information provided in the paragraph.

Table 5.1

Directions: Before you read this chapter, put an x in the *yes* or *no* column to show what you believe is true. After reading the chapter, check your answers to see if they are correct.

YES	NO	
		Spain, Andorra, and Portugal are located on the Iberian Peninsula.
		Greece is located on the Balkan Peninsula.
		Tourism is not important in the Mediterranean countries.
		Malta and Cyprus are independent nations.
		Vatican City is governed by the Italian government.
		Agriculture is unimportant to the Mediterranean countries.

Schemata for Text Structure

Authors use specific structures to organize the ideas presented in a reading selection. Structure refers to the ways ideas in a text are interrelated to convey a message to a reader. Some of the ideas in the text are of central importance to the author's message, while others are of less importance. Thus, text structure specifies the logical connections among ideas, as well as the subordination of some ideas to others (Meyer and Rice, 1984). Readers who identify and attend to structure, improve their comprehension (Richgels, McGee, Lomax, and Sheard, 1987; Fitzgerald and Spiegel, 1983; Mandler and Johnson, 1977). Students who follow the author's organizational structure as an aid to comprehension, tend to perform better on recall, summarization, and other comprehension tasks (Shannon, 1986). Schemata for text structure enable children to anticipate the author's ideas, which enhances comprehension. On the other hand, material that is unstructured is more difficult for students to comprehend.

Story grammar and the elements of literature (plot, theme, characterization, setting, and style) structure fiction. Five structural patterns are most commonly found in expository content. These include time order (chronological), list structure, comparison-contrast, cause-effect, and problem-solution (Horowitz, 1985). However, analysis reveals that these patterns are often combined.

Story Grammar

A story grammar is a structure that describes the parts of a well-formed story. It is also a schema, which permits readers to anticipate the elements of the story. Readers who have a sense of the ways stories are structured, understand and remember stories better. Children acquire a sense of story when well-formed stories are read to them, and when they have opportunities to read stories that have a well-developed story grammar.

Direct Instruction

Children can also learn story structure from direct instruction. One of the easiest story grammars to teach children is Mandler and Johnson's (1977). According to their grammar, a well-formed story should have these elements:

setting: this identifies who, where, and when;

beginning: the problem or conflict confronting the hero-protagonist;

reaction: the hero's response to the problem or conflict, which usually is manifested in what the hero says or thinks;

attempt: the hero attempts to solve the problem or conflict;

outcome: the hero succeeds or fails in solving the problem or conflict;

ending: the story wrapup.

This story grammar has been applied to *The Whipping Boy* by Sid Fleischman in the following example.

setting: Jemmy, the whipping boy, and Prince Brat lived in a far-away kingdom.

beginning: Prince Brat and Jemmy are kidnapped.

reaction: Jemmy is not overly concerned about the kidnapping, and hopes that he may escape living in the palace as a whipping boy.

goal: Jemmy believes he must protect the prince.

attempts:
1. Jemmy pretends they are ordinary youngsters, but the prince insists on telling the kidnappers that he is the prince.
2. Jemmy pretends that he is the prince, so the kidnappers will think the prince is the whipping boy, and will allow him to carry the ransom note to the king.
3. Jemmy escapes the kidnappers and the prince follows him, but they are recaptured.
4. Bear scares the kidnappers away.
5. Jemmy and the prince hide in the sewers. The kidnappers find them, but are chased off by rats.

outcome: The prince turns Jemmy in for the reward, so both are returned to the palace. The prince explained that Jemmy saved his life.

ending: The prince promises to behave so Jemmy will not be whipped.

Teaching a story grammar takes several lessons according to Spiegel (1985). She recommends a 1 hour introductory lesson, with 15–30 minute lessons on subsequent days; each of these lessons concentrates on one story part and reviews previously learned parts. In teaching story grammar, focus on the parts of the story rather than on spelling or grammar; children cannot concentrate on too many aspects at once. An introductory lesson follows (Speigel, 1985).

1. Prepare a chart of a well-formed story.
2. Read the story aloud from the chart.
3. Identify the specific story parts on the chart. A second chart, which shows the story parts, should be prepared for the students' reference. Read through the chart aloud to identify story parts.
4. Ask the children to help write a good story. Ask them to identify a setting, beginning, reaction, goal, attempt, outcome, and ending. Continue until children have formed a story and ask various students to read the story aloud.
5. Give the children story frames to practice writing individual stories. The following is an example of a story frame. It can be used to comprehend while reading, and to summarize after reading. Some children need to work example items.

(Who) Lived *(Where)* *(When)*. *(Character's Name)* had a terrible problem. This prob-

lem was *(Beginning)* and *(The Character Reacted)*. I want to *(Goal)*. So *(Attempt)*. And

(Outcome). And *(End)*.

Comprehending Expository Text

Identifying and using the author's organizational pattern are important aspects of comprehending. In fact, Bartlett (1978) found that students who were *taught* to use structure, recalled almost twice as much information from their reading assignments.

Five expository patterns

As stated earlier, five structural patterns are predominant in expository text. These patterns represent ways of organizing the main ideas and supporting details that comprise informational materials. Expository materials are discussed in Chapter 6. The following section describes expository patterns:

> *time order* (chronological): puts facts and/or events into a sequence;
>
> *list structure:* enumerates items like facts, events, and ideas;
>
> *comparison and contrast:* identifies likenesses and differences among facts, events, ideas, or people;
>
> *cause and effect:* shows how an event or happening occurs, due to another factor or factors;
>
> *problem-solution:* a question is stated and answered.

Teaching Structural Patterns in Exposition

Students develop a sense of the structure of exposition when they have many opportunities to hear their teacher read well-written exposition, or when they read well-written exposition. Therefore, teachers should frequently select informational materials, as well as fiction and poetry, when they read to students.

Direct instruction will help students learn the structural patterns of exposition. As always, when directly teaching a concept to students, include many examples of the concept, and allow many opportunities for students to practice applying their knowledge. In introducing the patterns, you may follow these guidelines.

1. Read a selection aloud that reflects one of the patterns. Ask children to listen to identify the pattern. You may write the text on charts, so the students can follow the text as you read.
2. Ask children to identify the specific characteristics of the pattern, such as the causes in cause-effect text.
3. Pattern guides, viewed on overhead screens, can be transferred to transparencies, charts, or chalkboard. Students can complete the guides as they listen or read the various structural patterns. (See Figure 5.8.)

Main Ideas and Details

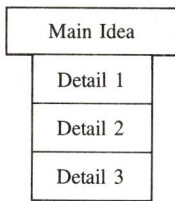

Main Idea
Detail 1
Detail 2
Detail 3

Cause and Effect

Cause	Effect
1.	1.
2.	2.
3.	3.

Problem Solution

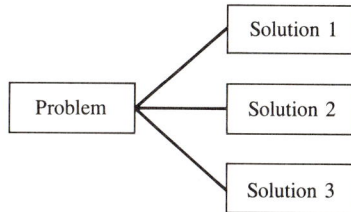

Problem → Solution 1 / Solution 2 / Solution 3

Compare–Contrast

Points of Comparison	Cat	Dog	Horse	Cow
Legs	4	4	4	4
Sound	meow	bark	neigh	moo
Tail				
Food				
Work				

Figure 5.8 Pattern guides

4. Read several selections and have students identify the ones that represent the pattern they are discussing.

Using Pattern Guides

Pattern guides are often completed during reading, which helps students learn to identify structural patterns. They learn to habitually look for structure in text, and to connect text information to the structure. Pattern guides alert students to the relationships in the text, and help students sort important ideas from unimportant ideas.

When introducing pattern guides, use the steps identified for teaching the various expository patterns.

Through discussion and questioning, teachers can encourage students to use what they know about structure to predict subsequent ideas and organization. Identifying the words that signal the various patterns of organization helps students make predictions about text.

SUMMARY

The following list summarizes the key points of this chapter.

1. Reading comprehension is the essence of the reading process. To comprehend, readers must understand written language, think about written content, and evaluate that content. Prediction plays an important role in reading. Competent readers are able to predict the author's language, ideas, and structure of the selection.
2. Readers' prior knowledge affects their understanding. The text is the author's blueprint for communicating ideas; however, he or she cannot tell readers everything they need to know. Readers follow the author's blueprint and use their experience to fill in the missing pieces.
3. Students need opportunities to practice applying comprehension strategies, since the more they process text, the more they will remember and understand.
4. Predictive abilities enable readers to anticipate the author's language, organization, and ideas. When readers make such speculations, they continue to read in order to confirm their predictions. Instruction should be directed toward developing this ability.
5. The reasons why students read, influence their understanding.
6. A variety of real and vicarious experiences will provide students with the experiential background necessary to comprehend a variety of written content materials. Experience can be developed through field trips, reading, movies, and television. Students should be encouraged to discuss their experiences as well as the new words that are associated with those experiences. Teachers should plan instruction that helps students relate their experiences to written content.
7. A large vocabulary is an enormous aid to comprehension. Therefore, teachers should plan systematic instruction to introduce vocabulary words. Both substantive words and connectives should be included in this instruction. One of the most important factors in developing vocabulary is the desire to know new words; thus, motivation to learn words should be one concern of instruction. Conceptual development and vocabulary are closely related, and many of the words in students' vocabularies represent concepts. To understand written content, children must relate words they read to their conceptual system.
8. Schemata are collections of ideas and concepts drawn from readers' experiences. Schemata enable us to structure our reading and our experiences.
9. Schemata supply readers with the information they need in order to understand.
10. Structural schemata include patterns for organizing both fiction (story grammar) and nonfiction. Students who can identify these schemata, can use them to structure their understanding.

SELF-TEST

Check your knowledge of the information presented in this chapter. The answer key is located in Appendix C.

1. What is the primary criterion for success in reading?
   a. the ability to decode words
   b. the extent of one's understanding of the material
   c. the number of pages read
   d. the number of questions the teacher asks

2. What aspects of comprehension are stressed by Carroll?
   a. decoding and word recognition
   b. art and music
   c. language and cognition
   d. attention and experience

3. What were the major components of reading comprehension that were identified by Davis?
   a. knowledge of word meaning
   b. sight words, phonics, structural analysis, context, and dictionary skills
   c. words, sentences, paragraphs, and selections
   d. synonyms, acronyms, and homonyms

4. How is structure related to reading comprehension?
   a. it is a new approach to vocabulary development
   b. it is a natural phenomenon
   c. it provides a framework for understanding and remembering content
   d. it is not related

5. What is a story grammar?
   a. a schema for a story
   b. it describes the parts of a story
   c. both a and b
   d. neither a nor b

6. How is teaching a process different from teaching a product?
   a. processes are easier to teach
   b. teaching a process is concerned with student output
   c. process-oriented instruction is concerned with improving the aspects of the process rather than the outward manifestation of reading
   d. processes are easier to observe than products

7. Why is reading comprehension considered a constructive process?
   a. the reader uses his or her experiences with data derived from the text to understand
   b. the reader must construct sentences in order to comprehend
   c. because it involves graphemes and phonemes
   d all of the above

8. What are the components of a story grammar?
   a. style, character, illustrations, and introduction
   b. setting, beginning, reaction, attempts, outcome, and ending
   c. beginning, middle, and end
   d. none of the above

9. What should teachers' questions do?
   a. activate background experience
   b. create a framework for understanding and remembering text
   c. ask children to support and explain their answers
   d. all of the above

10. What are the characteristics of poorly chosen questions?
    a. they emphasize insignificant details
    b. they distract attention from important ideas
    c. both a and b
    d. neither a nor b

11. What is *metacognition?*
    a. large thinking
    b. acting rather than thinking
    c. acting without thought
    d. monitoring one's thinking

12. What is the purpose of prereading comprehension instruction?
    a. to insure that students read every word in the text
    b. to create a bridge between the reader and the text
    c. to develop a faster reading rate
    d. to eliminate the use of schemata

13. What are schemata?
    a. experiences
    b. concepts
    c. expectations
    d. all of the above

14. What two factors are of paramount importance in reading comprehension, according to a synthesis of the data by Davis?
    a. knowledge of word meanings and reasoning with verbal concepts
    b. word recognition and vocabulary
    c. context clues and phonics
    d. structural analysis and sight words

15. What do words label?
    a. language arts
    b. concepts
    c. sounds
    d. oral reading

16. Which of the following statements describes the term concept?
    a. categories
    b. filing system
    c. based on previous experience
    d. all of the above

17. Which of the concepts included in a reading selection should be developed through instruction?
    a. all of them
    b. only those concepts necessary for comprehension
    c. all concepts that can be contrasted and compared
    d. only those concepts required for word recognition

18. What factors influence vocabulary development?
    a. height, weight, and hair color
    b. homonyms, synonyms, and acronyms
    c. experience, age, sex, socioeconomic status, education, and geography
    d. the amount of time spent talking

19. What approach is most effective for developing the range of vocabulary?
    a. direct instruction
    b. workbooks
    c. practicing correct pronunciation
    d. discourse analysis

20. What vocabulary strategy is based on making a list of words that the child likes to say?
    a. sensitivity to words
    b. word derivations
    c. etymology
    d. visualization

21. Which of the following contribute to children's ability to define words?
    a. writing
    b. synonym, antonym, classification, and example
    c. both a and b
    d. neither a nor b

22. What does connotative meaning refer to?
    a. meaning as defined by television
    b. meaning as defined by the teacher
    c. dictionary definition
    d. emotional reactions to a word

23. Why are thinking skills necessary for understanding reading content?
    a. because comprehension is essentially thinking
    b. because it is impossible to teach thinking skills
    c. both a and b
    d. neither a nor b

24. How can teachers facilitate the development of thinking skills in their students?
    a. by telling students to think every 15 minutes
    b. through questioning strategies
    c. by providing regular rest periods
    d. by cognitive induction

25. Is the question "Why do you think that?" a good one?
    a. it doesn't have an answer
    b. it avoids overstimulation
    c. it encourages a student to support and elaborate on the answer
    d. it is a cognitive-derivative question

26. What is the cognitive level of the question "Who is the main character in this story?"
    a. critical level
    b. literal level
    c. creative level
    d. interpretive level

27. What is interpretive thinking?
    a. this level of thinking is concerned with meanings not directly stated in the content
    b. this level of thinking is concerned with evaluation

     c. this level of thinking is concerned with meanings directly stated in the content
     d. this level of thinking is concerned with arriving at a new perspective of the content

THOUGHT QUESTIONS

1. Identify the various types of schemata readers use to comprehend and think of examples of each type.
2. How are words and intelligence related? Can students increase their intelligence by studying word meanings?
3. How is vocabulary related to experience?
4. What are some of the activities that teachers can use to increase and enrich schemata?
5. How do readers use schemata to comprehend?
6. How is a story map related to questioning?
7. How is exposition structured?
8. What is metacognition? How is it related to comprehension?

ENRICHMENT ACTIVITIES

1. Keep a personal vocabulary file for a semester or a quarter.
2. Read a lesson plan in a teacher's manual for a basal reader, and identify the levels of questioning that are used in the lesson.
3. Select a story in a basal reader and develop three questions at each level of thinking.
4. Analyze a chapter of a social studies textbook; determine whether the content is organized in a way that helps the reader comprehend the material.
5. Develop a semantic network for a concept.
6. Examine a basal reader story and identify the schemata that readers would need to comprehend the story.
7. Create a story map for a children's trade book; then create a map of a story in a basal reader. Do they both have a complete story grammar?
8. Develop a monologue that models inferencing for elementary students.
9. Create a vocabulary activity that could be used in an elementary classroom.

RELATED READINGS

Bagley, M. and K. Hess (1982). *200 Ways of Using Imagery in the Classroom,* Woodcliff Lake, NJ: New Dimensions in the 80's.

Baumann, J. (Ed). (1986). *Teaching Main Idea Comprehension,* Newark, DE: International Reading Association.

Bromley, K., and L. McKeveny (February 1986). "Precis Writing: Suggestions for Instruction in Summarizing," *Journal of Reading,* Vol. 29, 5, pp. 392–395.

DeMille, R. (1967). *Put Your Mother on the Ceiling,* New York: Penguin Books.

Fredericks, A. (October 1986). "Mental Imagery Activities to Improve Comprehension," *The Reading Teacher,* Vol. 40, 1, pp. 78–87.

Gambrell, L., B. Kapinus, R. Wilson (April 1987). "Using Mental Imagery and Summarization to Achieve Independence in Comprehension," *Journal of Reading,* Vol. 30, 7, pp. 638–642.

Gillett, J. and J. Kita (February 1979). "Words, Kids and Categories," *The Reading Teacher,* Vol. 32, pp. 538–542.

Hahn, A. (October 1985). "Teaching Remedial Students to be Strategic Readers and Better Comprehenders," *The Reading Teacher,* Vol. 39, 1, pp. 72–80.

Hansen, J. (1981). "The Effects of Inference Training and Practice on Young Children's Comprehension," *Reading Research Quarterly,* Vol. 16, pp. 391–416.

Heimlich, J. and S. Pitttelman (1986). *Semantic Mapping: Classroom Applications,* Newark, DE: International Reading Association.

Hirsch, E. D., Jr. (1987). *Cultural Literacy,* Boston: Houghton Mifflin.

Irwin, J. (Ed.) (1986). *Understanding and Teaching Cohesion Comprehension,* Newark, DE: International Reading Association.

Jensen, J. (Ed.) (1984). *Composing and Comprehending,* Urbana, IL: National Conference on Research in English.

Manzo, A. and A. Legenza (April 1975). "Inquiry Training for Kindergarten Children," *Educational Leadership,* pp. 479–483.

Manzo, A. (November 1969). "The ReQuest Procedure," *Journal of Reading,* Vol. 13, pp. 123–126.

McNeil, J. (1987). *Reading Comprehension,* Glenview, IL: Scott Foresman and Company.

Presseisen, B. (1986). *Thinking Skills: Research and Practice,* Washington DC: National Education Association.

Silvers, P. (March 1986). "Process Writing and the Connection to Reading," *The Reading Teacher* Vol. 39, 7, pp. 684–689.

Shoop, M. (March 1986). "InQuest: A Listening and Reading Comprehension Strategy," *The Reading Teacher,* Vol. 39, 7, pp. 670–683.

Sorenson, N. (October 1985). "Basal Reading Vocabulary Instruction: A Critique and Suggestions," *The Reading Teacher,* Vol. 39, pp. 80–89.

Spiegel, D. and J. Fitzgerald (March 1986). "Improving Reading Comprehension through Instruction About Story Parts," *The Reading Teacher* Vol. 39, 7, pp. 676–683.

Smith, S. (January 1985). "Comprehension and Comprehension Monitoring by Experienced Readers," *Journal of Reading,* Vol. 28, 4, pp. 292–300.

REFERENCES

Allen, J. (Fall 1985). "Inferential Comprehension: The Effects of Text Source, Decoding Ability, and Mode," *Reading Research Quarterly,* Vol. 29, pp. 603–615.

Anderson, R. and P. Freebody (1981). "Vocabulary Knowledge," in *Comprehension and Teaching: Research Review,* J. Guthrie (Ed.), Newark, DE: International Reading Association.

Anderson, R., E. Hiebert, J. Scott, and I. Wilkinson (1985). "Becoming a Nation of

Readers: The Report of the Commission on Reading," Urbana, IL: The Center for the Study of Reading.

Anderson, R. and P. D. Pearson (1984). "A Schema Theoretic View of the Reading Processes in Reading Comprehension," in *Handbook of Reading Research,* P. D. Pearson (Ed.), New York: Longman, pp. 255–291.

Baumann, J. and M. Schmitt (March 1986). "The What, Why, How, and When of Comprehension Instruction," *The Reading Teacher,* Vol. 39, pp. 640–647.

Beck, I. (1984). "Developing Comprehension: The Impact of The Directed Reading Lesson," in *Learning to Read in American Schools: Basal Readers and Content Texts,* R. Anderson, J. Osborn, and R. Tierney (Eds.), Hillsdale, NJ: Lawrence Erlbaum.

Beck, I., M. McKeown, E. McCaslin, and A. Burkes (1979). *Instructional Dimensions that May Affect Reading Comprehension,* Pittsburgh: University of Pittsburgh, Language Research and Development Center.

Beck, I., M. Perfetti, and M. McKeown (1982). "The Effects of Long-Term Vocabulary Instruction on Lexical Access and Reading Comprehension," *Journal of Educational Psychology,* Vol. 74, pp. 506–521.

Beers, T. (Summer 1987). "Commentary: Schema-Theoretic Models of Reading; Humanizing the Machine," *Reading Research Quarterly,* Vol. 22, pp. 369–379.

Berkowitz, S. (Spring 1986). "Effects of Instruction in Text Organization on Sixth-Grade Students' Memory for Expository Reading," *Reading Research Quarterly,* Vol. 21, pp. 161–178.

Bransford, J. (1979). *Human Cognition: Learning, Understanding and Remembering,* Belmont, CA: Wadsworth.

Carroll, J. (1985). "The Nature of the Reading Process," in *Theoretical Models and Processes of Reading,* 3d ed., H. Singer and R. Ruddell (Eds.), Newark, DE: International Reading Association.

Collins, A., J. Brown, and K. Larking (1980). "Inferences in Text Understanding," in *Theoretical Issues in Reading Comprehension,* R. Spiro, B. Bruce, and W. Brewer (Eds.), Hillsdale, NJ: Erlbaum.

Dewitz, P., E. Carr, and J. Patberg (Winter 1987). "Effects of Inference Training on Comprehension and Comprehension Monitoring," *Reading Research Quarterly,* Vol. 22, pp. 99–121.

Duffy, G., L. Roehler, and J. Mason (1984). *Comprehension Instruction,* New York: Longman.

Durkin, D. (1981). "Reading Comprehension in Five Basal Reader Series," *Reading Research Quarterly,* Vol. 16, pp. 481–533.

Durkin, D. (1978–1979). "What Classroom Observations Reveal About Reading Comprehension," *Reading Research Quarterly,* Vol. 14, pp. 481–533.

Ericsson, K. and H. Simon (1980). "Verbal Reports as Data," *Psychological Review,* Vol. 87, pp. 215–251.

Escondido School District (1979). *Mind's Eye,* Escondido, CA: Board of Education.

Fitzgerald, J. and D. Spiegel (1983). "Enhancing Children's Reading Comprehension Through Instruction in Narrative Structure," *Journal of Reading Behavior,* Vol. 15, pp. 1–17.

Flavell, J. (1976). "Metacognitive Aspects of Problem Solving," in *The Nature of Intelligence,* L. Resnick (Ed.), Hillsdale, NJ: Erlbaum, pp. 231–235.

Freebody, P. and R. Anderson (Spring 1983). "Effects of Vocabulary Difficulty, Text Cohesion, and Schema Availability on Reading Comprehension," *Reading Research Quarterly,* Vol. 18, pp. 277–294.

Feuerstein, R. and M. Hoffman (1985). "The Importance of Mediated Learning for the Child," *Human Intelligence International Newsletter,* Vol. 6, pp. 1–10.

Gillet, J. and J. Kita (February 1979). "Words, Kids and Categories," *The Reading Teacher,* Vol. 32, pp. 538–542.

Gordon, C. and P. D. Pearson (1983). "Effects of Instruction on Metacomprehension and Inferencing on Students Comprehension Abilities," Technical Report No. 269. Urbana, IL: Center for the Study of Reading.

Graves, M., C. Cook, and M. La Berge (1983). "Effects of Previewing Difficult Short Stories on Low Ability Junior High School Students' Comprehension, Recall, and Attitudes," *Reading Research Quarterly,* Vol. 18, pp. 262–276.

Green, G. (1984). "Some Remarks on How Words Mean," Technical Report No. 307, Urbana, IL: Center for the Study of Reading.

Hansen, J. (1981). "The Effects of Inference Training and Practice on Young Children's Comprehension," *Reading Research Quarterly,* Vol. 16, pp. 391–416.

Hayes, D. and R. Tierney (1982). "Developing Readers Knowledge Through Analogy," *Reading Research Quarterly,* Vol. 17, pp. 256–280.

Heiman, M. (1986). *Critical Thinking Skills,* Washington, DC: National Education Association.

Heimlich, J. and S. Pittelman (1986). *Semantic Mapping: Classroom Applications,* Newark, DE: International Reading Association.

Heller, M. (February 1986). "How Do You Know What You Know? Metacognitive Modeling in the Content Areas," *Journal of Reading,* Vol. 29, pp. 415–422.

Hirsch, E. D., Jr. (1987). *Cultural Literacy,* Boston: Houghton Mifflin.

Horowitz, R. (February 1985). "Text Patterns: Part I." *Journal of Reading,* Vol. 28, pp. 448–454.

Johnson, P. (1984). "Background Knowledge and Reading Comprehension Test Bias," *Reading Research Quarterly,* Vol. 19, pp. 219–239.

Johnston, P. and P. D. Pearson (1982). "Prior Knowledge, Connectivity, and the Assessment of Reading Comprehension," Technical Report No. 245, Urbana, IL: Center for the Study of Reading.

Johnson, D. and P. D. Pearson (1978). *Teaching Reading Vocabulary,* New York: Holt, Rinehart and Winston.

Kameenui, E., D. Carnine, and R. Freschi (1982). "Effects of Text Construction and Instructional Procedures for Teaching Word Meanings on Comprehension and Recall," *Reading Research Quarterly,* Vol. 17, pp. 367–388.

Langer, J. (Summer 1984). "Examining Background Knowledge and Text Comprehension," *Reading Research Quarterly,* Vol. 29, pp. 468–481.

Lawton, J. and S. Wanska (Summer 1979). "The Effects of Different Types of Advance Organizers on Classification Learning," *American Educational Research Journal,* Vol. 16, pp. 223–339.

Olshavsky, J. (1977). "Reading as Problem Solving: An Investigation of Strategies," *Reading Research Quarterly,* Vol. 12, pp. 654–674.

Mandler, J. and N. Johnson (1977). "Remembrance of Things Passed: Story Structure and Recall," *Cognitive Psychology,* Vol. 9, pp. 111–151.

McKim, R. (1980). *Experiences in Visual Thinking,* 2nd ed., Monterey, CA: Brooks/Cole.

McNeil, J. (1987). *Reading Comprehension,* Glenview, IL: Scott, Foresman and Company.

Meyer, B. (1981). "Basic Research on Prose Comprehension: A Critical Review," in *Comprehension and the Competent Reader: Inter-Specialty Perspectives,* D. F. Fisher and C.W. Peters (Eds.), New York: Praeger.

Meyer, B. and G. E. Rice (1984). "The Structure of Text," in *Handbook of Reading Research*, P. D. Pearson (Ed.), New York: Longman.

Meyer, F. (1982). "Reading Research and the Composition: Teacher: The Importance of Plans," *College Composition and Communications*, Vol. 33, pp. 37–49.

Patching, W., E. Kameenui, D. Carnine, R. Gersten, and G. Colvin (Summer, 1983). "Direct Instruction in Critical Reading Skills," *Reading Research Quarterly*, Vol. 18, pp. 406–418.

Potter, R. and C. Hannemann (March 1977). "Conscious Comprehension: Reality Reading Through Artifacts," *The Reading Teacher*, Vol. 30, pp. 644–668.

Presseisen, B. (1986). *Thinking Skills: Research and Practice.* Washington DC: National Education Association.

Pressey, G. (1976). "Mental Imagery Helps Eight-Year Olds Remember What They Read," *Journal of Educational Psychology*, Vol. 68, pp. 355–359.

Rasco, R., R. Tennyson, and R. Boutwell. (1975). "Imagery Instructions and Drawings in Learning Prose," *Journal of Educational Psychology*, Vol. 67, pp. 188–192.

Resnick, L. (1985). *Education and Learning to Think*, Pittsburgh: Learning Research and Development Center, University of Pittsburgh.

Richgels, D., L. McGee, R. Lomax, and C. Sheard (Spring 1987). "Awareness of Text Structures: Effects on Recall of Expository Text," *Reading Research Quarterly*, Vol. XXII, 2, 177–196.

Roe, B., B. Stoodt, and P. Burns (1987). *Secondary School Reading Instruction*, Boston: Houghton Mifflin.

Rohwer, W. and R. Matz. (1975). "Improving Aural Comprehension in White and Black Children: Picture Versus Print," *Journal of Educational Psychology*, Vol. 67, pp. 188–192.

Rosenshine, B. (1980). "Skill Hierarchies in Reading Comprehension," in *Theoretical Issues in Reading Comprehension*, R. Spiro, B. Bruce, and W. Brewer (Eds.), Hillsdale, NJ: Lawrence Erlbaum, pp. 535–554.

Rowe, D., and L. Rayford (Spring 1987). "Activating Background Knowledge in Reading Comprehension Assessment," *Reading Research Quarterly*, Vol. 22, pp. 160–176.

Sadoski, M. (Fall 1985). "Commentary: The Natural Use of Imagery in Story Comprehension and Recall: Replication and Extension," *Reading Research Quarterly*, Vol. 20, pp. 658–687.

Savell, J., P. Twohig, and D. Rachford (Winter 1986). "Empirical Status of Feuerstein's Instrumental Enrichment (FIE) Technique as a Method of Teaching Thinking Skills," *Review of Educational Research*, Vol. 45, pp. 346–401.

Shannon, D. (February 1986). "Use of Top-Level Structure in Expository Text: An Open Letter to a High School Teacher," *Journal of Reading*, Vol. 28, pp. 426–431.

Singer, H. (May 1978). "Active Comprehension: From Answering to Asking Questions," *The Reading Teacher*, Vol. 31, pp. 901–907.

Smith, C. (May 1978). "Evaluating Answers to Comprehension Questions," *The Reading Teacher*, Vol. 31, pp. 896–900.

Smith, F. (1978). *Understanding Reading*, 2nd ed., New York: Holt, Rinehart and Winston.

Sorenson, N. (October 1985). "Basal Reading Vocabulary Instruction: A Critique and Suggestions," *The Reading Teacher*, Vol. 39, pp. 80–89.

Spiegel, D. (October/November 1985). "A Story Grammar Approach to Reading and Writing," *Reading Today*, Vol. 3, p. 13.

Stahl, S. and M. Fairbanks (Spring 1986). "The Effects of Vocabulary Instruction: A

Model-Based Meta-Analysis," *Review of Educational Research,* Vol. 56, pp. 72–110.

Tierney, R. and J. Cunningham (1984). "Research on Teaching Reading Comprehension," in *Handbook of Reading Research,* P. D. Pearson (Ed.), New York: Longman, pp. 631–655.

Tuinman, J. (February 1980). "The Schema Schemers," *Journal of Reading,* Vol. 23, pp. 414–419.

Vygotsky, L. (1962). *Thought and Language,* Cambridge, MA: MIT Press.

Wisendanger, K. and J. Wollenberg (May 1978). "Prequestioning Inhibits Third Graders Reading Comprehension," *The Reading Teacher,* Vol. 31, pp. 892–895.

CHAPTER 6

Extending Comprehension

OVERVIEW   To comprehend, one must understand written language. Words which are an important aspect of written language were discussed in Chapter 5, while sentences, paragraphs and longer units of discourse are addressed in this chapter.

This chapter also explores comprehension strategies that readers employ during and following reading. In addition it presents *universal* comprehension strategies, which address the prereading, reading, and postreading processes.

Among the during-reading comprehension strategies students can use are metacognitive strategies, which readers use to control their own thinking and understanding. These strategies guide readers to self-question and to consciously examine their own understanding of text. Elaboration, which is embellishment of text, contributes to during-reading comprehension. Among the elaboration strategies that readers use are visualizing, summarizing, framing, paraphrasing, and and text applications. This chapter introduces strategies for developing discussion and writing in elementary classrooms, which are integral parts of comprehension instruction. Among the universal reading comprehension strategies explored in this chapter are the Directed-Reading-Thinking-Activity and The ReQuest Procedure.

Key Vocabulary

As you read this chapter, check your understanding of these terms:

anaphora
cloze procedure
cohesion
composing
Directed-Reading-Thinking-Activity
(DRTA)
discussion

elaboration
metacognition
paraphrase
Reciprocal Questioning Procedure
(ReQuest)
visualizing

Focusing Questions

As you read this chapter, think about these questions.

1. How do during-reading strategies differ from prereading strategies?
2. Why is discussion such a powerful comprehension strategy?
3. How does elaboration function in reading comprehension?
4. Which aspects of reading comprehension are addressed in the DRTA?

READING COMPREHENSION DURING READING

As you learned in Chapter 5, readers use their schemata to predict the text; then they read to confirm these predictions. Proficient readers perform many mental operations to understand written language. These operations reflect the interaction between readers' minds and the text to enhance both understanding and remembering. Readers' schemata provide them with a structure for remembering and integrating new knowledge.

The ability to recognize words is important to comprehension, but knowing words is insufficient for understanding. Readers must be able to use their word knowledge to construct an author's intended meaning. Words, sentences, paragraphs, and longer units of discourse (articles, stories, and poems) function in complex, interactive ways in the comprehension process. Therefore, understanding these elements facilitates comprehension. The following example clarifies this relationship. Notice the complexity of mental operations, as well as the reader's use of background knowledge, thinking skills, and written language. These few simple words convey surprisingly complex thoughts (see Table 6.1).

The balance of this section explores written language and reading comprehension. Both the reader and the author need to understand how meaning is constructed from the author's language. Readers who have these understandings can comprehend better. Authors who understand ways of expressing meaning create more comprehensible written language.

Sentence Meaning

Words are organized into sentences to express ideas. Thus, sentences are a basic unit of communication. The reader must understand sentences in order to comprehend. Syntax (word order) and semantics (word meaning) establish relationships among ideas in English sentences. Syntax is important to word meaning.

The order of words in the English language is critical to meaning. A reader

Table 6.1

Text	Reader's thoughts
It's true that we don't know what we've got until we lose it.	"Hmm. 'What we've got' is a vague statement. It could be material things, health, or emotions like love or contentment. I wonder which meaning is correct. I will have to read further to get more information." (The reader inferred material possessions, health, and emotions.)
But it's also true that we often don't know what we have been missing until it arrives.	"This sentence does not elucidate the nature of 'what we've got'. It does seem to eliminate health, since we usually don't realize its value until it departs. Therefore, it seems that the writer is referring to either material possessions or emotions. (Notice that the reader uses cultural literacy to eliminate health, which was one of the things included in the vague statement, "what we've got.")

may, in fact, be able to derive information from even a nonsense sentence—such as *the gindar zacked stently*—provided that the sentence follows basic structural rules. In analyzing this sentence, *the* is clearly an article modifying the noun *gindar*. Words such as *the* provide information about other words in the sentence. *Gindar* would be the subject. *Zacked* is a verb, and the *ed* ending tells the reader that the action occurred in the past. *Stently* seems to suggest how the subject *zacked*. Thus, the reader is able to decipher the meaning of sentences through his or her implicit knowledge of sentence construction.

According to Kamm (1979), instruction in sentence comprehension should include the following: identifying detail, developing sensitivity to sentence organization and word order, and realizing that there may be a number of ways to convey a single meaning. Paraphrasing is a sentence comprehension strategy that helps students understand the various ways of expressing a single meaning.

Paraphrasing

Paraphrasing is restating information or ideas in readers' own words. The restatement must be equivalent to the text—in other words—readers are not free to alter the author's ideas. Paraphrasing may involve semantics or syntax. A *semantic paraphrase* involves the substitution of synonyms for words in the original sentence or paragraph. A *syntactic paraphrase* involves changing word order. The following paraphrase activities are based on sentences, although paragraphs can be paraphrased too. The goal of paraphrasing is to help students understand and remember important ideas; therefore, the most important aspect of paraphrasing is to paraphrase the main idea; paraphrasing details has little value.

Paraphrasing Activities

1. Ask children to generate synonyms for specified words in a sentence.

> Example: The *large*, red *automobile ran* into a tree.
> Possible answers: *large*—big, enormous, gigantic; *automobile*—vehicle, car; *ran*—crashed, smashed

2. Provide students with several sentences and ask them to make a new sentence that has the same meaning.

3. *Sentence matching.* Ask students to identify the sentence that has essentially the same meaning as a sentence that is given by the teacher.

> Example: *It was Mary who painted the house.*
> a. The house was not painted.
> b. Mary painted the house.
> c. Mary painted a gray house.

4. Point out to students that looking for the answers to specific questions can aid in understanding sentences. *Who, what, when, where,* and *why* are questions that can be addressed in most sentences. Ask students to answer these questions for sentences provided by the teacher.

> Example: *Linda will go to the beach for a vacation tomorrow.*
> Questions: *Who*—Linda
> *What*—will go
> *Where*—to the beach
> *When*—tomorrow
> *Why*—for a vacation

5. Elaboration and transformation exercises can also aid in sentence comprehension. These activities may make use of sentences from in-class reading selections.

> a. Have students elaborate sentences in as many ways as possible.
> Example: *Susan is eating candy.*
> Possible answers: *Susan is eating a piece of candy.*
> *Susan is eating a small piece of chocolate candy.*
> *Susan is slowly eating a small piece of chocolate candy.*
> b. Transform sentences in as many ways as possible.
> Example: *Susan ate a piece of candy.*
> Possible answers: *Is Susan eating a piece of candy?*
> *Susan is not eating a piece of candy.*
> *What is Susan eating?*

Sentence Combining

Sentence-combining activities significantly increase students' comprehension (Combs, 1977). Sentence combining involves putting two or three short sentences together to form a new sentence. For example:

Susan saw the big dog running. (sentence 1)

She saw him run down the street. (sentence 2)

Susan could see the big dog running down the street. (combined sentence)

When teaching sentence combining, provide example sentences and group practice. Basal readers and content textbooks are excellent sources of sentence-combining activities. In addition to combining sentences, advanced students may identify the shorter sentences that comprise a longer sentence. For example, the sentence *One year Cheryl had new moccasins that Grandpa had made* comprises the sentences *One year Cheryl had new moccasins* and *Grandpa made them.*

Sentence questions

Questioning is another strategy for increasing sentence comprehension. When using this strategy, teachers select a sentence from the basal reader, children's writing, or a content textbook and ask students to answer questions regarding *who, what, when, where, why,* and *how.* For example:

One year Cheryl had new moccasins that Grandpa had made.

What—moccasins

Why—not stated in this sentence (we might infer that the moccasins were a birthday or Christmas present)

When—one year

Where—not stated in this sentence

Who—Cheryl had moccasins
Grandpa made them

Structured comprehension

Structured Comprehension, a procedure developed by Cohn (1969), is a means of practicing sentence comprehension as well as encouraging reading and thinking on the part of students. The suggested steps for this procedure are listed below.

1. Teachers should select factual content that is somewhat above the average reading level for the individual student or class.
2. Have the student read the first sentence of the selection.
3. Students should begin by asking themselves the question *Do I know what this sentence means?* They should then ask the teacher (or a fellow classmate) as many questions as are necessary to fully comprehend the meaning of the sentence. The student may refer to the selection during the questioning process.
4. The teacher should ask questions that are related to the initial sentence; students should write down the answers to these questions. Questions should stress literal meaning and should be concerned with pronoun antecedents, the meaning of figurative language, and individual word meanings.
5. Students score their own papers.
6. Students continue through the selection, using this pattern.

ReQuest

The Reciprocal Questioning Procedure (ReQuest), developed by Manzo, improves reading comprehension and helps students develop questioning skills (Manzo, 1969). The basic steps in ReQuest are included in the following summary.

The student and teacher silently read the first sentence of the text. The student asks the teacher as many questions as possible about the sentence with the text closed (these questions should be modeled after the kind the teacher normally poses to the class). The teacher answers all of the student's questions, asking the student to restate any poorly stated questions. If the student does not fully understand an answer, the teacher should restate the answer to clarify the student's understanding. After all of the student's questions have been answered, the second sentence is read—and the teacher asks thought-provoking questions to insure comprehension. At this point, the teacher should include questions that are related to the student's previous responses. For instance, when discussing a story, the teacher might ask whether the answer to a previous question is true in the light of new information acquired from the next sentence.

The ReQuest procedure continues until the student can confidently answer the question, *What do you think is going to happen in the rest of this selection?* and *What have you read that causes you to make this prediction?* Then the student reads to the end of the selection to determine if the prediction was indeed accurate.

When introducing ReQuest the teacher may model the procedure with a student to help students understand what is expected. Then students may work in pairs using the procedure.

Cohesion

When sentences are related or linked to one another, this relationship is called **cohesion**. Cohesive sentences are easier to understand because each sentence helps readers understand the next sentence (Irwin, 1986). When sentences are cohesive, readers are better able to create a text structure in memory. Sentences are more difficult to understand and remember if they have separate entities. Halliday and Hansen (1976) have identified five types of cohesion: reference, substitution, ellipsis, conjunction, and lexical cohesion, which are shown in Table 6.2.

ACTIVITIES FOR UNDERSTANDING SENTENCE RELATIONSHIPS

1. Identify the purpose of each sentence in the following paragraph.

Courage is the word that refers to the sense of bravery that may characterize a person who faces danger. But what word describes the actions of individuals who face a long and difficult struggle? To go out on one's own, to leave an old way of life and begin a new one, to learn to live by one's own wits and skill—all of these deserve the label of *courage.*

Possible answer: The first sentence defines the term *courage.* The second sentence is a question that the reader is asked to evaluate. The third sentence provides various examples of courage.

Table 6.2   TYPES OF SENTENCE COHESION

Type	Example
Reference (includes pronouns)	*Linda* went to the movie. *She* bought a box of popcorn.
Substitution (replacing one word or phrase within another)	Susan already *knows.* Everyone *does.* (Does substitutes for knows.)
Ellipsis (omission of a repeated word or phrase)	Would you like a *cake?* I have several. (Implied repetition.)
Conjunction (additive, adversative, causal, and temporal links)	I watered the lawn *before* the rain began.
Lexical (reiteration)	A peach is a *fruit.* All *fruits* contain seeds.
Lexical (collocation occurrences of words that regularly co-occur in the language)	The candy bar cost 50 *cents.* I had a *dollar.*

2. Ask students to write examples of different types of sentences.
3. Matching activities. Ask students to match sentences that contain related information, as in Figure 6.1.

Figurative Language

Understanding figurative language is important to reading comprehension. Figurative language may be expressed in sentences, paragraphs, or in entire selections, such as poetry. Figurative language is a picturesque, expressive, connotative use of language. Figurative language is used for vivid and interesting writing. It can also be utilized to influence readers' opinions—as in propaganda. Figurative language can sometimes express difficult ideas in concrete terms. The most common forms of figurative language are listed here:

Types of figurative language

A *metaphor* suggests a comparison of one item or idea with another that is dissimilar. The words *like* and *as* are not used in making this comparison. Example: *Mary is a peach.*

Figure 6.1

A *simile* is a comparison between two items or ideas that are dissimilar; however, the analogy suggests how the two are in fact alike. The words *like* and *as* are used in this comparison. Example: *The man walks like an elephant.*

A *personification* gives human characteristics to an animal or inanimate object. Example: *The cherry tree is wearing a lovely dress of blossoms.*

An *allusion* is an indirect reference to a person, place, or thing. Example: *That boy has a Cheshire cat grin.*

A *hyperbole* suggests extreme exaggeration. Example: *I am so tired that I may never get up again.*

A *euphemism* is an affectation used in order to appear agreeable or inoffensive. Example: A person who dies is said to have "passed away."

When teaching students to understand figurative language, they may illustrate the figurative expressions such as, *its raining cats and dogs.* They can also write explanations of figurative expressions. Titles of books like *Amelia Bedelia, The King Who Rained,* and *A Chocolate Moose for Dinner* provide humorous illustrations of figurative language.

Language and sentence comprehension present a variety of difficulties for children. Certainly, figurative language is confusing to the literal-minded student or the youngster whose native language is not English. Another common difficulty is anaphora. **Anaphora** is largely concerned with pronoun referents in sentences.

Anaphora is the relationship between referent and the reference item which is identified with the anaphoric term. Anaphora is an aspect of cohesion that presents comprehension problems to many students, especially beginning readers. A formal definition of anaphora is the use of a word as a regular grammatical substitute for a preceding word or group of words (Wolf, 1966). For example, in the sentence "Linda closed the car door and then she locked it," *she* is substituted for Linda and *it* is substituted for door.

The most common anaphoric terms are simple personal pronouns like *he, she, we, her,* and *them.* However, Bauman and Stevenson (1986) identify seven other items in their anaphora taxonomy.

Anaphora taxonomy

Pronouns.

Locative pronouns (here and there).

Deleted nouns replaced by adjectives. (The band members were supposed to be at practice by 9:00 A.M., but only a few were there.) The adjective *few* replaces band members.

Arithmetic anaphora are similar to deleted nouns but denote number. For example, in "Ann and Rose walked down the hall, the former is petite and cute and the latter is tall and willowy. *Former* refers to Ann and *latter* refers to Rose.

Class inclusive anaphora are shown in the example, "The small dog stalked the squirrel, and the little animal ultimately pounced on its prey." *Little animal* is a class inclusive term for small dog.

Inclusive anaphora are extensions of simple class inclusive anaphora; an anaphoric term refers back to an entire phrase, clause, or passage. For example, in a discussion of the civil war, the author summarizes "These factors led us into civil war." *Factors* represents an inclusive statement of the causes of the Civil War.

Deleted predicate adjective occurs when words such as *so is, is not,* or *is too* indicate a deleted complement, as in "Linda is ambitious. Kathy is not." *Ambitious* is deleted after *is not.*

Proverbs are analogous to pronouns: the verb is substituted by a generic term such as *can, will,* or *have.* For example, "Jane got a perfect score on her examination, and so will Dottie"; *so will* substitutes for *get a perfect score.*

Teaching Anaphora

Anaphora should be directly taught to students. Box 6.1 is the script of an example lesson designed for the latter part of first grade or early second grade. As a basis for independent practice activities, Bauman and Stevenson (1986) suggest using a book like *Nobody Listens to Andrew* by Elizabeth Guilfoile. Box 6.2 is an example for applying this suggestion, based on the book *Crictor* by Tomi Ungerer.

Paragraph Meaning

Sentences are arranged into paragraphs that express meaning. The majority of paragraphs are structures for developing ideas; therefore, all of the sentences within a paragraph develop an idea. Understanding the way that meaning is expressed in paragraphs enhances comprehension. Readers who see the relationships among sentences in a paragraph, and recognize the underlying structure that ties these sentences together, understand the text. Therefore, reading comprehension instruction should teach children the various patterns for organizing paragraphs.

Main ideas and details

The major structural aspects of paragraphs are main ideas and supporting details. Therefore, the ability to identify the main idea of a paragraph and its supporting details has a high priority in most reading programs.

Bauman (1986) identified a scope and sequence of main idea tasks which is summarized in Table 6.3.

When teaching main ideas, identify paragraphs that have well-stated main ideas. The main ideas in some paragraphs are implied, and some paragraphs do not have main ideas. Examples of main ideas can be selected from text materials that children are reading in class. Examining model main-idea paragraphs helps students understand the nature of main ideas. However, di-

Box 6.1

Objective: To teach students to understand personal pronoun anaphora. Specifically, boy/he and girls/they.

Introduction-example: In the stories I read to you and those in your readers, authors sometimes use words to stand for other words. For instance, look at the sentences I wrote on the chalkboard:

Tammy is my neighbor. She lives in that house.

Can you read these sentences aloud, Richard? [Student reads aloud.] Good. Find the word *Tammy* in the first sentence. [A student points to the word.] Now find the word *she* in the second sentence. [Student points to the word.] *She* stands for the word *Tammy*. Look at the sentences while I read them aloud, except that I will substitute *Tammy* for *she*. [Then the teacher reads the sentences aloud, substituting *Tammy* for *she*.] Notice that the second sentence has the same meaning as the first sentence, even when I change *she* to *Tammy*. This shows you how one word can stand for another word. But the meaning does not change.

Practice

I have written some sentences on this chart [uncover the chart]. In each pair of sentences, there is a word that stands for another word. Read the sentences and see if you can think which word the underlined word stands for.

These sentences were written on the chart.

1. *Keith baked a pie. It was good.*

2. *Today is Jerry's birthday. I gave him a shirt.*

3. *Joe and Sam are classmates. They are seven years old.*

4. *Janet left the party early. She was not feeling well.*

5. *"Come and play with me," said Chris. "No," said Michael, "You can play by yourself."*

Read the sentences in line 1 with your eyes. Now, Sue read them aloud for the class. [Student reads.] Good. Now think about what word stands for *pie* in the second sentence? What word is used instead of *pie*? [Student says, "it".] Yes, *it* stands for *pie*. Now we will read the sentences aloud, but we will read *pie* instead of *it* in the second sentence. [Teacher and students read aloud.]

Look at the sentences in line 2. What word is underlined in the second sentence? [Students respond *him*.] Rachel, will you read the sentences aloud for the group? What does the word *him* stand for? [A student answers *Jerry*.] That is correct. The teacher proceeds through the sen-

tences in this manner. When the students completed the sentences, the teacher showed them a chart story that included some underlined words.
Guided practice

1. *Jim, Mark, and Lauren are friends.*

2. *They always walk home from school together.*

3. *One day, they saw a purse laying on the sidewalk.*

4. *Jim said, "What should we do with it?"*

5. *Mark said, "I think we should leave it on the street."*

6. *But Lauren suggested, "We can give it to Officer Clancy."*

7. *He will know what to do.*

8. *They decided to give it to Officer Clancy.*

9. *He gave them a reward.*

"In this story you see some underlined words. All of the underlined words stand for another word, just like those in the sentences we just completed. Listen while I read the story to you, then we will figure out which words the underlined words stand for." After going through the story and identifying the words represented by the underlined words, the teacher gave the children a worksheet for independent practice.
Independent practice

To complete the worksheet, the children drew arrows from the underlined words to the word they represented. When the children read their next basal reader story, the teacher called their attention to the anaphoric terms.

rect instruction is necessary to fully develop this concept. Expository content is most appropriate for teaching main ideas because the main ideas of stories are expressed in the theme. Instruction should begin with explicitly stated main ideas, but after students can identify stated main ideas, they are ready to learn to identify unstated or implied main ideas. When inferring an unstated main idea, readers use the stated details along with their experiences to infer the main idea. The following paragraph illustrates an unstated main idea.

We had a delightful day. We saw birds, monkeys, elephants, zebras, lions, and tigers. Some of the animals were in cages, but some of them were in natural areas. We had hot dogs and a Coke at the lunch counter and then we saw giraffes and elands. We walked and walked, but we had fun.

The unstated main idea of this short paragraph is "a visit to the zoo."

When teaching students to identify main ideas, explain whether the main

---

Box 6.2   Words That Stand for Other Words

Directions: Read the following story and think of the word that each underlined word stands for. Then write the word it stands for in the blank above the word.

    Once upon a time in a little French town, lived an old lady whose

name was Madame Louise Bodot. <u>She</u> had one son who was in Africa

studying reptiles. One morning the mailman brought <u>her</u> a peculiar

O-shaped box. Madame Bodot screamed when <u>she</u> opened <u>it</u>. <u>It</u> was

a snake <u>her</u> son had sent <u>her</u> for <u>her</u> birthday.

---

idea is the topic, the gist of the selection, or a main-idea statement. Also, explain whether the main-idea statement should be a word, phrase, sentence, or more than a sentence. Students should generate their own main-idea statements; choosing among multiple-choice statements is not as effective. Present model main-idea statements, which will help students develop their own.

Identify and state main ideas

    After children learn how to identify and state main ideas, the teacher should help them transfer this concept to expository content. It is most important to transfer this skill to content textbooks. Activities like the following help students acquire and transfer this skill.

    Main ideas and supporting details can be presented in the following ways: chronological order; listing; comparison and contrast; cause and effect; and question-answer. Paragraphs serve many different functions in a selection. Some paragraphs introduce topics, while others summarize topics or illustrate ideas. Authors often combine various types of paragraphs in discussing their topics.

    Showing various paragraph models will aid the students' comprehension. Additionally, the teacher should have the students look for the various types of paragraphs in their assigned reading. After these steps, the students should be ready to write their own examples of the various types of paragraphs. The following sections explain these various types of paragraphs.

Chronological Order

    The cycle begins with the Year of the Mouse. Next is the Year of the Ox. Then comes the Year of the Tiger, the Rabbit, the Dragon, the Serpent, the Horse, the Sheep, the Monkey, the Cock, and the Dog. Last comes the year of the Pig. Then the cycle starts all over again.

Table 6.3

Main-idea task	Description	Grades
Main ideas in lists of words	Students acquire basic concept of main idea. They analyze lists of related words to determine category (shirt, pants, dress = clothing).	1 and up
Main ideas in sentences	Students generalize main idea to larger unit of text, sentence (main idea = topic + what is said about the topic).	2 and up
Main ideas and details in paragraphs—explicit	Students generalize the main idea to paragraphs.	3 and up
Main ideas and details in paragraphs—implicit	After students understand explicit main ideas, they are ready for implicit ideas.	3 and up
Main ideas and details in short passages—explicit	After mastering paragraphs, move to short passages at explicit level.	5 and up
Main ideas and details in short passages—implicit	After explicit passages, move to implicit ones.	5 and up
Main idea outlines for short passages—explicit	An extension of preceding tasks.	6 and up
Main idea outlines for short passages—implicit	An extension of preceding tasks.	6 and up
Main ideas in long passages	Generalize main ideas in longer selections.	7 and up

Source: Based on J. Baumann, "The Indirect Instruction of Main Idea Comprehension Ability," in *Teaching Main Idea Comprehension*, J. Baumann (Ed.), Newark, DE. International Reading Association, 1986. Reprinted with permission of James Baumann and the International Reading Association.

1. What year starts the cycle?
2. What year ends the cycle?
3. *What type of paragraph is this?*

Listing

Musical instruments are often played together in an orchestra. There are four main kinds of instruments used: string, woodwind, brass, and percussion (Fay et al., 1978).

1. What is the purpose of this paragraph?
2. What is enumerated in this paragraph?

Comparison

Another string instrument is the cello. This instrument looks like a big violin, and it has a beautiful, deep sound that makes you think of colored leaves and the warm days of fall (Fay et al., 1978).

1. What is the cello compared with?
2. Did this comparison help you understand this instrument?

Cause and Effect

The sound of your voice is also caused by vibrations. When you talk or sing or shout, the air passes between the vocal cords in your throat and makes them vibrate, and this is what makes the sound of your voice. You can press your fingers against your throat when you speak, and feel the vibrations (Fay et al., 1978).

1. What causes the sound of your voice?
2. What is the effect of pressing your fingers against your throat?

Question-Answer

The word *automobile* comes from two Greek words: *auto,* meaning *self,* and *mobile,* meaning *moving.* An automobile is something that moves itself. This, however, is not quite true because a driver and some gasoline are required to make it move.

1. What word is defined in this paragraph?
2. What two Greek words are combined to make this word?

A teacher who is instructing children to find the main idea of a paragraph should be certain that there in fact is a main idea in the paragraph—not all paragraphs have a main idea. Informational materials are most suitable for main-idea exercises because the organization of fiction does not usually include main ideas and supporting details.

One teacher introduced main ideas and supporting details by comparing them with a *Big Mac.* She explained that the meat in the *Big Mac* could be compared to the main idea, while the bun, sauce, lettuce, onion, and pickles were like supporting details. This analogy made the main-idea concept very clear to students.

ACTIVITIES FOR UNDERSTANDING THE CONCEPT OF MAIN IDEAS

1. The concept of *main idea* can be introduced to young children through the use of pictures. Teachers can show pictures to children and ask them to make up sentences that describe the most important point of that picture. They should also list the details that helped them identify this main idea, as shown in Figure 6.2.
   a. What is the main idea of the picture? (Possible answer: A birthday party.)
   b. What are the supporting details? Why did you say this was a birthday party? (Possible answer: Birthday cake, party hats, decorations, and presents.)

Figure 6.2

2. Main ideas can also be taught through the key words in sentences. Students could, for example, be directed to compose their own telegrams. A full message could be given to the class with the request that they rewrite it in telegraphic language. Telegrams are composed of key words—which are usually nouns and verbs, although other parts of speech may also be important in certain messages. A child's telegram might read like this: "Arriving, October 31, United 103."

3. Activities that involve locating key words in sentences can be expanded to finding key words in a paragraph. Once the key words in the sentences of a paragraph have been identified, the student can relate them to one another to determine the main idea that is suggested. For example:

Pigs are *useful* animals. About *three-tenths* of the *meat eaten* in the *United States* comes from *hogs*. Pigs give us *bacon, ham, sausage,* and *pork chops*. Other *parts* of the *pig* are *used* to make *lard, leather, brushes, soap, glue,* and *medicines*. *Every part* of the pig is *used* except its squeal.

The main idea of this paragraph—*Pigs are useful animals*—is in the first sentence. The key words in each sentence of this passage clearly support this conclusion.

4. Categorization activities help students understand the concept of main ideas.
   a. Children could be given pictures of objects and asked to identify those items that do not belong in the picture, as in Figure 6.3.
   b. Ask students to make up a sentence about the objects that reflects the main idea of the picture. (For example, *Things I use when I get*

Figure 6.3

ready for bed.) Have students compose a complete paragraph based on this main idea, using the objects as supporting details.

Example: *When I get ready to go to bed I need several things. I use soap and a washcloth to wash myself. I use a toothbrush and toothpaste to brush my teeth. Then I am ready for bed.*

5. Some general in-class strategies for main-idea instruction are suggested below.
   a. Encourage students to ask themselves the following questions:
      What is this sentence, paragraph, or selection about?
      What idea do most of the key words suggest?
      Which words are repeated in the passage?
      What is the summary sentence saying?
   b. Have students read paragraphs and select the best statement of the main idea from multiple-choice answers that are provided.
   c. Encourage students to look for words and phrases that indicate the main idea, such as *first, last, the most important factor,* and *the significant fact.*
   d. Create a diagram to illustrate the main ideas and supporting details. Figure 6.4 is an example of such a diagram.

Forms of Discourse

Paragraphs are organized into larger chunks of discourse, which may be fiction (narrative) or nonfiction (expository). To comprehend longer segments of discourse, a reader has to be able to impose some form of organization on the

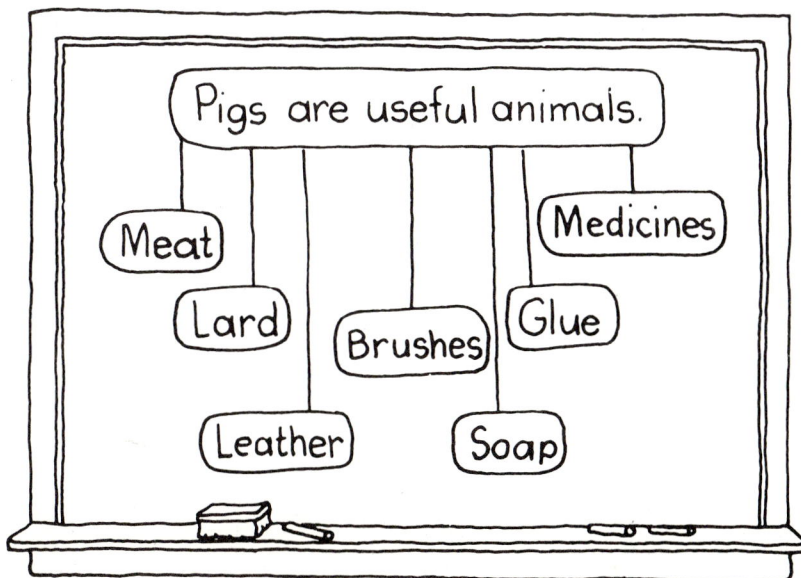

Figure 6.4 A diagram of main ideas and supporting details.

material being read (Tuinman, 1980). Understanding the ways in which authors organize fiction and nonfiction helps the reader anticipate the presentation of ideas. Understanding discourse organization allows the reader to relate ideas to one another, and enables the reader to think about the larger concepts under discussion.

One approach to understanding the structure of discourse is discourse analysis, which is based on the premise that different types of discourse require different schemata. Thus, readers will make correct responses to reading material only if they approach that material from the perspective of its overall writing pattern, that is, its form of discourse (rhetoric). The reader's recognition of the particular type of discourse facilitates comprehension of the selection (Marshall and Glock, 1978–1979).

Catterson (1979) suggests that comprehension instruction through discourse analysis should use the directed reading activity. In this activity, questions are posed that help readers comprehend. Some examples of these questions are listed in the following.

QUESTIONS FOR NARRATIVE

1. Who is the most important character in this story? Why do you think this?
2. What is the climax in this story?
3. Could this story occur in any other setting?
4. How many episodes are in this story?
5. What was the author saying to the reader in this story?

QUESTIONS FOR EXPOSITION

1. What is the main idea addressed in this selection?
2. How does the author support or explain the main idea?
3. How does the author organize the important ideas (cause and effect, comparison, and the like)?

Comprehending Nonfiction

Well-written nonfiction begins with an *introductory* paragraph, which introduces the topic in broad, general terms and then narrows to a more specific point. The *body* is the second part of a selection. The body develops the ideas that were identified in the introduction. Each paragraph usually has one main idea, which may be presented in one of the paragraph styles—such as example, enumeration, or comparison. The selection usually ends with a *summary* paragraph, which pulls together the ideas developed in the body and contains a general concluding statement. The diagram of a nonfiction selection is shown in Figure 6.5.

Paragraph organization

The overall organization of a selection may follow the same organization as paragraphs. In other words, the selection may make a point through examples, cause and effect, comparison, and the like. The organizational pattern is

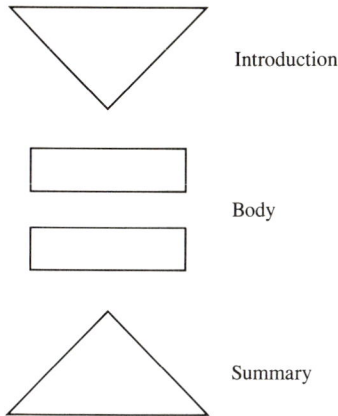

Figure 6.5   A diagram of a nonfiction selection.

often implied in the introduction, with the author offering examples or comparisons. Most frequently, a combination of patterns is used. The words and phrases that serve as clues to these various patterns were presented in Chapter 5. The following activities will help children understand nonfiction organization.

1. Give children a selection in which the paragraphs have been scrambled. Ask them to put them into order.
2. Give students a selection with a missing introduction or summary. Ask them to write their own version of the missing part.
3. Ask students to read a nonfiction selection and locate the introduction, body, and summary.

Additional suggestions for the comprehension of nonfiction materials are discussed in Chapter 9.

Comprehending Fiction

The structure of fiction is based on setting, theme, plot, characters, and the author's style. The *setting* refers to the location for the story and the time period in which it takes place. *Theme* is the author's idea, on which the story is based (Huck, 1987). The *plot* is the general plan of the story, and it consists of a series of episodes that move the action toward the climax. The *characters* are the animals or people around whom the story is centered. *Author style* refers to the author's use of language in telling the story.

Research indicates that children expect a story to be structured (Guthrie, 1977). They understand and remember a story in terms of this structure. As children grow older, their expectations of story structure become more specific.

Story structure   Teachers can help children comprehend fiction by providing stories that have a clear structure, which can be easily identified. Directed questions can also help children to understand story structure. (Examples of such questions are discussed in Chapter 10.) Children should be encouraged to complete the structure diagram presented in Figure 6.6 for all fiction selections they read.

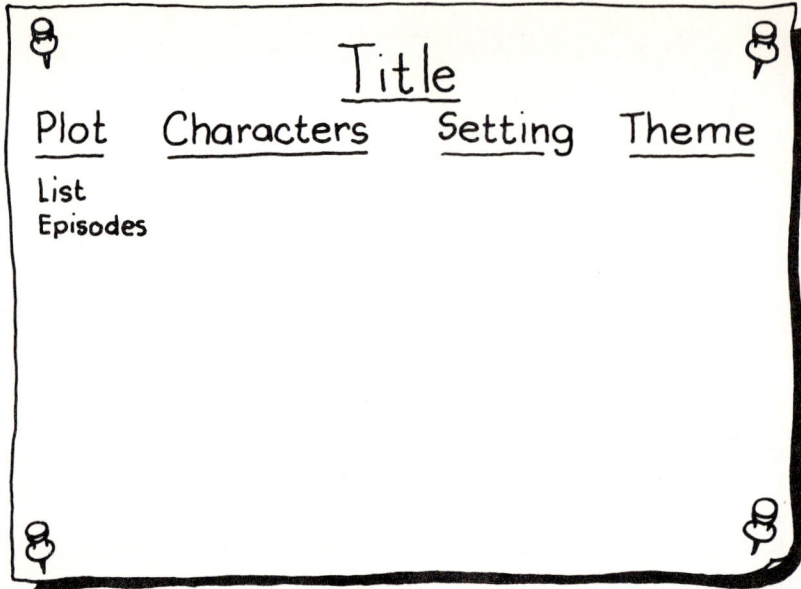

Figure 6.6 A diagram of a fiction selection.

Another device to facilitate comprehension is the use of *story maps.* These are visual representations of a story, similar in construction to semantic maps or networks (Reutzel, 1985). They graphically organize and integrate the concepts and events included in a story. Story maps help teachers organize reading instruction; in turn, they help students perceive the organization of their reading material. Story maps can be used as prereading activities to introduce a story; they can also be used as a visual aid to postreading reflection, review, and discussion. Initially, teachers may map stories, but as children become acquainted with the technique, they may create story maps.

Story map

Reutzel (1985) suggests these steps for designing story maps.

1. Make a summary list in sequence of the main idea, major events, and major characters in the story.
2. Locate the main idea in the center of the map.
3. Draw lines projecting out from the main idea to accommodate the major events and characters on the list.
4. Teachers and students may create their own designs for illustrating the story events and characters (see Figure 6.7). Reutzel suggests entering the major concepts or events in circles attached to the ties, which are sequenced clockwise around the center circle. Then, enter subevents or subconcepts clockwise around the circles containing the major events or concepts in the story map.

COMPREHENSION STRATEGIES TO USE WHILE READING

When they are reading, students should use comprehension strategies that enhance their mental operations, which facilitate understanding. The reading

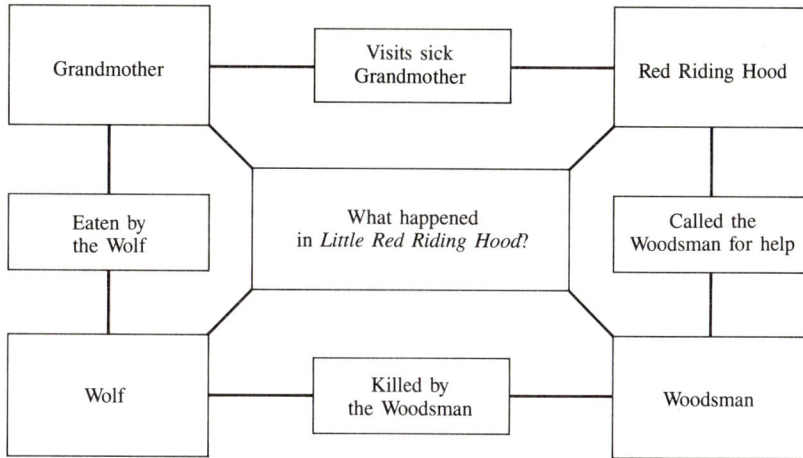

Figure 6.7 Semantic web based on *Little Red Riding Hood.*

comprehension strategies used *during* reading emphasize active engagement with the text. These strategies include activating the appropriate schemata, which enable students to build connections between their existing knowledge and text content. The metacognitive and elaboration strategies that build connections between readers and text are discussed in the following section.

Metacognitive Strategies

Metacognition means monitoring and regulating one's own cognitive processes, as well as the products of those processes (Flavell, 1981). "Learning to learn" strategies are also often included in discussions of metacognition; when students "learn to learn," they are acquiring the ability to control their own reading and learning processes. Metacognitive skills enable readers to attend to the text, to track their own understanding, and to use this information to help themselves. In other words, readers can identify their own comprehension problems, and select possible solutions to comprehension failure.

By monitoring their own comprehension skills, readers are aware of their own understanding or lack of understanding. To do this, readers must adjust their reading to their reading purpose. For example, to prepare for an examination, students read closely and carefully, but to survey an article, readers may choose to skim.

Teaching Metacognitive Skills

Metacognition is concerned with "knowing what you know," "knowing what you don't know," and "knowing how to help yourself when you don't know." Fluent readers are aware of their understanding, and they consciously coordinate thought and reading. Teachers help them develop this awareness. Poor readers are unaware of comprehension. They often read the assignments, but do not examine their own comprehension (Brown, 1978). The following example illustrates metacognitive instruction, which is intended to increase students' awareness of their own comprehension.

Jimmy, a fourth grader, was assigned reading in a mathematics text that explained long division; then the teacher demonstrated long division on the chalkboard. But when Jimmy tried to work a problem, he could not remember the process. He asked the teacher for assistance; when his teacher asked him to explain the technical vocabulary (divisor, remainder, and so forth) he could not. She told him to use the text's glossary and label each part of the problem with the appropriate term. She established a purpose for rereading by having him label each part of the problem. After rereading and labeling, Jimmy worked the problem successfully.

Through metacognitive instruction, Jimmy learned to monitor his comprehension process. Competent readers are able to identify and focus on the important parts of the text. By having Jimmy label the parts of the problems, the teacher demonstrated the importance of focusing on terms related to the process. Jimmy's understanding was sharpened when he worked the problem successfully. He was in the process of acquiring metacognitive skills.

Direct teaching

Metacognitive skills should be taught directly, and gradually related to the content areas (Presseisen, 1986). Teachers have several strategies at their disposal for teaching students to monitor their own comprehension. Each of these strategies is designed to cause active reading, which involves readers with the content. One strategy is modeling the metacognitive process. Such a demonstration is accomplished with a "think-aloud," which was illustrated in Chapter 5. Other strategies include:

> *Summaries* of the content read. They are concerned with identifying main ideas and writing them succinctly in one's own words. Summaries are examined later in this chapter.
>
> *Self-questioning* about important ideas in the content. A number of researchers have studied students' questions (Wong, 1985; Smith, 1978; Singer, 1978; Wisendanger and Wollenberg, 1978); they concur that having students ask questions of and about text induces active reading. These questions create a purpose for reading, which provides for more thought during reading, and promotes student-centered discussions after reading. Students learn to formulate questions from the questioning model their teacher presents. Provide students with guided practice to help them develop self-questioning skills.
>
> Examples of during-reading self-questions are "What did this paragraph tell me?" or "What did the author say in this paragraph (sentence or selection)?" Some readers find it useful to stop after every paragraph to self-question.

Singer (1978) recommends that teachers ask questions like "What would you like to know about this _____ (picture, story, topic and so forth) ? This initiates student questioning. The answers to students' questions should be read aloud. If students discover that their questions are not answered in the text, they should try to obtain the answers in outside reading.

Reread

When self-questioning reveals that the reader is not comprehending, he or she should return to the point in the selection where understanding was lost. Then the youngster should reread to obtain meaning.

Another aspect of metacognition and of self-questioning is making students aware of where they obtain the information necessary for answering questions. Raphael (1982) designed an instruction strategy to increase the quality of students' answers. This strategy directs students to determine whether a question is answered in the text (right there), whether they need to check other sources, such as reference materials (think and search), or whether they should think of an answer using their own experiences and knowledge (on my own). Such a strategy could be presented to students on an overhead transparency or on a chart, with teacher explanation and demonstration. Box 6.3 illustrates this strategy. It is based on the story *My Robot Buddy,* introduced in the preceding chapter.

Heller (1986) developed a metacognitive strategy for helping children "know what they know," which is appropriate for both fiction and nonfiction. It is illustrated in Box 6.4, which is based on the story *Not Just Any Ring* by Danita Ross Haller.

Active reading

The metacognitive strategies just presented encourage active reading and text elaboration. The deeper a reader processes the text, the more he or she will

---

Box 6.3

Directions: After you read the story, read each question and put a check mark beside the correct phrase.

1. Did Jack expect Danny One to rescue him from the robotnappers?

   Right there _____
   Think and search _____
   On my own _____

2. Why did the doctor warn Jack about robotnappers?

   Right there _____
   Think and search _____
   On my own _____

3. What parts are needed to build a robot?

   Right there _____
   Think and search _____
   On my own _____

4. Why was Jack robotnapped?

   Right there _____
   Think and search _____
   On my own _____

Box 6.4

Topic: Types of magic
Reading Purpose: Where was the real magic in this story? Is this real magic?

A	B	C
What I already know	What I now know	What I don't know
About magic tricks	Jessie thought the ring was magic. She was afraid without her ring.	Whether this is real magic. This seems like supersitition.

remember and understand, since deep processing involves more thinking than superficial processing—hence facilitating comprehension. Both elaboration and following the author's organizational framework facilitate understanding (McNeil, 1987).

Elaboration

Elaboration is an embellishment of text; it is accomplished by drawing on prior knowledge, inferring, creating mental images, paraphrasing text, and summarizing text. These thought processes increase comprehension. Instruction improves elaboration strategies (Reder, 1980). The following sections address strategies for encouraging elaboration.

Visualizing Text

Comprehension increases when readers create images. Seeing, imaging, and drawing contribute to the visual thinking process (McKim, 1980). Research shows that visual images do aid understanding (Rohwer and Matz, 1975). For instance, Pressley (1976) found that eight-year-olds could learn to construct mental pictures for the sentences and paragraphs they read, and they recalled more story events than students who had not had this training. Rasco et al. (1975) found that imagery significantly aided the comprehension of fourth- and fifth-grade students. In a program developed by the Escondido Union School District (1979) the children learned to recognize important words, develop mental images for them, and to discuss and verify their images through oral reading. This program resulted in significant reading comprehension gains. Research shows that readers who develop visual imaging skills improve their comprehension. Furthermore, students can learn to translate words into visual pictures as they read. A planned sequence of activities is necessary to help students learn to create mental images of story settings, characters, and story action, as well as to understand the information in expository materials. Mental imagery can be taught using teacher modeling, guided practice, and independent practice (Gambrell, Kapinus, and Wilson, 1987). These should be incorporated with the following instructional steps, specified by Mundell (1985).

Give children opportunities to create images of concrete objects. For example, students may create images of objects that are in the classroom, such as bulletin boards, books, and exhibits, or teachers may bring objects into the classroom for use in imaging instruction. Encourage students to visualize specific characteristics, such as color, shape, and size. After imaging, students can compare their images with the real objects to verify them. Gamelike activities are appropriate at this level. For instance, students may focus on creating an image of an object in the classroom. The object should then be removed to discuss its image, and then returned to compare it to the image created while it had been removed. Similar activities can be developed with photographs.

Activities

Encourage students to visualize and recall familiar objects, scenes, or past experiences outside the classroom. For instance, students may close their eyes and create images of their bedroom; then they may answer questions about this image. The questions might include, "Where is your bed located in the room?" "What color are the walls?" and "Where are the windows located?" Students may draw pictures of their images to compare to the actual room. Activities like those described in the book *Put Your Mother on the Ceiling* by Richard DeMille are useful at this stage. Castillo (1972) researched the activities in this book. He found that they promoted imagination, listening skills, language, and comprehension. In the book, children were asked to imagine the color of a jacket that a child wore. They were then told to mentally change this color. Other activities encouraged children to imagine such activities as walking on the ceiling.

Have students listen to high-imagery stories that use common experiences or knowledge. For example, read trade books that include action, descriptive scenes, and well-developed characters. After completing the selection, students can create illustrations based on their images; they should have opportunities to compare and discuss their illustrations. Play tapes of music, stories, or radio shows, and encourage students to create images from what they heard. Oral reading is also a good imaging activity at this state. Students should discuss the images they create.

Mental images

By following steps 1–3, students should be ready to create their own mental images as they read. Teachers should encourage pupils to create images as they read. This should help them discover the relationships between their images and the text. Have the students read vivid plays, stories, riddles, and jokes, while focusing on the mental images they create to accompany these readings. Provide opportunities to discuss and compare these images. I recommend the following books.

PRIMARY LEVEL

Byrd Baylor, *The Desert is Theirs*
Jan Garten, *The Alphabet Tale*

Carol Carrick, *Lost in the Storm*

Steven Kellog, *Can I Keep Him?*

Leo Lionni, *Swimmy*

Robert McCloskey, *Time of Wonder*

David McPhail, *The Bear's Toothache*

John Steptoe, *The Story of Jumping Mouse*

Lynd Ward, *The Biggest Bear*

INTERMEDIATE LEVEL

Lucy Boston, *A Stranger at Green Knowe*

Betsy Byars, *The House of Wings*

Lynne Reid Banks, *The Indian in the Cupboard*

Eleanor Cameron, *That Julia Redfern*

Eleanor Cameron, *A Room Made of Windows*

Kathryn Lasky, *Oklahoma*

Jean Merrill, *The Pushcart War*

Philippa Pearce, *Tom's Midnight Garden*

Jill Paton Walsh, *Lost and Found*

Guidelines

Fredericks (1986) offers the following guidelines for imaging instruction.

1. Students should understand that individuals have different images, which are influenced by their individual experiences.
2. There are no right or wrong images. Teachers should avoid attempting to change students' images; however, teachers may help children re-create images by rereading a piece, or giving students opportunities to rehear a tape or record. Student-created images develop understanding.
3. Children should have sufficient opportunities to create images before discussion. Children who require long periods of time to create images, should be encouraged to draw illustrations of their images.
4. Provide adequate time for students to share and discuss images in a supportive atmosphere. This activity should not be viewed as an attempt to "correct" images.
5. Stimulate image development through questions such as, "What do you see?" "Tell us more." "What does it look like?"
6. Art activities represent the images, ideas, and feelings gained from listening to a story, and allow the students to participate in an imaging exercise. The art form could be collage, painting, sculpture, and so forth. Art helps children formulate and clarify what they have learned,

and increases their ability to express the content they understand (Cooke and Haipt, 1986).

Summarizing

Summaries condense original content while retaining its information, essence, and point of view. Written summary statements enhance recall and comprehension of both fiction and information (Bromley 1985; McNeil and Donant, 1982). In writing summaries, readers reorganize text information in a manner that is meaningful to them; therefore, students facilitate integration of text information with their existing knowledge. Effective summaries are based on skills that students can develop. When learning to generate summaries, students need to recognize the relative importance of different parts of the text. The skill of identifying main ideas is also a prerequisite skill for summarizing. Summaries should not be rambling recapitulations of the entire text.

Modeling and practice

Summarizing can be taught using teacher modeling, guided practice, and independent practice (Gambrell, Kapinus, and Wilson, 1987). The first step is to teach students the characteristics of a good summary: it is brief, it has the important ideas of a passage, and it does not include supporting details (Armbruster, Anderson, and Ostertag, 1987). To achieve this, teachers may choose to have students read a passage and then present an example summary of that passage. Teachers can describe the process involved in generating the model summary.

Researchers have found that the process of creating summaries can be taught; they have developed processing rules that children can use to improve their summarizing ability (Brown and Day, 1983). First, students should examine their summaries to identify and eliminate all unnecessary material, including trivial information. Then they should identify and delete any redundant material. When a series or list of items is included in the summary, students should substitute a superordinate term for the list. For example, if the summary includes a list such as *cats, dogs,* and *gerbils,* students could substitute the superordinate term, *pets.* Finally, summary writers should include the topic sentence of the text; if there is no topic sentence in the material, they should invent one.

The teacher may provide several example summaries and have students select the best ones. These summaries may include ones that are too brief, too long, and ones that include too many details. Students should have opportunities to discuss the characteristics of these various summaries.

After students learn the attributes of a good summary, they should have guided practice. While they are practicing writing summaries, the teacher should circulate around the classroom to answer students' questions. Finally, students should have many opportunities for independent practice in summarizing. All practice should occur in a meaningful context; children should write summaries of content that is relevant to them. Students should have authentic purposes for reading and summarizing the text. Through direct application of their summarizing skills, students develop greater appreciation of their value.

The following paragraphs address additional formats that can be used to abstract reading content.

Study guides are teacher-constructed instruments that are designed to guide students' reading. They are most frequently used with content textbooks, but they can be used with literature, or as guides to studying a theme or unit, such as important ideas, concepts, and vocabulary. Study guides give students a different form for summarizing. Three-level study guides, which are the most common types, include literal, inferential, and application questions, based on the text. Students use study guides while they are reading. Study guides are examined in greater detail in Chapter 8.

Frames provide students with a model and structure for summarizing text. Frames are useful in teaching students how to summarize, before they are able to generate their own summaries. A story frame is a sequence of spaces hooked together by key language elements (Fowler, 1982; Nichols, 1980). In most cases, these language elements are transition words and often reflect a specific line of thought or argument. Once a frame is constructed, it can be used with new passages, if the new passages can support the line of thought or argument implied with the frame. Frames are relatively open-ended, since no specific words or answers are intended for each space.

Listening

Frames can be used as a listening activity before students read fluently. In this context, a story frame is displayed after students listen to or read a story. Students look at the first line or set of key words in the frame, then they discuss possible responses. The teacher moves the discussion to subsequent lines in the frame. The children are instructed to think back to the first line to identify ideas that will make the lines relate to one another (cohesion). Once students can use story frames effectively in a directed teaching situation, they can begin to use them individually.

Teachers can use the following guidelines to construct frames.

1. Read a passage or story and identify the problems, facts, or text structure on which you want students to focus.
2. Sketch a paragraph that addresses this point.
3. Take the completed paragraph and delete all words, phrases, and sentences, except those needed to sustain the purpose of the paragraph. You will probably need to make notations under certain spaces so that students will be able to follow the frame.
4. Try the frame with other passages or stories that are similar to the passage on which the frame is based. Modify the frame so that it can be used in several selections.

Examples of frames are illustrated in Figure 6.8.

Applying Reading Content

Depth of processing is enhanced when readers think of examples and/or applications of the concepts and ideas about which they are reading. These activi-

Figure 1 Story summary with one character included

Our story is about _____ . _____

_____ is an important character in our story. _____ tried to

_____ . The story ends when _____

_____ .

Figure 2 Important idea or plot

In this story the problem starts when _____

_____ . After that, _____ . Next,

_____ . Then, _____

_____ . The problem is finally solved when _____

_____ . The story ends _____

_____ .

Figure 3 Setting

This story takes place _____ . I know

this because the author uses the words " _____

_____ ." Other clues that show when the story takes place are _____

_____ .

Figure 4 Character analysis

_____ is an important character in our story. _____ is

important because _____ . Once,

he/she _____ . Another time, _____

_____ . I think that _____

_____ is _____

    (character's name)   (character trait)

_____ because _____ .

Figure 5 Character comparison

_____ and _____ are two characters in our story.

_____ is _____

                (character's name)

_____ while _____

          (trait)   (other character)

_____ is _____ . For instance,

                       (trait)

_____ tries to _____ and _____

_____ tries to _____ learns a lesson when

_____ .

Figure 6.8 Sample story frames. (*Source:* Gerald Fowler, "Developing Comprehensive Skills in Primary Students Through the Use of Story Frames," *The Reading Teacher,* Vol. 36, No. 2 (February 1982) 176–179. Reprinted by permission of Gerald Fowler and The International Reading Association.)

ties improve recall and comprehension. For example, students who are study-ing forms of government can think of examples of governments like those included in their text. Primary-grade children who are reading about "People Who Help" may think of other examples of people who supply important services to others. Children who are reading the story *My Friend Jacob* by Lucille Clifton could think of additional ways that friends can help each other. They might also identify additional stories or poems about friends that are similar to this story.

COMPREHENSION AFTER READING

Follow-up activities are a successful means of promoting thinking skills. **Dis-cussing** and **composing**, both of which contribute to deep processing of ideas and information, are the most important follow-up activities. These activities improve and reinforce understanding, as they cause readers to consciously examine written content. They also allow students to see how other members of the class think about a selection. Rarely do two readers understand and react to a selection in exactly the same manner.

Follow-up

Follow-up activities tend to be product-oriented and teacher-directed; the teacher identifies the product that will exhibit understanding. For example, in a discussion, the product is students' answers, in composing, the product is a composition.

Discussion is an important means of developing reading comprehension. Students' interpretations of text and points of view are shared through discus-sion and new meanings are developed as students talk and listen to one another. Discussion encourages students to enrich and refine their understandings of the text (Bridges, 1985) by introducing them to ideas that may not have occurred to them while reading. It also permits them to see facts in the light of others' interpretations. Meanings shared in discussion groups are not merely a collec-tion of individual meanings; they are part of new sets of meanings developed as members talk and listen to one another (Pinnell, 1984).

Memory

Memory is reinforced by discussion because students elaborate ideas as a result of talking about them. Students who articulate their ideas have a good chance of recalling the information later (Alvermann, Dillon, O'Brien, 1987).

Discussion strategies require teacher planning, modeling, and student preparation. Teachers plan for discussion through planning questions that focus students on the important ideas in the reading selection. They need to plan model questions because their questions will help students learn to ask good questions of one another.

Reading comprehension instruction involves asking and answering ques-tions, and commenting on selections read (Manzo and Manzo, 1987). Both teacher and students must master the art of asking, answering, and comment-ing to establish the reciprocity—or give and take—necessary to permit lan-guage and thought to be modeled and shaped (Manzo and Manzo, 1987). Dis-cussion questions were included in Chapter 5. The topics of levels of questioning, think time, and the use of teaching questions rather than testing questions were included in that presentation. However, answering questions and commenting during discussions, which are important to successful comprehension, are discussed in the following sections.

Students are rarely directly taught how to ask questions, answer questions, or how to comment during discussions, but they should be. Children need to acquire strategies for asking questions, answering questions, and commenting. The following strategy was used successfully in a recent research project with first- and second-grade students (Stoodt and Costello, 1985).

1. Stop and listen to the question.
2. Think of an answer.
3. Hold up your hand to let the teacher know you have an answer.
4. Listen carefully to other students' questions and answers.

After the teacher in this project demonstrated the strategy, the students practiced until they performed each step automatically. The first- and second-grade children in this project significantly increased their reading comprehension after learning *how* to answer questions.

L-R-D

The *Listen-Read-Discuss* strategy is a discussion strategy developed by Manzo and Casale (1985). This strategy builds students' confidence, thus encouraging them to participate in discussions. For this strategy the teacher should begin with a well-structured text. Then the teacher explains the text by briefly presenting the important ideas and concepts. The class then reads the text that the teacher explained. They may read to locate words, ideas, or facts that are difficult to comprehend or that are inconsistent with the information presented by the teacher. After reading, the students discuss the text. First, basic meanings should be clarified. After a discussion of the main ideas, the students and teacher should raise questions that were unanswered in the text. Two questions help guide this discussion: What did you understand best from what you heard and read? What questions or thoughts did the topic raise in your mind? The order of the questions, the form of the questions, and the number of questions will differ from teacher to teacher and from class to class.

Example

The Listen-Read-Discuss strategy is illustrated with this example. Mr. Healy, a fifth-grade teacher, previewed a reading assignment regarding hurricanes. In planning his discussion, he remembered that the class exhibited a wide range of achievement from slightly above average to well below average. He examined the text to identify the main ideas presented and the organization of those ideas, and he considered the erroneous ideas that his students might have regarding hurricanes. He had two objectives for the lesson: to master the subject matter and to help the students learn to participate in a discussion.

He presented the main ideas in a graphic organizer on an overhead transparency. The transparency looked like this:

```
┌─────────────────────────────┐        ┌──────────────┐        ┌──────────────┐
│ Form over the ocean in the  │────────│  HURRICANE   │────────│  Destructive │
│          tropics            │        └──────────────┘        └──────────────┘
└─────────────────────────────┘                │                      │
            │                          ┌──────────────┐        ┌──────────────┐
            │                          │Whirling storms│       │ Loss of life │
            │                          └──────────────┘        └──────────────┘
┌─────────────────────────────┐       ╱              ╲                 │
│ Move west gathering momentum│ ┌──────────────┐ ┌──────────────┐ ┌──────────────┐
│ Turn toward pole            │ │Southern      │ │Northern      │ │Loss of property│
│ When reach temperate        │ │hemisphere    │ │hemisphere    │ └──────────────┘
│ latitudes go east           │ │Clockwise     │ │Counter clockwise│
└─────────────────────────────┘ └──────────────┘ └──────────────┘
                                        ╲              ╱
                                       ┌──────────────┐
                                       │     Eye      │
                                       └──────────────┘
```

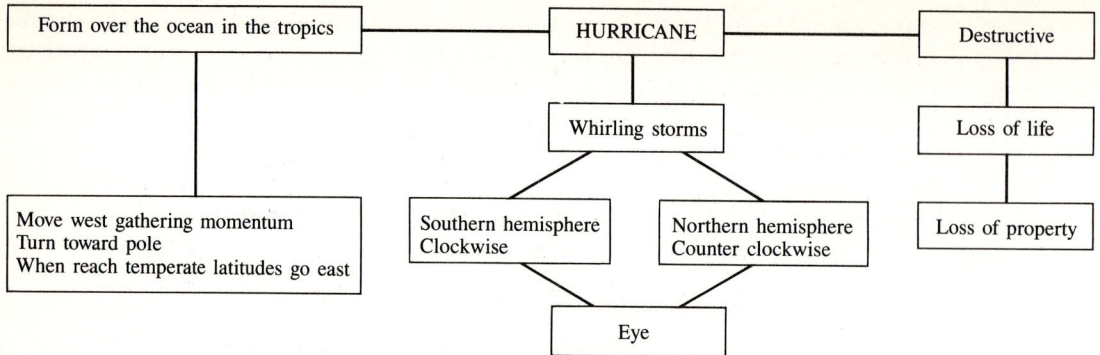

After defining tornadoes, he explained each part of the graphic organizer. Then the students read the text. After reading, the group discussed the selection. The following is an excerpt from this discussion.

> *Teacher:* What is the most interesting fact that you learned about hurricanes?
>
> *Kelly:* That they form over oceans. I thought we had a hurricane down in Red Bank.
>
> *Jerry:* That wasn't a hurricane. It was a tornado.
>
> *Kelly:* How do you know the difference?
>
> *Sara:* Hurricanes form over the ocean and tornadoes form over land. Isn't that right Mr. Healy?
>
> *Teacher:* Yes. Can you think of any other differences after reading the text?
>
> *Mitchell:* Hurricanes have slower winds than tornadoes.
>
> *Richard:* Tornadoes have funnel clouds.
>
> *Teacher:* What is a funnel cloud over the ocean called?
>
> *Teacher:* No one knows? Let's look back at the text and see if you can find out.

Retelling

Retelling, like discussion, is a postreading strategy based on oral language as a vehicle for increasing reading comprehension. Reading comprehension is enhanced when children are encouraged to talk about what they read (Koskien, Gambrell, Kapinus, and Heathington, 1988). Retelling requires readers to organize the story or information in order to recount the content. Research shows that comprehension is significantly increased after four experiences with retelling (Koskinen, Gambrell, Kapinus, and Heathington, 1988).

Teachers commonly use the following format when incorporating retellings in comprehension instruction. They explain retelling, identify the goals of retelling, and model it for students. The students silently read a text or a portion of a text; then they pair up with another youngster to engage in retelling. One student is the storyteller who tries to tell all of the important ideas in the selection, while the other student listens. Partners usually take turns being the storyteller and the listener. The quality of retellings is improved through instruction.

Explain and model

Retelling instruction should include an explanation of the purpose for retelling and guided practice. The teacher should model effective retelling of text. For example, the teacher might read a fable like "The Fox and the Grapes" and explain to the students that after she reads it aloud, she will retell the fable, including all of the important ideas. While the teacher reads the fable aloud, the students listen for the important parts. After teacher modeling of retelling, students should have opportunities to practice.

Retelling prompts

Students' retellings can be guided through question prompts that are appropriate for the type of text being read. The following prompts were suggested in an article by Koskinen, Gambrell, Kapinus, and Heathington (1988).

Prompts for Encouraging Retelling

Narrative text
    Who are the main characters?
    When did the story take place?
    Where did the story take place?
    What important events happened in the story?
    How did the story end?

Expository text
    What is the topic of the selection?
    What are the important ideas in the selection?

Source: P. Koskinen, L. Gambrell, B. Kapinus, and B. Heathington, "Retelling: A Strategy for Enhancing Students' Reading Comprehension," *The Reading Teacher,* Vol. 41 (May 1988) 892–898. Reprinted by permission of the authors and the International Reading Association.

After students have experiences with guided retelling, they may work independently to refine their skills. Students commonly use materials from basal readers, content text books, and trade books for retelling practice.

Reaction Guide

Evaluation or reaction guides help students evaluate themselves and one another. Reaction sheets help them understand what is expected and to evaluate their retellings as a basis for improvement. The following reaction sheet illustrates one approach to evaluation of retelling.

Example of a Retelling Reaction Sheet

Name _____   Date _____
I listened to _____

Choose one thing your partner did well.
    He or she told about the characters.   ____
    He or she told about the setting.   ____

He or she told about events in the story.   ____

His or her story had a beginning.   ____

His or her story had an ending.   ____

Tell your partner one thing that was good about his or her story.

Source: P. Koskinen, L. Gambrell, B. Kapinus, and B. Heathington, "Retelling: A Strategy for Enhancing Students' Reading Comprehension," *The Reading Teacher,* Vol. 41 (May 1988) 892–898. Reprinted by permission of the authors and the International Reading Association.

The Directed-Reading-Thinking-Activity

The **Directed-Reading-Thinking-Activity (DRTA)** approach to reading comprehension, developed by Stauffer (1975), stresses reading as a thinking process. Children are divided into groups of eight or ten, based on their reading skills. Students read from the same textbook, identify purposes for reading, and look for proof in the text to support their responses. The reading group itself determines whether the proof that has been presented is adequate. The teacher is the catalyst in this activity, directing questions to encourage children's interpretation and formation of inferences. The basic steps in the DRTA are included in the following outline.

1. Establish purposes for reading the selection. Encourage children to establish their own purposes as well, providing assistance as required.
2. Reading rate should take into account the purpose of the reading, the nature of the content (for example, literature, science, or social science material), the level of the content, and students' familiarity with the content.
3. Reading should take place.
4. Facilitate reading comprehension.
   a. Have students answer the purpose questions.
   b. Examine the "proof" for the answers by rereading those passages that support or refute student answers.
   c. Stauffer (1975) suggests that teachers must essentially ask *What do you think? Why do you think so?* and *Prove it!*

The Cloze Procedure

The **Cloze Procedure** is useful for both teaching and evaluating comprehension. This discussion focuses on the instructional uses of the cloze. (The assessment of this procedure will be discussed in Chapter 8.) The Cloze Procedure is a method of systematically deleting words from a selection. The reader must then supply those words that were deleted. When using the Cloze Procedure, students should be asked to explain why they selected their particular words. The basic steps in the Cloze Procedure are included in the following outline.

1. Selections will vary in length, since older students can work with longer selections than younger ones. Cloze selections are usually composed of passages that are a minimum of 250 words.
2. The first and last sentences of the selection should be left intact. After the first sentence, every fifth word should be deleted and replaced with a 15-space line—so that each blank provided is of equal length.
3. Students are to fill in the blanks with the words they think were in the original passage.
4. Scoring: 57 percent accuracy is the equivalent of an independent reading level, 45 percent to 56 percent is the equivalent of an instructional reading level, and 44 percent or less is the equivalent of a frustration reading level. (Spelling does not count in scoring.)

CLOZE VARIATIONS

1. For younger students, use a book such as *Alexander and the Terrible, Horrible No Good, Very Bad Day* by Judith Viorst. This book is humorous; children can easily relate this story to their own experiences.
2. Read the cloze passage aloud to young children, allowing them to tell you what word to insert in the blank. Children may also listen to a tape-recorded reading of a selection.
3. Selective deletions are useful for instruction at all grade levels. (In this situation, the teacher would simply ignore the fifth-word blank rule and would delete all selected parts.) The following selected parts of speech may be deleted in different exercises: nouns, verbs, adjectives, adverbs, prepositions, and conjunctions.
4. Have children supply synonyms in addition to the exact words that were deleted from the original passage.
5. Instead of every fifth word, delete every tenth word.
6. *Zip* is a technique that was developed by Blachowicz (1977). A chart, book, or overhead transparency may be used as the reading selection. Masking tape should block out the selected words. Children should initially skim over the passage for a general understanding before supplying the masked words. After each word response has been given and discussed, the tape should be pulled off or *zipped* so that the reader can receive immediate feedback.
7. A *listening cloze* is useful with young children and poor readers. This procedure is basically the same as the written cloze, except that the content is read to children and they in turn supply the words orally.

The cloze procedure is a valuable instructional tool for reading comprehension. However, systematic application is necessary in order to realize the full value of this strategy.

Composing and Comprehending

Reading and writing are similar processes because they are essentially processes of meaning construction (Applebee, 1984). In comprehending text, the reader is constructing meaning; in composing text, the writer is constructing meaning. Readers use their background of experience with the text to think about and understand the text. Writers use their background of experience to generate ideas and to produce a text. Both reading and writing are cognitive processes, concerned with processing language. Writing supports the reading process and reading supports writing.

Box 6.5 compares the processes of comprehending and composing (Squire 1984).

Children learn to read by reading, and they learn to write by writing; they also learn to read by writing, and to write by reading. Dorothy Grant Hennings (1984) points out that "In learning to organize informational content for writing, students gain insight into how authors handle complex ideas on paper; in so doing, they are refining their schemata for comprehending this type of content."

Writing and comprehension

It is apparent that writing can play a prominent role in developing reading comprehension; therefore, students should have many opportunities to write during reading instruction. They should write about the stories and information they read. They should also read and write literature that represents the various forms and functions that they are to comprehend and compose. Many of the

---

Box 6.5 Composing and Comprehending

Prereading:
> Reader uses prior experiences.
> Reader anticipates author's ideas, organization, and vocabulary.
> Reader establishes purpose.

Prewriting:
> Writer uses experiences to generate ideas, including ideas acquired from reading.
> Writer organizes ideas using story grammar and exposition grammar as basis for organization.
> Writer identifies audience.

During comprehending and composing:
> Writer composes—reader comprehends.
> Reader and writer actively engage with text.

After reading:
> Reader analyzes text, evaluates text, discusses text.
> Compares text to other texts.

After composing:
> Writer reads to evaluate, edit, and revise.
> Writer shares by publishing, reading orally, asking others to read.

comprehension strategies introduced in Chapters 5 and 6 involve writing. The majority of reading lessons should include writing activities, just as the majority of writing activities are dependent on students' reading during each stage. They read to prepare to write, they read what they have written as they write, and they reread during the revision and editing processes.

In addition to writing strategies like paraphrasing and summarizing, which were suggested earlier, teachers can ask students to write predictions about a selection they are preparing to read. They may write the prediction in a single sentence or in several sentences; after reading the selection, students should compare their predictions with the actual text. Students may also be asked to write about the most exciting part of a story, a description of the main character, or identify the new facts they acquired from reading a text.

Journals

Journal writing should begin in kindergarten and continue throughout the grades. Journals give students opportunities to reflect, summarize, and ask questions. Journals may be personal or interactive. In an interactive journal, the teacher engages in written exchanges with the student. Journals are also valuable indicators of pupils' growth in writing. Both teacher and students can look through the journal to identify patterns of growth.

Children who have opportunities to read and discuss realistic fiction, traditional literature, fantasy, poetry, and biography are acquiring a sense of the structure of these various literary forms, which will help them write these various forms. In addition, as children read various plots, characterizations, settings, and so forth, they are learning how to write these elements of literature. Previously read text is a model and an incentive for writing. For example, children who understand a story's story grammar, can create story grammars to structure the stories they write. Box 6.6 is an example story grammar composed by a third-grade class. After creating the story grammar, the students wrote individual stories based on the story grammar.

Box 6.6 Story Grammar for Writing

Setting: Mars in the future; the main character is a robot named Michael.
Problem: Michael is stuck on Mars because he cannot get his space ship to fly. He is afraid his batteries will wear out before he gets back to earth.
Episodes:
1. He tried to repair his spaceship, but could not find the parts he needed.
2. He tried to radio for help, but he could not get anyone on the radio.
3. He tried to locate someone on Mars who had a battery recharger to recharge his batteries.

Resolution: When he did not return to earth at the expected time, his owner got worried and sent out a search party; they found him and got him back to earth before his batteries ran down.

Exposition   Hennings (1981) recommends several strategies for relating reading and writing of expository content.

1. Factstorming, which is the process of calling out phrases that come to mind on a topic. Factstorming may occur as the result of reading, listening to a selection read, or seeing a film.
2. Categorizing the facts that were stormed into related groups.
3. Collaborative drafting of paragraphs, based on groups of interrelated facts.
4. Sequencing paragraphs into an interrelated whole.
5. Drafting introductions and conclusions.
6. Organizing the parts into a cohesive report, complete with headings, introductions, and concluding sections.
7. Interpreting similar pieces of discourse.
8. Summarizing, synthesizing, and judging.

SUMMARY

This chapter examined comprehension processes during reading and after reading. The following list summarizes the key points of this chapter.

1. During reading, readers must be actively involved with the text. The depth of processing influences recall and understanding. Elaboration of the ideas and information read enables readers to integrate newly acquired data with existing knowledge.
2. Elaboration is enhanced by mental imagery, writing summaries, completing frames, paraphrasing the text, thinking of examples and applications of the text, and self-questioning.
3. Understanding the *structure* of written texts enhances the readers' comprehension. Text is structured in various ways, such as story grammar and exposition grammar, which were explored in Chapter 5. In this chapter, structure was examined from the perspective of sentence, paragraph, and discourse.
4. Anaphora, pronoun referents in sentences, presents comprehension problems for some students.
5. At the paragraph level, main ideas and supporting details were discussed, as well as the patterns most frequently used in presenting main ideas and supporting details.
6. Follow-up discussion after reading is very important to comprehension; discussion should be a part of every reading comprehension lesson.
7. Certain reading strategies are valuable throughout the comprehension process: before reading, during reading, and after reading.
8. These strategies include DRTA, ReQuest, cloze, and composition.
9. Composing and comprehension are two sides of the same cognitive process; therefore, composition should be a consistent aspect of reading comprehension instruction.

SELF-TEST

Check your knowledge of the information presented in this chapter. The answer key is located in Appendix C.

1. What is the focus of during-reading comprehension strategies?
   a. building vocabulary
   b. increasing readers' control of strategic behaviors
   c. increasing decoding skills and word pronunciation
   d. all of the above

2. Why is integrating new information with existing knowledge so important?
   a. it facilitates higher-order cognitive processes
   b. it makes thinking unnecessary
   c. it places readers in the position of reading each sentence as a separate entity
   d. it is a paraphrase

3. Why is deep processing important in reading?
   a. it involves more thinking than superficial processing
   b. it increases understanding
   c. it increases recall
   d. all of the above

4. What is elaboration?
   a. making written language more elegant
   b. embellishment of text
   c. highlighting important sentences
   d. all of the above

5. Which of the following strategies contribute to elaboration of text?
   a. creating mental images
   b. paraphrasing text
   c. summarizing text
   d. all of the above

6. Which of the following statements describes mental imagery?
   a. writing paragraphs that describe textual illustrations
   b. using television in reading classes
   c. creating mental images of text
   d. choosing appropriate colors for black and white illustrations

7. What are the components of a comprehension lesson?
   a. modeling
   b. guided practice
   c. independent practice
   d. all of the above

8. What is the first stage of mental imagery instruction?
   a. creating images of concrete objects
   b. creating mental images while reading
   c. altering mental images
   d. all of the above

9. Why is discussion an important aspect of mental imagery instruction?
   a. it isn't
   b. it helps students realize that classmates' images may differ from their own
   c. it helps them create correct images
   d. it alters their individual experiences

10. What is the purpose of summaries?
    a. to model word recognition
    b. to read aloud expressively
    c. to conform to semantic and syntactic rules of English
    d. to condense original content

11. What are the major characteristics of effective summaries?
    a. they are rambling recapitulations of the entire text
    b. they retain the information, essence, and point of view of the text
    c. they embellish the information presented in the original text
    d. they are written in outline form

12. Which of the following is not a rule for preparing a sound summary?
    a. delete unnecessary material
    b. delete redundant material
    c. select a topic sentence
    d. avoid using the author's terms

13. What are frames?
    a. an empty square in which the reader writes a summary
    b. a sequence of spaces hooked together by key language elements
    c. a series of blanks requiring completion with specific answers
    d. all of the above

14. What is paraphrasing?
    a. altering the author's ideas
    b. diagramming main ideas and details
    c. phrasing found in exposition
    d. restating information in the reader's words

15. What are considered the structural elements of text?
    a. punctuation
    b. sentences and paragraphs
    c. discourse
    d. all of the above

16. What word is used to identify the relationship between sentences?
    a. punctuation
    b. cohesion
    c. cognitive-derivative
    d. all of the above

17. Which main idea task is taught first?
    a. implicit main ideas
    b. main ideas in lists of words
    c. explicit main ideas
    d. main ideas in short passages

18. How can a student identify an unstated main idea?
    a. by studying the details
    b. by using typography

c. meditation

d. selecting the first sentence in the paragraph

19. What is anaphora?

a. a new type of word-recognition skill

b. substituting a word for a preceding word or words

c. a part of the request procedure

d. instruction before reading

20. Which answer represents DRTA?

a. Decoding-Reading-Thinking-Activity

b. Department-Recording-Thinking-Act

c. Directed-Reading-Thinking-Activity

d. none of the above

21. What is the ReQuest Procedure?

a. a questioning strategy during which the student and the teacher ask questions

b. an exercise that only involves questioning by the teacher

c. a type of workbook exercise

d. a way of requesting assistance in reading comprehension

22. What are the most important organizational factors in paragraphs?

a. punctuation and capitalization

b. main ideas and supporting details

c. both a and b

d. neither a nor b.

23. What are the two major types of postreading strategies?

a. follow-up discussions and composition

b. reading orally

c. decoding the words

d. workbooks and worksheets

24. What is the purpose of the ReQuest procedure?

a. reading with expression

b. teaching students to ask and answer questions

c. to develop students' reference skills

d. to practice speed reading

25. Why are reading and writing so closely related?

a. because they are both concerned with constructing meaning

b. because both are concerned with written language

c. both a and b

d. neither a nor b

THOUGHT QUESTIONS

1. Explain the concept of deep processing in your own words.

2. How are deep processing and elaboration related?

3. Why is it important for readers to integrate new knowledge with existing knowledge?

4. How does the ReQuest procedure contribute to learning to ask and answer questions?
5. Explain the Directed-Reading-Thinking-Activity.
6. How does the cloze procedure function as a comprehension strategy?
7. Discuss the relationship between composing and comprehending.
8. Why should writing be an aspect of most reading comprehension lessons?

ENRICHMENT ACTIVITIES

1. Make a lesson plan for teaching anaphora.
2. Look at a trade book and identify examples of cohesion.
3. Prepare a lesson for teaching the ReQuest procedure. If possible, teach this lesson in an elementary classroom; afterward, identify the strengths and weaknesses of the lesson.
4. Identify a chapter in a content textbook and use the approach suggested by Dorothy Grant Hennings to plan a lesson.
5. Create a story grammar that could be used as a basis for writing a story.
6. Plan a main idea lesson for expository material.
7. Compare the DRTA with a lesson plan in a basal reader teacher's manual. How are the lessons alike and how are they different? How could you change the basal lesson to make it more like the DRTA?

RELATED READINGS

Alvermann, D., D. Dillon, and D. O'Brien (1987). *Using Discussion to Promote Reading Comprehension,* Newark, DE: International Reading Association.
Applebee, A. (Winter 1984). "Writing and Reasoning," *Review of Educational Research,* Vol. 54, pp. 577–596.
Baumann, J., Ed. (1986). *Teaching Main Idea Comprehension,* Newark, DE: International Reading Association.
Blatt, G. and L. Rosen (October 1984). "The Writing Response to Literature," *Journal of Reading,* Vol. 28, pp. 8–12.
Combs, W. (January 1977). "Sentence-Combining Practice Aids Reading Comprehension," *The Reading Teacher,* Vol. 32, pp. 18–24.
Davey, B. (October 1983). "Think Aloud—Modeling the Cognitive Processes of Reading Comprehension," *Journal of Reading,* Vol. 27, pp. 44–47.
Gordon, C. (February 1985). "Modeling Inference Awareness Across the Curriculum," *Journal of Reading,* Vol. 29, pp. 444–447.
Heller, M. (February 1986). "How Do You Know What You Know? Metacognitive Modeling in the Content Areas," *Journal of Reading,* Vol. 29, pp. 415–422.
Holmes, B. and N. Roser (March 1987). "Five Ways to Assess Readers' Prior Knowledge," *The Reading Teacher,* Vol. 40, pp. 646–649.
Irwin, J., Ed. (1986). *Understanding and Teaching Cohesion Comprehension,* Newark, DE: International Reading Association.
Jensen, J., Ed. (1984). *Composing and Comprehending,* Urbana, IL: National Conference on Research in English.

Koskinen, P., L. Gambrell, B. Kapinus, and B. Heathington (May 1988). "Retelling: A Stratcgy for Enhancing Students' Reading Comprehension," *The Reading Teacher*, Vol. 41, pp. 892–898.

Manzo, A. and U. Casale (April 1985). "Listen-Read-Discuss: A Content Heuristic," *Journal of Reading*, Vol. 28, pp. 732–734.

Pinnell, G. (1984). "Communication in Small Group Settings," *Theory into Practice*, Vol. 23, 246–254.

Shoop, M. (March 1986). "InQuest: A Listening and Reading Comprehension Strategy," *The Reading Teacher*, Vol. 39, pp. 670–674.

Uttero, D. (January 1988). "Activating Comprehension Through Cooperative Learning," *The Reading Teacher*, Vol. 41, pp. 390–395.

Winograd, P. and L. Smith (December 1987). "Improving the Climate for Reading Comprehension Instruction," *The Reading Teacher*, Vol. 41, pp. 304–310.

Wong, B. (Summer 1985). "Self-Questioning Instructional Research: A Review," *Review of Educational Research*, Vol. 55, pp. 227–268.

REFERENCES

Alvermann, D., D. Dillon, and D. O'Brien (1987). *Using Discussion to Promote Reading Comprehension*, Newark, DE: International Reading Association.

Applebee, A. (Winter 1984). "Writing and Reasoning," *Review of Educational Research*, Vol. 54, pp. 577–596.

Armbruster, B., T. Anderson, and J. Ostertag (Summer 1987). "Does Text Structure/ Summarization Instruction Facilitate Learning from Expository Text?" *Reading Research Quarterly*, Vol. 22, pp. 331–346.

Baumann, J. (1986). "The Direct Instruction of Main Idea Comprehension Ability," in *Teaching Main Idea Comprehension*, J. Baumann (Ed.), Newark, DE: International Reading Association.

Baumann, J. and J. Stevenson (1986). "Identifying Types of Anaphoric Relationships," in *Understanding and Teaching Cohesion Comprehension*, J. Irwin (Ed.), Newark, DE: International Reading Association.

Blachowicz, C. (December 1977). "Cloze Activities for Primary Readers," *The Reading Teacher*, Vol. 31, No. 3, pp. 300–307.

Bormuth, J. (1968). "The Cloze Readability Procedure," in *Readability in 1968, a Research Bulletin*, J. Bormuth (Ed.), Champaign, IL: National Council of Teachers of English, pp. 40–47.

Bridges, D. (April 1985) "Quality of Understanding in Classroom Discussion," Paper presented to the annual meeting of the American Educational Research Association, Chicago.

Bromley, K. (January 1985). "Precis Writing and Outlining Aids to Learning Content Materials," *The Reading Teacher*, Vol. 38, No. 4, pp. 534–539.

Brown, A. and J. Day (1983). "Macrorules for Summarizing Texts: The Development of Expertise," *Journal of Verbal Learning and Verbal Behavior*, Vol. 22, No. 1, pp. 1–14.

Bull, B. and M. Wittrock (November 1973). "Imagery in the Learning of Verbal Definitions," *British Journal of Educational Psychology*, Vol. 43, pp. 55–70.

Castillo, G. (1972). "Eight Months in the First Grade," in *Human Teaching for Human Learning*, G. Brown (Ed.), New York: Viking-Compass, pp. 131–193.

Catterson, J. (1979). "Comprehension: The Argument for a Discourse Analysis Model," in *Reading Comprehension at Four Linguistic Levels,* C. Pennock (Ed.), Newark, DE: International Reading Association.

Cohn, M. (February 1969). "Structured Comprehension," *The Reading Teacher,* Vol. 22, No. 5, pp. 440–444.

Cooke, J. and M. Haipt (1986). *Thinking with the Whole Brain: An Integrative Teaching/ Learning Model (K–8),* Washington, DC: National Education Association.

Combs, W. (January 1977). "Sentence-Combining Practice Aids Reading Comprehension," *The Reading Teacher,* Vol. 21, pp. 18–24.

DeMille, R. (1967). *Put Your Mother on the Ceiling,* New York: Penguin Books.

Fay, L., R. Ross, and M. LaPray (1978). *The Young America Reading Program.* Chicago, IL: Rand McNally.

Flavell, J. (1981). "Cognitive Monitoring," in *Children's Oral Communication Skills,* W. Dickson (Ed.), New York: Academic Press.

Fowler, G. (November 1982). "Developing Comprehension Skills in Primary Students Through the Use of Story Frames," *The Reading Teacher,* Vol. 36, No. 2, pp. 176–179.

Fredericks, A. (October 1986). "Mental Imagery Activities to Improve Comprehension," *The Reading Teacher,* Vol. 40, No. 1, pp. 78–83.

Guthrie, J. (February 1977). "Story Comprehension," *The Reading Teacher,* Vol. 30, pp. 574–577.

Guthrie, J., M. Seifert, N. Burnham, and R. Caplan (November 1974). "The Maze Technique to Assess, Monitor Reading Comprehension," *The Reading Teacher,* Vol. 28, No. 2, pp. 161–168.

Halliday, M. A. K. and R. Hansen (1976). *Cohesion in English,* London: Longman.

Harrison, C. (1982). "The Nature and Effect of Children's Rewriting School Textbook Prose," paper presented at the Ninth World Congress on Reading, Dublin.

Hennings, D. (1984). "A Writing Approach to Reading Comprehension—Schema Theory in Action," in *Composing and Comprehending,* J. Jensen (Ed.), Urbana, IL: National Conference on Research in English.

Huck, C. (1987). *Children's Literature in the Elementary School,* 4th ed., New York: Holt, Rinehart and Winston.

Huffstetler, S. (March 1979). *Main Idea Strategy,* Greensboro, NC: The University of North Carolina at Greensboro.

Irwin, J., Ed. (1986). *Understanding and Teaching Cohesion Comprehension,* Newark, DE: International Reading Association.

Kamm, K. (1979). "Focusing Reading Comprehension Instruction: Sentence Meaning Skills," in *Reading Comprehension at Four Linguistic Levels,* C. Pennock (Ed.), Newark, DE: International Reading Association, pp. 44–56.

Koskinen, P., L. Gambrell, B. Kapinus, B. Heathington (May 1988). "Retelling: A Strategy for Enhancing Students' Reading Comprehension." *The Reading Teacher,* Vol. 41, pp. 892–898.

Manzo, A. (November 1969). "The ReQuest Procedure," *Journal of Reading,* Vol. 13, No. 2, pp. 123–126.

Manzo, A. and U. Manzo (May 1987). "Asking, Answering, Commenting: A Participation Training Strategy," paper presented at the International Reading Association, Anaheim, CA.

—— (April 1985). "Listen-Read-Discuss: A Content Heuristic," *Journal of Reading,* Vol. 28, pp. 732–734.

Marshall, N. and M. Glock (1978–1979). "Comprehension of Connected Discourse: A Study into the Relationships Between the Structure of Text and Information Recalled," *Reading Research Quarterly,* Vol. 24, pp. 10–56.

McKim, R. (1980). *Experiences in Visual Thinking,* 2nd ed., Monterey, CA: Brooks/Cole.

McNeil, J. (1987). *Reading Comprehension,* 2nd ed., Chicago: Scott, Foresman and Company.

McNeil, J. and L. Donant (1982). "Summarization Strategy for Improving Reading Comprehension," *New Inquiries in Reading Research Instruction,* 31st Yearbook of the National Reading Conference, J. Niles and L. Miller (Eds.), Rochester, NY: The National Reading Conference.

Mundell, D. (1985). *Mental Imagery: Do You See What I Say?* Oklahoma City, OK: Oklahoma State Department of Education.

Nichols, J. (December 1980). "Using Paragraph Frames to Help Remedial High School Students with Written Assignments," *Journal of Reading,* Vol. 33, No. 2, pp. 228–231.

Oaken, R., M. Wiener, and W. Cromer (1971). "Identification, Organization and Reading Comprehension for Good and Poor Readers," *Journal of Educational Psychology,* Vol. 62, pp. 71–78.

Pinnell, G. S. (1984). "Communication in Small Group Settings," *Theory into Practice,* Vol. 23, pp. 246–254.

Presseisen, B. (1986). *Thinking Skills: Research and Practice,* Washington, DC: National Education Association.

Pressey, G., "Mental Imagery Helps Eight-Year Olds Remember What They Read," *Journal of Educational Psychology,* Vol. 68, pp. 355–359.

Raphael, T. (November 1982). "Question-Answering Strategies for Children," *The Reading Teacher,* Vol. 36, pp. 186–190.

Singer, H. (May 1978). "Active Comprehension: From Answering to Asking Questions," *The Reading Teacher,* Vol. 31, pp. 901–907.

Smith, C. (May 1978). "Evaluating Answers to Comprehension Questions," *The Reading Teacher,* Vol. 31, pp. 896–900.

Spiegel, D. and J. Fitzgerald (March 1986). "Improving Reading Comprehension Through Instruction About Story Parts," *The Reading Teacher,* Vol. 39, No. 7, pp. 676–683.

Squire, J. (1984). "Composing and Comprehending: Two Sides of the Same Basic Process," in *Composing and Comprehending,* J. Jensen (Ed.), Newark, DE: International Reading Association, pp. 23–32.

Stauffer, R. (1975). *Directing the Reading-Thinking Process,* New York: Harper & Row.

Stoodt, B. and J. Costello (May 1985). "Remedial Readers Learn How to Learn," paper presented to the International Reading Association, New Orleans, LA.

———— (March 1985). "Writing to Learn," Greensboro, NC: University of North Carolina at Greensboro.

Tuinman, J. (February 1980). "The Schema Schemers," *Journal of Reading,* Vol. 23, pp. 414–419.

Wisendanger, K. and J. Wollenberg (May 1978). "Prequestioning Inhibits Third Graders' Reading Comprehension," *The Reading Teacher,* Vol. 32, pp. 892–895.

Viorst, J. (1972). *Alexander and the Terrible, Horrible No Good Very Bad Day,* New York: Atheneum.

PART

III

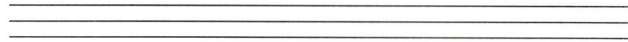

THE
ELEMENTARY
READING PROGRAM

CHAPTER 7

The Elementary Reading Program

OVERVIEW   This chapter guides your synthesis of reading knowledge with teaching and management skills to create a classroom reading program. Chapter 2 addressed the nature and function of groups and lesson planning; subsequent chapters discussed reading skills and abilities. Based on the material presented in the previous chapters, we now create a reading program and select instructional materials. Reading materials are further examined in Chapter 8.

Teachers are the most powerful factors in the reading program. They function as program managers, responsible for teaching approximately 26 students to read each school year. They must plan a year-long reading program, based on daily instruction that helps each youngster develop his or her reading ability to the fullest. Teachers must perform this feat in a limited amount of time and with a variety of distractions. They must "keep school"; that is, manage and discipline children, see to their work habits, collect and count lunch money, complete attendance reports, collect and count magazine subscription money, send children who are ill to the nurse (or home), wipe drippy noses, soothe upset youngsters, break up fights, serve on curriculum committees, attend professional meetings, take courses to update teaching certificates, *and* teach children to read. Such a list would make the most sophisticated CEO (chief executive officer) of a major corporation turn pale, but teachers do manage all of these activities and many others. Teachers are indeed executives, the more successful the teacher, the better his or her managerial skills.

This chapter examines the management skills teachers need for effective reading instruction. They must develop a classroom reading program that meshes with the school's reading philosophy. Once a reading program is established, the most important aspects of management are reading groups, and the "other children"—those who are not a part of the reading group that is receiving direct instruction. The "other children" probably present the greatest problem for teachers; they must be involved in independent learning activities that engage their attention so as *not* to disrupt group instruction.

Finally, assessment plays an important role in reading instruction and pro-

269

gram development. Teachers must be prepared to assess the reading process, which differs from assessing a discipline that includes a prescribed body of knowledge. Reading is assessed by examining the various parts of the reading process. Both assessment and instruction are controlled by teachers' conceptions of reading; they must ask themselves "Should reading be taught as a process or as a set of separate subskills?" This chapter answers this question by synthesizing the reading knowledge you have acquired thus far.

Key Vocabulary

As you read this chapter, check your understanding of these terms:

assessment	**individualized reading**
basal reading program	**interactive theories**
"bottom up" theories	**IRI**
cooperative learning	**norm-referenced tests**
criterion-referenced tests	**reading skills management systems**
holistic	**subskills**
independent activities	**whole-language theory**

Focusing Questions

As you read this chapter, try to answer these questions;

1. Why is management a pivotal factor in reading instruction?
2. Why are the "other children" the most difficult aspect of reading instruction?
3. How does a whole-language program differ from a basal reading program?
4. How is assessment related to instruction and management?

THEORIES OF ELEMENTARY READING

The elementary reading curriculum develops the reading skills and abilities students will use the remainder of their lives to gather information, to entertain themselves, to find spiritual sustenance, and to learn. The reading curriculum usually specifies the reading skills to be learned and the order in which those skills will be introduced.

A sound elementary reading program is characterized by children who read competently and frequently, for pleasure and information (Winograd and Greenlee, 1986). Reading requires more than mastery of a series of subskills; fluent reading combines skills, motivation, knowledge, and experiential background. According to contemporary theory, there are three predominant explanations of reading: holistic or "top down" explanations; subskills or "bottom up" explanations; and combination or interactive explanations.

Holistic Theory

A **holistic** or **"top down"** theory of reading maintains that reading should be taught as a language process, not as a series of skills. Whole-language proponents believe that reading is greater than the sum of its parts. According to this theory, constructing the meaning of print is the goal of reading; in turn, understanding the meaning of print is the driving force in the reading process. Reading is taught as an active process that derives meaning from written language. Teachers who subscribe to a holistic theory of reading believe that children learn words through meaningful, written language (Anderson et al., 1985; U.S. Department of Education, 1986). A holistic approach emphasizes reading as an aspect of the language arts; therefore, speaking, listening, and writing play important roles in a "top down" theory of reading instruction. Children's literature usually provides much of the reading content in a holistic approach.

Individualized
Language
experience
Whole-language

Among the more popular holistic or "bottom up" approaches are individualized reading, language-experience, and whole-language instruction. These approaches are discussed later in this chapter. The continuum of holistic and subskills approaches are shown in Figure 7.1.

Subskills Theory

A **subskills** (**"bottom up"**) theory is at the opposite end of the continuum from holistic approaches. This theory is based on the notion that reading ability is a summary of its parts or skills. A "bottom up" theory of reading acquisition is based on students mastering and coordinating word-recognition and comprehension subskills. Thus, reading is a summary of reading skills. In this approach, instruction focuses on a specific set of reading skills. Students progress through a series of reading subskills, with each skill building on previously mastered skills. They master these skills and practice them so they can fluently coordinate them.

Specific skills

Subskills approaches to reading instruction usually begin with students learning letter names and sounds, then they learn to blend these sounds (phonemes) into words. Proponents of a subskills approach believe that pronouncing

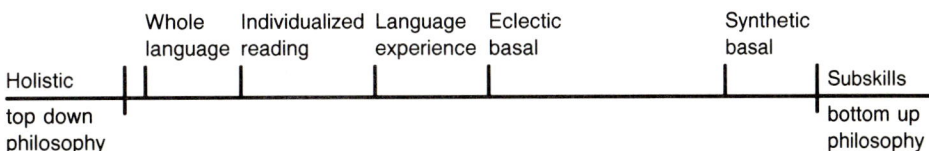

	Whole language	Individualized reading	Language experience	Eclectic basal		Synthetic basal	
Holistic	| |	|	|	|		|	| Subskills
top down philosophy							bottom up philosophy

Figure 7.1   A holistic-subskills continuum.

words enables students to associate meaning with them. For example, students learn the phonemes c/a/t, which they blend to form the word *cat.* After saying the word, students are expected to associate the printed word with the animal that meows. Students in subskills reading programs are introduced to letters, sounds, and words, as well as the rules and exceptions to rules for decoding words. Subskills approaches usually include synthetic or explicit phonics, which include decoding words in isolation. After learning to decode isolated words, students then learn to decode words in sentences.

Comprehension instruction in a subskills approach is also based on carefully sequenced, specific skills. For example, students develop comprehension skills by activities such as identifying stated main ideas and stated supporting details.

Combination or Interactive Theories

Combination or **interactive** approaches to reading are founded on the notion that reading is a process involving aspects of both "top down" and "bottom up." This theory recognizes that reading is a meaning-driven process—meaning often enables readers to recognize specific words in the text. However, there are instances when readers cannot recognize a word that is essential to comprehension; when this occurs, readers must use "bottom up" processes to decode the word so they can comprehend the text.

The most common examples of a combination or interactive approach to reading are seen in eclectic basal readers. Eclectic basal readers emphasize meaning from the outset of reading instruction, but they also include direct instruction. The text in eclectic basal readers is usually comprised of adapted trade books.

WHOLE LANGUAGE

The major theoretical premise supporting whole language is that babies acquire a language through using it, not through practicing its separate parts until some later date, when the parts are assembled and the totality is finally used (Altwerger, Edelsky, and Flores, 1987). Language is used to create meaning. Readers process written language. Therefore, students should acquire reading skills in situations that require them to make meaning. Language is used as a tool for making sense of the world; it is needed for content area learning as well as literacy. A number of writers and researchers in the field of literacy have described whole language (Weaver, 1988; Edelsky, 1986; Newman, 1985; Goodman, 1986; Harste, Woodward, and Burke, 1984; Smith, 1984).

Whole-language theory has emerged from the past decade of research and educational thought regarding effective teaching of reading. However, whole-language approaches to literacy have already withstood the test of time. For example, language-experience instruction and individualized reading (personalized reading) are both long-used, whole-language approaches. Individualized reading was first used in the early 1900s, gaining popularity in the 1960s. The majority of language arts textbooks have endorsed an integrated approach to the language arts for many years. Thus, whole language is an existing theory dressed in new clothing, very much like *The Emperor's New Clothes.* What exactly is the current conception of whole language?

Whole language is a philosophy of teaching, rather than a method. This philosophy maintains that readers must be able to understand written language as an integrated whole—in order to construct a message from print, which substantially matches that of the writer. Students learn through real reading and writing, not just through reading and writing exercises. Skills are not neglected; they are taught within a meaningful context to assist the comprehension process. Whole-language approaches emphasize an early, natural exposure to literature through reading stories to children, as well as offering them many opportunities to read "real" literature.

Whole-language today

The most common conceptualization of whole language and the one endorsed in this text is:

Whole-language instruction is integrated, simultaneous listening, speaking, reading, and writing instruction, presented in a meaningful context.

Whole-language instruction is characterized by the following factors:

1. Curriculum that is meaningful for students, based on their interests, strengths, and needs.
2. Incorporation of children's literature in the literacy program. Teachers should read or tell stories and poetry *every* day.
3. Students must participate in authentic writing *every* day.
4. Students read literature *every* day.
5. Students learn to reflect on and control their own reading and writing processes (metacognition).
6. Cooperative learning, which promotes literacy, through such activities as paired reading, peer tutoring, peer writing conferences, team activities, and the like.

Whole-language classrooms tend to use the following methods and materials, although nothing in this philosophy dictates these particular methods.

1. Literature (in significant amounts).
2. Language-experience instruction.
3. Writing.
4. USSR or DEAR (uninterrupted sustained silent reading; drop everything and read).
5. Paired reading.
6. Interest inventories.
7. Directed-Reading-Thinking-Activity (DRTA).
8. Metacognitive skills (monitoring one's own learning and or understanding).
9. Discovery learning.

Strengths of Whole Language

Reading is language—as are listening, speaking, and writing. Indeed the language arts cannot be separated, even when they are taught separately. A whole-language program uses writing, drama, speaking, listening, discussing, and similar activities in conjunction with children's exploration of books. An integrated approach to literacy is efficient because each of the language arts enhances the others.

Whole language *empowers* teachers, encouraging them to rely on their professional knowledge and experience. Teachers do not merely deliver a program designed by someone else—they invent curriculum and instruction. Teachers use their professional background of experience to develop curriculum.

Literature

Whole-language approaches make use of the excellent literature available, which motivates both teachers and students. Furthermore, research shows that literature develops comprehension and is an effective model for writing. Children develop a story grammar from reading and listening to literature. They build a frame of reference about how stories and information are written. Literature helps children discover what to anticipate in the pattern and language of books. Of course, this knowledge enables them to structure the pattern and language of their own writing.

A whole-language philosophy keeps children as the central focus of literacy instruction. They learn best through material that has meaning for them, and when they read to discover answers to their own questions. Thus, teachers must get acquainted with students' interests early in the school year and use this knowledge to identify reading materials.

A whole-language approach enables children to use all they know about language, as well as their world knowledge. Listening, telling, reading, and writing stories develops all aspects of language; they build children's confidence in their own abilities. This confidence will motivate them to use their language skills. A whole-language approach gives children many opportunities to read, write, speak, and listen. Clearly, the more children read, the better they read. The more children write, the better they write. This approach immerses children in language.

Basals are a springboard

When basal readers are used, they should function as a springboard into a whole-language program. The majority of basal readers are based on selections from the best of children's literature. Furthermore, a sound basal reader incorporates speaking, listening, writing, and reading. The thematic approach used in some basal readers permits children to explore their interests, while acquiring the world knowledge and cultural literacy that enables them to read and understand any book they choose to read. Reading and discussing a common story in a reading group or whole class expands children's ability to recognize words, which enables them to comprehend. Many of the activities associated with basal readers lead children to literature outside of the basal reader. In addition, reading groups give children opportunities to discuss and to work cooperatively.

Box 7.1 illustrates a whole-language approach to literacy, based on combining basal reader materials with children's literature. The basal reader literature is a preprimer (first-grade) story from *The Riverside Reading Program,* while the trade book used to introduce this story is *Swimmy* by Leo Lionni.

Whole language is equally valuable in the intermediate grades. Middle-grade lessons can by styled like the example in Box 7.1, using literature appropriate to the higher grade levels. Some intermediate-grade lessons may extend over three days of instruction, while a unit may cover several weeks.

All types of literature

In addition to narrative literature and poetry, students at the intermediate-grade level are exposed to considerable expository literature; they are expected to study topics in depth and to write reports. Teachers should read aloud from informational literature, and should encourage students to choose informational materials for independent reading. As they read and write on a variety of subjects, students refine their literacy skills. Specific themes, topics, or units can be developed to enhance learning. These themes or units may grow out of the textbook, students' interests, or current events.

The example shown in Box 7.1, presents only a few of the possibilities for developing whole-language literacy instruction. As teachers well know, there are no simple formulas for success. When teachers use their professional knowledge and experience, the sky is the limit. Simple exposure to print is not sufficient. Children need carefully designed instruction in order to develop reading, writing, listening, and speaking abilities. There is no substitute for a thoughtful, perceptive, and skillful teacher.

Weaknesses of Whole Language

A whole-language philosophy of teaching is valuable; it is the ideal toward which many teachers strive. However, to implement this philosophy, teachers need to understand both its strengths and weaknesses. This section addresses the weaknesses that teachers must compensate for, in a whole-language program.

Time is an impediment to whole-language reading instruction. Teachers need considerable time to plan instruction and select appropriate materials. They must analyze students' interests. Furthermore, in order to plan instruction, teachers must have extensive knowledge of children's literature and language development. Successful whole-language teachers often devote the entire summer to reading and selecting materials for the school year. The whole-language approach is the most demanding of all the instructional philosophies.

Students need considerable time to process the print necessary to develop an understanding of written language. They need time to figure out the words in written language. Children learn to read by reading and to write by writing, *but* first, they must know *how* to read and *how* to write. Only then can they read to develop reading ability and write to refine writing ability.

Whole language programs also present some problems for teachers. Class

Box 7.1   Whole Language in First Grade

This is a two-day lesson based on the story "The Big Splash," which is the introductory story in the unit "Going Up."

Day One

In the example, Miss Robinson introduces the book *Swimmy* by Leo Lionni to the entire class, explaining that the story is set in the ocean, and the main character, Swimmy, has a problem. She explains that many stories are based on problems and solutions. The children listen to the story to identify the problem and the solution to the problem (Chapter 6). She also points out that the author uses some interesting words in the story and suggests that they listen carefully to understand what the words mean (Chapter 5). After listening to the story, they discuss Swimmy's problem (he is afraid of being eaten by the bigger fish), then they discuss the solution (he teaches the little fish to swim together like a big fish). Then they discuss the interesting words the author used. Finally, Miss Robinson asks a reading group to go to the reading table to prepare for reading "The Big Splash." She sends the other children to their seats to write a story about Swimmy.

She explains to the reading group that the story is an ocean story about a seal and a whale with a problem, although the problem is different from Swimmy's problem. She asks them to think about the kinds of problems the seal and whale might encounter. After a brief discussion, she introduces the new vocabulary with the sentences in the children's textbooks (Chapter 5).

The next step is guided silent reading. This step uses the suggested silent reading purposes and follow-up discussion from the text. During the discussion, they identify the story problem and problem solution. After the discussion, the children return to their seats to write letters of advice to the little whale.

Day Two

On the second day, Miss Robinson has the children dictate a language-experience story to review "The Big Splash." She asks them to include some of the interesting words they heard in *Swimmy* when dictating the story (Chapter 4).

The teacher's edition includes skills instruction related to the long e (Chapter 5). Students who need to develop this skill can identify long e words in the story, and can write additional words that include the long e sound.

The teacher's edition also includes antonym instruction. Words from the story like *big, little, up,* and *down* can be used to initiate antonyms. Then children can dictate lists of antonyms or draw illustrations of antonyms.

> A choice of avenues to reading are available to teachers. The children may work in pairs rereading "The Big Splash" to one another, they may read the language-experience story, or the teacher may obtain for the children sets of books like:
>
> *How High Is Up* by Bernice Kohn
> *The Ups and Downs of Marvin* by Barbara Shook Hazen
> *Pirates, Pirates over the Salt, Salt Sea* by Patty Wolcott

size is often too large for effective whole-language instruction. Teachers need large numbers of books to develop a whole-language program. Just to start a whole-language program, a minimum of 10 books per child is needed. These books must be in the classroom, in addition to the resources provided by a centralized school library. The amount of time and effort involved in program planning and development is prohibitive for many teachers. In addition evaluation is more complex.

Higher reading achievement is attained through direct instruction. Proponents of whole language advocate attitude, enthusiasm, and the numbers of books read, rather than reading achievement. Combing the best aspects of whole language and direct instruction seems to be the best approach. The commonly used whole-language approaches, language experience, and individualized reading are discussed in the next sections.

THE LANGUAGE-EXPERIENCE APPROACH

The basic philosophy of a **language-experience** approach is summarized in the following list (Lee and Van Allen, 1963).

1. Children can talk about their thoughts.
2. Children's thoughts can be expressed in painting, writing, or some other form.
3. Anything the child writes, can be read.
4. Children can read what *they* write, as well as what *other people* write.
5. As children record the sounds that they make in speech, they use the same letters over and over.

The language-experience approach to reading instruction, which was thoroughly discussed in Chapter 3, may be used as a reading program for all grade levels. Charts are adapted for intermediate-grade children by writing in cursive letters rather than in typed manuscript form. The guidelines discussed in Chapter 3 are also useful for older children. The language-experience approach may be combined with either a basal reader or individualized reading. The language-experience approach lends itself to individualized instruction; it has the advantage of being based on the child's own experiences (Fields and Lee, 1987).

INDIVIDUALIZED OR PERSONALIZED READING INSTRUCTION

Individualized reading instruction is a holistic approach to literacy, which involves children choosing many of the materials they read. The reading selections include a wide array of children's literature, informational books, magazines, and other printed materials. Children choose reading materials that have meaning for them; therefore, this approach is also called personalized reading. This approach has four basic characteristics. First, children use their own language in learning to read; this approach emphasizes the complementary role of reading and writing, by giving children many opportunities to write. Second, individual students self-select the materials they will read. They read at their own pace, which some authorities believe enhances reading growth (Veatch, 1978). Third, they meet individually with their teacher to discuss their reading. Finally, specific need groups are formed when direct instruction is required to teach a specific skill. Students with similar needs are grouped together.

The advantages of individualized reading instruction have been identified by researchers. Veatch (1978) summarized this research and identified five major advantages of this approach:

- Attitudes toward reading are significantly improved when this approach is implemented.
- The teacher-pupil conference is a valuable aspect of this program.
- Children tend to read a greater volume of material when they participate in these programs.
- Children can learn to choose books they are capable of reading. This is an important factor because some teachers feel that children will choose books that are too difficult.
- Children's self-concepts improve.

When implementing an individualized reading program, teachers should begin with diagnosing students' reading level, identifying their reading interests, and identifying their strengths and weaknesses in reading.

Teachers also must gather a variety of printed materials for students to read. These materials may include fiction, nonfiction, poetry, newspapers, magazines, brochures, and so forth. Students should have access to these materials, as well as those in the school media center. A minimum number of books for initiating an individualized reading program is 10 per student, thus a class of 26 students should have access to a minimum of 260 books (Barbe and Abbott, 1975).

Four activities most commonly occur during individualized reading instruction. Students have a silent reading period during which they read independently from materials of their own choosing. This period is similar to SSR (sustained silent reading) or USSR (uninterrupted sustained silent reading); students are encouraged to read independently, but they may ask for assistance with word identification or similar problems. While students are reading silently, others participate in individual pupil-teacher conferences. Subsequently, students may have opportunities to share their reading with their classmates. Students also participate in special need groups.

Some teachers express concerns about having individual conferences with students, as they are not able to read all of the books that the students are reading. Although teachers cannot possibly read every book available to children, they should, nevertheless, be prepared to discuss books that are unfamiliar to them. Teachers who are conducting conferences on unfamiliar stories may open the discussion with a statement like this one: "Since I have not read this book, what do you think I should know about it?" or "Do you think I should read this book? Why or why not?" Discussions can also focus on plot, theme, characterization, or setting of the book. The following areas may be discussed in the individual conference.

1. Affective areas.
    a. Why did the child select this book?
    b. How did the child react to the book?
    c. Would the child enjoy experiences similar to those in the book?
    d. Does the youngster know someone else who might enjoy this book?
2. Comprehension.
    a. Did this book contain words the child did not understand?
    b. Could this story actually happen? How does the child know this?
    c. Ask the child to retell the story. Discuss plot, theme, characterization, setting, and style.
    d. If the book is an informational one, ask the child if he or she learned any new facts?
3. Word-recognition skills.
    a. Were there any new words that the child was unable to identify (pronounce)? The teacher should ask the child to identify words that could present problems for other readers.
4. Oral reading.
    a. Ask the child to read his or her favorite part of the story, or a section that describes a character, setting, or climax.

Teacher-pupil conferences should be scheduled at regular intervals. These conferences help teachers diagnose individual needs and enables the teacher to provide the necessary instruction. Conferences also give students a feeling that the teacher has a genuine interest in their reading development.

Time is a major element in pupil-teacher conferences. A teacher and child may become so engrossed in the book discussion that the schedule for the remaining conferences is too short. A three-minute egg timer is a helpful reminder of the time allotted for individual conferences.

Group conferences are also useful in an individualized reading program. These conferences can be arranged when several children who have read the same book meet with the teacher. Group discussions effectively enhance reading comprehension. In a group discussion, one or more individuals usually bring up unique ideas, which, in turn, stimulate thinking.

Children participating in an individualized reading program should regularly share some of the books they have read with the rest of the class. Books can be shared through art, music, drama, writing, and so forth.

Both teachers and pupils should be involved in the record-keeping tasks that are associated with individualized reading. Teachers should maintain a file for each child, which includes individual observations. Figure 7.2 shows a sample entry from a teacher's file.

File folders should be maintained, so students can record the titles they read and their reactions to the books. Figure 7.3 is a sample entry from a child's file.

As stated earlier, both conferences and special needs groups are important aspects of individualized reading. Special needs groups are formed for a specific purpose. They are disbanded when that purpose is achieved. For example, a group of students may be formed when they need to learn how to identify main ideas and supporting details. This group may meet for a week or two until they master this skill, then they disband. New groups are formed to develop other skills or to provide guided practice of skills. Special needs groups meet for short periods each day, usually for no longer than 10 to 15 minutes.

BASAL READERS

Basal readers are books designed for use in teaching children to read. Each basal reading program offers a set of reading skills that are presented and reviewed

Date: 12/4
Book: *The Endless Steppe* by Hautzig
Progress: Word-by-word reading
Comment: Interested in story but may need easier book.

Figure 7.2 An entry from a teacher's file.

Title: A Bear Called Paddington

Author: Bond

Date Started: 6/12

Date Completed: 6/15

Was this a good book? Why? Yes, it was funny.

Figure 7.3 An entry from a child's file.

in a specific sequence. Reading instruction is presented through student texts comprised of fiction, nonfiction, and poetry. In many basal reading programs, the majority of the students' texts are derived from children's trade books, some of which are reproduced exactly; others are abridged because they are too lengthy for a reader; and others are adapted so that the reading difficulty of the text gradually increases as students move through the program. The teacher's edition of a basal reading series provides explicit instructions for teaching the skills included in the program.

Basal reader authors generally agree that reading skills are important, but that skills alone will not assure comprehension. The skills must be taught in a context that encourages students to read and to love reading (Aaron, 1987). The basic philosophy behind most basal reading programs is that children must be taught to read. They need systematic reading instruction in conjunction with skills practice in order to achieve and maintain proficiency. Extensive reading leads to increased vocabularies, enlarged knowledge (cultural literacy and schemata), broader interests, greater appreciation of writing techniques and styles, and improved speed of comprehension. Furthermore, enjoyment and appreciation of literature are increased by wide reading (Aaron, 1987).

Basal readers are "springboards" into reading. No basal series was ever intended to be a complete, self-contained reading program. Individual basal reader texts do not include enough material to meet children's needs. Additional reading from children's literature gives students opportunities to enjoy reading, and enables them to practice implementing the skills they have acquired.

The majority of schools in the United States have an adopted basal reading program that teachers are expected to use. In 90 to 95% of the elementary schools, an adopted basal reading series is ordinarily used for a minimum of five years (Aukerman, 1981). School systems usually chose basal readers that parallel the local reading curriculum. However, teachers are expected to follow the skills sequence in the series, and to use the tests accompanying the program. The tests determine whether students have sufficiently learned the skills necessary for moving into the next level of readers.

Types of Basal Readers

Among current basal readers, there are two major types: eclectic basal readers and synthetic (or phonics first) basal readers. To the eye of a novice, basal readers look very much alike, but closer scrutiny reveals differences.

Eclectic basal readers include basic instruction to teach children sight words, context clues, structural analysis, and phonics. Comprehension skills are developed from the outset of reading instruction, beginning with the readiness level of materials. Both sight words and the word-identification skills are introduced in context, which enables children to associate meaning with words. Basal readers include study skills and content reading instruction in the middle grades. Throughout the program, word meanings and background knowledge are developed. The student texts are largely comprised of children's literature, like those described in the preceding section.

Synthetic basal readers introduce phonics first, beginning with phonemes (sounds), and moving on to words that can be blended from the sounds they have learned. The students' texts are comprised of selections that are based on words that can be formed from the sounds that students have learned. For example, students who have learned the short a, the /n/, and the /t/ would be limited to a text comprised of words like, *tan, ant, an, at,* and *Nat.* Synthetic basal readers stress phonics as a means of decoding words, and the students spend considerable time "sounding out" words in isolation. The philosophy behind this approach is that students will understand the meaning of a word after they pronounce it. Therefore, this approach teaches the sounds and the rules necessary for pronouncing English words.

Comprehension is not neglected in a synthetic basal, but it is stressed later, with the greatest emphasis occurring at the upper-grade levels. In the early stages, the basal text is limited to sounds that students have learned, which of course, limits the text. Comprehension is not as prominent in the early stages of reading, as the early text stresses the decoding of words, rather than the development of comprehension.

Using the Basal Reader: A Basal Lesson

Basal readers are discussed in depth in Chapter 8; however, this section addresses enriching the basal reading program with supplemental literature. Since basal readers are not complete reading programs, authors and publishers of these programs expect that teachers will use their own professional knowledge and experience to enrich them. This is why so many basal reading programs incorporate reading selections from children's literature.

Teachers can use the text selections to encourage students to read trade books. When selections have been abridged or adapted, students can read the original selections. Students should be encouraged to compare the basal reader text with the original trade book. In other instances, when a complete trade book or poem is reproduced, the students may read other selections by the same author. Students may want to do an in-depth study of an author, which will help them understand the author's choice of subject and writing style.

Some basal readers are developed around thematic units, which can be used to encourage students' reading. The teacher can identify additional books related to the unit. Frequently, the teacher's edition suggests additional readings on the same subject. Reading stories aloud that are based on the theme encourages students to read, and some teacher's manuals include lists of books to read aloud that are related to the theme.

Many basal readers include example selections of different types of literature, such as realistic fiction, biography, historical fiction, poetry, traditional literature, and information. These selections can be used to introduce different types of literature, and to develop students' appreciation of them. In addition, teachers can use these selections to lead students into reading other examples of the various types of literature. When the selections are arranged in thematic units, students can compare the treatment of a subject in the various literary forms.

Literature and basal readers can be further explored through the arts. Children should have opportunities to respond to literature in a variety of ways such as art, music, and drama.

Combining basal reading instruction with whole language, individualized reading, and/or language experience offers students the best of each approach. Overall instruction can be built on the basal reader, along with assigned individualized reading, which can enhance reading development. In individualized reading, the students read trade books of their choice, and discuss their reading in teacher-student conferences. When combining language experience with the basal reader, teachers use student-written materials to enhance basal reader lessons. As a foundation for composing stories, students can use topics and concepts developed in the basal. No matter what approach is used, teachers should read to students every day, and students should discuss the selections the teacher reads. As well, the students should read silently, and then discuss their reading in conferences.

Combination approaches usually involve extensive use of children's literature; therefore, teachers should refer to Chapter 9 for additional suggestions regarding the use of children's literature. The following vignette illustrates a combined approach.

WRITING

You may find it unusual that writing is included in a discussion of reading programs. The reason for this is an important one: I believe that along with hearing stories, one of the most powerful influences on proficient readers is writing stories. Students who hear many stories again and again, and who have opportunities to write again and again, will do so, and in the process, become excellent readers. Listening, speaking, reading, writing, and thinking comprise the literacy cycle. Whole-language approaches to literacy stress the importance of students participating in authentic (purposeful, meaningful) writing activities every day.

The writing process comprises *prewriting* or preparation for writing, *composing,* which is the actual writing of text, *revision,* which is the rethinking and rewriting of text, and the *editing* process, which permits students to refine handwriting, spelling, punctuation, and capitalization. In some classrooms, the final aspect of writing is *publishing,* or making writing products public. Students may do this through reading aloud, preparing bulletin boards, and making hardback books.

Children *want* to write. Most of them come to school believing they can write because they have experimented with pencils, Magic Markers, chalk, crayons, and pens. Children know that adults write for specific purposes, as they have observed them making grocery lists, leaving notes, copying recipes, and writing letters and greeting cards. They expect adults to obtain meaning from written language.

Box 7.2   Third-Grade Vignette

Rose Wilson is in her second year of teaching. She has 26 third-grade students, including Jerry, who reads at a fourth-grade level, and Kristen, who reads only a few words. Her class is divided into three reading groups, but she incorporates whole-class instruction as well. Basal reader instruction in this vignette is based on the selection "Blackout," which was adapted from a book by Anne and Harlow Rockwell. We will visit Ms. Wilson's average reading group.

On *Monday,* Ms. Wilson introduced the story to her class by explaining that "Blackout" is a story about a winter storm, and how a family meets the problems created by the storm. Then she asked the students to think of problems that might arise as a result of a winter storm. She wrote the problems that students identified on the chalkboard, which gave her an opportunity to teach the new words introduced in the story (storm, shivered, faucet, emergency, exhausted, and radiator). *Notice that she used students' own language as a basis for developing reading vocabulary.* This is a whole-language strategy. Then Ms. Wilson reviewed the consonant digraph, *sh* (initial and final position), and the *ed* ending on verbs. Rose instructed the students to identify words in the story that included the *sh* digraph and *ed* verbs.

Then the students read "Blackout" silently to identify the emergencies in the story, while Rose moved on to teach the next group.

On *Tuesday,* Ms. Wilson reviewed the new words and the silent reading purpose. Then the group discussed the emergencies that arose in the story and read sections of the story aloud to support their discussion of emergencies (oral language and listening development). When the students completed their discussion, Ms. Wilson asked them to think about emergencies they had experienced. After a few minutes of thinking, she had the students brainstorm the concept, emergency (oral language and listening development). After the discussion, the students returned to their desks to write about emergencies they had experienced (composition).

On *Wednesday,* the students worked in pairs reading their compositions aloud to one another. Then they revised their emergency stories and read them aloud to the reading group (reading, writing, oral language, and listening). Some of the students wanted more writing time, while others were satisfied with their drafts. Some of the students chose to read trade books on the same theme as "Blackout." These books included *The Mushroom Center Disaster, Bus Ride,* Growing Time, and *A Bowl.*

On *Thursday,* Ms. Wilson introduced the next story in the basal reader unit to the reading group.

What do children learn from writing? They learn that written language should make sense, which helps them make sense of texts that they read and write. When listening to and writing stories, children expand their knowledge of story language (Weaver, 1988) and their sense of story grammar. When they read, their knowledge of story language and story grammar enables them to comprehend characters, settings, theme, plot, and author's style. Children learn to attend to print as they construct meaning. After constructing meaning in written language, they better understand how authors express meaning. Writing expands their knowledge of sound/symbol relationships. By encoding their ideas, students learn to decode written words. When students write, they use thinking skills. Writing is a thinking process. During composing, writers think their topic through, and reflect on their experiences. Furthermore, through writing, teachers can observe the ways students handle problem-solving, cause and effect, main ideas and supporting details, descriptions, and comparisons. Writing these patterns helps students comprehend them. While composing and revising, students read and reread their compositions many times, which enhances reading development.

Children should draw or write their ideas on the first day of kindergarten and on every subsequent school day. For example, kindergarten teachers may invite children to draw pictures or write stories about themselves. Later the teacher may invite them to read their stories aloud. Children who are encouraged to write every day, generate many ideas; they are further encouraged when the teacher shows that he or she values their writing. Elementary-school students, including kindergarten and first-grade students, enjoy reflecting on the events in their lives as they write in journals every day.

Intermediate-grade students can reflect on topics, classes, and textbooks, and respond to them in interactive journals. Then the teacher reads and responds to the students' journals. Teachers' questions, responses, and comments in the journals encourage students' learning, and demonstrate the value they place on students' writing.

Older students who have not had opportunities to write are more reluctant writers, but in time, they will develop the trust that permits them to write. Teachers of these students need to assure them that their ideas will be valued; this will help convince the students that they can translate those ideas into written language.

Writing is an important aspect of *all* reading programs. Developing their writing skills will enhance students' reading skills.

READING SKILLS MANAGEMENT SYSTEMS

One of the difficulties in individualized reading programs and whole-language programs is managing and monitoring reading skill development. However, teachers can create their own skill checklists or they can use those provided in texts (Barbe and Abbott, 1975); their local school system may also provide an inventory of reading skills for each grade level. Another means of managing reading programs is a skills management system.

Reading skills management systems were developed to provide teachers with the data necessary to manage and monitor reading skill development. A management system is an organizational and monitoring approach for teaching reading skills. It is a system for "diagnosis and prescription" (Bagford, 1977). Many reading management systems are computerized today, with the majority of basal reading programs providing a management system. They furnish information on student progress for teachers, parents, and administrators. Standardized tests determine which children have mastered the reading objectives in the system and which have not. The main value of management systems lies in helping teachers organize word-recognition skills instruction.

Management systems include the following components:

1. Behavioral objectives for reading skills, which are organized into hierarchical order.
2. Tests designed to assess mastery of the objectives. These tests are usually criterion-referenced tests, as they include criteria for various levels of mastery.
3. A resource file, which suggests skill development exercises and lists published materials that can be used for teaching each objective.
4. A bookkeeping system for assisting teachers in determining children's mastery of the behavioral objectives. This helps teachers plan their instruction and provides information about students' progress.

Unfortunately, management systems have some important weaknesses. They tend to equate reading with a set of isolated skills and view learning to read as essentially a mastery of a specific set of skills. One management system identifies more than 450 discrete skills (Johnson, 1977). Educators who follow a holistic approach to reading disagree with a management systems view of reading. They believe in a holistic approach to reading, because reading is greater than the sum of its parts. Management systems, like many reading programs, also depend on arbitrary hierarchies of reading skills, and, as yet, there is no researched proof that reading skills should be learned in a specific order.

Reading groups are also important aspects of classroom management. The following section addresses this component of the reading program.

MANAGING READING GROUPS

Reading groups and their formation are discussed in Chapter 2; however, the complexity of managing groups is addressed in this chapter. Management of reading groups is a particularly important topic, since time spent on behavior management is negatively correlated with learning (Brophy, 1979). Teachers need to organize and instruct groups in ways that minimize the difficulties of group instruction. Researchers have identified a series of characteristics that potentially inhibit learning in groups (Allington, 1980; Gambrell, Wilson, and

Gantt, 1981). They found considerable differences in the instruction provided for high-, average-, and low-ability groups. For instance, low-ability groups spend more time on decoding tasks, oral reading, and behavior control, while high-ability groups spend more time on meaning-related activities and silent reading, and their teachers are less likely to interrupt them.

Students who are assigned to low reading groups exhibit more negative feelings and have low self-evaluations. Teachers who are aware of these pitfalls and who plan carefully can overcome these problems and cause their students to have better attitudes and achievement.

The major goal of reading instruction is to develop students who can and do read and enjoy reading for information and pleasure. By now you have some sense of the nature of the task; therefore, we come to the next hurdle, teaching reading in a limited amount of time. The average school in the United States has a 180-day calendar. Teachers find that they often do not have the full eight hours a week that is allocated for reading instruction. Children are sometimes ill; some children are involved in "pull-out" programs, such as Chapter One reading programs and remedial math programs; middle-grade children often serve as crossing guards in some schools; and students have instrumental music instruction during the school day.

Goodlad's (1983) research reveals that an average of 1 hour and 45 minutes per school day are scheduled for reading and language arts instruction. This means that teachers must plan carefully, so they are prepared for interruptions. They must also teach the children who are in the classroom at that moment. Waiting for all members of a reading group to return wastes precious moments. Teachers must be prepared for a less than ideal teaching environment. Flexibility is one answer to this dilemma.

Flexible reading groups produce good results and positive attitudes (Unsworth, 1984). Teachers who have flexible reading groups usually have two or three groups within a classroom; each group includes 9 or 10 pupils. Group membership is not fixed; it varies according to students' needs and teachers' purposes. Groups are periodically created, modified, or disbanded to meet new needs as they arise. These groups may function to read a unit of stories, to acquire specific skills, to develop content area concepts, or to read the works of an individual author.

In a flexible grouping system, pupil commitment is enhanced when students know what the goals are and what is expected of them. The students in these groups should recognize and evaluate their own progress. In-group activities may focus on the basal reader, language experience activities, or discussions of trade books read in an individualized or whole-language approach. The following material illustrates the weekly instruction for a primary and an intermediate reading group.

One Week's Instruction in a Primary Group

Monday:
  Introduce unit of stories about dreams. Discuss students' dreams of the future. Introduce new vocabulary. Guided *silent reading* of "Dreams at Work."

Write an experience story about dreams. The story should have a beginning, middle, and end. These stories will be typed into the computer and printed out for later reading.

Students will select one story from the "Dreams" collection to *read independently.*

Tuesday:

Review the story, "Dreams at Work."

Students may tell about the "dreams" story they read independently. Group will discuss different kinds of dreams.

Students practice oral reading in of "Dreams at Work" for reader's theater. They may do this in pairs.

Students write about their personal dreams in their journals.

Wednesday:

Introduce the story, "Casey and the Clock," which is also in the dreams unit. Initiate the discussion by asking why the author of "Dreams at Work" compared dreams to a kite. Then explain that they are to think about why the new story is like a kite.

Introduce the new vocabulary in context. Review value of context in decoding. Have students identify context that helped them identify each word.

Guided silent reading of "Casey and the Clock." Follow-up discussion about why this story is like a kite.

Children read the story orally to one another in pairs.

Thursday:

Review the story read yesterday. Evaluate students' knowledge of the new words.

Review their knowledge of short vowel sounds.

Discuss synonyms. Students will identify synonyms for words in the story.

Students read the story aloud for specific purposes and discuss the dream in this story.

Students may write dream poems independently.

Friday:

Students read their dream poems aloud to the reading group.

Then they compare their dreams with those they read about during the week.

Discuss the ways they used synonyms when writing their poems.

Have students look over the stories read this week and identify words containing short vowels. They may categorize words containing short vowels

One Week's Instruction in an Intermediate Group

Monday:

Introduce the "Secrets" unit. Discuss what "secrets" are and the fact that each story will have a different secret.

Introduce the story, "Mysterious Secrets of Magic."

Guided silent reading of the story.

Teach vocabulary in context and context clues skill lesson.

Students write compositions about their favorite magic tricks.

Tuesday:

Students read their compositions about magic tricks to the class.

Then they read the story aloud for specific purposes that the teacher identifies. Each student explains how he or she used context clues in reading the story.

Students independently read books about magic tricks.

Wednesday:

Introduce the selection, "Can Animals Predict Earthquakes?"

Guided silent reading of the selection.

Discuss and review main ideas. Have students identify the main idea in each section of the reading assignment.

Students then identify a little known fact about an animal and write a paragraph about that fact. Students should be certain each paragraph has a main idea.

Thursday:

Discuss the ways that the two selections read this week are similar and why they both fit into a "secrets" unit.

Students share their paragraphs aloud and group identifies the main idea in each paragraph.

Discuss revising paragraphs and making a bound book of their little known facts. The students can present the book to the school library and take turns reading it aloud to other classes.

Friday:

Discuss the fact that both selections read this week are informational. Then introduce an Encyclopedia Brown story and compare it to the information selections read earlier.

Introduce vocabulary in context.

Gomplete guided silent reading. Then discuss the comparison of this mystery story with the expository selections.

Students work in pairs practicing oral reading of this story.

For independent reading, they may select another Encyclopedia Brown story.

Cooperative learning activities, seatwork for the "other children," and recreational reading are important reading group activities. These dimensions of group instruction are discussed in the next sections.

COOPERATIVE LEARNING

Cooperative learning involves activities in groups of two or three students. Cooperative activities encourage active student involvement (Uttero, 1988); therefore, these activities contribute to learning. This instructional design leads students to take responsibility for their own learning. They develop independence and confidence in their own abilities, and a more positive attitude toward school (Uttero, 1988).

When implementing cooperative-learning strategies, teachers should explain the process and its purpose to their students. They need to understand the importance of staying on task and avoiding socializing. The cooperative process involves discussing and sharing ideas; students become active participants in the learning process. At this point, students benefit from a demonstration or a role play that models cooperative learning. Students need to understand exactly what is expected of them during group activities. Then the teacher should assign the students to pairs or triads; often weak students are placed with strong students, or heterogeneous groups are formed. After groups are formed, the teacher gives the students their assignments. The teacher should observe group activities and adjust group membership, as well as assignments when necessary.

Students can gradually take over more group responsibility. They may identify groups with which to work and choose group activities.

Following are some suggested cooperative-group activities.

1. Students read aloud to one another, page by page, until a story is completed.
2. Students discuss a story the group has read silently. They should discuss answers and agree before responding (quiz-show style).
3. They map words or stories.
4. They do categorization activities.
5. Students do "think-alouds" while other group members identify the types of thinking used.
6. They engage in guided independent reading, which includes: asking and answering questions; paraphrasing content; outlining; mapping; summarizing; completing study guides; and dramatizing stories.

THE "OTHER CHILDREN" AND SEATWORK

As you learned in Chapter 2, reading groups are the major delivery system for reading instruction. The majority of elementary-school classrooms in the United States have three reading groups: high, average, and low. When one group is having teacher-directed reading instruction, the other students need to be actively involved with learning, but they must not interrupt the teacher or students who are engaged in direct instruction. They are usually engaged in independent seatwork, which may be comprised of workbook pages, ditto sheets, copying activities from the chalkboard, and so forth.

Effective seatwork reinforces skills that were introduced during direct instruction. These activities must be difficult enough to reinforce skills, and easy enough to be completed independently, without making too many mistakes. When children make mistakes, they are practicing skills that we do not want them to acquire. Due to the time involved in planning seatwork, teachers tend to use the same seatwork for *all* students. This means that it is often too difficult for less able students, and too easy for the fluent readers in the class. Therefore, teachers should consider planning *different* seatwork for each instructional group. Planning different seatwork for each reading group results in better learning. The following paragraph discusses the creation and use of seatwork.

The most effective seatwork involves reading and writing, rather than completing worksheets or copying from a chalkboard. For example, students may write in journals about a story they have read, or one of their experiences. They may read language-experience stories or trade books that relate to a subject or theme they are studying. These activities reinforce reading skills without making additional work for the teacher (the work involved in creating worksheets). Frequently, it takes the teacher longer to make an activity than it does the children to complete it.

I strongly discourage exercises that involve copying from the chalkboard; young children (those in kindergarten through third grade) usually have difficulty tracking their eyes well enough to copy accurately, and the educational value of such activities is limited. Even middle-grade students may copy incorrectly and make errors due to copying failure, not because they fail to understand.

The most valuable activities for the "other children" include independent reading, writing, paired reading, and carefully planned skills practice. The teacher's manuals that accompany basal readers include more suggestions for reading activities than most teachers have time to use in class, but many of these activities are creative and useful learning activities that children can complete outside of reading group while the teacher is instructing another reading group.

RECREATIONAL OR INDEPENDENT READING

This section explores recreational or independent reading, which is the reading students do *without* teacher direction. By contrast, the reading completed in reading groups, in preparation for reading groups, and in content textbooks is usually directed reading because the teacher introduces vocabulary and helps students develop silent reading purposes. Recreational reading gives children opportunities to read selections that they enjoy without having to report or complete written assignments related to the content. These activities give students opportunities to develop reading fluency, which enables them to enjoy reading.

In developing the independent or recreational reading program, teachers need to schedule time for reading during each school day—and at every grade level. Time for reading is precious; there are so many demands on students' time that they often do not have time or encouragement for reading outside of school.

Teachers need to motivate their students to read for recreation. They can do this by analyzing students' interests, and introducing them to materials that are related to their interests. Teachers should provide a broad array of materials, which include interesting magazines, newspapers, phamplets, and so forth. Bulletin-board and classroom displays of books, authors, and subjects motivate students to read. Independent reading should never be the subject of reports either written or oral. Reports are punishment for reading and discourage further reading.

Uninterrupted sustained silent reading (USSR) or (drop everything and read (DEAR) are recreational reading programs during which everyone in the classroom or the entire school reads. In classrooms that have a USSR program, the teacher reads, as do any visitors. In schools with a DEAR program, the principal, secretary, and cafeteria workers read at the same time as the children. These programs are highly motivating for students and teachers alike.

During USSR, everyone reads silently and there are no interruptions. Initially, the silent reading period may be only 5 minutes in length, but this time should be gradually increased, as the children learn to concentrate.

Linda Gambrell (1978) suggests the following guidelines for a USSR program.

1. Lay a groundwork for the program by promoting student interest before it actually begins.
2. Collect reading materials that are of interest to the students, including books, magazines, and newspapers.
3. Develop guidelines that insure reading is a silent activity, and be certain that students do not interrupt one another.
4. Everyone should read during the period, including teachers themselves.

ASSESSMENT

An important aspect of any reading program is assessing students' progress, which is an indication of the program's success. Assessment data helps us make decisions regarding programs, instruction, and materials. This section addresses the subject of assessment.

Gathering information regarding students' reading achievement is an integral part of instruction. Teachers must assess children's reading development to determine their reading levels. They must also assess specific student strengths and weaknesses in order to plan instruction. Assessment is especially important at the beginning of the school year in order to group children for instruction. Assessment data enable teachers to design individual instructional plans. Assessment helps teachers monitor children's progress in acquiring reading skills and abilities. Assessment should be continuous because children's skills—and needs—change over the course of time.

Teachers need data regarding students' performance from multiple sources. Multiple sources of data create a framework of information; some information corroborates other information, while other data may contradict, which suggests the need for a closer look. Reading is difficult to assess because it is a covert activity that occurs in the brain; thus, it is not directly observable and not directly measurable. Because reading is a process, the products that are examined will never be completely accurate.

The purposes of reading evaluation are summarized in the following list.

1. Assessment helps teachers organize classes into groups. Formal tests are one factor that should be considered in grouping. Teachers need to know students' reading level and their skill development in order to organize their classes.
2. Assessment allows teachers to address students' individual needs. Item analysis of standardized tests can provide information about specific strengths and weaknesses. Most tests given today are machine-scored, and computer printouts provide much information about student performance on specific test items. The diagnostic-prescriptive cycle should reflect the sequence suggested in Figure 7.4.
3. Assessment is important for accountability, a concern of the community as well as the teaching profession. Test data can be used in discussions with parents about the reading program.
4. Tests can be used to assess individual growth and development in reading. Test scores should always be considered in relation to the individual's socioeconomic level, I.Q., and such other factors as the education of the parents and the child's experiential background.

   Assessment may be informal or formal. **Informal evaluation** involves observation, checklists, and teacher-made tests. **Formal assessment** includes standardized tests and criterion-referenced tests.

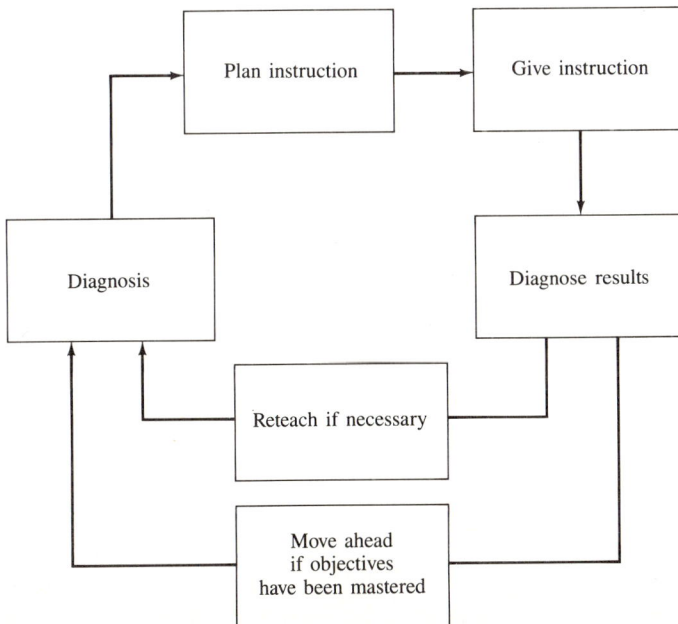

Figure 7.4 The diagnostic presciptive instruction cycle.

Observation

When *observation techniques* are systematically applied, they can help teachers understand students' strengths and weaknesses in reading. Systematic observation requires that the teacher establish objectives and record accurately

Take notes —————— what is seen and heard (Miccinati and Pine, 1979). Several observation periods should be scheduled because one observation is rarely sufficient to analyze reading behavior. The observer should be prepared to take rapid notes without attracting undue attention.

The following suggestions will help teachers develop observation skills for informal assessments.

1. Establishing specific objectives for observation is crucial for this procedure. For example, the teacher may establish such goals as learning sight words, recognition of inflected endings, or the development of literal comprehension skills.
2. Schedule observation for a time when the child will display the behavior you wish to study. This time should be relatively free from distractions. Schedule several observations so that you are certain that the behavior observed is representative. A child may make an error in one observation that will not be repeated in subsequent observations. Periodic observations provide a longitudinal picture of reading growth (Miccinati and Pine, 1979).
3. Select a setting that is appropriate for observation.
4. The observer should look for strengths as well as weaknesses. Observers should make an effort to observe as objectively as possible. One way of controlling objectivity is to write down the supporting evidence for all inferences made.
5. In recording observations, the following formats may be used:
   a. A running commentary records everything that has been observed in the situation.
   b. A checklist of skills and/or behaviors may be used to aid observation.
   c. Anecdotal records are a documentation of systematic checks to gain knowledge about a child (Miccinati and Pine, 1979). A sample anecdotal record might read: *Susan decodes words accurately in the basal reader using phonics skills and structural analysis. She decodes words very slowly. Susan has a limited sight vocabulary. Her comprehension is about 50 percent in oral and silent reading. I need to test her sight-word vocabulary and use strategies to extend her knowledge of sight words. Her decoding skills should also be improved through practice exercises.*

Teacher-Made Tests

Informal *teacher-made tests* are instruments that also aid in student assessment. One of the most useful informal aids is the **IRI (Informal Reading Inventory)**. An IRI usually consists of reading passages taken from a basal reading series. It may include a list of words that children must be familiar with in order to read the books in that series.

The reading passages selected for the IRI should be chosen from the middle section of the book, which is the part closest to the designated grade level. Two passages are selected at each grade level—one selection is for oral reading and the other is for silent reading. These selections are arranged sequentially by grade level, beginning with preprimer and proceeding through the sixth grade. The preprimer selections should include 40 words. This number

Questions

gradually increases at each level, so that the sixth-grade reader passage should include 150 words. The teacher should construct four or five questions for each passage. Questions should address the literal, interpretive, and critical levels of thinking.

The selections should be typed so that both the teachers and students have a copy. Teachers mark the child's errors on their copies, or they may tape record the child's reading for later analysis.

When administering the IRI, teachers should begin below the grade level at which they believe the child is reading. Thus, the child begins with rather easy content.

The coding system associated with the IRI provides data on the reader's use of context, self-correction, and use of phonic cues. Teachers should also observe the following factors (Pflaum, 1979):

1. Is the error self-corrected?
2. Does the error change the meaning of the sentence?
3. If the error does change the meaning, can the sentence be sensibly completed?
4. Is it possible to evaluate the use of phonic cues?

Table 7.1 presents a suggested coding system for use with the IRI.

Teachers should take detailed notes on the behavior of the child being examined. For example, signs of tension, pointing, subvocalizing, unnatural voice, and holding the book close to the eyes should be recorded.

Scoring the IRI

Analyze errors

After the errors (or miscues) have been recorded, the teacher should examine them to determine whether or not the errors were self-corrected, whether they changed the meaning of the content, or whether they were dialect-related; finally, the teacher should analyze the use of phonic cues. For example, a child who reads the sentence *I am here* as *I be here* is using dialect. The child who reads the sentence *Father ran into the forest* as *Dad ran into the woods* is substituting miscues that do not change the sentence meaning. Thus the following miscues should not be counted as errors:

self-corrected errors

miscues that do not alter sentence meaning

dialect miscues

Table 7.1   A SUGGESTED CODING SYSTEM FOR THE IRI

Error	Code
Omissions	Cross out the omission. (Linda is ~~very~~ excited.)
Words pronounced following a five-second hesitation	Write a *P* above the word. (Susan cannot $\overset{P}{go}$ to the beach.)
Added word	Mark a caret in the sentence where the word was inserted and write the word above the sentence. (Susan can $\overset{not}{\wedge}$ come.)
Substitution	Write the substituted word above the sentence. (We will come to the $\overset{park}{party}$.)
Repetition	Write an *R* above the word. (Muffin $\overset{R}{is}$ outside.)
Ignores punctuation	Write an *X* on the punctuation that was disregarded. (We picked corn$\underset{\times}{,}$tomatoes$\underset{\times}{,}$and cucumbers.)
Hesitations	Put a check mark above the word in the sentence. (It is $\overset{\checkmark}{raining}$ very hard.)
Child self-corrects an error	Write a lowercase *c* above the word in the sentence. (Will it $\overset{c}{snow}$ tomorrow?)

Look for patterns

Phonics cues may be analyzed by examining the words that the child substituted for the actual words in the selection. For example, a child who pronounced *sat* for *set* and *pine* for *pin* might be demonstrating a problem with vowels. Teachers should look for patterns in word recognition errors.

An IRI is scored by determining the percentage of correct answers in the following manner.

1. The percentage of correct answers is determined for each passage (omitting self-corrections, miscues that do not alter meaning, and dialect miscues).
2. The word-recognition score is computed by dividing the number of words in the selection into the answer, obtained by subtracting the number of errors from the total number of words in the selection. For example:

50 words in the selection
$\underline{-10}$ errors recorded
40

$$50\overline{)40.00} \quad 0.80 = 80\% \text{ word-recognition score}$$

3. A word-recognition score is not given for the silent reading passage.
4. The comprehension score is computed by determining the percentage of correct answers. For example:

10 questions based on the selection
$\underline{-3}$ errors in answering questions
7

$$10\overline{)7.00} \quad 0.70 = 70\% \text{ comprehension score}$$

The standards of performance for the IRI, designed by Betts, are as follows (Betts, 1946):

Reading levels

The *instructional level* is achieved when the student reads with 75 percent comprehension and 95 percent word recognition. This is the highest level at which the child can read with teacher assistance. Infrequent errors and good comprehension are associated with this level. This level is used for basal reading instruction.

The *independent level* is the level at which the reader achieves 95 percent to 100 percent comprehension and 100 percent word recognition. This is the highest level at which a child can read fluently with infrequent errors and excellent comprehension. Materials at this level are used for recreational reading.

The *frustration level* is the level of reading where comprehension falls to 50 percent and word recognition to 90 percent. Reading skills are weak, fluency disappears, and there are frequent errors and poor comprehension. The reader is usually tense when reading at the frustration level.

Auding level

The *listening comprehension* (auding level) is determined by reading a selection to children and having them respond orally to questions based on the passage. This provides a measure of the child's listening comprehension as well as an estimate of the level at which the child understands content.

Comprehension on the IRI may be further analyzed by asking the following questions (Kavale, 1979):

Can the student read content with more ease, speed, and understanding than on past reading occasions?

Has the student's ability to paraphrase content increased?

Has the student's ability to recall facts from reading content increased?

Has the student's ability to answer thought questions based on the reading content increased?

The Cloze Procedure

The cloze procedure is an informal test of reading comprehension that was described in Chapter 6. A cloze procedure is an excellent means of measuring comprehension. The following is a brief example of a passage that could be used for this testing approach.

> It is time for winter weather to arrive. The birds have flown _____ , the leaves have fallen, _____ the sky has grown _____ . Soon the snow will _____ . We must prepare for the cold weather.

Answers: *south, and, dark, fall*

Children tend to find the cloze test somewhat more difficult than a multiple-choice test, because it is difficult to guess answers on the cloze. Some of their difficulty with cloze testing can be overcome by practice with sample exercises.

Norm-Referenced Tests

Formal evaluation usually involves published testing materials. The two major types of published testing instruments are standardized or norm-referenced tests and criterion-referenced tests.

Survey and diagnostic

Norm-referenced reading tests include *reading achievement (survey) tests* and *diagnostic tests.* These tests compare a child's reading performance with the achievement level established for average children at the same grade level. For example, if Susan is enrolled in third grade, she would take a reading test that contained second-, third-, and fourth-grade content. Her grade equivalent score of 5.7 would indicate that she can perform second-, third-, and fourth-grade reading tasks as well as the average students in the seventh month of the fifth grade (Pyrczak, 1979). Norm-referenced tests are standardized in terms of administration procedures and normative information. Standardized reading survey tests at the primary level usually include word-recognition and comprehension subtests. Such tests at the intermediate level usually include vocabulary (word meaning) and comprehension subtests.

In-depth analysis

Diagnostic reading tests are used to answer specific questions about reading performance. A diagnostic test breaks the reading process into specific skills for an in-depth analysis. These tests are used after achievement tests and teacher observation indicate that the youngster has reading difficulties. A diagnostic test may include subtests on oral reading, comprehension, word analysis skills, visual and auditory discrimination, reading rate, or reading study skills. These tests are frequently administered by special instructors rather than the classroom teacher, as they are individual tests that require specialized interpretation.

Grade equivalent scores are provided by standardized reading achievement tests and diagnostic reading tests. Unfortunately, many teachers misinterpret these scores. A grade equivalent score of 3.9 does *not* mean that the child can read content written at the ninth month of the third-grade level. In fact, grade equivalent scores are usually one to two grade levels higher than the child's actual ability to read content. Scoring for these tests should probably be revised so they do not cause confusion in interpretation.

Standardized tests should be examined carefully to determine their reliability and validity. The following sections discuss the importance of these factors.

Reliability

Consistency

Reliability is an important attribute of any test. The *reliability* of a test indicates that the test score is stable when it is given repeatedly. Good tests are consistent in their measurement of students' skills. Reliability is illustrated in the following example. A teacher administered a word-recognition test to three students on Monday and found that one student had excellent skills, while the other two had poor skills. The teacher readministered the same test on Friday—with the same results; thus, the teacher had used a reliable test. In the classroom, we do not normally use the same test repeatedly to determine reliability; therefore, test-makers should provide us with reliability data that they have developed as a result of standardizing the test. A good test should have a reliability coefficient of at least 0.90 for a single age or grade level, or a standard error of measurement of not more than three months for grade equivalent scores.

Validity

Test **validity** is concerned with whether the test measures what it purports to measure. For example, a test of reading comprehension should test *all* of the factors that are related to reading comprehension. Kavale (1979) suggests that teachers take tests themselves to help them determine the validity factor.

Criterion-Referenced Tests

Criterion-referenced tests are becoming popular due to the concern today with individualized instruction. These tests compare the student's performance to "some absolute standard, usually some specified behavioral criterion or performance. The focus is on what the student can do." For example, a score of 90 percent may mean that the teacher can assume adequate learning has occurred. Thus the primary concern in these tests is whether the student has demonstrated a required level of proficiency in a particular skill.

Criterion-referenced tests do have some weaknesses. One of the most important weaknesses is that not all skills and abilities can be stated in behavioral form. Another problem is that mastery levels differ for individual students.

A third significant problem of these tests is that they are based on the notion of a hierarchy of reading skills; however, no such hierarchy has ever been established.

Basal Reader Tests

The majority of basal readers available today are part of an instructional system for reading that includes tests. These tests are designed to determine how well students have mastered the skills taught in a unit, level, or book within the basal reading system. These tests are specific to a particular basal reading program. They are generally not norm-referenced tests.

Basal reader tests have a specific place in the reading program. They help teachers determine whether students have mastered the content that was taught. They point out those students who need reteaching of material already covered, and those students who are ready to move ahead and who should be accelerated in the reading program. One word of caution is in order regarding these tests: they usually are not truly diagnostic, so it may be necessary to do more extensive testing of children who are having difficulty in the reading program.

USING STANDARDIZED READING TESTS

When selecting standardized tests, teachers should consider the following factors:

1. What is the purpose of testing? The test that is finally selected should provide the specific information desired by the user.
2. Consult references to determine what tests are available for various assessment purposes. The two standard references for reading tests are: O. K. Buros, Ed. (1968). *Reading: Tests and Reviews,* Highland Park, NJ: Gryphon Press.
   ———— (1968). *The Eighth Mental Measurements Yearbook,* Highland Park, NJ: Gryphon Press.
3. Examine tests that appear to serve your purposes. You can order specimen sets from most publishing companies. Study the specific skills tested and the format of testing.
4. Study the standardization data that is reported in the preceding standard references. This information should always accompany the test.
5. Consider the overall cost per child. A less expensive test may provide just as much data as a costly one.

All standardized tests exhibit some strengths and some weaknesses. Some of the salient factors that should be considered in the decision to use a standardized test are listed below (Kavale 1979).

1. A test designed for large numbers of children is not as valuable as tests designed for individuals. Keep in mind that a test may be too difficult or too easy for specific students.
2. Standardized tests are in a multiple-choice format, and some children may have inflated scores due to guessing.
3. Standardized tests are timed, which creates a problem for children who do not respond well to this kind of pressure.
4. Some children may have difficulty correctly completing the separate answer sheets that may accompany various tests (such as machine-scored tests). Children may accidentally mark incorrect answers.
5. Tests at upper-grade levels may assume lower levels of ability. Children may score a baseline reading score—such as third-grade level—for simply writing their names on the test booklet.
6. Be aware that standardized tests overestimate children's instructional reading levels by a factor of one to two years.
7. Longer tests are usually more reliable than shorter tests.

Test Administration

When administering tests of all types, teachers should observe the following principles.

Provide a quiet place without distractions for students taking tests.

Minimize the amount of writing required on tests.

Teach children how to take tests (for example, how to follow directions or how to use answer sheets that are separate from the testing booklet).

Try to find out why children responded as they did.

Do an item analysis to identify the specific items missed.

ASSESSING LITERATURE-BASED READING INSTRUCTION

Teachers are sometimes puzzled by how to monitor students' progress in literature-based programs, since they do not use workbooks or tests that accompany basal readers. However, there is a variety of valid ways to gather assessment data, although these data are usually informal. The following list provides a few suggestions (Aiex, 1988).

1. Teachers can develop checklists to complete as they listen to students read.
2. Students can tell a familiar story.
3. Students can point to individual words on a page or chart.
4. Teachers can observe behaviors like the following:
   a. Do children demonstrate an interest in words?
   b. Do children turn the pages at the appropriate time when a story is being read?

    c. Can the youngster locate a familiar book on the shelf?

    d. Do the students choose to read or write during free time?

    e. Do children notice words in their environment (billboards, advertising, bulletin boards, and the like)?

    f. Do children invent spellings that are appropriate to their development in their own writing?

    g. Do children enter into book discussions?

    h. Do they ask questions about print?

    i. Do they demonstrate the awareness that print has meaning?

5. Do the children spontaneously tell others about books they have enjoyed?

6. Do the children predict story events before reading?

Teachers can also choose an informal inventory from those currently published to administer to their students. The majority of informal inventories are administered on an individual basis, so teachers need to arrange for the time to administer these instruments.

SUMMARY

The elementary reading program is multifaceted; teachers must be excellent managers to insure their students' success. Teachers have to develop and implement a reading program that parallels the philosophy of the local school system. The following list summarizes the key points of this chapter.

1. Current reading philosophies are holistic, subskills, or interactive. Holistic approaches emphasize context meaning as a means of acquiring reading fluency; subskills emphasize learning specific skills, which are integrated to acquire reading fluency. Interactive approaches combine both holistic and subskills approaches.

2. The most common approach to reading instruction is the basal reader approach; however, holistic strategies like the whole-language, individualized reading, and language-experience approaches are popular.

3. Children's literature fulfills an important role in all reading programs; however, it is particularly important in the whole-language and individualized programs because instruction is based on literature. Nevertheless, literature can be used to enrich any instructional approach.

4. Managing reading groups is necessary in successful reading programs. A particular concern in reading instruction is planning effective seatwork for the "other children" who are not a part of the group receiving direct instruction.

5. Teachers gather assessment data from various sources to help in grouping children and designing programs that will meet individual needs. They use assessment data from both informal and formal instruments to plan reading instruction.

6. Literature-based reading programs rely more heavily on informal assessment data gathered from teachers' observations.

SELF-TEST

Check your knowledge of the information presented in this chapter. The answer key is located in Appendix C.

1. Which of the following are characteristics of a whole-language program?
   a. extensive use of workbooks and seatwork
   b. copying material from the chalkboard
   c. extensive use of children's literature
   d. subskills

2. Which approach to reading is founded on teaching students skills that build on each other and practicing those skills until students can use them in an interrelated manner?
   a. holistic
   b. subskills
   c. language experience
   d. individualized

3. How is recreational reading related to the reading program?
   a. it provides students with reading practice
   b. it should include written and oral reports
   c. students read materials that are listed by the teacher
   d. it detracts from the developmental reading program

4. Which of the following approaches are holistic?
   a. individualized reading
   b. language experience
   c. whole language
   d. all of the preceding

5. Which of the following characteristics are associated with a synthetic approach to reading instruction?
   a. letter sounds are taught first
   b. students decode words in isolation
   c. comprehension is emphasized later in the program
   d. all of the preceding

6. Why is writing related to reading?
   a. children learn how authors express their ideas
   b. children read and reread as they write
   c. both a and b
   d. neither a nor b

7. What is the purpose of testing?
   a. motivation
   b. to insure that students complete their homework
   c. to record test information regarding students' reading achievement levels
   d. to record test information in permanent records

8. Which of the following factors characterize a sound elementary reading program?

a. reading for information
b. reading for pleasure
c. frequent recreational reading
d. all of these

9. What is the focus of a "bottom up" explanation of reading?
a. decoding words
b. separate reading skills
c. both a and b
d. neither a nor b

10. What is the focus of a "top down" theory of reading?
a. The meaning of written language
b. the interaction of the language arts
c. both a and b
d. neither a nor b

11. What is the focus of an interactive theory of reading?
a. language meaning
b. reading skills
c. both a and b
d. neither a nor b

12. What is the major theoretical premise of a whole-language approach to reading instruction?
a. subskills can be integrated to achieve understanding
b. language is acquired through use
c. a synthetic approach to phonics
d. none of these

13. Why does a whole-language approach empower teachers?
a. they are delivering a program developed by another person
b. They do not have to think
c. they use their professional background to develop curriculum
d. they do not have to take as many reading courses

14. How can basal readers function with a whole-language approach?
a. they contain literature for students to read
b. they function as a springboard into reading
c. they incorporate reading, writing, listening, and speaking
d. all of these

15. Which of the following are not whole-language approaches to reading instruction?
a. language experience
b. individualized reading
c. synthetic (explicit) phonics
d. shared book experiences

16. How many observations of students are necessary to draw conclusions regarding their reading skills?
a. one
b. three
c. multiple
d. fifty

17. What tools should teachers use when conducting an informal assess-
    ment?
    a. anecdotal records
    b. checklists
    c. scheduled observations
    d. all of these

18. What is an IRI?
    a. a basal reading series
    b. an informal reading inventory
    c. an independent reading intake
    d. an interpretive reading instruction

19. Which level on the IRI is the level at which the reader achieves 95 percent
    to 100 percent comprehension and 100 percent word recognition?
    a. frustration
    b. independent
    c. listening
    d. instructional

20. Which words are deleted in a cloze procedure?
    a. every second word
    b. every fifth word
    c. every fifteenth word
    d. every vowel

21. How do norm-referenced tests function?
    a. they compare a student with himself or herself
    b. they compare students to a standard developed by reading authorities
    c. they compare students with the achievement level of average stu-
       dents
    d. they compare students with themselves

THOUGHT QUESTIONS

1. Compare a holistic approach with a subskills approach. Which do you prefer?
   Why?

2. Identify an example that clarifies the interactive or combination approach to
   reading instruction.

3. Why are the "other children" a particular problem in reading instruction?

4. Identify three ways to engage the "other children" in active learning situations.

5. Why is assessment in a literature-based approach different from that in a
   basal reading program?

6. How do formal and informal assessment differ? What is the value of
   each?

7. Why did the author compare teachers with chief executive officers in business?

8. How is writing related to the reading program?

ENRICHMENT ACTIVITIES

1. Interview three elementary teachers regarding their philosophy of reading instruction. Ask them which philosophy they endorse and why. Ask them to explain how their philosophy of reading influences the way they teach reading.

2. Use a basal reader lesson as a basis for creating a whole-language lesson.

3. Identify a unit theme or concept, and then create a list of trade books to read aloud and books for students' independent reading.

4. Administer an informal inventory to a child and analyze his or her reading strengths and weaknesses.

5. Write your own philosophy of reading. How does it influence your teaching?

6. Observe a class that does little or no writing, and then observe a class that writes regularly. How do the reading skills of the children differ?

7. Prepare a bulletin board to stimulate recreational reading.

8. Examine several standardized reading tests. What levels of reliability and validity do the tests have? What skills are tested? Do the tests provide information that would be helpful in planning a reading program? If so, what information is provided?

RELATED READINGS

Altwerger, B., C. Edelsky, and B. Flores (November 1987). "Whole Language: What's New?" *The Reading Teacher*, Vol. 41, pp. 144–153.

Altwerger, B., J. Diehl-Faxon, and K. Dockstader-Anderson (September 1985). "Read-Aloud Events As Meaning Construction," *Language Arts*, Vol. 62, 5, pp. 476–484.

Anderson, R., E. Hiebert, J. Scott, and I. Wilkinson (1985). *Becoming a Nation of Readers: The Report of the Commission on Reading.* Urbana, IL: The Center for the Study of Reading.

Berglund, R. and J. Johns (February 1983). "A Primer on Uninterrupted Sustained Silent Reading," *The Reading Teacher*, Vol. 36, pp. 534–539.

Brophy, J. (1979). "Teacher Behavior and Student Learning," *Educational Leadership*, Vol. 37, pp. 33–38.

Dreher, M. and H. Singer (March 1985). "Parents Attitudes Toward Standardized Reading Test Results," *The Reading Teacher*, Vol. 38, 7, pp. 624–632.

Eldridge, J. and D. Butterfield (October 1986). "Alternatives to Traditional Reading Instruction," *The Reading Teacher*, Vol. 40, pp. 32–37.

Fields, M. and D. Lee (1987). *Let's Begin Reading Right*, Columbus, OH: Merrill.

Gambrell, L., R. Wilson, and W. Gantt (1981). "Classroom Observations of Task-Attending Behaviors of Good and Poor Readers," *Journal of Educational Research*, Vol. 74, pp. 400–404.

Gaus, P. (December 1983). "The Indispensable Reading Teacher," *The Reading Teacher*, Vol. 37, 3, pp. 269–273.

Henke, L. (January 1988). "Beyond Basal Reading: A District's Commitment to Change," *The New Advocate*, Vol. 1, pp. 42–51.

Hoffman, J. (Ed.) (1986). *Effective Teaching of Reading: Research and Practice*, Newark, DE: International Reading Association.

Johns, J. (Winter 1983). "Improving What Goes on in the Reading Group," *Prime Areas,* Vol. 25, 2, pp. 25–32.

Johns, J. and R. Berglund (Winter 1982). "Repeated Readings: Help for Poorer Readers," *Tar Heel Reading Journal,* Vol. 2, 1, pp. 26–30.

Johnson, M., R. Kress, and J. Pikulski (1987). *Informal Reading Inventories,* 2d ed., Newark, DE: International Reading Association.

Kann, R. (February 1983). "The Method of Repeated Readings: Expanding the Neurological Impress Method for Use with Disabled Readers," *Journal of Learning Disabilities,* Vol. 16, pp. 90–92.

Newman, J. (1985). *Whole Language Theory in Use,* Portsmouth N.H.: Heinemann.

Pikulski, J. (1982). *Approaches to the Informal Evaluation of Reading,* Newark, DE: International Reading Association.

Rhodes, L. and M. Hill (March 1985). "Supporting Reading in the Home—Naturally: Selected Materials for Parents," *The Reading Teacher,* Vol. 38, 7, pp. 619–623.

Samuels, A. (March 1979). "The Method of Repeated Readings," *The Reading Teacher,* Vol. 32, 6, pp. 403–408.

Taubenheim, B. and J. Christensen (November/December 1978). "Let's Shoot 'Cock Robin'! Alternatives to 'Round Robin' Reading," *Language Arts,* Vol. 55, pp. 975–977.

Taylor, B. and L. Nosbush (December 1983). "Oral Reading for Meaning: A Technique for Improving Word Identification Skills," *The Reading Teacher,* Vol. 37, 3, pp. 234–237.

Unsworth, L. (December 1984). "Meeting Individual Needs Through Flexible Within-Class Grouping of Pupils," *The Reading Teacher,* Vol. 38, pp. 298–304.

Venezky, R. (1974). *Testing in Reading,* Urbana, IL: National Council of Teachers of English.

Weaver, D. (1988). *Reading Process and Practice.* Portsmouth, N.H.: Heinemann.

White, J., J. Vaughn, and I. Rorie (October 1986). "Picture of a Classroom Where Reading Is for Real," *The Reading Teacher,* Vol. 40, pp. 84–87.

REFERENCES

Aaron, E. (1987). "Enriching the Basal Reading Program with Literature," in *Children's Literature in the Reading Program,* B. Cullinan (Ed.), Newark, DE: International Reading Association.

Allington, R. (1980). "Teacher Interruption Behaviors During Primary Grade Oral Reading," *Journal of Educational Psychology,* Vol. 72, pp. 371–374.

Anderson, L., C. Evertson, and J. Brophy (1979). "An Experimental Study of Effective Teaching in First-Grade Reading Groups," *The Elementary School Journal,* Vol. 79, pp. 193–223.

Anderson, R., J. Mason and L. Shirey (1984). "The Reading Group: An Experimental Investigation of a Labyrinth," *Reading Research Quarterly,* Vol. 20, pp. 6–38.

Altwerger, B., C. Edelsky, and B. Flores (November 1987). "Whole Language: What's New?" *The Reading Teacher,* Vol. 41, pp. 144–154.

Aukerman, R. (1982). *The Basal Reader Approach to Reading,* New York: John Wiley.

Bagford, J. (May 1977). "Management Systems and Comprehension Do Not Mix!" *Language Arts,* Vol. 54, 8, pp. 517–520.

Barbe, W. and S. Abbott (1975). *Personalized Reading Instruction,* West Nyack, NY: Parker Publishing Company.

Betts, E. (1946). *Foundations of Reading Instruction.* New York: American Book Co.

Bond, G., M. Tinker, and B. Wasson (1979). *Reading Difficulties—Their Diagnosis and Correction,* 4th ed., Englewood Cliffs, NJ: Prentice-Hall.

Brecht, R. (October 1977). "Testing Format and Instructional Level with the Informal Reading Inventory," *The Reading Teacher,* Vol. 31, pp. 57–59.

Brophy, J. (1979). "Teacher Behavior and Student Learning," *Educational Leadership,* Vol. 37, pp. 33–38.

Brzeinski and H. Driscoll (1971). "Early Start in Reading—Help or Hindrance?" in *Parents and Reading,* C. Smith (Ed.), Newark, DE: International Reading Association.

Chall, J. (1983). *The Stages of Reading Development,* New York: McGraw-Hill.

Durkin, D. (1983). *Is There a Match Between What Elementary Teachers Do and What Basal Reader Manuals Recommend?,* Reading Ed. Rep. No. 44, Urbana, IL: University of Illinois, Center for the Study of Reading.

Edelsky, C. (1986). *Writing in a Bilingual Program: Habia Una Vez,* Norwood, NJ: Ablex.

Fields, M. and D. Lee (1987). *Let's Begin Reading Right,* Columbus, OH: Charles Merrill.

Gambrell, L. (December 1978). "Getting Started with Sustained Silent Reading and Keeping It Going," *The Reading Teacher,* Vol. 32, pp. 328–331.

Gambrell, L., R. Wilson, and W. Gantt (1981). "Classroom Observations of Task-Attending Behaviors of Good and Poor Readers," *Journal of Educational Research,* Vol. 74, pp. 400–404.

Goodland, J. (1983). *A Place Called School,* New York: McGraw-Hill.

Goodman, K. (1986). *What's Whole in Whole Language,* Richmond Hill, Ontario: Scholastic-TAB.

Harste, J., V. Woodward and C. Burke (1984). *Language Stories and Literacy Lessons,* Exeter, NH: Heinemann.

Johns, J. (Winter 1983). "Improving What Goes on in the Reading Group," *Prime Areas,* Vol. 25, 2, pp. 25–32.

Johns, J. and R. Berglund (Winter 1982). "Repeated Readings: Help for Poorer Readers," *The Tar Heel Reading Journal,* Vol. 2, 1, pp. 26–28.

Johnson, D. (May 1977). "Skills Management Systems: Some Issues," *Language Arts,* Vol. 54, pp. 511–516.

Kavale, K. (1979). "Selecting and Evaluating Reading Tests," in *Reading Tests and Teachers: A Practical Guide,* R. Schreiner (Ed.), Newark, DE: International Reading Association, pp. 11–34.

Komoski, P. (1982). *Affecting the System Through Productive Evaluation,* ED 217 071, Arlington, VA: ERIC Document Reproduction Service.

Lee, D. and R. Van Allen (1963). *Learning to Read Through Experience,* 2nd ed., East Norwalk, CT: Appleton & Lange.

Miccinati, J. and M. Pine (1979). *Observing Students' Reading Skills,* York, PA: The College Reading Association.

Pflaum, S. (December 1979). "Diagnosis of Oral Reading," *The Reading Teacher,* Vol. 33, pp. 278–284.

Pyrczak (1979). "Definitions of Measurement Terms," in *Reading Tests and Teachers: A Practical Guide,* Newark, DE: International Reading Association, pp. 72–80.

Ransom, P. and R. Mitchell (1980). "Curriculum and Objectives," in *Teaching Reading,* P. Lamb and R. Arnold (Eds.), Belmont, CA: Wadsworth, pp. 107–131.

Rauch, S. (January 1974). "Administrators Guidelines for More Effective Reading Programs," *Journal of Reading,* Vol. 17, pp. 297–300.

Rowell, E. (January 1976). "Do Elementary Students Read Better Orally or Silently?" *The Reading Teacher,* Vol. 29, pp. 367–370.

Schreiner, R. (Ed.) (1979). *Reading Tests and Teachers: A Practical Guide,* Newark, DE: International Reading Association.

Smith, F. (1984). "The Creative Achievement of Literacy," in *Awakening to Literacy,* H. Goelman, A. Oberg and F. Smith (Eds.), Exeter, NH: Heinemann.

Unsworth, L. (December 1984). "Meeting Individual Needs Through Flexible Within-class Grouping of Pupils." *The Reading Teacher,* Vol. 38, 298–304.

U.S. Department of Education (1986). *What Works: Research about Teaching and Learning,* Washington, DC: U. S. Department of Education.

Veatch, J. (1978). *Reading the Elementary School,* 2nd ed., New York: John Wiley.

Winograd, P. and M. Greenlee (April 1986). "Students Need a Balanced Reading Program," *Educational Leadership,* Vol. 43, No. 7.

CHAPTER 8

Selecting and Using Reading Materials

OVERVIEW   Teachers implement the elementary reading program based on their interpretation of the adopted reading philosophy and the reading curriculum. Among the many instructional decisions they have to make is choosing appropriate materials to implement the reading program. Basal readers and workbooks are commonly used for teaching reading. However, sound reading instruction incorporates a wide variety of printed materials including trade books, newspapers, magazines, and children's writing. In addition, media such as computer software, video cassette recorder (VCR) programs, films, and filmstrips can be used to develop reading skills. For example, teachers can use programs they have recorded with a VCR to build students' schemata for comprehending text. Teachers can use these programs twice in a classroom lesson; first, to introduce the subject, and second, to review the concept.

Teachers need to choose appropriate materials for reading instruction and to use those materials effectively with their students. This chapter describes and examines reading materials, as well as guidelines for choosing materials and incorporating them into the classroom reading program.

Key Vocabulary

As you read this chapter, check your understanding of these terms:

basal reader   **instructional materials**
computer   **media**

Focusing Questions

As you read this chapter, think about these questions:

1. What are the strengths and weaknesses of basal readers?
2. How can a teacher develop a combination approach to reading instruction?

READING MATERIALS

Current educational theory provides basic notions regarding reading instruction that impinge on the materials we use for teaching. Reading instruction focuses on student-directed activities and guiding students to understand the processes and strategies they need to use to comprehend text. Reading materials should help students understand how to create meaning through written language. Students need to realize that ideas are more important than printed words, and that skilled readers use the language cues in print and their background of knowledge stored in memory to comprehend. Their reading instruction should begin with whole units—stories, poems, articles, and so forth (Glazer, Searfoss, and Gentile, 1988).

Reading can be taught with any printed material; there is no magic in a special program or in a particular book. However, the majority of teachers, particularly, novice teachers feel more comfortable with materials developed specifically for teaching reading. Selecting appropriate reading materials is a particularly important topic for teachers, because the majority of school systems give teachers input into this decision, and new teachers are frequently assigned to text adoption committees. In the following discussion, the trends in reading materials, as well as the pros and cons of various types of reading materials will be examined.

Children can learn to read with any printed material. Successful teachers use newspapers, magazines, and trade books with many students. However, these materials work best when teaching one child at a time or with students who are fluent readers. Materials that are specifically designed for reading instruction provide a controlled vocabulary, which means that a smaller number of new words are introduced in a single reading selection. Well-designed reading materials provide for a gradual buildup of reading vocabulary and decoding skills. Otherwise, students may be exposed to texts that contain only unknown words, thus overwhelming students and turning them off to reading.

Reading materials must hold students' interests, motivate them to read, be readable, include well-structured selections, and relate to their experiences so they can construct understanding. Obviously, this perfection is difficult, if not impossible, to achieve. Nevertheless, teachers can successfully select and organize reading materials for their classes.

SELECTING MATERIALS FOR WHOLE-LANGUAGE, LANGUAGE EXPERIENCE, AND INDIVIDUALIZED READING

Contemporary philosophies of reading emphasize the role of children's literature in reading instruction. A growing body of research emphasizes the importance of extended silent reading and vocabulary development to achieve reading fluency (Anderson et al., 1985). Increased use of trade books encourages extended silent reading (Henke, 1988). The movement to increase the use of children's literature in reading instruction is gaining momentum from teachers and parents, who recognize the importance of literature in developing lifelong readers. Current basal reading programs incorporate literature selections in reader content, and recommend extended independent reading of trade books as well as supplemental literature for teachers to read aloud. Alternative approaches to reading instruction like whole-language, language-experience, and individualized reading are also based on extensive use of literature.

A whole-language approach to reading is based on students reading literature every day and on teachers reading to children every day. A language-experience approach to reading is based on children writing and reading their own materials, as well as materials their classmates have written. In a language-experience program, students also read literature, as they acquire the sight words and decoding skills that permit them to read stories. An individualized reading program is founded on the notion that children will read from trade books that they choose, followed with individual student-teacher conferences.

Teachers need considerable knowledge about children's trade books in order to develop classroom book collections. This knowledge also enables them to suggest books for the school librarian to purchase, since children need both a classroom book collection and a well-developed centralized school library (media center). Teachers also must know enough about children's trade books to develop webs, like those in Chapter 10, to develop thematic units, to suggest books that will interest individual students, and to choose literature to read aloud to their classes.

In order to prepare themselves for using children's literature, teachers need to read children's books regularly. More than 3000 new children's trade books are published each year. Obviously, teachers cannot read all of them, so they must rely on book selection aids like the following.

> *Best Books for Children: Preschool Through Middle Grades,* 3rd ed., John T. Gillespie and Christine Gilbert, Eds., R. R. Bowker.
>
> *The Best in Children's Books: The University of Chicago Guide to Children's Literature,* 1973-1978, Zena Sutherland, Ed., University of Chicago Press.
>
> *Building a Children's Literature Collection,* 3rd ed., Harriet Quimby and Margaret Mary Kemmel, Eds., *Choice Magazine.*
>
> *Easy Reading: Book Series and Periodicals for Less Able Readers,* Michael Graves et al., Eds., International Reading Association.
>
> *The Elementary School Library Collection,* 14th ed., Lois Winkel, Ed., Bro-Dart Foundation.

Teachers can also obtain assistance from periodicals like *Horn Book, Language Arts, The Reading Teacher, School Library Journal,* and *Journal of Reading.* Each of these periodicals publishes reviews of children's books and bibliographies of trade books that teachers find helpful.

What qualities should teachers seek in the books they select for classroom use? First, the books that children read and those the teacher reads to them should include fiction, nonfiction, and poetry. The literature should be well structured with a complete story grammar or a complete expository grammar; poetry should communicate with children. You can refer to Chapters 5 and 6 for information regarding story grammar. Chapter 10 includes guidelines for selecting nonfiction and poetry.

In selecting and organizing their own materials, teachers must consider a number of factors. They must select materials with a range of difficulty that approximates the reading abilities of their students. For instance, a second-grade class usually includes students who are still at a readiness stage, students who read first-grade materials, those who read average second-grade materials, and those who read third- and fourth-grade materials. Teachers can use readability formulas to evaluate reading materials (the Fry Readability Graph is found in Appendix B). As discussed in Chapter 2, a minimum of 10 books is necessary for initiating a trade book program. This means that a teacher of an average classroom would need to examine the readability of a minimum of 300 trade books, because some of them may be too difficult or too easy for class use.

Then they must read the books to identify the interests addressed and the background of experience needed to comprehend them. A classroom trade book collection should include books that address a broad range of interests, experiences, and types of literature. Some children have a broad range of experiences and interests; others need to acquire more interests and experiences to use as they read. Some children enjoy fantasy, others poetry, and others informational books. Teachers frequently organize their reading selections into thematic units, because each reading selection can lead into the next, which helps students build comprehension abilities. In most instances, teachers obtain multiple copies of the books they choose, so that small groups of children can read and discuss the books. When a reading program is based on trade books, it is important not to underestimate the number of books needed, because a basic tenet of such programs is learning to read through reading many books.

After the materials are selected, teachers make teaching plans. First, they plan ways of motivating children to read the books. Then they plan to introduce the words necessary to read the books as in the list of book words included in Chapter 4. Teachers must plan to introduce decoding skills that students need to achieve independence. In addition, they must build the background of experiences needed for comprehension of the reading selections. They also need to plan for developing important comprehension skills such as identifying main ideas and supporting details. Discussion enhances understanding; therefore, questions to guide the discussion of each story should be prepared in advance. Teaching plans should include reteaching of skills and abilities that students have not mastered. Finally, teachers should compile a list of books on subjects related to the ones they have selected for their reading program. This enables them to suggest books to students for further reading. One of the advantages of a trade book program is that students usually spend more time reading complete books; therefore, teachers need lists of books to suggest for further reading.

Many teachers choose to spend their summers selecting materials and making plans for teaching with trade books. Summer planning is advantageous, because they have fewer interruptions and more time to read and assess the readability of the books they are considering. Librarians are very cooperative in suggesting books and lending large numbers of books for review.

Both classrooms and libraries should include newspapers, magazines, and periodicals that appeal to children. Children find materials like the following interesting.

Children's Digest
Cricket Magazine
Ebony Jr.
Highlights for Children
Humpty Dumpty's Magazine for Little Children
Owl: The Outdoor and Wildlife Discovery Magazine for Children
National Geographic World
Ranger Rick's Nature Magazine
Scholastic
Weekly Reader

Both teachers and children must select trade books. Children need to have opportunities to make independent book choices. Some teachers encourage students to choose their own books, while others suggest several books from which students may choose the one they want to read. One useful technique for selecting books that students will be able to read is to have them open a book in the middle and read a page, holding up a finger for each word not recognized. When they have five fingers raised, they should return the book to the shelf because it is too difficult. Older students may simply count unknown words until they reach five.

SELECTING BASAL READING MATERIALS

Basal readers are the most widely used reading materials in this country. They were described in Chapter 2, although the strengths and weaknesses of basals and their selection were not addressed earlier. This section explores these topics and builds a foundation for selection of basal reading materials.

Strengths and Weaknesses of Basal Readers

Basal readers offer direct, systematic reading instruction. They provide for the introduction of a certain set of skills in first grade, another set in second grade, and so forth. Furthermore, some basal readers provide for reteaching, review, and maintenance of reading skills as students move through the program. When a basal reading program is not used, teachers must work harder to devise plans to monitor students' progress in the acquisition of reading skills.

Publishers of school materials study research and teachers' preferences in order to prepare basal readers and instructor's manuals that meet teachers' specifications. Teachers designing their own reading programs and locating and preparing all of the materials needed to teach an average class of 26 students would have a long, arduous task. Publishers have done much of this work for teachers. Of course, teachers must have the expertise to choose appropriate materials and to tailor these prepared materials in ways that enable them to meet the particular needs of their students. Subsequent sections of this chapter offer suggestions for adapting basal reader lessons to meet students' needs. For example, teachers must elaborate and enrich basal reading materials with language experience and with trade books.

No basal reading program was ever intended to be a self-contained reading program (Aaron, 1987). The pupil texts do not include enough reading material to fully develop students' reading competence. Therefore, teachers must supplement basal readers with other interesting reading material. The use of children's literature in the reading program was addressed in Chapter 10. Over the years, basal readers have been criticized for a variety of reasons. Critics have expressed concern regarding the simplistic language and the trite stories in these texts. Another concern is the fact that basal readers are designed for average children; they do not provide enough assistance for teachers who must meet the needs of students who progress faster or slower than average. Current basal readers bear little resemblance to those of the past.

Among the strongest criticisms leveled at basal readers in recent years are racism (McCutcheon, Kyle, and Skovira, 1979), sexism (Britton and Lumpkin, 1977), middle-class orientation (McCutcheon, Kyle, and Skovira, 1979), and ageism (Nilsen, 1978). Traditional basal readers told us "to live in a house in the suburbs with a mommy who stayed at home and a daddy who worked." We were to be white and middle-class (McCutcheon, Kyle, and Skovira, 1979). Youngsters who did not fit this description found little with which to identify in basal readers.

Racism

Avoiding racism is an important factor in developing sound basal readers. In the past, basal reader characters were largely white, Anglo-Protestant, white-collar, middle-class people who lived in single-family dwellings. Father wore a business suit when he went to his office each day, while Mother stayed at home

Multiracial and multiethnic

cooking, cleaning, and minding the children. However, much criticism has been raised in regard to this portrayal of American life for children. Most basal reader publishers have responded to this criticism by including characters from different racial and ethnic backgrounds in their textbooks.

In contemporary basal readers, one can easily find characters from these groups, and, in many cases, they are now the main characters in stories. Today these characters are portrayed in a favorable light. They participate in activities that are attractive to all children. This portrayal makes it possible for all children to identify with the characters. For example, a current basal reader includes black children who start a "pet-sitting business" and rescue a cat who is stranded in a tree.

Another study reveals that the representation of black people in children's books has improved (Chall et al., 1979). Current literature now includes black characters in the text as well as the illustrations. Black characters are placed in more contemporary settings and have more prominent roles. However, much remains to be done in improving the quality and quantity of black characters in children's books. Researchers have suggested that the best way to improve this situation is to encourage and recognize talented writers from various minority groups to create literature based on their own experiences (Chall et al., 1979).

Racial balance

Thus, racial balance in basal readers is achieved when children from different races are included as important characters who participate in activities that are attractive to children. Stereotypes should be avoided in the portrayal of various racial groups. Race should be incidental to the story line, and children from other races should be the kinds of persons with whom all children can empathize. No distinct dialect or actions differentiate these characters from others. Thus it still appears that there is room for improvement in basal reader characterizations.

Room for improvement

Sexism

Women frequently have been portrayed either in a passive or negative fashion (Simpson, 1978). For example, Frasher and Walker found that girls were shown in quiet games 60 percent of the time, but boys only 20 percent of the time. They also found that girls were generally depicted in passive situations that demonstrated lack of creativity, initiative, and independence. Boys, on the other hand, were pictured as assertive, brave, curious, and independent (Frasher and Walker, 1972).

Has this situation changed? Research does indicate that there have been some changes in the portrayal of women and girls. More females appear in basal reader stories today and they are portrayed in a greater variety of roles. However, sexual identities have been changed in basal readers without significant differentiation in behavior, "suggesting that boys and girls are very alike in what they say and do" (McCutcheon, Kyle, and Skovira, 1979). Again, it appears that the changes have generally been related to names and illustrations. This author recently examined a basal reader that illustrates this situation. The publisher of this basal reader had changed the ice-cream man to an ice-cream woman in order to avoid sexism. One researcher suggests that we find a way to portray girls and boys as equal but, at the same time, allow for differences (McCutcheon, Kyle, and Skovira, 1979).

Equal but different

The Committee on Sexism and Reading of the International Reading Association (1977) has developed a checklist to assist teachers in analyzing sexism in school materials. This checklist includes the following points.

1. balanced representation
2. participation in both physical and intellectual activities
3. positive recognition
4. both males and females participating in domestic chores
5. both males and females having a variety of choices and goals to which to aspire
6. both males and females portrayed as independent persons
7. both men and women shown in a variety of occupations
8. the avoidance of self-deprecation by characters
9. illustrations that avoid stereotyping
10. the usage of inclusionary language, such as chairperson and police officer.

Ageism

Youth-oriented society

Concern with the portrayal of old people in children's reading materials has recently been voiced. Nilsen (1978) points out the fact that in our youth-oriented society, we do not like to think about or talk about growing old. She also identifies the stereotyped old woman who is constantly the butt of jokes. Phrases such as *that funny little woman* and *foolish old lady* are common in children's stories (Nilsen, 1978).

Contemporary basal readers have attempted to improve the portrayal of old people. They are now shown as interesting people who children can enjoy accompanying—which seems realistic, since many children do enjoy the company of their grandparents.

Selecting A Basal Reader

It is apparent that basal reader selection is an important issue in reading instruction because basal readers have considerable impact on day-to-day reading instruction. The basal reader determines the literature children will read, the specific reading skills taught and the sequence for introducing those skills, the words students will learn, the type of practice activities they will complete, and the instructional pattern for developing reading maturity. Furthermore, once basal readers are chosen, they are used for five to ten years. Obviously, this is an important decision.

Contemporary teachers have greater input in choosing basal readers than previous generations of teachers. Teachers serve on selection committees, and in many school districts, each teacher has an opportunity to vote for the basal reader he or she believes will best meet students' needs. This means that teachers must learn how to examine basal readers in order to identify the characteristics that will result in reading success for their students.

The most common method of textbook selection is to use a textbook adoption committee and an evaluation form (Cotton et al., 1988). Committee members use guidelines to analyze an array of basal readers from various

Box 8.1　Basal Reader Evaluation Guidelines

Publisher _____　　Date _____

Copyright Date _____　　　Grade Level _____

Directions: Rate each of the following considerations as follows: 1 for excellent, 2 for average, 3 for poor.

I. Objectives
  A. Do the basal reader objectives parallel those of the school's reading curriculum?
  B. Does the sequence of objectives parallel those of the reading curriculum?
  C. Are word-recognition skills presented in a balanced manner?
  D. Is comprehension emphasized?
  E. How much attention is devoted to higher-order thinking skills?
  F. Do the middle-grade objectives include content reading and study skills in the intermediate grades (middle)?
II. Reader Content
  A. Are the selections arranged in thematic units?
  B. Does the content include fiction, nonfiction, and poetry?
  C. Does the content include literature with literary merit?
  D. Are the adaptations of trade books well written?
  E. Are the selections well structured?
  F. Are the selections interesting to children?
  G. Does reader content develop cultural literacy?
  H. Are racism, sexism, and ageism avoided in the selections?
  I. Are stereotypes avoided?
  J. Are the format and illustrations attractive?
  K. Is new vocabulary presented in context in the student's editions?
  K. Are books suggested for independent reading?
III. Teacher's Editions
  A. Is the teacher's edition easy to use?
  B. Is reading related to the other language arts?
  C. Are read-aloud books suggested?
  D. Are instructional adaptations suggested to meet the needs of excellent readers and of disabled readers?
  E. Are teachers encouraged to use their professional expertise?
  F. Does the program actually develop skills or does it merely label those skills and fail to develop them?
  G. Can the basal be adapted to both whole-class instruction as well as small-group instruction?
IV. Teaching and Learning Strategies
  A. Are teaching and learning strategies appropriate to children's development?
  B. Is adequate material included for reinforcement of skills?

C. Do questions encourage higher-level thinking skills?
D. Are students encouraged to read independently?
E. Is silent reading encouraged as preparation for oral reading?
F. Are skills introduced, practiced, reviewed, and maintained?
V. Workbooks and other Ancillary Materials
    A. Do the workbooks and other ancillary materials provide for practice of skills introduced in the basal?
    B. Are the directions easy to understand and follow?
    C. Which ancillary materials are essential to the program?
VI. Assessment
    A. Does the program provide readiness assessment at each level, end-of-level tests, and an informal inventory for placing students in the series?

publishers. The guidelines usually lead the committee to examine the following areas: objectives, content, scope and sequence of skills, teaching and learning strategies, evaluation procedures, physical characteristics of the text, and supplementary components and cost (Middleton, 1987).

Some schools choose to pilot reading programs they are considering. Piloting a basal reader simply means that the materials are tried out in various classrooms in the school system.

Box 8.1 is an evaluation form that illustrates commonly used guidelines for basal reader selection.

In addition to evaluation guidelines, some schools employ a "skills trace" when examining basal readers. In a skills trace, an evaluator isolates one skill that is taught in the series (Cotton et al., 1988). For example, a skill such as main ideas or the short vowel sound of *e* might be the object of a skills trace. The scope and sequence charts and indexes from the teacher's editions and workbooks are analyzed to identify the grade levels where the skills are taught. All references to the skill are analyzed. Each member of the committee is usually responsible for tracing different skills. Each evaluator is responsible for analyzing how the skill is introduced, taught, practiced, and evaluated throughout the elementary grades. This information is recorded and compared across all of the series being considered.

A skills trace makes teachers aware of the nature of the textbooks they are using. However, they are very laborious and overlook some very important aspects of a basal reader. All basal readers include a common set of reading skills. These skills are introduced in sequences that are unique to the program, but the sequences do not differ significantly. The real difference among basal readers is in *how* skills are taught, reviewed, and maintained. Teachers also need to be aware that some skills have more value at the primary level than at the intermediate level. For example, primary-grade students need direct instruction to learn the short *e* sound, but intermediate-grade students need to use this knowledge automatically. Such concepts could be overlooked in a skills trace.

Ultimately, the most important aspect of basal readers is the skill with which teachers use them in the classroom.

Using Basal Readers Effectively

Successful reading programs depend on teachers' ability to adapt and supplement reading material to meet individual needs. The following suggestions should guide teachers' use of basal readers.

1. Avoid making the basal reader the total reading program. Basal readers should be springboards into reading, and students should be encouraged to read a variety of interesting materials.
2. Every classroom should have a collection of trade books that reflect a variety of interests and reading levels, in addition to access to a central library.
3. Make a record of the basal readers each child reads; make this record a part of his or her permanent school record so that subsequent teachers know what basal readers they have read.
4. Become acquainted with the skills, attitudes, and abilities developed at each grade level in order to monitor children's progress. You may create a chart of each youngster's progress.
5. Select appropriate strategies from the teacher's manual. It is not necessary to do all of the activities suggested for each lesson. Teacher's manuals are suggestive rather than prescriptive.
6. Do not spend too much time on a single story in a basal reader because students may become bored.
7. Plan lessons that do not introduce any new skills or words, so students have opportunities to develop fluency.
8. Read an entire story or episode at one time in order to avoid fragmentation.
9. Avoid practices such as "round robin" or "barbershop" style reading.
10. Skip stories or lessons that are uninteresting or that do not serve a valid purpose. The following section suggests ways of adapting basal reader lessons.

Adapting Basal Reader Lessons

The first step in adapting basal reader lessons is to examine the scope and sequence of skills developed in the series, then to rank these skills by importance. All reading skills do not have equal importance. For example, the authors of the Report of the Commission on Reading (Anderson et al., 1985) state that some reading programs try to teach too many letter-sound relationships; therefore, phonics instruction drags out over too many years.

Comprehension skills are a different matter. They do not vary much from grade level to grade level; as children move through the reading curriculum, they are applying comprehension skills to increasingly more complex and abstract reading content. Nevertheless, some comprehension skills are more important than others. For instance, identifying main ideas and predicting outcomes are more important than some other skills. In general, beginning teachers have greater difficulty knowing which skills are crucial. They may refer to professional books for assistance in assigning importance to various reading skills. Experienced teachers are helpful in this task. The following rating scale will help you rank the importance of skills.

1. Crucial
2. Important
3. Helpful
4. Unecessary—delete

After ranking the skills, identify those skills that students have already developed. This will help you know which skills are crucial and developed, and which should be a focal point in teaching, since they are crucial and un-developed. In identifying skills that students have developed, you may examine permanent record files and tests, as well as conferring with preceding teachers when possible. This analysis could result in a chart like the following one.

Skill	Rating
1. Prefixes: *pre* and *dis*	2
2. Stated main ideas	1
3. Predicting outcomes	1
4. The consonant *p* in final position	Delete
5. The consonant *gh* in final position	3

The fourth skill in the preceding chart is identified as a "delete," because students who know the sound of *p* in the initial position are very likely to know the sound of *p* in the final position. Therefore, instructional time would be better spent studying an unknown sound, or recognizing stated main ideas, which is crucial to comprehension and should be taught at every grade level.

Once you have identified the reading skills that you will focus on during the school year, the next step is to sequence these skills. Generally speaking, in first and second grade it is very difficult to alter the order of lessons because each lesson builds on the words and sounds taught in preceding lessons; this means that usually, lesson emphases will be changed rather than the order of introduction. The teacher who decides to change the sequence of, or omit lessons, should plan to teach any words and skills that students will need in order to read subsequent selections before attempting to teach these materials. Otherwise, students will be confused.

In the middle or intermediate grades, reading materials and students are somewhat more flexible, so a teacher may alter and omit lessons that do not fit the needs and interests of his or her students. However, these teachers should also be alert to any words, word meanings, and skills that were in the omitted or reordered lessons, so they avoid expecting students to know things that they have not been taught.

After thinking through the scope and sequence of skills and ranking them as to importance, teachers must schedule time for reading instruction. Current teachers' editions contain almost overwhelming amounts of instructional material from which teachers must choose. An average class cannot complete all of the suggested activities accompanying the average reading lesson. Teachers should refer to their chart of important skills and already mastered skills to identify those needing emphasis. Generally speaking, basal reader lessons are taught in two to three days. A thoughtful analysis of skills and students' mastery of skills helps teachers identify reading selections that need three days of instruction and those that should be done in two days. Rarely can lessons be completed in one day; equally rare are the lessons meriting four days. Therefore, teachers should examine the basal readers carefully before deciding to spend four days on a given selection. Such lessons can usually be shortened by eliminating unnecessary activities. Lessons that continue over too long a period of time become boring; they diminish the time students have to read interesting content, which reinforces reading skill development.

Instructional Materials

Reading workbooks, worksheets, practice books, skills sheets, mastery lessons, and ditto masters all constitute **instructional materials.** Workbooks and other practice materials are widely used in reading instruction. The quality of these materials is very important to the quality of reading instruction, since students spend up to 70 percent of their class time in independent practice or seatwork using workbooks and skill sheets (Fisher et al., 1978).

These materials are marketed as parts of the basal reader program, although practice materials are not essential to the reading program, because practice can be provided through wide reading and teacher-made activities. However, students spend so much time in independent practice and seatwork that preparing these materials is a formidable task for most teachers. Osborn (1984) has studied workbooks extensively and suggests that "well-designed workbooks containing useful activities can be partners with teachers in the initial teaching of what is new and the maintenance of what has already been taught."

The purpose of workbooks, practice books, skills sheets, mastery lessons, ditto (duplicating, black line) masters, and many computer programs is reinforcement and review of the reading skills introduced in the lesson, as well as practice in following directions. In addition, these materials can be used to give students opportunities to work independently and to learn how to take tests.

Workbooks and similar kinds of activities could be improved if publishers would include more comprehension exercises, particularly those addressing higher-level thinking skills. In addition, some workbook activities should be designed to prepare students to read selections. These workbook activities could develop vocabulary, prediction, and the word-recognition skills needed in reading the selection.

Osborn (1984) and Owens (1986) have developed guidelines for selecting workbooks, which are summarized in the following list. These guidelines are appropriate for evaluating and selecting other types of practice materials as well.

1. The language of written directions should be clear, easy to follow, and unambiguous. Osborn (1984) points out that brevity is a virtue in workbook instructions. Some current workbooks are more difficult to read than the basal readers they accompany.
2. Workbook tasks should reflect reader content and the skills developed in conjunction with the lesson.
3. Workbooks should provide for systematic and cumulative review of what has been taught.
4. Workbooks should reflect the most important aspects of what is being taught in the basal reader. Activities for the less important aspects of reading should be placed in the teacher's edition, for use as teachers see fit.
5. The vocabulary, language, and concept level of workbook tasks should reflect that of the basal reader program.
6. Workbook format and response modes should be consistent from lesson to lesson.
7. Workbook tasks should supply opportunities for students to apply reading skills. Osborn (1984) points out that lack of application activities is one of the greatest weaknesses of current workbooks.

Using Workbooks

Appropriate use of workbooks is as important as the workbooks themselves. The first consideration in using workbooks and other such materials is to realize that they are *adjuncts* to direct instruction, rather than substitutes for it. Then teachers must make sure that students have acquired the reading skills necessary for working independent activities prior to using them. They must select among the available activities (such as workbooks, duplicating masters, computer software) those that will reinforce the desired skills and understandings. Some students need many practice activities, while others need little or no practice; therefore, it is inappropriate to have all of the students in the class complete all of the pages in a workbook. They should complete only those pages that will reinforce important, needed skills.

Independent activities should be introduced to students so they understand the objectives of the work and what they must do to complete it. Often this involves completing an example for the purposes of clarification. Skills that are reinforced through independent activities should be transferred to actual reading situations. For example, students who complete workbook exercises identifying main ideas, should transfer this skill to content textbooks by locating main ideas in their social studies or science textbooks.

Evaluation of independent activities presents problems for some teachers. However, since these are reinforcement activities, they should not be considered a part of students' grades. Therefore, students may self-check papers by comparing their responses to those in an answer key, or the teacher may informally look the paper over to identify areas needing further practice.

Designing Seatwork

Seatwork is a major instructional component in most elementary reading programs. Whether using a basal reading program, an alternative approach, or a combination approach to reading, teachers need to design seatwork that reinforces the reading skills they are developing. Seatwork provides students with opportunities to practice the skills and abilities they are learning. Seatwork is usually completed independently, while another group of students is working directly with the teacher. Students often spend a large percentage of time working independently in the average classroom; therefore, it is important for teachers to develop effective seatwork.

The two most effective seatwork activities for reading are independent silent reading and writing. These activities grow out of a whole-language philosophy. These activities necessitate collecting large amounts of relatively easy reading materials for students to read independently. Students also must be self-directing when participating in these activities. However, the most popular seatwork activities are worksheets.

All basal reading programs include seatwork activities and suggestions for developing independent activities. Seatwork activities can be developed to accompany basal reader stories or trade books. They can be used to reinforce comprehension skills, word-recognition skills, word meanings, content reading skills, and so forth. Rupley and Blair (1987) point out that there are two major concerns related to seatwork. The first is concern for their content; the second is for the quality of instruction used with them. The issue of content is addressed in the following guidelines, adapted from those developed by Scheu, Tanner, and Au (1986).

- Page layout should be easy to follow. For example, do not combine horizontal with vertical layout.
- Instructions should be clear, easy to follow, and unambiguous. Keep instructions brief.
- Student responses should require reading and writing complete thoughts.
- Worksheets should contain enough content to teach students something. The activity should be as much like the reading and writing act as possible.
- Do not mix activities on a single sheet. For example, do not mix activities like phonics and main ideas on a given sheet.
- Students should have sufficient command of the skill in question so they can do the task with a minimum of incorrect responses. They should be successful 90% of the time while doing seatwork or workbook activities (Berliner, 1984).
- But worksheets should be complex enough to develop students' skills and understandings.

Box 8.2 illustrates a worksheet that could be used with a variety of stories. Box 8.3 illustrates a worksheet to use with expository content.

Box 8.2   Story Worksheet

Name _____   Date _____

Story Title _____

Story Author _____

Write the new words you learned on the lines below.

_____   _____

_____   _____

_____   _____

Use the new words you wrote to write three sentences that tell important ideas about the story.

Box 8.3   Expository Content Worksheet

Name _____   Date _____

Selection (book) _____

Author _____

Write three new facts you learned.

_____

_____

_____

Why are these facts important?

When using seatwork in the classroom, teachers should provide students with both written and spoken instructions (Rupley and Blair, 1987). This permits the children to review instructions without interrupting the teacher, who is usually instructing a reading group while the other children are completing the seatwork tasks. Written directions also provide students with opportunities to practice reading skills and to learn words.

Students should understand the purpose of seatwork, which should be reinforcement of a skill that was taught earlier. Seatwork cannot function as an instrument for initial teaching of reading skills. Students who understand this purpose are better able to complete assignments in an acceptable manner. When seatwork is used as reinforcement, it sometimes reveals that some students need reteaching or clarification of skills previously introduced.

Included among the printed material students read in contemporary classrooms is computer software. The next section addresses the problem of selecting computer programs for classroom use.

CHOOSING AND USING COMPUTER SOFTWARE

Students, teachers, and parents are enthusiastic about the applications of **computers** in education. During the next decade the computer will find its way into most classrooms. Some states have already passed legislation mandating computer literacy for all students in the state. There is no doubt that computers are wonderful tools for writing and managing information. The are motivating vehicles for drill and practice of reading skills, and they foster active student involvement. Because computer programs are merely sets of instructions, they can be changed and modified instantly. Computers can tutor students, test students, present games, provide drill and practice, manage information, present simulations, provide word processing capabilities, and calculate grades (Blanchard, Mason, and Daniel, 1988).

Current computer software for reading instruction can be used to develop reading readiness, word-recognition skills, comprehension skills, and remedial reading skills. Word-processing software makes it possible for even kindergarten and first-grade students to compose on the computer; the interrelation of reading and writing suggests that word-processing programs can contribute to reading development.

Among current software, word identification is the most popular domain for computerized applications. Students can learn phonics, sight words, structural analysis, and context clues with the computer. Programs also exist for developing comprehension skills and content reading skills. Comprehension instruction is one of the most challenging kinds of computerized instruction, because students must learn that reading is a "meaning getting" process. Computer program designers find it more difficult to design effective comprehension programs.

Programs like CARIS can be used in language experience approaches. In this program, children dictate stories to a teacher or aide who types them into a computer. The computer then provides a typed copy of the story for the student, followed by an alphabetical list of all the words in the story. DOVACK serves as a teacher resource, maintaining a lot of the stories and all the words used by each student. The teacher can use these word lists to review students' word knowledge. The *word banks* maintained by students in a language-experience approach can be computerized for easy access.

The majority of computerized comprehension programs rely on short readings, after which students respond to questions with multiple-choice responses. Some programs are limited because they merely provide questions and multiple-choice answers. However, programs like *The Story-Maker,* and *Textman,* developed by Andee Rubin, demonstrate greater complexity than the usual comprehension programs.

The cloze procedure is one of the more effective procedures for computer use. Cloze activities can be used to develop context clue knowledge and comprehension skills. When using a cloze activity, readers must infer the missing words from the surrounding context. Deleting every fifth word is the most frequently used cloze pattern. The word-processing capacity of computers makes it easy to create cloze procedures for students to complete.

Students can use word-processing programs to produce class newspapers, literary magazines, reports, stories, personal dictionaries, thesauruses, and to collect and organize notes for reports. The great flexibility of computers is one of their most attractive characteristics.

Simulation programs demonstrate this flexibility. Simulation programs convey information through experiences that imitate reality (Blanchard, Mason, and Daniel, 1988). Students analyze the data, evaluate possibilities, make decisions, and reevaluate the situation on the basis of the results (Edwards, 1983). One such simulation is *Temple of Asphai* (Automated Simulations), which requires problem-solving in a dungeon. These adventures are excellent recreational reading and are useful for teaching study skills (Hayes, Lancy, and Evans, 1984). Some simulations teach significant concepts and have accompanying text-based materials that support the school curriculum (Blanchard and Mason, 1985). Examples of this type of simulation include:

The Market Place—Lemonade (MECC [Minnesota Educational Computer Consortium])

Oregon Trail (MECC)

The Odell Lake (MECC)

In addition to the various types of software discussed in preceding paragraphs, teachers can use software to create reading materials for their students. For example, they can use *Crossword Magic* (L and S Computerware) to create crossword puzzles and *Adventure Programs* (Spinnaker) to create adventure programs. Drill, practice, and review programs can be created with programs like *Teacher Utilities* for the Apple computer, which was created by the Minnesota Educational Computer Consortium, and *Author,* which is a Radio Shack

---

Box 8.4   Guide for Selecting Computer Software

Program Title _____   Date _____

Company _____

Cost _____

Overall Impression _____

A. Does the school have the computer and peripherals needed to run this software?
B. Do the objectives of this program match the objectives of the adopted reading curriculum?
C. Does the program provide practice of skills being developed in the reading curriculum?
D. Is the price of this software reasonable?
E. Does this software go beyond typical workbook activities?
F. Does this program give children opportunities to read and write rather than identify multiple-choice responses?
G. Are words introduced in a meaningful context?
H. Do comprehension programs emphasize higher-level thinking skills?
I. Does this program have instructional value?
J. Is this material pedagogically sound?

---

program for the TRS 80. Of course, the programs mentioned in this section are simply a few examples of the many programs from which teachers can choose.

Selecting computer software to complement reading instruction is a complex task due to the wide variety of reading software available to schools. When choosing computer software, teachers should avoid materials that are merely mechanized workbooks. Box 8.4 illustrates an instrument teachers can use to guide their selection of computer software. This instrument is designed for use when previewing computer software, since that is the recommended approach for selecting programs.

Using Computers in the Classroom

Now that we have discussed the exciting prospects for using computers in the classroom, it is time to examine the realities of the situation. The best way to become computer literate is to spend time with a computer, learning what it can and cannot do. Once students know how to turn a computer on and off, and how to keyboard, they need to use a discovery approach to learning about computers. Unfortunately, the majority of schools lack the numbers of computers necessary for such exploration. Some schools have one or two computers for each classroom; others have one or two for the entire school, and some have larger numbers of computers.

Schools that have large numbers of computers can give students the needed exploration, but schools with limited resources must make choices. They may choose to pool all of their computers in a computer lab and schedule classroom groups of students into the lab. Another option is to place a few computers in each classroom and to schedule time on the computer for the children in that classroom. When schools do not have a computer for each student, teachers and students must plan their work carefully, so they make the best use of the time available. For instance, when using the word-processing program, teachers should have completed prewriting and drafting of the composition before scheduling computer time.

Computer Fatigue

Frequent computer use can lead to visual fatigue. A series of research studies revealed that visual fatigue is a common result of reading the video display terminal (Blanchard, Mason, and Daniel, 1988). Reading an electronic display is more fatiguing than reading paper print. The reading rate is significantly slower for text presented electronically (Muter et al., 1982). According to a research study by Chapman and Tipton (1985), comprehension of paper print is better than with electronic print.

A number of factors may contribute to the difference in reading an electronic display and reading paper print. For example, the difference in amount of experience with reading electronic display may contribute to this reading variation. Physical factors like the difference in the luminosity of the display or an individual's sensitivity to flicker since most video displays flicker may contribute to reading differences. Such issues cannot be resolved here, but it is clear that children should not spend long periods of time in front of a computer during the school day. Teachers need to plan and monitor computer time.

USING MEDIA IN THE READING PROGRAM

Film, film strips, flat pictures, and so forth can be used to good advantage in reading instruction. The various forms of **media** can be used to build background experience, and to activate schemata for reading specific stories, poems, or expository text. Because schemata play such an enormous role in competent reading, the selected media are also important. Film can also motivate students to read. Many students who have seen the "Little House" series on television have been moved to read the books, just as reading a book to students motivates them to read the same book, or another one by the same author.

When using media with children, it is important that the teacher preview the material before presenting it. Then the students who will see the media, should be prepared to participate. They should learn any new words or expressions included in the media, and the instructor may alert them to key words (or expressions) or concepts that they will encounter in the media. In some instances, the teacher should identify listening or observing purposes to aid students' comprehension. It is also instructive to compare ideas and modes of presentation when information is presented in media and in written language.

SUMMARY

The following list summarizes the key points of this chapter.

1. Reading instruction is based on the selected approach, which indicates what materials are to be used in conjunction with the specified approach. Basal readers are used in 90 to 95% of the schools in the United States; therefore, they are a powerful factor in reading instruction.
2. The most common approaches to contemporary reading instruction are the basal reader, language-experience, individualized reading, and whole-language. Each of these approaches has strengths and weaknesses. Because materials are so important to the reading curriculum, teachers must choose both basal materials and materials for independent work very carefully.
3. Therefore, the most effective approach is probably a combination of these approaches. Combination approaches are usually organized around a basal reader, which provides the systematic structure for reading development. However, the other approaches incorporate the language arts, and invite students into the wide reading necessary for developing reading skill.
4. Teachers must choose basal readers carefully because they use these materials so often. In addition, once chosen, basal readers are used for five to ten years.
5. Basal readers are usually selected by a teacher committee using specific selection guidelines. A skills trace is a useful way of evaluating basal readers.
6. The materials used in whole-language, individualized reading, and language-experience approaches include trade books, children's writing, newspapers, magazines, and so forth.
7. Computers are widely used in the United States to supplement reading instruction; therefore, computer software should be selected that enhances the reading curriculum.

SELF-TEST

Check your knowledge of the information presented in this chapter. The answer key is located in Appendix C.

1. What is the major goal of basal reading programs?
   a. to provide systematic reading instruction
   b. to make teacher planning unnecessary
   c. to teach all of the students in the class the same skills at the same time

    d. so the other students in the reading group can follow the text when a student reads aloud

2. What percentage of American schools use basal readers?
    a. 25 to 30%
    b. 50 to 55%
    c. 90 to 95%
    d. 100%

3. What is the major goal of seatwork activities and workbook exercises?
    a. to introduce new skills
    b. to reinforce and practice previously taught skills
    c. both a and b
    d. neither a nor b

4. Why are basal reading programs so important in American reading instruction?
    a. teachers are expected to use them
    b. they are components of the curriculum
    c. they present a systematic approach to reading instruction
    d. all of the above

5. What is the function of reader content?
    a. it is a springboard into reading
    b. it should entice children to read
    c. it provides the substance necessary for developing comprehension
    d. all of the above

6. Which statement describes the skills developed by basal readers?
    a. all basal reading series develop reading skills in the same order
    b. each series of basal readers differs in the sequence of skills introduced
    c. basal readers develop skills as students indicate they need the skills
    d. all of the above

7. Why do teachers need to rank the importance of the reading skills included in their adopted basal reader?
    a. so they can adapt the basal to their students' needs
    b. so they can locate games for teaching
    c. so they will know when to fail students
    d. none of the above

8. How long does it take to teach an average basal reader lesson?
    a. four days
    b. two to three days
    c. one day
    d. five days

9. How can teachers shorten basal reader lessons?
    a. by skipping them completely
    b. by substituting literature for the reading content
    c. by omitting unnecessary activities
    d. all of the above

10. What is the purpose of workbooks and worksheets?
    a. to keep the students quiet
    b. to introduce new skills

       c. to reinforce and practice skills
       d. to test students' reading knowledge

11. How can teachers use workbooks more effectively?
    a. by introducing the activities to students so they know what is expected of them
    b. by using only those activities that provide needed practice
    c. both a and b
    d. neither a nor b

12. Which answer describes computer software?
    a. mechanized workbook
    b. challenging presentation of higher-level thinking skills
    c. well-developed comprehension programs
    d. all of the above

13. What kinds of materials are the basis for an individualized reading program?
    a. workbooks
    b. trade books (literature)
    c. basal readers
    d. children's writings

14. Why is children's literature important to contemporary reading instruction?
    a. it is used in basal readers
    b. it is used for independent reading
    c. because teachers are expected to read aloud to students
    d. all of the above

15. What are the major sources of trade books for children's reading?
    a. classroom collections of books
    b. the school media center
    c. both a and b
    d. neither a nor b

16. What materials are the basis for a language-experience approach to reading?
    a. trade books
    b. basal readers
    c. computer programs
    d. children's writings

17. What kinds of reading materials are used in a combination approach to reading?
    a. literature
    b. children's writings
    c. basal readers
    d. all of the above

THOUGHT QUESTIONS

1. Why do you think basal readers play such an important role in American reading instruction?

2. Identify substitutes for seatwork that students can complete independently while the teacher is working directly with reading groups.

3. Discuss the strengths and weaknesses of workbooks and identify ways of overcoming the weaknesses.

4. What do you think is the role of computer literacy in schools? How could your philosophy be implemented in elementary schools?

5. Examine the guidelines for evaluating basal readers. Identify any points that you think could be eliminated and any points that should be added.

6. How can reading materials be related to the school philosophy of reading?

ENRICHMENT ACTIVITIES

1. Work with another class member and compare two basal reading programs using the guidelines in this chapter. Decide which of the programs better meets students' instructional needs. Be prepared to explain why you chose the particular program.

2. Prepare a skills trace for one skill in one basal reading series.

3. Prepare a worksheet to reinforce and/or practice one skill that was previously introduced to a class. Then prepare the script for introducing this worksheet to a class.

4. Select a workbook that accompanies one level of a basal reading program. Examine each page and compare it with the text it is intended to accompany. Which activities are most valuable and which could be omitted?

5. Working in a group, use the guidelines presented in this chapter to plan the skills and the order of their presentation for a grade level of a basal reading program.

6. Prepare seatwork activities that could be used with a specific reading group (high, average, or low ability).

7. Analyze a workbook or a set of worksheets. What are the strengths and weaknesses of these materials?

8. Use the guidelines suggested in this chapter to analyze the scope and sequence of skills at one grade level of a basal reading series. Create a chart that shows the points of emphasis and the omissions.

9. Analyze a package of computer software designed for reinforcing reading skills.

RELATED READINGS

Aaron, R. (1987). "Enriching the Basal Reading Program with Literature." in *Children's Literature in the Reading Program,* B. Cullinan (Ed)., Newark, DE: International Reading Association, pp. 126–138.

Anderson, R., J. Osborn, and R. Tierney, Eds. (1984). *Learning to Read in American Schools: Basal Readers and Content Texts,* Hillsdale, NJ: Lawrence Erlbaum.

Blair, T. and W. Rupley (February 1988). "Practice and Application in the Teaching of Reading," *The Reading Teacher,* Vol. 41, pp. 536–543.

Blanchard, J. and G. Mason (November 1985). "Using Computers in Content Area Reading Instruction," *Journal of Reading,* Vol. 29, pp. 112–117.

Blanchard, J., G. Mason, and D. Daniel (1988). *Computer Applications in Reading,* 3rd ed. Newark, DE: International Reading Association.

Cotton, E., C. Casem, M. Kroll, E. Langas, A. Rhodes, and J. Sisson (February 1988). "Using a Skill Trace to Solve the Basal Reader Adoption Dilemma," *The Reading Teacher,* Vol. 41, pp. 550–555.

Cullinan, B., Ed. (1987). *Children's Literature in the Reading Program,* Newark, DE: International Reading Association.

Dasch, A. (January 1983). "Aligning Basal Reader Instruction with Cognitive Stage Theory," *The Reading Teacher,* Vol. 36, No. 4, pp. 428–435.

Geoffrion, L. and O. Geoffrion (1983). *Computers and Reading Instruction,* Reading, MA: Addison-Wesley.

Goodman, K. (1988). "Look What They've Done to Judy Blume!: The Basalization of Children's Literature," *The New Advocate,* Vol. 1, pp. 29–41.

Heald-Taylor, G. (October 1987). "Predictable Literature Selections and Activities for Language Arts Instruction," *The Reading Teacher,* Vol. 41, pp. 6–13.

Henke, L. (1988). "Beyond Basal Reading: A District's Commitment to Change," *The New Advocate,* Vol. 1, pp. 42–51.

Flood, J. and D. Lapp (May 1987). "Types of Writing in Basal Readers and Assessment Tests: An Imperfect Match," *The Reading Teacher,* Vol. 41, pp. 880–883.

Martinez, M. and W. Teale (February 1988). "Reading in a Kindergarten Classroom Library," *The Reading Teacher,* Vol. 42, pp. 568–573.

Miller, J. (October 1986). "Evaluation and Selection of Basal Reading Programs," *The Reading Teacher,* Vol. 40, pp. 12–17.

Rude, R. (1986). *Teaching Reading Using Microcomputers,* Englewood Cliffs, NJ: Prentice-Hall.

Scheu, J., D. Tanner, and K. Hu-pei Au (October 1986). *The Reading Teacher,* Vol. 40, pp. 18–27.

Scott, D. and J. Barker (May 1987). "Guidelines for Selecting and Evaluating Reading Software: Improving the Decision-Making Process." *The Reading Teacher,* Vol. 40, pp. 884–887.

REFERENCES

Aaron, R. (1987). "Enriching the Basal Reading Program with Literature," in *Children's Literature in the Reading Program,* B. Cullinan (Ed.), Newark, DE: International Reading Association, pp. 126–131.

Anderson, R., E. Hiebert, J. Scott, and I. Wilkinson. (1985) *Becoming a Nation of Readers: The Report of the Commission on Reading,* Urbana, IL: The Center for the Study of Reading.

Anderson, R. (1984). "The Environment of Instruction: The Function of Seatwork in a Commercially Developed Curriculum," in *Comprehension Instruction: Perspectives and Suggestions,* G. Duffy, L. Roehler and J. Mason (Eds.), New York: Longman, pp. 93–103.

Aukerman, R. (1981). *The Basal Reader Approach to Reading,* New York: John Wiley & Sons.

Bagford, J. (May 1977). "Management Systems and Comprehension Do Not Mix!" *Language Arts,* Vol. 54, No. 8, pp. 517–520.

Baumann, J. (1985). *Whole Language Instruction and Basal Readers,* Columbus, OH: Silver, Burdett and Ginn.

Blanchard, J. and G. Mason (November 1985). "Using Computers in Content Area Reading Instruction," *Journal of Reading,* Vol. 29, pp. 112–117.

Blanchard, J., G. Mason, and D. Daniel (1988). *Computer Applications in Reading,* 3rd ed. Newark, DE: International Reading Association.

Brophy, J. (1983). "Classroom Organization and Management," *Elementary School Journal,* Vol. 83, pp. 265–285.

Britton, G. and M. Lumpkin (October 1977). "For Sale: Subliminal Bias in Textbooks," *The Reading Teacher,* Vol. 31, No. 1, pp. 40–45.

Chall, J., E. Radwin, V. French, and C. Hall (February 1979). "Blacks in the World of Children's Books," *The Reading Teacher,* Vol. 32, No. 5, pp. 527–533.

Chapman, A. and Tilton, J. (1985). *The Presentation of Written Passages on Television: A Comparison of Three Methods.* Lexington: The Kentucky Network.

Committee on Sexism and Reading of the International Reading Association (December 1977). "Guide for Evaluating Sex Stereotyping in Reading Materials," Vol. 31, No. 3, p. 288.

Cotton, E., C. Casem, M. Kroll, E. Langas, A. Rhodes, and J. Sisson (February 1988). "Using A Skill Trace To Solve the Basal Reader Adoption Dilemma," *The Reading Teacher,* Vol. 41, pp. 550–555.

Dishaw, M. (1977). "Descriptions of Allocated Time to Content Areas for the A–B Period," Beginning Teacher Evaluation Study. San Francisco, CA: Far West Regional Laboratory for Educational Research and Development.

Editors (1980). "Why Comprehension," *Reading Research Quarterly,* Vol. 25, No. 2, pp. 181–182.

Educational Products Information Exchange (1977). "Report on a National Study of the Nature and the Quality of Instructional Materials Most Used by Teachers and Learners," New York: EPIE Institute.

Edwards, L. (1983). "Teaching Higher Level Thinking Skills Through Computer Courseware," *AEDS Monitor,* Vol. 21, No. 11, pp. 28–30.

Fisher, C., D. Berliner, N. Filby, N. Marliave, R. Cohen, L. Dishaw, and J. Moore (1978). "Teaching and Learning in Elementary Schools: A Summary of the Beginning Teacher Evaluation Study," San Francisco: Far West Laboratory for Educational Research and Development.

Frasher, R. and A. Walker (May 1972). "Sex Roles in Early Reading Textbooks," *The Reading Teacher,* Vol. 25, No. 8, pp. 741–749.

Geoffrion, L. and O. Geoffrion (1983). *Computers and Reading Instruction,* Reading, MA: Addison-Wesley.

Goodman, K. (1988). "Look What They've Done to Judy Blume!: The Basalization of Children's Literature," *The New Advocate,* Vol. 1, pp. 29–41.

Harris, A. (February 1976). "Practical Applications of Reading Research," *The Reading Teacher,* Vol. 29, No. 5, pp. 559–565.

Hayes, B., D. Lancy, and B. Evans (December 1984). "Computer Adventure Games and the Development of Information Processing Skills," paper presented at the Fifth Annual Meeting of the American Reading Forum, Orlando, FL.

Henke, L. (1988). "Beyond Basal Reading: A District's Commitment to Change," *The New Advocate,* Vol. 1, pp. 43–51.

Hughes, A., S. Bernier, N. Thomas, C. Bereiter, V. Anderson, L. Gurren, J. Lebo, and J. Overberg (1982). *The Headway Program,* LaSalle, IL: Open Court.

Komoski, P. (1982). "Affecting the System Through Productive Evaluation," ED 217 071, Arlington, VA: ERIC Document Reproduction Service.

Mason, J. and J. Osborn (1982). *When Do Children Begin "Reading to Learn"? A Survey of Classroom Reading Instruction Practices in Grades Two Through Five,* Champaign, IL: University of Illinois.

McCutcheon, K. and S. (January 1979). "Characters in Basal Readers: Does 'Equal' Now Mean 'Same'?" *The Reading Teacher,* Vol. 32, No. 4, pp. 438–441.

Middleton, Y. (May 1987). "Perspectives on Textbook Adoption Procedures," paper presented at the International Reading Association Conference, Anaheim, CA.

Nilsen, A. (February 1978). "Old Blondes Just Dye Away: Relationships Between Sexism and Ageism," *Language Arts,* Vol. 55, pp. 175–179.

Osborn, J. (1984). "The Purposes, Uses, and Contents of Workbooks and Some Guidelines for Publishers," in *Learning to Read in American Schools: Basal Readers and Content Texts,* R. Anderson, J. Osborn, and R. Tierney (Eds.), pp. 45–112.

Owen, S. (1986). "A Study of Fourth Grade Reading Workbooks," unpublished Doctoral Dissertation, Greensboro, NC: The University of North Carolina at Greensboro.

Rupley, W. and T. Blair (January 1987). "Assignment and Supervision of Reading Seatwork: Looking in on 12 Primary Teachers," *The Reading Teacher,* Vol. 40, pp. 391–398.

Scheu, J., D. Tanner, and K. Hu-pei Au (October 1986). "Designing Seatwork to Improve Students' Reading Comprehension Ability," *The Reading Teacher,* Vol. 40, pp. 18–27.

Shannon, P. (1982). "Some Subjective Reasons for Teacher's Reliance on Commercial Reading Materials," *The Reading Teacher,* Vol. 40, pp. 12–17.

Shannon, P. (1983). "The Use of Commercial Reading Materials in American Elementary Schools," *Reading Research Quarterly,* Vol. 19, pp. 65–85.

Simpson, C. (February 1978). "Educational Materials and Children's Sex Role Concepts," *Language Arts,* Vol. 55, No. 5, 161–167.

Stoodt, B. (March 1980). "Racism, Sexism, Ageism, and Middle-Classism in Basal Readers," unpublished research, Greensboro, NC: The University of North Carolina at Greensboro.

Weiner, R. (March 1974). "A Look at Reading Practices in Open Education," *The Reading Teacher,* Vol. 27, No. 5, 438–442.

THE INDIVIDUAL AND THE ELEMENTARY READING PROGRAM

CHAPTER 9

Reading and Comprehending Content Materials

OVERVIEW Have you ever heard of the "fourth-grade slump" (Chall, 1983)? Sometimes fourth graders who were excellent readers in the early grades encounter difficulties when they encounter the textbooks and expository materials that characterize middle-grade (intermediate-grade) reading. Although content textbooks are used prior to fourth grade, the writing style used in them changes in the middle grades. Teachers expect students in the middle grades (and beyond) to read text and learn independently. In general, middle-grade teachers expect children to learn *how* to read in the primary grades; therefore, they expect students to use their reading skills to acquire new knowledge. Expository reading material and content textbooks may be used at all grade levels, but intermediate-grade students are expected to learn independently from them. These students must learn *how* to use reading as a functional tool. They will need content reading skills throughout life. This chapter prepares teachers to teach the strategies that will help their students develop the skills and abilities necessary to understand expository text.

Key Vocabulary

As you read this chapter, check your understanding of these terms:

exposition	**three-level study guide**
narrative	**technical vocabulary**
SQ3R	

Focusing Questions

As you read this chapter, think about these questions:

1. How are the demands of intermediate-grade or middle-school reading different from those of primary-grade reading?

339

2. What writing patterns are commonly found in social studies, science, and mathematics?
3. What strategies will help students understand content textbooks?

THE CONTENT-AREA READING PROGRAM

The content reading program is concerned with teaching students to read expository text, which is written to convey information and to explain. Expository text plays an important role in all of our lives. Content textbooks are largely comprised of expository text; they are written to inform and to teach students factual material. During the school years, teachers can convey only a small portion of the massive amount of information available in our "information age." All of us must become lifelong learners—continually updating our store of knowledge throughout life. The skills that enable us to do this are the functional reading skills. These skills enable us to acquire new knowledge and concepts from reading; students must learn how to use these important skills.

Beginning in the intermediate grades (or the middle school) and continuing through high school and college, a major part of school time is spent reading content textbooks to acquire information. Typically, teachers assign pages for students to read; later students take tests to demonstrate their knowledge of assigned material. Teachers take responsibility for identifying the information students know and do not know, but they do not take the responsibility for teaching students how to learn that information.

Many teachers, school administrators, and parents incorrectly assume that children master reading skills in the primary grades; then they use these skills in the middle grades to acquire knowledge (Chall, 1975). Because they assume that children have well-developed reading skills, middle-grade teachers tend to devote more attention to social studies, science, and mathematics concepts. They do not realize that they need to further and refine the reading skills necessary to understand this content (Arnold and Sherry, 1975; Hash, 1974). Durkin (1978–1979) examined reading comprehension and content reading instruction in her observational study and concluded that middle-grade teachers paid little or no attention to content reading. She found that teachers were not teaching new vocabulary or how to understand text which are important factors in comprehending expository text. The most common instructional approach identified in this study was "round robin" reading, which means the students were taking turns reading aloud from sections of the text. This was followed with assigned questions to which the students wrote answers. This study underscores the great need for content reading and study skills instruction. Middle-grade teachers must accept the responsibility for this instruction.

Research

Current research also emphasizes the need for content reading instruction. Armbruster and Gudbrandsen (1986) found that direct instruction in social studies was rare; reading, studying, and thinking skills were primarily taught through practice or application of skills that students had presumably acquired. Their research showed that new knowledge about developing reading comprehension is not included in social studies textbooks.

In view of the importance of content reading and study skills, the logical time for students to begin learning study strategies would be when they first encounter content area textbooks, which is in the intermediate grades or middle school. Some primary-grade teachers use content textbooks, but these books are written in a narrative style, which is very similar to trade books and basal readers. It is not until fourth grade that students have a content text written in the style of the discipline.

Teachers cannot assume that children who have learned to read in the primary grades are able to understand content materials. These materials require specialized reading skills. Primary-grade reading materials are largely comprised of **narrative (story) content** and are designed to develop basic reading skills. These materials progress from simple to more advanced levels. This narrative content contains interesting characters and dialogue, is well illustrated, and is often written in a humorous style. Dulin (1977) states that "such material often almost teaches itself." Primary reading instruction emphasizes learning and practicing reading skills, and does not focus on the ideas and concepts presented in the content. Narrative reading does *not* prepare children for functional reading.

Comparing and contrasting the content in the following excerpts from a basal reader and a science text will reveal some of the basic differences between narrative material and **expository (informational) writing.** The first passage is from a basal reader.

> The statue of the black soldier had stood in the park for many years. Below the rain-streaked stone and the weather-stained musket a small crack indented one leg. The muscles stood out, strong fibers that had helped carry Silas into battle. He had been only sixteen when he went away to war to become a hero.
>
> Silas did not remember how long he had stood looking across the grass to the trees and the ridge. Children played about him season after season, pretending to fire his gun or fall in step with him.
>
> A sigh like fragile wind escaped Silas. He was filled with memories of days when dark gold leaves had clung to his face and slid and stuck to his uniform like so many tarnished medals. The birds in springtime had pecked at his cracks, looking for juicy ants, and summer suns had beat upon his head. Now it was fall again, and dry leaves drifted about the pedestal, heaping in little mounds.
>
> The only black man in his company, he had won a medal for saving six men from enemy fire from an abandoned mill. The engraved name of the battle was blurred— time left no sharp edges on anything, including memory. Yet the day was still fresh when the entire company had drawn up at attention and General Washington had read the citation in a voice that was stern and commanding. His own feet had been wet from the snow creeping into his worn-out shoes.
>
> " 'To Militiaman Silas Tanner for Bravery under fire at the Battle of Peeks Mill, given to him this twenty-second day of December, 1775.' "*

The second passage is from a science textbook.

Earth's Place In Space

> You, too, are in orbit. Right now you are on a space station. It is in orbit around the Sun. It is moving along its orbit and is spinning as it goes. Your station is space planet

*From Helen Olian, "Silas Tanner," in *Soaring Plateaus,* comp. Leo Fay and Paul S. Anderson, Young America Basic Series, Chicago: Rand McNally, 1978, pp. 294–295. Reprinted by permission of the publisher.

Earth. And the Earth is about 93 million miles away from the Sun. Scientists use the metric system to measure our distance from the Sun.

You know that scientists use metric units to measure weight and mass. When scientists measure length, they use other units of the metric system—the *meter,* the *centimeter* and the *kilometer.*

Look at the photograph of a yardstick and a meter stick. Which of the two is longer? A meter is actually equal to about 39 inches, a little more than a yard (or three feet).

You can divide a meter into 100 equal parts called centimeters. The photograph compares sections of two rulers. The ruler on the top is marked in inches and the other is marked in centimeters. Compare the inch marks with the centimeter marks. Do you agree that 1 inch is equal to about 2½ centimeters?

You can use centimeters and meters to measure short distances—your height or the length of a car. But the distance to the Sun is very large. It must be measured by a larger ruler, the kilometer. A kilometer is equal to 1,000 meters or about six-tenths of a mile. The distance to the Sun is 93 million miles. The distance to the Sun is also 150 million kilometers."†

The author of the basal reader story creates a mood in the selection—through such descriptions as *rain-streaked stone, weather-stained musket,* and *The muscles stood out, strong fibers that had helped carry Silas into battle.* The story is told from the point of view of the statue, which is also of interest to children. Silas talks about experiences and feelings that children can understand. The descriptive parts of the selection are especially vivid, and this helps readers identify with the character and the story action. The words used in this story are common, easily identified words. The reader will undoubtedly be able to comprehend this selection.

Compact

The science passage is quite compact but contains a large number of ideas. This selection contains no descriptions. The reader must understand the following technical words: *metric units, weight, mass, meter, centimeter,* and *kilometer.* Photographs must be related to the written content in order to understand the concepts that are introduced. Comparison and contrast is used to explain the concept of *meter.* Previous knowledge of inches, yards, and feet is necessary in order to comprehend this explanation.

Examination of the preceding selections illustrates some of the demands that content reading places on the reader. The following discussion examines these reading demands in more detail.

THE DIFFICULTIES OF CONTENT READING

Content textbooks are written to help children learn the basic concepts of such disciplines as science, social science, mathematics, and language. These concepts range from the abstract (such as *freedom*) to the concrete (such as *river*). Many of the concepts taught in content textbooks are unrelated to students'

†Excerpt from *Concepts in Science,* Newton Edition, Grade 5, Purple, by Paul F. Brandwein, et al., Copyright © 1975 by Harcourt Brace Jovanovich, Inc., reprinted by permission of the publisher.

previous experiences. These concepts are often developed in a pyramid-like fashion. Students must understand and remember various key concepts that serve as a basis for material introduced later in the textbook. For example, the reader of the preceding science passage would be expected to remember the metric measurement concepts for use in later reading. Smith, Goodman, and Meredith (1970) state that "The reader must have certain associations with the language symbols in common with the writer. But he must also have some experiences in common with the writer and must have reached a level of concept development that makes communication possible."

Vocabulary

*Technical
vocabulary*

The concepts presented in content textbooks are linked to vocabulary development because words often serve as labels for concepts. The vocabulary in basal readers is controlled, so that the reader does not encounter too many new words at one time. Basal reader vocabulary is more closely related to the reader's experience than the **technical vocabulary** in content textbooks. Each discipline, however, has an extensive vocabulary list all its own. Some examples of technical vocabulary words and their respective disciplines are listed in the following.

Social studies: *culture, urban, economic, archaeologist, anthropologist, monetary.*

The information in a science book is organized in a particular manner. Readers who can identify that organization have a better chance of understanding what they read. *(Courtesy Jean-Claude Lejune)*

Science: *satellite, revolution, protoplanets, orbit, radiation, nuclei, protrons, neutrons.*

Mathematics: *Notation, regrouping, estimate, operation, multiples, denominators.*

Language: *pronoun, adjective, determiner, article.*

The technical vocabulary used in content materials must be directly taught to students during regular classroom instruction. (See Chapter 5 for teaching suggestions.)

The vocabulary introduced in content materials also includes common words used with special meanings. For example, *mouth* may mean an opening in the face or the opening of a river, cave, or harbor. *Revolution* may refer to a political uprising in social studies or a movement of the earth in science. Readers must be prepared for such shifts in meaning.

Writing Style

Writing in content textbooks is compact and often difficult to read. Many ideas are compressed into a few lines of print. Every word is important to understanding; therefore, readers cannot skip words they do not recognize. One paragraph may cover a hundred-year period. The accomplishments of a figure like John F. Kennedy may be discussed in a single paragraph. Clearly, the complexity of significant historical figures cannot be fully explored in such brief text. Scientific discoveries that involve a number of concepts are often treated with the same brevity.

Structure

The information and explanations in content texts are structured in specific ways, since the knowledge associated with each discipline is more than a mere collection of facts; structure expresses the interrelationship of facts. Expository grammars (structures) explain and inform through the organization of main ideas and details, which are structured in several ways. The prevalent structures are *cause and effect, comparison, problem-solution, sequential order, listing,* and *description* (Piccolo, 1987). Students who can recognize these structures, read with greater understanding (Niles, 1974).

The compact writing style, presentation of concepts, technical vocabulary, and expository grammar all contribute to the high readability level that characterizes content textbooks. High readability level is a matter for concern because it makes comprehension difficult. Students who have difficulty understanding the text are not likely to acquire new knowledge from it. A number of research studies have explored the reading difficulty of content textbooks. Heddens and Smith (1964) examined elementary mathematics textbooks and found a high readability level. Johnson and Vardian (1973) found the same problem in social

Table 9.1   MAJOR DIFFERENCES BETWEEN BASAL READERS AND CONTENT TEXTBOOK MATERIALS

Basal readers	Content textbooks
Are generally stories with story grammar.	Expository structure.
Controlled vocabulary.	Technical vocabulary.
Reader can identify with characters.	Reader must understand and retain the information presented.
Concepts are often related to reader experience.	Concepts are often abstract or unrelated to reader experience.
Writing style is descriptive.	Writing style is compact.
Can be read for pleasure.	Read to learn information or solve problems.
Content and pictures convey information.	Graphic aids and content convey information.
Controlled readability.	Readability generally above the grade level that has been determined.
Purpose is to entertain.	Purpose is to explain and inform.

studies textbooks. Peters (1975-1976) studied concept presentation in social studies textbooks rather than readability. He found that comprehension could be increased by changing the style of explaining concepts. Generally speaking, *Difficult content* content textbooks have a higher readability level than the grade in which they are used. Therefore, even an average reader can experience difficulty with this material.

Students must be able to understand 75 percent of the ideas and 90 *Instructional level* percent of the vocabulary in a social studies selection in order to read it at an instructional level (Herman, 1969). Of course, this means that even higher levels of vocabulary knowledge and understanding are required if independent reading is to be achieved. Such demands are obviously very difficult for students to meet. Bormuth (1972) found that 65 percent of the students in the intermediate grades gain little information from reading content textbooks. This data should make teachers realize the crucial need for content reading instruction.

Graphic aids Readers of content materials must also be able to read and interpret the graphic aids that are often used to convey information in content materials. Pictures, graphs, charts, tables, and maps express various relationships in a condensed format. Readers must interpret these aids in terms of the accompanying written content. Students appear to have a tendency to disregard graphic aids.

Table 9.1 summarizes the major differences between basal reader and content textbook materials.

TEACHING CHILDREN TO READ CONTENT MATERIALS

Content reading instruction is necessary and important for intermediate-grade and middle-school students. This section introduces principles of content reading and helpful reading strategies. Content reading requires application of comprehension skills to content materials; therefore, the skills and strategies introduced in Chapters 5 and 6 are appropriate to content reading. In addition, specific skill applications are also discussed in this section.

The teaching tasks involved in content reading instruction are:

1. Matching reading materials to children's reading abilities.
2. Motivating students to read content materials.
3. Developing the skills and strategies necessary for comprehending content materials.
4. Direct application of content reading skills to content text.

Matching Materials to Children's Abilities

When selecting instructional materials, teachers must consider the child's reading ability as well as the level of reading difficulty (**readability**) of the materials themselves. A child's reading ability can be estimated from a reading achievement test or an informal inventory (see Chapter 10).

Readability of content materials is based on such factors as vocabulary, sentence length, sentence complexity, abstractness of concepts, writing style, reader interest, reader experience, and type of print. However, vocabulary and sentence length are the factors that are most often assessed for readability.

A number of excellent formulas are available for estimating the readability of content. The **Fry Readability Graph,** however, is one of the quickest and easiest for teachers to use. Calculating readability according to the Fry graph involves selecting three 100 word samples, determining the number of sentences in the sample to the nearest tenth of a sentence, the average number of syllables, and the average number of sentences in a 100-word selection. This information is used to determine the approximate grade level of the selection. The Fry Readability Graph can be examined in the Appendix.

Cloze

Another way of matching children and the appropriate reading materials is by the cloze procedure. The cloze is used for assessing and teaching comprehension as well as measuring readability. In this approach, the child's ability to read specific materials is evaluated. The **cloze precedure** is also easy to construct, administer, and score. The application of the cloze procedure to content materials is reviewed below.

1. Select materials that represent those you would use in the classroom. Select a 520-word passage. (Burron and Claybaugh, 1974)
2. The first and last sentences should be left intact. Begin counting with the first word of the second sentence and delete every tenth word until you come to the last sentence. Replace these deleted words with blank lines of equal length.
3. Administer the cloze by having children fill in the blanks. (Note that spelling does not count.)
4. Compute the score by calculating the percentage of correct answers.
5. Interpret the score as follows:

57 percent or above is equated with an *independent* reading level
45 to 56 percent is equated with an *instructional* reading level
44 percent and below is equated with a *frustration* reading level

Alternatives to the textbook

After assessing readability, the teacher may discover that some children in the class are unable to read the textbook. Therefore, alternatives must be sought. A wide variety of interesting and well-written informational books are available on the market today. These trade books can be substituted for textbooks because some of them have a lower readability level. Magazines may also provide information at lower readability levels. Teachers frequently find that they can cover the same topics and information from trade books and magazines as that found in textbooks.

Audiotapes

Some children have such limited reading skills that it is necessary to provide them with an alternative source of information. These children work with audiotapes of their textbooks. Teachers should not allow poor reading skills to inhibit learning. These children may be able to acquire information from the written content at a later date but, in the meantime, they should be permitted to learn as well as successful readers.

Motivating Children to Read Content Materials

Motivating students to read content materials is usually more challenging than motivating them to read narrative content. Teachers must plan instruction that will encourage children to read these materials. Films, photographs, directed questions, advance organizers, and bulletin-board displays all play a role in motivating students. Motivational strategies also help to build students' experiential background. Sartain (1973) suggests that "almost no learning occurs if the student does not intend to learn." He further states that many of our middle-school students today are not convinced that book learning has much value for them. By implementing specific teaching strategies, children should recognize that reading is essentially a functional skill.

Projects and activities help build enthusiasm for reading. Some of the projects and activities listed below may be used to help motivate students to read.

1. Arrange debates and discussions of local controversial issues. Students should research these issues prior to the class discussion.
2. Field trips to important local places of interest should be scheduled. Teachers should take pictures on these trips that can be discussed once they are developed.
3. Teach students how to do genealogical research and generate their own family trees (Criscuolo, 1977).
4. Design an exhibit featuring souvenirs from visits to various countries or plan a display that is related to a specific historical period.
5. Organize news teams in which students are assigned to a particular story. Students should read information related to this topic and present their findings (Criscuolo, 1977).

An individual project can motivate students to read with enthusiasm and purpose. *(Courtesy Elizabeth Crews)*

6. Have children act as newspaper sleuths. Students should prepare questions that can be answered by reading newspaper stories. These questions should then be duplicated and distributed to other students.
7. Encourage students to think of ways to use the information they are to read or values that this material has in their lives. For example, geographic data is helpful if one is taking a trip, while scientific information can solve problems in the home.

COMPREHENDING CONTENT MATERIALS

The skills for reading and comprehending content materials should be developed in a functional manner. According to this approach, skills should be developed as they are needed for learning specific materials. Skills should be developed directly in response to working with content textbooks. Teaching random skills is not effective because children do not automatically transfer skills from one situation to another. Study guides, structured overviews, vocabulary development instruction, and other strategies should be components of

Functional instruction

any program that aspires to teach children how to comprehend and retain content material. The strategies suggested in this chapter should be used in conjunction with content textbooks. Functional instruction is meaningful for students.

Reading expository materials requires both general and specific skills. Some of these required skills and abilities are:

word recognition

technical vocabulary and concepts

identifying main ideas and supporting details

following directions

adjusting rate

recognizing common thought (organizational) patterns used in non-fiction

using graphic aids

reading widely

Teaching Vocabulary

Vocabulary is a well-known factor in reading comprehension. It is particularly important in content reading because these materials incorporate a significant number of new terms that are often abstract. Equally well known is the fact that copying definitions from a dictionary does not help students learn word meanings. The following guidelines are most helpful in teaching the technical vocabulary used in content text (Carr and Wixson, 1986).

Instruction should help students relate new vocabulary to their background knowledge. Students should be encouraged to use context to associate meaning with words, as context use depends on background knowledge. For instance, students who have have been to the beach can associate the term *undertow* with their beach experience. Teachers' questions and classroom discussion give students opportunities to associate experience with the target word or the context of that word. Asking students to use the context to define a term in their own words is helpful. Beck and McKeown (1983) developed activities in which students were asked to describe a situation involving the target word such as, "Tell me about a *theory* of yours," "describe that *mime*," or "Tell me why you would like to see a *mime*."

Instruction should help students develop elaborated word knowledge. Elaborating word meanings helps students acquire understandings that go beyond mere dictionary definitions. Word meanings are elaborated when words and concepts are introduced together. Introducing words in multiple contexts also elaborates word knowledge. For example, introducing the words *circular, column, funnel, moisture,* and *vapor* in a science lesson about tornadoes gives students opportunities to associate meaning and context with the words, which will help them "stick" in children's minds.

Instruction should provide for active student involvement in learning new vocabulary. The harder one works to process stimuli by constructing a relationship rather than by memorizing one, the better one's retention (Blachowicz, 1985). Brainstorming words that are associated with a concept is an excellent strategy; after brainstorming, the words are categorized to extend understanding. This activity can be used to develop word meanings and as a prewriting

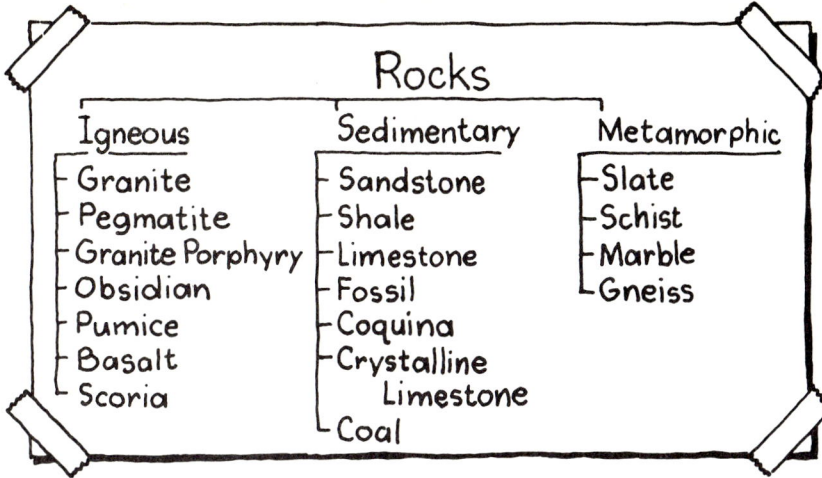

Figure 9.1 Structural overview for a science textbook.

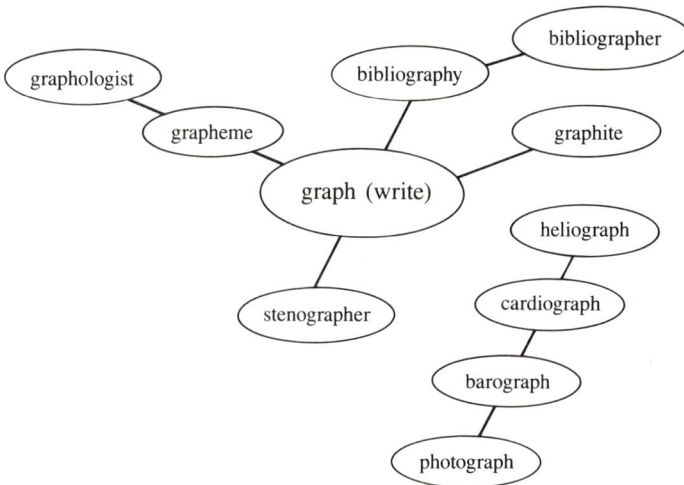

Figure 9.2 Root word web.

activity to generate the words and concepts that will be developed during composing. This strategy is illustrated in Figure 9.1. It is an example of a structured overview prepared for a chapter in a science textbook. Figure 9.2 illustrates a web of words generated from the root word *graph*. Figure 9.3 illustrates a matrix that helps students identify the significant attributes of concepts and compare them. Word maps encourage student involvement.

Preparing to Learn from Text

Learning the vocabulary to understand the concepts in a text is one way of preparing to read. In addition, readers need the background that will help them

	Vortex	Funnel	Duration	Causes	Where
Hurricane			*Days*		
Tornado		*X*	*Seconds –Minutes*		*Inland*

Figure 9.3 Word map matrix for science content.

understand the text, and they need to use their background experiences to understand. A short brainstorming session of 5–10 minutes is a good way to develop background and activate schemata (Jones, Palincsar, Ogle, and Carr, 1987). The brainstorming can be followed by having students complete an anticipation guide. To prepare an anticipation guide, the teacher establishes the objectives for the reading assignment and then creates items for the anticipation guide that will help students achieve those objectives. The objectives for a fifth-grade reading assignment about Jeannette Rankin, the first woman elected to Congress were: to understand that Jeannette Rankin was educated as a teacher and later as a social worker; to understand that she wanted to correct social wrongs, particularly in regard to women and children; she worked for women's suffrage and for child labor laws. Box 9.1 is an anticipation guide illustrating the implementation of these objectives.

Box 9.1 Anticipation Guide for Jeannette Rankin

Directions: Before reading this selection, read each sentence and in the first column write yes if you think the sentence is true or no if you think it is untrue. After you read, write yes or no in the second column.

	Before reading	After reading
1. Jeannette Rankin was a teacher.	_____	_____
2. Jeannette Rankin believed there were no social wrongs in the United States.	_____	_____
3. Jeannette Rankin is famous because she was the first woman elected to Congress.	_____	_____
4. Jeannette Rankin did not think women should vote.	_____	_____
5. Jeannette Rankin worked for child labor laws.	_____	_____
6. Jeannette Rankin wanted an eight-hour work day for women.	_____	_____
7. The voters thought women belonged at home.	_____	_____

Comprehension skills   Content reading requires students to use the comprehension skills discussed in Chapter 6. Teaching strategies can help students by preparing them to anticipate concepts, ideas, language, and organization used by the author. A **structured overview** can be used to introduce words and concepts. A structured overview shows the relationships among concepts and between concepts and words. Teachers can use the following steps to develop a structured overview.

Identify the concepts and vocabulary that are necessary for understanding the selection.

Organize the words into a structure that illustrates relationships.

A **directed reading lesson** for content textbooks can also be used to help students understand the material they read. A sample lesson for a science textbook is described in the following.

A DIRECTED READING LESSON FOR CONTENT TEXTBOOKS

I. *Preparing the class for the reading lesson.* In this section of the lesson, the teacher introduces the ideas being studied and attempts to motivate students to read the lesson. The teacher could introduce the lesson by explaining how our bodies need food for energy and for growing. The teacher could then tell the students that they will learn how food is changed into energy, and that this process will be illustrated by conducting an experiment with yeast, which is a living plant.

II. *Introduce vocabulary and concepts.* The following explanation should be given for the new vocabulary and concepts that will be presented in the lesson: *Yeast* is made up of millions of tiny plants. (Show students a photograph of a yeast slide.) Yeast plants are not green. Yeast plants are composed of tiny balloons. Each balloon is a cell. When the yeast cell *reproduces*, it creates a new cell. When yeast cells are put into a sugar solution, they make carbon dioxide gas. *Carbon dioxide* is a combination of carbon and oxygen.

III. *Establish the purposes for silent reading.*
    a. How do we know that yeast is a living thing?
    b. What substance enables yeast to grow and reproduce?
    c. How does the yeast use sugar to grow?

IV. *Have students read the selection silently.*

V. *Conduct a discussion.*
    a. Discuss the silent reading purposes that were established.
    b. Raise additional discussion questions. (Children should be able to support their answers.)
      1. How does the process of yeast growth and reproduction relate to human growth?
      2. Does the human body get energy only from sugar?
      3. Can you think of uses we might have for reproducing yeast?

VI. *Application.* This section is directed toward the application of the knowledge that was learned in the lesson.
    a. Conduct the experiment suggested in the textbook.
    b. Make a clay model of a yeast cell and show the stages of growth.

Facilitate
comprehension
A second aid for facilitating the comprehension of content materials is a **three-level study guide** which students complete while they read. This guide includes liberal, interpretive, and application questions. This concept was developed by Herbert (1978). The following is an example of this type of study guide. This example is based on a chapter from a fifth-grade social studies textbook.

I. *Literal questions can be verified by checking the text.*
   a. What is the *monetary system?*
   b. What word is used to describe the money that people are paid for their work?
   c. Why are some people paid more money for their work than others?
   d. Where do people learn skills?
II. *Interpretive questions require that the reader try to understand the author's intended meaning from the written content.*
   a. How is the banking system related to the monetary system?
   b. How is the banking system related to labor?
   c. Do you think a monetary system is better than a system of barter? What are the advantages and disadvantages of both?
III. *Application questions (or activities) encourage children to apply the knowledge they acquire.*
   a. Visit a local bank and have students investigate the following:
      1. What interest rates are available for savings?
      2. What interest rates are available for loans?
      3. Why do these rates differ?
   B. Examine "help-wanted" advertisements in the local newspaper.
      1. What kind of training is required for different jobs?
      2. What kinds of skills appear to command the highest pay?
   C. Have students create a diagram that shows the relationship between salary (wages) and the monetary system.

Using Structure to Comprehend

Expository text structure (expository grammar) refers to the patterns authors use to represent main ideas and supporting details. Research shows that using knowledge of text structure as a teaching and learning strategy helps students comprehend content area texts (Englert and Hiebert, 1984; Horowitz, 1985; Slater, 1985; Piccolo, 1987). Knowledge of structural patterns can be used in reading, listening, and writing; graphic organizers can be used in each of these situations. The most common expository grammars are description, enumeration, sequence, cause and effect, comparison and contrast, and problem-solution.

1. The descriptive paragraph presents a main idea and the attributes are the supporting details.
2. The enumerative paragraph (listing) has a main idea, which is the topic, and the details in the listing, support it. This structure is signaled by words like *first, second, third, next, last,* and *finally.*

3. The sequence paragraph, which makes a statement about a main idea, is supported by the details in a specific order. This paragraph may include the same signal words as the enumerative paragraph.
4. The cause-and-effect paragraph makes a statement about a subject; the details identify causes and effects. This structure may be signaled by words like *so, so that, because of, as a result of, since, in order to,* as well as the terms *cause and effect.*
5. The comparison-and-contrast paragraph explores the main idea and identifies the subject; the details show how the subjects are alike and/or different. The signal words may include *different from, same as, alike, similar to, resembles, compared to,* and *unlike.*
6. The problem-solution paragraph identifies a problem and the supporting details describe the problem—its causes and the solutions. The signal words include *a problem is, a solution is, the problem is solved by.*

Structure Lessons

The lessons described in this section should be taught with content-area text materials and are appropriate for fourth-, fifth-, and sixth-grade students. The lessons described herein are adaptations of those developed by Piccolo (1987).

FIRST LESSON

1. Explain that the paragraphs in content materials and other types of informational materials have structures that differ from the structure of stories.
2. Explain that the students will learn the six expository grammars over the next few weeks; they will focus on one expository grammar at a time. Introduce the first one selected and explain the structure. Show the students a graphic organizer like those illustrated in Box 9.2, which illustrates the structure being studied. Graphic organizers may be presented on an overhead screen or a chart.
3. Distribute copies of a paragraph that corresponds to the graphic organizer. The class and teacher read the paragraph together. Then ask the class to identify the signal words or phrases that are clues to the structure. Make a list of the words that are clues to the target structure and display with the graphic organizer.
4. Identify the main idea of the paragraph.
5. Using another example of a paragraph with the same pattern, give the class a copy of a graphic organizer that illustrates the structure. As a group, compose a paragraph that follows the graphic organizer. Make sure that the appropriate signal words are included in the paragraph.
6. As homework or seatwork, have students identify paragraphs that follow the pattern in their content textbooks. The main idea and the signal words will help them.

> *Descriptive:*
> Do you want to tell the reader what something is?

Box 9.2   A Graphic Organizer

A. Problem-solution structure

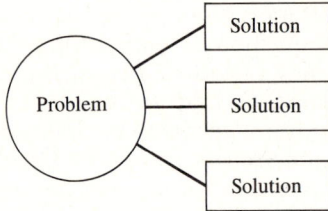

B. Cause-and-effect structure

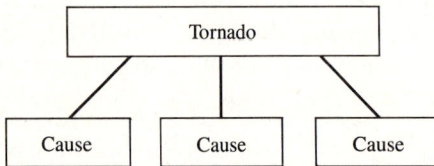

C. Sequential structure

Main Idea: To make hot chocolate

Ingredients	Equipment
sugar	pan
cocoa	spoon
salt	egg beater
water	
milk	

Steps

1. Combine sugar, cocoa, salt, and hot water.
2. Add milk, stir, and heat.
3. Beat with egg beater.
4. Pour into cups.
5. Top with marshmallows.

D. Description

Main Idea: Tornadoes are violent, twisting, wind storms.

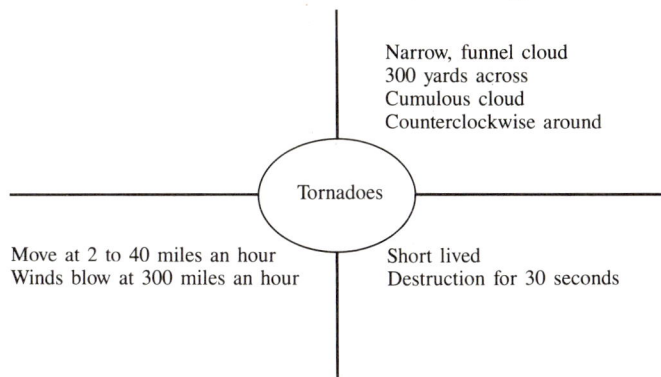

Narrow, funnel cloud
300 yards across
Cumulous cloud
Counterclockwise around

Tornadoes

Move at 2 to 40 miles an hour
Winds blow at 300 miles an hour

Short lived
Destruction for 30 seconds

E. Cause and effect

Main Idea: Tornadoes have destructive effects.

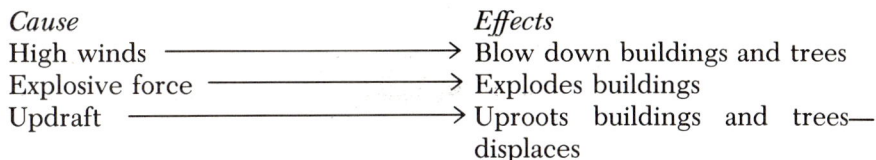

Cause	Effects
High winds ⟶	Blow down buildings and trees
Explosive force ⟶	Explodes buildings
Updraft ⟶	Uproots buildings and trees—displaces

Sequence:
Do you want to tell someone how to do or make something?
Enumerative:
Do you want to give a specific list of things that are related to the topic and tell about each?
Cause and effect
Do you want to give reasons why something happens or exists?
Problem-solution
Do you want to state some problem related to the subject and offer some solutions?
Comparison/contrast
Do you want to show the similarities or differences between two ideas, places, things, people, or the like?

SECOND LESSON

1. Students identify a topic they want to write about.
2. Each student makes a list of the details that he or she plans to include in the paragraph.
3. Give each student a graphic organizer—a blank one that does not include the details. Then students organize a paragraph by stating a main idea and writing the details in the blanks.

4. When the organizer is completed, students compose original paragraphs.

THIRD LESSON

1. Choose good and poor examples of the structure and share them. They can be written on the overhead for sharing. Identify good main-idea statements, signal words, and details. With poor paragraphs, go through the revision process.
2. Then hand papers back to students for their revisions.

FOURTH LESSON

1. This lesson is to show students how to extract information from a paragraph and put it into simple terms using a graphic organizer as a guide. Using another model paragraph, make a copy for each student and make a transparency of a blank organizer. As a class, read the paragraph and fill in the organizer. This activity prepares them for using graphic organizers for note taking.

FIFTH LESSON

1. Give students additional practice locating the pattern in content-area texts, encyclopedias, or other reference books. Once students understand this pattern, follow this lesson plan for introducing each of the other patterns.

Major ideas and relationships

Generally the following activities are helpful in learning text structure. **Textbook organizers** help children to focus on major ideas and relationships (Aulls, 1978). They preorganize content for the student, which aids understanding. The following are the steps for developing a textbook organizer.

1. Identify the important ideas in the textbook chapter.
2. Organize these ideas into a hierarchy that distinguishes between the superordinate and the subordinate ideas.
3. Have children write a 50 to 300 word selection that is based on the organization of important ideas that were understood from the reading.
4. Have students read the textbook organizer before reading the actual chapter. Discuss the organizer with the class.

Following Printed Directions

Following *printed directions* can be a problem for adults as well as children. Every adult has had the experience of purchasing an item and being unable to follow the set of printed directions that was enclosed. We usually have to read directions in order to solve problems. Many children, however, experience frustration in reading directions and carrying them out.

Students must learn that each step in a set of directions is important, and that directions usually must be followed in the prescribed sequence. The inability to complete one step—or completing a step out of sequence—may cause failure in the end. The following procedure is recommended for having children read directions.

1. Read the entire set of directions to understand the general nature of the task.
2. If diagrams accompany the directions, study these in relation to the written directions.
3. Read the directions step by step, taking note of the sequence of the steps. Words such as *first, second, third, next,* and *last* are helpful in following a sequence. Underlining key words is also helpful.
4. Visualize the directions.
5. Reread the directions.
6. Perform the directions in the correct sequence.

The following are suggested worksheet activities for teaching children to read and follow written directions.

WORKSHEET FOR READING AND FOLLOWING DIRECTIONS
Directions: Read all the information presented here before doing anything. You have 20 minutes to complete this worksheet.

1. Write your name in the top left-hand corner of this paper.
2. Draw two squares in the top right-hand corner of this paper.
3. On the back of this paper, write the following sentence: *The small black dog barked.*
4. Draw a line under the verb in the sentence that you wrote in Step 3.
5. Draw a circle around your first name.
6. Say your name aloud.
7. Write your initials on the back of this paper.
8. Count aloud by 10s until you reach 100.
9. Walk to the chalkboard and write today's date.
10. After reading all of the directions, complete Steps 1, 2, and 3.

Directions: Complete the following set of directions to identify a good vacation site. Rewrite the word in the blank space provided, following the suggested changes. Use the new word formed in the next step. The beginning words are *Funny Word.*

1. Write the words. _____
2. Replace the *F* with the fourth letter of the alphabet.
3. Delete the vowel *u* and replace it with the vowel in the word *sit.*
4. Change the first *n* to the 19th letter of the alphabet.
5. Place the vowel in *set* between the *n* and the *y.*
6. Place the 12th letter of the alphabet between the *r* and the *d* in the second word.

Adjusting Reading Rate

Students should be taught to adjust their **reading rate** as they read different types of material with different purposes in mind. Otto, Barrett, and Harris (1966) conducted research that indicates that intermediate-grade students can learn to adjust their reading rates. They found that fourth graders were more able to respond to training in rate adjustment than older students. Thus, it appears that fourth grade is a good time to introduce rate adjustment instruction.

Rate is determined by the type of content, the purposes for reading, and student interest and familiarity with the topic. Students read more slowly when preparing for a test than they do when reading a chapter to prepare for class. Students generally read newspapers and magazines most rapidly, and they read fiction material a bit more slowly. Rate may decrease, depending on the type of content being read. Social studies is read more slowly than fiction, science is read more slowly than social studies, and mathematics is usually the slowest

Familiarity read of all the disciplines. Students read theoretical content—such as a discussion of culture—more slowly than a comic book. When students are familiar with a subject they read more rapidly than when reading unfamiliar material.

Children can read at rates that range from study reading to skimming and scanning. **Study reading** is a very slow rate of reading, which permits the reader to think and to make notes. **Skimming** is reading rapidly to get an overview of the content and to identify the main ideas. **Scanning** is reading rapidly to identify specific bits of information: for example, looking up a telephone number in a directory. There are obviously rates other than the three discussed here as well—and these tend to fall somewhere in between the cautiousness of study reading and the speed of skimming and scanning.

"Mind-wander-ing" Students should be taught that "mind-wandering" is a major deterrent to reading rate. They should learn to concentrate on the content of the printed page as they read—because this will increase their rate as well as their comprehension. The following activities can be used for determining and adjusting reading rates.

1. Have students read short selections and time their reading rates. The length of these selections can be increased as students' reading abilities become more developed. Ask students follow-up questions about the selection. The students' accuracy in answering questions will help you determine whether they read at an appropriate rate. Students should identify appropiate rates and work toward increasing their individual reading rates. Graphs can be used to chart progress.
2. Give students various sample materials and ask them to discuss the reading rates that are appropriate for each piece of content. For example, provide a mathematics problem, a paragraph from a science book, and selections from a basal reader, a catalog, or a newspaper story.
3. Ask children what rate should be used in the following situations: looking up a word in a dictionary, finding the time of a favorite television show in the newspaper, and reading instructions to conduct a science experiment.

4. Ask children to skim through a chapter in a textbook and list the main ideas.

5. Have students scan their social studies textbook for a specific place, name, or date.

6. Give students a list of questions related to the content of a chapter and ask them to scan that chapter in order to locate the answers.

Using Graphic Aids

Graphic aids are widely used in content textbooks. Graphic aids include maps, charts, graphs, tables, and pictures. Each of these aids presents compressed information, which must be understood and interpreted in relation to the content. A large amount of information presented in a small amount of space confuses many readers. The first task in teaching the use of graphic aids is to instruct children to examine them carefully. They should recognize that these aids will increase—or in some cases lead to—their comprehension of the content. Unfortunately, many children choose to ignore the graphic aids in the text in order to reduce their reading chores.

Purpose

Teachers should include information drawn from graphic aids in their class discussions. Children should be asked to identify the purpose of the particular aid being discussed. (The title will reveal the purpose.) Children should also learn to recognize and interpret any symbols used. Last, they should be encouraged to draw conclusions based on the information that is provided.

Content textbooks contain various kinds of graphs. *Picture graphs* make comparisons using pictures. *Circle* or *pie graphs* show the relationship of individual parts to the whole. *Bar graphs* use vertical or horizontal bars to show comparisons, while *line graphs* make use of lines for the same purpose. Teachers should ask questions about different types of graphs. The following are questions that could be raised for a discussion of a graph that illustrates the distribution of family income.

What does each vertical bar represent on this graph?

What do the numbers on this graph mean?

What category represents the greatest expense, in terms of family income?

What category represents the least expense in terms of family income?

What generalization can you make based on this graph?

Maps are a common graphic aid. Maps that are commonly included in social studies content include relief maps, weather maps, general reference maps, and road maps. Thus students must be able to interpret different types of maps as they read content materials. Most maps have a key legend that the reader should study carefully in order to determine such information as the scale of distances used. The legend also indicates the meaning of the symbols used on the map; for example, a star may represent a capital city.

Teachers should devise questions such as the following to help children learn to read maps effectively.

1. What is the capital of Ohio?
2. Locate the Mississippi River. Where does it begin and where does it end?
3. How many miles are represented by one inch on this map?
4. Which state is larger: Texas or Arkansas?
5. Is New York City closer to Miami, Florida, or to Los Angeles, California?
6. Identify the largest cities in the United States and locate them in relation to bodies of water. Can you think of a generalization about cities and bodies of water? Explain your answer.

READING A VARIETY OF MATERIALS

Children who are studying content selections should have many opportunities to read a variety of materials. Books, magazines, and newspapers expand, enrich, and clarify ideas that are introduced in textbooks. Trade books are frequently easier to read than content textbooks. Children who have difficulty reading textbooks can acquire concepts from trade books. Many excellent informational books are available from publishers today. Teachers should also survey the books available in their school's library in order to supplement the chapters in content textbooks.

The following trade books could be selected to supplement the content textbook readings on an energy unit.

Asimov, I. *How Did We Find Out About Nuclear Power?* Walker, 1976.

Berger, M. *Energy from the Sun.* Crowell, 1976.

Black, H. *Dirt Cheap.* William Morrow, 1979.

Dennis, L. *Catch the Wind.* Four Winds-Scholastic, 1976.

Gallant, R. *Explorers of the Atom.* Doubleday, 1974.

Hoke, J. *Solar Energy.* Watts, 1979.

Kiefer, I. *Underground Furnaces.* William Morrow, 1976.

Pringle, L. *Energy: Power for People.* Macmillan, 1975.

Newspapers and Magazines

Newspapers and magazines are valuable for reading because they can be used as materials for motivating students. Furthermore, newspapers and magazines deal with issues that are important to students. Current issues should be made available to intermediate-grade students.

Activities such as the following can be used for exposing students to newspaper and magazine selections.

1. Have students read classified advertisements and cut out those objects or services that are of interest to them.
2. Ask children to locate the time and station for a favorite television or radio show listed in the newspaper.
3. Have students select an interesting story and do an in-depth study of the topic.
4. Have students do crossword puzzles found in the children's magazines.
5. Separate headlines from stories and have students read them and match them accordingly.
6. Discuss a particular news item as it is reported in various newspapers.
7. Cut apart comic strips and have children reassemble them in the correct sequence.
8. Identify main ideas and supporting details in a newspaper story.
9. Analyze the kinds of advertisements that appear in different magazines.
10. Have students write their own newspaper articles.

Daily newspapers and television newscasts provide opportunities to examine controversial issues. For example, a review of various newspapers might reveal that a number of cities are considering building convention centers, which in turn has created local controversy. Students may discuss the pros and cons of such issues. They can also examine their own attitudes on the subject. The following is a newspaper lesson plan that can be used in class.

A SAMPLE LESSON PLAN FOR USING THE NEWSPAPER

Objectives:

To identify fact and opinion in a news story

To identify reporter bias in a news story

To discuss personal position related to a news story

Materials:

Newspaper articles on a controversial issue

Introduction:

Ask students to list all of the information they may already know about the topic. Ask them to tell where they found this information. Ask them to write an *F* alongside every item they consider a fact and an *O* alongside every opinion.

Guided practice:

Does the story appear to agree with your knowledge of the matter?

Do the reporters state mostly fact or mostly opinions?

Identify each fact and each opinion.

Do you think the reporters are biased? How do you know?

Did this report influence your own opinion? Why or why not?

Follow-up discussion:

Discuss the purposes of silent reading.

Discuss any other relevant points about the story that members of the class might raise.

Independent practice:

Conduct a poll of class opinion. Ask children to tell why they feel as they do about the news story. Ask them to state what would change their opinions.

Reading Mathematical Materials

Many children experience difficulty in reading mathematical materials. In fact, some children who are capable of doing computations have difficulty reading this material. They do not appear to understand the language used in verbal problems, and this prevents them from conceptualizing the mathematics involved. A number of researchers have shown that children's success in mathematics is directly related to their abilities to read and interpret written content (Fay, 1967).

Format and style differ

"The arithmetic text departs from others in format and style, with primary concern placed upon the logical sequence of arithmetic skills and principles, less emphasis upon theme organization and literary style, and the use of non-story-type written exercises to illustrate or provide practice in mathematic concepts and rules" (Coulter, 1972). Mathematical content is concise, abstract, and complex. Moulder (1969) points out that there are more ideas per line and per page than in other forms of writing. Every word is critical in reading mathematics.

Language

Since language is such an important aspect of reading all content material, teachers should provide assistance in developing the language skills associated with this discipline. Practice sessions should include the use of sight words, context clues, phonics, and structural analysis. Keeping a glossary of mathematical terms will help children learn to recognize and define key words. Attempts to visualize mathematical concepts will also aid comprehension. For example, a child could visualize that *a dozen* is equivalent to 12 items. Children should create diagrams that help them conceptualize verbal problems. If the children were asked to take 7 apples away from 14 apples, for example, they could draw 14 pieces of fruit and cross out half of this amount.

The following mathematics problem exemplifies the language and conceptualization that is required to read a simple verbal problem.

If a dozen eggs cost 79 cents, how much would three dozen eggs cost? The reader must conceptualize the following: a dozen, three dozen, 79 cents, and that multiplication is the operation required to solve the problem. It might also be helpful for readers to estimate an answer.

Systematic approach A systematic approach to verbal problems aids readers. The following steps were devised by Aaron (1965) to guide the reading of word (verbal) problems. Problem: *John had 25 marbles and lost 18 on the way to school. How many marbles does he have left?*

1. Read quickly to get an overview of the problem.
2. Reread the problem, this time at a slower rate to determine what facts are given.

> Facts: *John had 25 marbles.*
> *John lost 18 marbles.*

3. Think of the specific question that needs to be resolved.

> Question: *How many marbles does he have left?*

4. Think about the order in which the facts should be used in answering the question.

> Order: *The first figure to consider is 25.*
> *The second figure to consider is 18.*

5. Think about the operations that are required for solving the problem.

> Operation: *Subtraction*

6. Estimate an answer that seems reasonable.

> Estimate: *The answer is more than 5 (or less than 10).*

7. Work out the problem by performing the appropriate operation.

> Computation: *25 − 18 = 7*

8. Compare the computed answer with the estimated result.
9. Go back to the first step and think the problem through again if the answer seems unreasonable.

Metacognitive Strategies

Metacognition is monitoring one's cognitive processes and products as well as regulating these processes. The ultimate goal of content reading and study skills instruction is to develop independent readers who comprehend. To reach this goal, readers must not only recognize that their purpose determines how they should read, which may range from deep, active reading to skimming, but they must also monitor their own comprehension; in other words, they should be conscious of when they have comprehended and when they have not. When they are aware that they have lost understanding, they must "debug" the process.

For example, a student reads a selection in a science text that introduced

---

Box 9.3

Topic: Cell division
Purpose: To understand the mitosis process.

A	B	C
What I already knew	What I now know	What I don't know
Mitosis is cell division. One cell divides into two cells.	There are four stages in mitosis which are. . . .	Why cell division happens.

---

the mitosis process. Her purpose was to learn the stages in the mitosis process. After reading, she mentally reviewed the stages (prophase, metaphase, anaphase and telophase); then she drew a diagram of each stage. When drawing the diagrams, she found that she needed to review the last two stages in order to complete the drawings. Therefore, she monitored her own understanding and reread selectively to fill in the missing pieces, so she "debugged" the process.

Self-monitor

Teachers can help students monitor their own reading comprehension through activities like modeling with a reading selection on the overhead; through making summaries (see Chapter 6); through a study method like SQ3R; and through completing worksheets like the one in Figure 9.3. Box 9.3 is an example of a metacognition worksheet.

WRITING TO LEARN CONTENT

Writing increases students' learning and improves students' ability to learn. In the content areas, students are expected to read and extract major ideas and then to synthesize them (Cunningham and Cunningham, 1987). Therefore, teachers must instruct students in strategies for extracting and organizing critical information from text. Activities, like those described in this chapter, will help students extract and organize information. However, composing (writing) is a major means of organizing, thinking, and learning.

A good writing lesson is one in which the teacher introduces the important ideas in the prewriting stage, then provides time for students to compose; during the revision stage, the teacher gives students help in rethinking and reorganizing their ideas; finally, students have time to edit their writing. Teachers can help students develop writing skills in the content areas by modeling what they expect of students, by giving them guided practice, and providing feedback that helps students (Cunningham and Cunningham, 1987). Students should have opportunities to share what they have written with their classmates. This can be accomplished by pairing students or assigning them to small groups.

Students may write various structures as described in the structural lessons. They may write summaries like those discussed in Chapter 6. Students may write to state and prove points. They may use webs, graphic organizers, timeliness or other organizational devices during the prewriting period to organize for writing. Students may use these devices to organize ideas that they read, and to guide their synthesis of ideas in preparation for writing.

After writing, students should share what they have written. This can be accomplished in small groups or pairs, and on occasion in whole-group situations.

STUDY SKILLS

Study skills are as valuable as content reading skills; they enable students to read and recall the details of reading materials. We will examine the following study skills: use of a study method, recognizing the organization, and parts of a book, locating and organizing information, and using reference materials.

Successful instruction

Shores (1967) conducted a series of studies designed to develop a plan of instruction for study skills. The following conclusions were reached as a result of his studies.

> The success of a study skills program depends largely on a commitment to include study skills in the curriculum.
>
> Study skills should be emphasized in the language arts program throughout the intermediate grades, with opportunities for practice in the specific areas of content.
>
> Supplemental materials and a well-stocked school library are important components of the study skills program.

A Study Method

How many times have you heard students say, *I read the assignment, but I don't remember a thing I read.* Students often have difficulty selecting a study method that is appropriate for them. Students need to establish their own strategies to guide their study hours. Such methods help students to learn more efficiently. Even very able students can benefit from learning new study methods for retaining ideas.

Some teachers and students hesitate to follow a study method simply because they do not fully understand it. They may feel that teaching or learning a study method will be time-consuming. However, students can perfect methods and feel confident and comfortable using them. Students should have a minimum of 20 teacher-directed practices for any study method that is introduced.

SQ3R is a very effective study method (Robinson, 1974). The basic components of SQ3R are:

S for *Survey*
Q for *Question*
R for *Read*
R for *Recite*
R for *Review*

Anticipate ideas

Survey refers to skimming through the content so the reader has a general idea or overview of the selection. Surveying allows the reader to anticipate the ideas that will be introduced by the author later in the selection. The reader should make use of headings and subheadings in order to survey the author's main ideas and organization of the content. The introduction and the summary also provide an overview for students. Graphic aids, if included in the discussion, should also be examined during the survey.

During the *questioning* phase, readers identify purposes to guide and organize their reading. They can change headings and subheadings into questions. If the selection does not have these features, the reader should develop questions from the introductory and/or the summary paragraph. Readers should keep a written record of their questions.

Students should *read* to answer the questions developed in the previous step.

Answer questions

Students should *recite* aloud to answer questions. Many students benefit from taking a pause in their reading to recite answers to questions about the selection. Thus, reciting helps the reader clarify ideas. Readers should always recite answers in their own words and should think of examples to support their responses.

Students should *review* the assignment immediately following the reading activity to reinforce any ideas and thoughts they may have. During this step, readers should make notes or outlines summarizing the author's important ideas. Any paragraphs that were unclear should be reread. An additional review within 24 hours is very effective for material retention.

The SQ3R study method is applied to a selection in the following example.

APPLICATION OF THE SQ3R STUDY METHOD

Food

Food is an important daily requirement of human beings. Food provides us with the energy we need for work and play. Food makes us grow. All living things need food to live and grow.

Kinds of Food

There are many kinds of food in the world. Foods are derived from plants and animals. Pineapples, tomatoes, oranges, and potatoes are some examples of foods from plants. Eggs, meat, and cheese are foods from animals. A supermarket is a storehouse of food from various parts of the country.

Survey: Read the title and subtitle. The article is about food and kinds of food.

Question: Why is food important? What are the major sources of food?

Read.

Recite: Food is important because it gives us energy and makes us grow.

Review: Try to recall the ideas discussed without looking again at the selection. Give examples of different types of food. Be sure to review the lesson again within 24 hours.

ORGANIZING INFORMATION

Organizing information helps students comprehend and recall content. Outlines and summaries are important aids for organizing. The first step in **outlining** is to examine chapter titles and subtitles, because this is the key to the author's underlying organizational pattern (Lunstrum and Taylor, 1978). The next step is to identify the main ideas and supporting details (see Chapter 6). Students should understand that information is condensed in an outline, so that they avoid rewriting the text. The ideas in an outline are stated as key words and phrases. The following ideas are important in outlining:

Main ideas

> Scan chapter headings and subheadings.
> Identify main ideas and details.
> Condense information.

The importance of an idea should be indicated by letters, numbers, and indentation. *Roman numerals* indicate main ideas, *capital letters* represent details, and numbers or lowercase letters are equated with the lesser details.

> Do not include unimportant details in an outline.
> An outline should clarify the relationships among ideas.
> Paraphrase the author's ideas.

An example of an outline format is provided below.

A SAMPLE OUTLINE

I. Igneous rocks
  a. Extrusive rocks
    1. obsidian
    2. pumice

      3. scoria
      4. basalts
      5. felsites
   b. Intrusive rocks
      1. granites
      2. syenites
      3. gabbros

Some activities for teaching outlining are listed below.

1. Give children a blank outline form in which spaces appear next to Roman numerals, letters and numbers and have them outline a chapter in a textbook.
2. Ask children to write a one-page summary of a content selection.
3. Practice summarizing sections of a chapter as a group activity. Ask children to identify organization, key words and phrases, and to compress information.

Locating Information

Children must learn to predict where information might be located and how to go about locating it if they are to engage in independent study. Independent study skills require that students be self-directed; thus, the ability to locate and use sources of information is the basis for independent study. Sources of information include textbooks, reference books, *The Reader's Guide to Periodical Literature,* atlases, newspapers, magazines, and filmstrips.

The following aspects of books should be discussed with children:

The *preface,* which explains the author's purpose and organization.

The *table of contents,* which is an outline of the topics and subtopics in the book. It is an excellent guide for outlining and organizing information.

The organizational pattern of the *chapters.*

The *index,* which helps students locate specific information.

Teachers can aid students' understanding of textbook organization by asking them specific questions and providing directed activities that involve textbook examination. The following are suggested examples of questions and activities.

1. In what chapter is _____ (a specific topic) found?
2. Have students write an outline of Chapter 2 using the table of contents.
3. On what page is _____ (a specific idea) located?
4. On what page does Chapter 3 begin?
5. What does the word _____ mean in the context of this book?
6. Under what topic is the subtopic _____ located in Chapter 4?

Topics and subtopics

The **index** is a particularly useful aid for locating information. Children should learn how to use alphabetical order to locate words, to identify key words for locating information, and to understand the relationships between topics and subtopics. One of the best ways to teach children to use the index is to provide them with activities that require using an index. Some examples of index activities are listed below.

1. What is ostracoderm?
2. What did Harrison Schmitt do?
3. How do bacteria reproduce?
4. Where is the Kong Chow Temple located?
5. Who was Patrick Henry?
6. What is a polygon?

The preceding questions should be rather easy to answer with the assistance of an index. However, some information is much more difficult to locate because it requires that the reader think about the relationships that exist among topics. The following questions require this type of thinking.

1. Why is Patrick Henry's name listed as *Henry, Patrick?*
2. What are the subentries under *renaming?*
3. Under what entry would you expect to find information about city government?
4. Under what entry would you expect to find *DNA?*
5. If an entry lists several different pages, such as *horses, 211, 313–314,* which entry would you first use in looking up the information?
6. Why is there a comma after *24* and a dash between *26* and *27* in the following entry: *Solar system, 24, 26–27?*

Using a Media Center

The student who has learned to use the index efficiently is well on the way to understanding how to make use of the **media center** (**library**). The *card catalog* is the major source for locating information in a library. Children should learn that the cards are organized by alphabetical order according to three categories: author, title, and subject. Show children examples of these different types of cards.

Learn the system

The organization of media centers is based on the *Dewey Decimal System* or the *Library of Congress numbering system.* Children should learn the system implemented in their own center and should familiarize themselves with the location of various materials within that media center. Having children make a floor plan indicating the numbering system and the location of materials is one method of familiarizing them with this system.

Providing children with purposeful activities can teach children to use the card file in a functional way. Teachers could pose some of the following problems to teach use of the file.

1. When would you use a subject card instead of an author or title card?
2. When would an author card be most useful?
3. Who is the author of the book _____ ?
4. What company published this book?
5. How many pages are in the book?
6. In what year was the book published?
7. What subjects are covered in this book?
8. What system of numbering books in the card catalog is used in this center?

Reference Materials

Encyclopedias, dictionaries, and other reference materials are located in the media center. Children should become acquainted with the different types of reference materials available to them and the wealth of information that can be found in these materials. Topics are arranged in alphabetical order in reference works. Each reference contains introductory pages that explain the organization, abbreviations, and codes utilized in the book. Children should learn to read and use this information comfortably. Use of reference materials can be taught in a problem-solving approach with such questions and activities as those developed for the use of a textbook and an index.

Guide words are used in encyclopedias and dictionaries. The guide word in the upper left-hand corner of a dictionary page shows the first word defined on the page, and the word in the upper right-hand corner indicates the last word defined on that page. The guide words on an encyclopedia page identify the topic that is discussed on the page.

After students locate information related to a subject, they should skim the material to determine if it is relevant to the topic they are studying. For example, a child who is studying George Washington's presidency needs to recognize that all content that is not directly related to the topic should be eliminated. The student may find information about Washington's role in the revolutionary

Relevant information

war and his life at Mount Vernon, but these are not directly related to his role as president. Teachers should provide practice exercises for children in identifying relevant pieces of information in reference materials.

SUMMARY

The following list summarizes the key points of this chapter.

1. Content reading and study skills are associated with the comprehension of nonfiction materials. These skills are especially important to students in the intermediate grades. These students should receive direct instruction in using these functional reading skills. Comprehension of expository writing (nonfiction) differs from narrative writing because concepts are developed in expository writing. Expository content has

the following characteristics: uses technical vocabulary, uses common vocabulary in different contexts, knowledge is organized in a variety of ways, readability is at a higher level, graphic aids are used, and readers are expected to understand concepts.

2. In teaching children to read content materials, teachers have three tasks: (1) matching content to children's reading level, (2) motivating children to read content, and (3) teaching the necessary reading and study skills. Strategies that are useful for teaching content reading include vocabulary activities, the structured overview, the direct-reading-and-thinking activity, and the three-level study guide.

3. Reading verbal mathematics problems presents a particular problem to some children. Students can be assisted in reading these types of problems by teaching the vocabulary associated with this material and helping them to conceptualize the problem.

4. Content reading instruction should also include instruction in following directions, adjusting reading rate, reading graphic aids, reading a variety of materials, and the use of newspapers and magazines.

5. Study skills instruction should include such study methods as SQ3R and approaches to organizing and locating information.

SELF-TEST

Check your knowledge of the information presented in this chapter. The answer key is located in Appendix C.

1. What is *functional reading?*
   a. reading content materials
   b. reading informational materials
   c. both a and b
   d. neither a nor b

2. What does research show about content reading and study skills instruction?
   a. they receive too much attention
   b. they are unnecessary
   c. they receive inadequate attention
   d. they can be taught through the use of the basal reader

3. How are content reading materials different from basal reading materials?
   a. characters are included in the basal reader
   b. there is dialogue in the basal reader
   c. content materials include a large amount of information
   d. all of the above

4. Why is reading content materials a demanding task?
   a. because of the number of concepts, the technical vocabulary, the patterns of writing, the graphic aids, and the readability level
   b. because of the narrative style
   c. the size of the book is discouraging
   d. none of the above

5. What factors influence readability of content materials?
   a. vocabulary and concepts
   b. sentence length and complexity
   c. reader interest, experience, and type size
   d. all of the above

6. What is the purpose of the cloze procedure?
   a. to evaluate a child's ability to read specific materials
   b. to measure and teach comprehension
   c. both a and b
   d. neither a nor b

7. Why should children with limited reading skills use audiotapes?
   a. they are more entertaining than reading
   b. tapes are less expensive than books
   c. poor reading skills will not prevent learning
   d. all of the above

8. What kinds of activities can be used to build motivation for reading content materials?
   a. lectures and tests
   b. displays, films, pictures, bulletin boards, purpose-setting questions, and advance organizers
   c. selecting materials that are difficult to read
   d. none of the above

9. What is the objective of content reading?
   a. very rapid reading
   b. comprehension of specialized material
   c. effective television viewing
   d. preparing effective notebooks

10. What types of questions are included in a three-level study guide?
    a. literal, interpretive, and critical
    b. organizing, facilitating, and application
    c. literal, interpretive, and application
    d. all of the above

11. What is the purpose of a textbook organizer?
    a. to focus the learner on major ideas and relationships
    b. to reconstruct poorly organized textbooks
    c. for library use
    d. it is a substitute for the table of contents

12. Why do verbal mathematics problems give some children difficulty?
    a. they are not capable of doing the computation
    b. they cannot read numbers
    c. they do not read well enough to understand the mathematics involved
    d. they have dysgraphia, which prevents their understanding the computations involved

13. What organizational patterns commonly occur in content materials?
    a. narrative
    b. sequence, cause and effect, classification, comparison and contrast, and definition

    c. narrative, expository, oral, and graphic
    d. none of the above

14. What is one of the most important factors in reading directions?
    a. sequence
    b. dyscalculia
    c. rewriting them
    d. all of the above

15. What factors influence rate adjustment?
    a. reading machines
    b. the number of students in the class
    c. content, purpose, interest, and familiarity
    d. narration, exposition, and argument

16. Which of the following statements describes *skimming?*
    a. reading rapidly to get an overview of the content and main ideas
    b. reading rapidly to identify specific pieces of information
    c. reading at rates above 20,000 words a minute
    d. it inhibits comprehension

17. What kinds of information are presented by graphic aids?
    a. colorful information
    b. unnecessary information
    c. creative types of information
    d. compressed information

18. What kinds of graphic aids are commonly used in content textbooks?
    a. audiotapes
    b. charts, graphs, maps, tables, and pictures
    c. teacher's manuals, bulletin boards, and advance organizers
    d. all of the above

19. What is the purpose of reading a variety of materials in content reading instruction?
    a. to help children understand and remember concepts
    b. to expand, enrich, and clarify ideas
    c. neither a nor b
    d. both a and b

20. What do the letters and numbers in *SQ3R* represent?
    a. sight, questioning, read, read, and read
    b. stop, query, review, read, and rest
    c. survey, question, read, recite, and review
    d. none of the above

21. What is the value of outlines and summaries?
    a. they provide handwriting practice
    b. they force students to read the content
    c. they help the reader organize the content
    d. they are excellent homework assignments

22. What skills helps students engage in independent study and solve problems?
    a. reading the basal reader
    b. learning how to locate information

c. literature skills

d. all of the above

THOUGHT QUESTIONS

1. Why is content reading instruction essential for middle-grade students?

2. Compare expository grammar with story grammar? How do they function to increase comprehension?

3. Discuss the role of composing in comprehending content materials.

4. How does metacognition relate to content-area reading?

5. Why is content reading a special case of reading comprehension? How are content reading and comprehension similar?

6. Why is vocabulary instruction particularly important in content-area reading?

ENRICHMENT ACTIVITIES

1. Obtain social studies, science, and mathematics textbooks and analyze a chapter from each to identify the reading skills necessary for students to read and understand them.

2. Make a list of technical vocabulary from content textbooks.

3. Using the model for a directed content reading lesson discussed in this chapter, develop a lesson plan for teaching a chapter in a content textbook.

4. Develop a lesson plan for teaching children reference skills.

5. Develop a three-level study guide for a chapter in a content textbook.

6. Compare a chapter in a basal reader with a chapter in a content textbook.

7. Use the Fry Readability Graph to determine the estimated readability levels of various content textbooks.

RELATED READINGS

Clark, R. (1987). *Free to Write,* Portsmouth, NH: Heinemann.

Cunningham, P. and J. Cunningham (February 1987). "Content Area Reading-Writing Lessons," *The Reading Teacher,* Vol. 40, No. 6, pp. 506–513.

Graham, K. and H. A. Robinson (1984). *Study Skills Hand Book,* Newark, DE: International Reading Association.

Horowitz, R. (March 1985). "Text Patterns: Part II," *Journal of Reading,* Vol. 28, No. 6, pp. 534–542.

Hoskins, S. (March 1986). "Text Superstructures," *Journal of Reading,* Vol. 29, No. 6, pp. 538–543.

Manning, M., G. Manning, and R. Long (May 1986). "When the Book Is Not a Story," *Early Years,* Vol. 16, No. 9, pp. 29–31.

Manzo, A. (March 1985). "Expansion Modules for the ReQuest, CAT, GRP, and REAP Reading/Study Procedures," *Journal of Reading,* Vol. 28, No. 6, pp. 498–503.

McGee, L. and D. Richgels (April 1985). "Teaching Expository Text Structure to Elementary Students," *The Reading Teacher,* Vol. 38, No. 8, pp. 739–748.

Moore, D., J. Readence, and R. Rickelman (1982). *Prereading Activities for Content Area Reading and Learning,* Newark, DE: International Reading Association.

Piccolo, J. (May 1987). "Expository Text Structure Teaching and Learning Strategies," *The Reading Teacher,* Vol. 40, No. 9, pp. 838–847.

Shannon, A. (November 1984). "Monitoring Reading Instruction in the Content Areas," *Journal of Reading,* Vol. 28, No. 2, pp. 128–134.

Sinatra, R., J. Stahl-Gemake, and N. Morgan (October 1986). "Using Semantic Mapping After Reading to Organize and Write Original Discourse," *Journal of Reading,* Vol. 30, No. 1, pp. 4–13.

REFERENCES

Aaron, R. (May 1965). "Reading Mathematics," *Journal of Reading,* Vol. 9, pp. 391–395.

Armbruster, B. and B. Gudbrandsen (Winter 1986). "Reading Comprehension Instruction in Social Studies Programs," *Reading Research Quarterly,* Vol. 21, No. 1, pp. 36–48.

Arnold, R. and N. Sherry (Winter 1975). "A Comparison of the Reading Levels of Disabled Readers with Assigned Textbooks," *Reading Improvement,* Vol. 12, pp. 207–211.

Aulls, M. (1978). *Developmental and Remedial Reading in the Middle Grades,* Boston: Allyn and Bacon.

Beck, I. and M. McKeown (March 1983). "Learning Words Well—A Program to Enhance Vocabulary and Comprehension," *The Reading Teacher,* Vol. 36, pp. 622–625.

Bormuth, J. (1972). "Literacy in the Classroom," Paper Presented at the University of Chicago's Annual Reading Conference.

Burron, A. and A. Claybaugh (1974). *Using Reading to Teach Subject Matter,* Columbus, OH: Charles Merrill.

Carr, E. and K. Wixson (April 1986). "Guidelines for Evaluating Vocabulary Instruction," *Journal of Reading,* Vol. 29, No. 7, pp. 588–595.

Chall, J. (1975). "Reading and Development," Keynote Address at the Twentieth Annual Convention of the International Reading Association, New York, NY.

Chall, J. (1983). *Stages of Reading Development,* New York: McGraw-Hill.

Clark, R. (1987). *Free to Write,* Portsmouth, NH: Heinemann.

Coulter, M. (1972). "Reading in Mathematics: Classroom Implications," in *Reading in the Content Areas,* J. Laffey (Ed.), Newark, DE: International Reading Association.

Criscuolo, N. (December 1977). "Convincing the Unconvinced to Read: Twelve Strategies," *Journal of Reading,* Vol. 21, pp. 219–221.

Dulin, K. (1977). "Reading in the Content Areas," in *Views in Elementary Reading,* T. Barrett and D. Johnson (Eds.), Newark, DE: International Reading Association.

Durkin, D. (1978–1979). "What Classroom Observations Reveal About Reading Comprehension Instruction," *Reading Research Quarterly,* Vol. 14, pp. 481–533.

Englert, C. and E. Hiebert (February 1984). "Children's Developing Awareness of Text Structures in Expository Materials," *Journal of Educational Psychology,* Vol. 76, pp. 65–74.

Fay, L. (1965). "Reading Study Skills: Math and Science," in *Reading and Inquiry,* J. Figurel (Ed.), Newark, DE: International Reading Association.

Hash, R. (1974). "The Effects of a Strategy of Structured Overviews, Levels Guides and Vocabulary Exercises on Student Achievement, Reading Comprehension, Critical

Thinking and the Attitudes of Junior-High-School Classes in Social Studies," Ph.D. dissertation, State University of New York.

Heddens, J. and K. Smith (1964). "The Readability of Elementary Mathematics Textbooks," *Arithmetic Teacher*, Vol. 11, pp. 466–468.

Herber, H. (1978). *Teaching Reading in the Content Areas*, 2nd ed., Englewood Cliffs, NJ: Prentice-Hall.

Herman, W. (1969). "Reading and Other Language Arts in Social Studies Instruction: Persistent Problems," in *A New Look at Reading in the Social Studies*, R. Preston (Ed.), Newark, DE: International Reading Association.

Horowitz, R. "Text Patterns: Part 2," *Journal of Reading*, Vol. 28, pp. 534–541.

Johnson, R. and E. Vardian (February 1973). "Reading, Readability, and the Social Studies," *The Reading Teacher*, Vol. 26, pp. 483–488.

Lunstrum, J. and B. Taylor (1978). *Teaching Reading in the Social Studies*, Newark, DE: International Reading Association.

McGee, L. and D. Richgels (April 1985). "Teaching Expository Text Structure to Elementary Students," *The Reading Teacher*, Vol. 38, No. 8, pp. 739–748.

Moulder, R. (1969). "Reading in a Mathematics Class," in *Fusing Reading Skills and Content*, H. A. Robinson and E. Thomas (Eds.), Newark, DE: International Reading Association.

Niles, O. (1974). "Organization Perceived," in *Perspectives in Reading: Developing Study Skills in Secondary Schools*, H. Herber (Ed.), Newark, DE: International Reading Association.

Otto, W., T. Barrett, and T. Harris (1966). "Transfer Effect of Training Intermediate Grade Pupils to Adjust Reading Purpose," Cooperative Research project, no. 3137, Committee for Research on Basic Skills, University of Wisconsin.

Peters, C. (1975–1976). "The Effect of Systematic Restructuring of Material Upon the Comprehension Process," *Reading Research Quarterly*, Vol. 11, pp. 87–111.

Piccolo, J. (May 1987). "Expository Text Structure: Teaching and Learning Strategies," *The Reading Teacher*, Vol. 40, No. 9, pp. 838–847.

Robinson, F. (1974). "Study Skills for Superior Students in Secondary School," in *Improving Reading in Middle and Secondary Schools*, L. Hafner (Ed.), New York: Macmillan.

Sartain, H. (October 1973). "Content Reading—They'll Like It," *Journal of Reading*, Vol. 17, pp. 47–51.

Schwartz, R. and T. Raphael (November 1985). "Concept of Definition: A Key to Improving Students' Vocabulary," *The Reading Teacher*, Vol. 38, pp. 198–205.

Shores, H. (1967). "Teaching the Research Study Skills, Phase II," Urbana, IL: Report of Grolier.

Smith, E., K. Goodman, and R. Meredith. (1970). *"Language and Thinking in the Elementary School*, New York: Holt, Rinehart and Winston.

10

Literature and the Reading Program

OVERVIEW Frequent, pleasurable experiences with literature motivate children to read, which can lead to the lifelong desire to read. This chapter explores the relationship between children's literature and the elementary reading program. Literature is the content of the reading program; it makes children want to read. Literature exposes children to beautiful, rich language, which serves as a model for their writing. Literature provides models of thinking and multicultural understanding. Most important, literature is valuable because it gives pleasure.

Children's literature is gaining new prominence in reading because of the widespread interest in the whole-language approach to reading instruction. In addition, many contemporary basal readers are comprised of excerpts from literature. Therefore, effective teachers need to know and use children's literature because literature is the *heart* of the reading program.

Key Vocabulary

As you read this chapter, check your understanding of these terms:

argument   literature
creative dramatics   poetry
exposition   readers' theater
interest inventories   web

Focusing Questions

As you read this chapter, think about these questions:

1. How are reading skills and literature related?
2. What is the greatest value of literature?
3. What are the qualities of good children's literature?

CHILDREN'S LITERATURE

"All that people have ever thought, done, or dreamed lies waiting to be discovered in a book" (Huck, 1979). Children should experience literature every day of their school lives. **Literature** must be at the center of the reading program; otherwise, reading is merely a collection of learned skills. Reading skills are of little worth if students do not have the desire to read. Literature can motivate children and instill in them a lifelong desire to read.

If children learn to read but never choose to read, we will have failed as teachers. "If we teach a child to read, yet develop not the taste for reading all our teaching is for naught. We shall have produced a nation of 'illiterate literates'—those who know how to read, but do not read" (Huck, 1979). McKenzie (1977) writes of a more specific concern: "To be given phonics lessons before one has discovered stories is one sure way to know reading failure." Literature is a major asset in a reading program. What child could resist the humor of the friendship between a mouse and a whale in *Amos and Boris* by William Steig or fail to sympathize with the bear in *The Bear's Toothache* by David McPhail or Imogene's peculiar problem in *Imogene's Antlers* by David Small. "Children never fully become persons until they discover delight in books" (Huck, 1979).

Good stories give teachers the right materials for teaching reading comprehension. Children attend to good stories; understand them better than stories that do not "grab" their attention. Good stories are easier to remember. Well-structured stories are also important to reading comprehension. A good story must have setting, problem, attempts to solve the problem, and problem-resolution; otherwise, children will have difficulty understanding the story.

Pupil texts of basal reader series often contain selections from the best children's writers (Aaron, 1987). These selections, which are often abridged and adapted, give students opportunities to read fine literature. This serves as a springboard into a broader appreciation of literature. After reading a selection they enjoy, many children are motivated to read the complete story; for instance, the book *My Robot Buddy* by Alfred Slote, which appears in a fourth-grade basal reader, is so interesting to many fourth graders that they go to the library, obtain the book, and read it in its entirety. Basal reader selections also introduce students to other selections by the same writer. A selection from a Beverly Cleary story will call attention to her other books such as *Ramona Quimby Age 8, The Mouse and the Motorcycle,* and *Dear Mr. Henshaw.*

Since much of the literature included in basal readers is adapted, students can learn quite a lot from comparing stories, poems, and informational articles with the originals. They can identify the adaptations and raise questions about the logic and/or accuracy of the adaptations. The illustrations in basal reader versions of literature may not be the same as those in the original version, so students can compare these as well. Comparisons of text and illustrations create good opportunities for teaching critical thinking.

When basal reader selections are arranged according to theme or topic, students are given opportunities to explore topics from various perspectives. Teachers can expand on these themes by introducing other books with the same theme. In one basal series, a theme is "gifts." Readers are led to a broader concept of gifts as they consider the gift of "The Statue of Liberty," a gift that is earned, a gift that is made for another person, and gifts with which we are born.

Literature in the basal reader offers teachers opportunities to compare various types of literature on the same theme or topic. For instance, when students compare a poem, an informational article, a folk tale, and a contemporary story on the same topic they are acquiring an understanding of theme and structure.

According to Huus (1975) literature is used in classrooms in six general ways:

1. Free reading, which occurs during the time set aside for students to read books that they choose on their own.
2. Reading aloud to children. Children should be prepared for these readings and selections should be carefully chosen.
3. A guided and supplementary reading program in which students receive assistance in selecting books. Students may be directed in this approach to read content materials that will enhance their studies.
4. Topical units of study, which may focus on such topics as *Christmas in other lands* or *Arbor Day.* During this unit, students read fiction, nonfiction, and poetry that are related to the selected topic.
5. Creative sharing of literature among classmates. This approach will be discussed in detail later in the chapter.
6. The total literature program incorporates all of the preceding approaches in a flexible instructional plan. This type of program encourages students to appreciate literature. The total literature program should include instruction on the elements of fiction, nonfiction, and poetry (Huus, 1975).

The Values of Literature

Books add immeasurable richness to our daily lives. They expand our knowledge and experience, help us solve problems, and provide pleasure and relaxation. We see the fun of literature in Audrey Wood's *The Napping House,* and everyone has had a day like Alexander's in *Alexander and the Terrible, Horrible, No Good, Very Bad Day. The Indian in the Cupboard* and *The Return of the Indian,* both by Lynne Reid Banks, are guaranteed to excite the most blasé readers.

Reading literature is a way to learn and develop language skills. Elkind (1978) points out that children "who from an early age are exposed to good literature begin to get a sense of the power and beauty of language." Thus, literature models language development. As children listen to or read stories and poems, they experience this "power." Savoring the language in books such as *Dandelions Don't Bite* (Adelson, 1972), *The Most Beautiful Word* (Vasiliu, 1970), *Sound Words* (Hanson, 1976), *Ounce, Dice, Trice* (Reid, 1961), and *Who,*

Said Sue, Said Whoo? (Raskin, 1973) gets children into the habit of responding to written language. Their understanding, in turn, enables them to understand the meaning of other written materials.

Literature helps children understand others. Literature allows us to walk in another's shoes for a time and to think about their good times and problems. Literature develops our sensitivity; we feel the pain of a friend's death in *Bridge to Terabitha* by Katherine Paterson. Gilly, in the *Great Gilly Hopkins,* also by Katherine Paterson, is a young rebel struggling to understand the mother who deserted her. Literature helps youngsters understand children with special problems in books like *I Have a Sister, My Sister Is Deaf* by Jeanne Peterson. Literature is about life, and the problems and struggles individuals encounter in life are frequent themes in literature.

Literature can stimulate the imagination and develop children's appreciation of literature. Literature is an art form that allows us to view the world and our experiences from a new perspective; thus, literature can "expand the horizons" of its readers. Books such as *The Sun Is a Golden Earring* (Belting, 1962) and *The Earth Is on a Fish's Back* (Belting, 1965) focus on the beauty of nature. *The Terrible Troll Bird* (d'Aulaire, 1976) introduces readers to imaginary characters; *The Shadow of the Gloom World* (Eldridge, 1978) beckons children into the future. Fantasy plays on one's imagination and thus adds another dimension to children's lives.

One of the most important values of children's books is developing understanding, appreciation, and evaluation of characters' feelings and actions (Aaron, 1987). As children identify with characters, they develop a deeper involvement with the story, which makes reading a more enjoyable and meaningful experience. For example, in the book *Ramona and Her Mother,* Beverly Cleary shows readers Ramona's feelings about adjusting to a working mother. Paula Fox helps readers understand Ned and his problems with guilt and his minister father in *One-Eyed Cat.*

Knowledge is another value of literature for children. Informational books give children knowledge and stimulate their interest in the subjects explained in the books. Well-written fiction is carefully researched and also adds to their knowledge. Expository books like *Popcorn* by Millicent Selsam, *The Smallest Life Around Us* by Lucia Anderson, and *Jet Journey* by Mike Wilson and Robin Scagel spark children's interests. *Pets in a Jar* and *Look to the Night Sky* by Seymour Simon make children active participants in the learning process.

INTEREST IN READING

The desire to read is created in a variety of ways: a stimulating environment, selecting books carefully, reading aloud to children, giving book talks about books, providing time for children to read and respond to literature, parents who demonstrate interest in reading, motivational activities, and integrating literature into the curriculum. In this chapter, we will explore these topics.

Environment

Interest in reading is created by an environment that immerses children in literature. Teachers create such environments when they have interesting, attractive books displayed in classrooms. Children also need to *own* good books. The paperback phenomenon makes it possible for many children to own books.

Listening centers with tapes and records of books give children additional opportunities to listen to stories. Bulletin board displays and art work enhance the reading environment. A reading center in the classroom provides a special place where students can read and relax. Reading centers can include such equipment as rocking chairs, beanbag chairs, bathtubs painted bright colors, and soft cushions. This author visited one classroom in which an old telephone booth was used as a site for pleasure reading.

The literature used in elementary classrooms must be carefully selected, so that it reflects the best in children's literature. In addition, this literature should be related to children's interests and experiences. These important topics are addressed next.

Selecting Literature

Teachers who enjoy literature themselves are the best models of reading for students. Enthusiasm for reading is contagious; therefore, teachers should freely share their good feelings about reading with their students. A good reading and literature program requires an enthusiastic as well as a knowledgeable teacher. Teachers must have an in-depth knowledge of children's literature, and they should make an effort to learn about new books that are published. Sources of information on children's literature include:

Adventuring with Books—published by National Council of Teachers of English (1111 Kenyon Road, Urbana, IL 61601).

Booklist—published semimonthly by the American Library Association (50 East Huron Street, Chicago, IL 60611).

Children's Catalog—published by H. W. Wilson Company (950 University Avenue, Bronx, NY 10452).

Beyond Fact: Nonfiction for Children and Young People—published by the American Library Association (50 East Huron Street, Chicago, IL 60611).

Bulletin of the Center for Children's Books—published by the University of Chicago (5801 Ellis Avenue, Chicago, IL 60637).

The Elementary School Library Collection—published by The Bro-Dart Foundation (P.O. Box 3488, Williamsport, PA 17705).

The Horn Book Magazine—published by Horn Book Inc. (585 Boylston Street, Boston, MA 02116).

Language Arts—published by the National Council of Teachers of English (1111 Kenyon Road, Urbana, IL 61601).

The Reading Teacher—published by the International Reading Association (800 Barksdale Road, Newark, DE 19711).

The School Library Journal—R. W. Bowker Company (1180 Avenue of the Americas, New York, NY 10036).

Children's appreciation of literature often is a result of their exposure to books. Children should experience quality literature; therefore, teachers must familiarize themselves with a wide range of trade books. That discussion includes a list of references that are useful in choosing trade books for classroom use. In addition, the following guidelines will help teachers select literature. These guidelines are adapted from *Children's Literature in the Elementary School* by Charlotte Huck, et al. (1987).

FICTION:

Does the book tell a good story that children will enjoy?

Are the characters developed in the story? Can children identify with these characters?

Does the story leave children with positive feelings? (Some children's stories are sad, but they should not leave children in despair.)

Is the setting realistic for the story?

Is the theme significant for children?

Is the writing style suited to the content? Is the style appropriate for the age group for whom the book is intended?

NONFICTION:

Do the facts in the book appear to be authentic?

Does the book effectively explain the topic that is discussed?

Does the book adequately cover the topic?

Is the information well organized?

Is the writing style suited to the topic?

Is the writing style suited to the audience?

Does the book explain interrelationships and implications rather than merely listing facts?

Does the book offer reference aids so the reader can find further information?

Do the illustrations extend and clarify the text?

The literature that is read aloud to children and used for book talks should meet all previously discussed criteria.

INTEREST AND APPRECIATION FOR READING

Interest is probably one of the most important factors of reading literature because teachers must continually tap children's interests if they are to learn how to read. Thus teachers are generally agreed that interest in reading is of paramount importance. Interests are learned, and "they arise from the interaction of our basic needs and the means that we discover for satisfying them" (Dechant and Smith, 1977). Huus (1979) suggests that interest is based on a peculiar combination of factors that includes developmental state, experience, and curiosity. In order to develop the interests of children, teachers must have knowledge of these three considerations in regard to children in their classes. This knowledge will permit teachers to bring children and literature together in a productive and satisfying relationship.

Interest in literature precedes appreciation. Interest develops as a result of one's opportunities with reading a variety of materials and through listening to interesting stories. The interested reader reads indiscriminately, but appreciation evolves into critical, in-depth reading. Thus the appreciative reader is both discriminating and informed.

Huus (1979) summarized the research on reading interests and found that children's interests were influenced by the following factors:

Sex. Boys and girls have different reading interests. These differences emerge at approximately the ages of nine or ten.

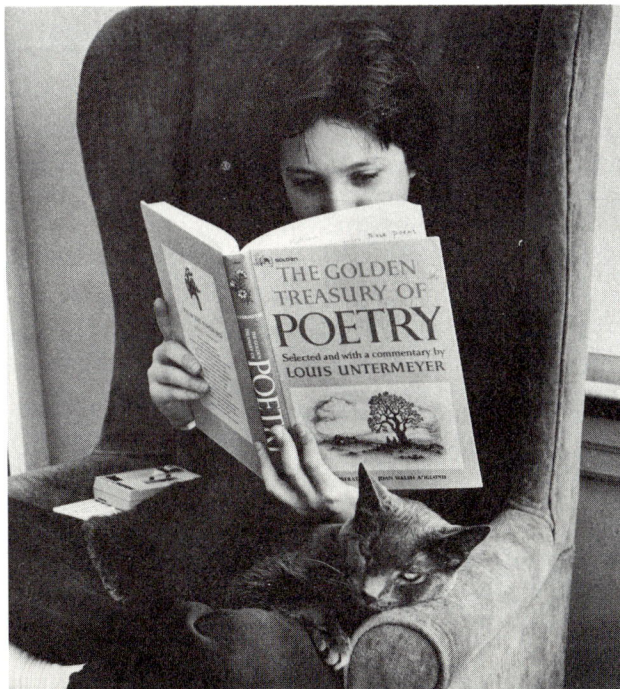

Skillful teachers are able to tap children's interest in and appreciation of literature. *(Courtesy Jean-Claude Lejune)*

Age. Younger children's interests differ from those of older children.

Literary quality. Children prefer well-written literature.

Language. Children prefer books written in standard English.

Authors. Children tend to read books written by well-known authors.

Reading program. The type of instructional program can influence children's interest in reading.

Relevance

"Relevance is a very important factor in motivating children to read" (Stanchfield, 1971). Teachers must become familiar with children's interests, as well as encourage the development of additional interests. **Interest inventories** are one way of learning about children's interests.

Interest inventories

Interest inventories may take a variety of forms. They may be as simple as asking children the titles of their favorite books to having them identify the topic they most like to read about. Incomplete sentences or multiple choice questions may be designed to assess children's interests. A sample multiple-choice inventory is listed below.

If you had nothing else to do, which of the following would you choose?

reading   watching television   playing a game

If you could read on any topic, which of the following would you choose?

sports   humor   history   adventure

Children in the intermediate grades can easily follow an incomplete sentences inventory and write in their own answers. This kind of inventory should be read aloud to young children and disabled readers, with the teacher writing in the answers. The following is an example of an incomplete sentence inventory.

1. I like to read about _____
2. I go to the library _____
3. I like to read when _____
4. I would rather read than _____
5. I like to watch television _____
6. I like television shows about _____
7. Books about sports are _____
8. I think horse stories are _____
9. Mystery stories are _____
10. My favorite author is _____
11. Books bore me when _____
12. I read funny stories _____
13. When I have free time, I _____
14. I like to read in _____
15. Good books make me feel _____

16. Good stories are about _____

17. I am happiest when _____

In scoring the inventory, assign one point for each positive statement about reading. Children who score 13 to 17 points have a positive attitude toward reading, those who score from 9 to 12 points have average attitudes toward reading, and children who score below 9 points need some assistance in developing reading interests. An item analysis of these responses reveals specific reading interests, which can help the teacher to plan reading selections and class projects.

Reading to Children

"The single most important activity for building the knowledge required for eventual success in reading is reading aloud to children" (Anderson et al., 1985). Teachers should read to children *every day.* Reading to children builds their motivation to read, develops language skills, builds interest in specific topics, and gives them information. Children of all ages enjoy listening to good stories. Reading aloud to students is important for students at all levels; students in sixth, seventh, and eighth grades enjoy being read to just as much as young children. There is a great difference between what children can read independently and what they can listen to, understand, and enjoy. Students' ability to understand and enjoy stories usually goes well beyond their ability to decode words; therefore, teachers who read aloud to children are maintaining their interest in literature until their ability to read expands to the level of their interests.

Teachers should select books of literary quality to read, and they should read books that children either cannot or do not read for themselves. Reading these books aloud to children enables them to enjoy selections that they would otherwise miss.

Teachers should read fiction, nonfiction, and poetry to students every school day. Reading these types of literature develops children's understanding of the structure of each; it prepares them to comprehend when they read for themselves. The following guidelines will assist teachers as they implement a read-aloud program.

1. Choose quality literature that addresses children's interests. Books that have received awards are not necessarily interesting to students. Awards are usually given by adults for quality of writing. Do not continue reading a book that turns out to be a poor choice. Simply explain to students that the book is not as good as you thought, so you are replacing it with another. Refer to books like *Choosing Books for Kids* by Oppenheim, Brenner, and Boegehold and *The Read-Aloud Handbook* by Jim Trelease. Good read-aloud books are described in Table 10.1.

2. Make students comfortable for listening. Children should be in a listen-

Table 10.1 GOOD READ-ALOUD BOOKS

Books	Stories	Informational	Poetry
Fast-paced	X	X	X
Well-developed characters	X		
Short description	X	X	X
Easy-to-read dialogue	X		
Worthwhile theme	X	X	X
Clear language	X	X	X
Accurate information	X	X	
Interest level appropriate	X	X	X

ing attitude. Allowing them to play with toys, pencils, complete homework, and the like while the teacher is reading interferes with appreciation and comprehension.

3. Read at a special time each day.
4. Read smoothly, naturally, and expressively.
5. Read a complete picturebook to young children (showing the pictures as well).
6. As children mature and their listening comprehension grows, by the end of second grade or in third grade, you can begin to read episodic stories like those in Beverly Cleary's books. When you read stories that will extend over a number of reading sessions, briefly review the preceding story. Be sure to break the story at an appropriate point—stopping in midepisode interferes with comprehension.

Book Talks

Book talks are short presentations that highlight interesting or exciting aspects of a book in such a way that listeners will want to read the book. A book talk might be considered a commercial or an advertisement for a book; it is an effort to share one's enthusiasm for a book. Book talks can be presented by a teacher or a student, and they are useful at any grade level.

Book talks may be as simple or complex as the presenter wishes. Gener-
ally, book talks are short and to the point; they are not oral book reports. The style should be informal and conversational. The presenter may hold the book and show illustrations to enhance the presentation. Sometimes, props are used to build interest in a book. Following is a script for a book talk that was delivered to a fifth-grade class. This book talk is based on the book, *Salted Lemons* by Doris Buchanan Smith.

This is a story about an eleven year-old girl named Darby who moves from Washing-
ton D.C. to Georgia. Darby is shocked when the neighborhood children are prejudiced against her. The following quotation shows how Darby feels.

Here was nowhere, this strange place where they called her a Yankee and used strange words and acted hateful to Mr. Kaigler because he used strange words.

> Maybe they called him a spy just like they called her a Yankee. Why were they so afraid of anyone who wasn't exactly like they were?

Darby is a spunky girl, she stands up to the neighborhood children. She is also very sensitive to others' feelings. When she does better on the school entrance exam than her sister who is very smart, she feels superior, but when she realizes that her sister is very upset, she is understanding.

Finally, Darby makes friends with Yoko, a Japanese-American girl. One of their favorite activities is sitting in a tree and eating lemons with salt on them. The author describes Yoko and her family in this quotation.

> Darby was entranced by the beauty of this family with the sleek black hair and the golden skin. Americans, she thought with pleasure. Americans are all kinds of people.

Unfortunately, the friends are separated. To learn about their friendship and what finally separates them, you will have to read the book.

Response to Literature

Children should have opportunities to listen to, read, and respond to literature, so they can share their perceptions of stories. The classroom environment, read-aloud activities, opportunities to respond to literature, and opportunities to read should stimulate children's interest in literature and their motivation to read. For example, *The Amazing Bone* (Steig, 1976) is simply a story about a dog and a bone, if examined on an unimaginative level. However, teachers can ask questions about the pig's adventures with the bone that will prompt children to think about the significance of friendship in the story. Older children, are stimulated to read through exploring thematic units like one on hardship and survival that could include books like *The Cay* (Taylor, 1969), *The Cats* (Phipson, 1976), and *Two That Were Tough* (Burch, 1976).

Children's responses to literature should be thoughtful and honest. Each individual's responses should be based on his or her personal experiences, interests, and attitudes; therefore, no two responses will be exactly alike. Teachers need to understand how activities can extend students' responses to literature in ways that foster the growth of imagination and understanding. Response to literature may take many forms ranging from thinking to discussion, writing, dance, art, and drama. Students may respond to fiction, nonfiction, and poetry. The activities suggested in the following sections can be adapted to the various forms of literature.

Written Responses

Literature stimulates writing in a number of ways. Children may use the structure of a book, or its plot, or its characters as models for writing. They may choose to write a new ending, a new beginning, or an additional character. The subject matter or knowledge acquired from reading may provide the basis for writing.

Reading and writing are intricately related. Good writers read more than poor writers (Stotsky, 1984). Some authorities describe reading and writing as two sides of the same process (Squire, 1983). Certainly both are concerned with language and with constructing meaning through language. Each process involves interaction between individuals and language. Reading literature develops children's sensitivity to and understanding of language, which enables them to choose the words and construct the syntax to express their thoughts. Reading fiction, exposition, and poetry helps children develop a sense of the structure of the various forms of discourse. This gives them a structure for remembering what they have read, as well as a structure for organizing their own writings.

Because reading is so important to writing, students should read and be read a wide variety of literature. They should be exposed to well-structured literature with rich language. Literature in the classroom should create a model for writing that stimulates children to write. Literature develops children's sensitivity to language. Discussing the writing styles of authors will enable children to be sensitive to what they write themselves, and this will affect their learning (Wilcox, 1977). Teachers can help children understand such elements as plot, theme, characterization, setting, and writing style through instruction with literature. Writing stories, paragraphs, and even sentences allows students to think about the structure of written language.

Children need a stimulus for writing, and literature can often provide the ideas and inspiration that is necessary. Moss (1977) reports on a literature and writing unit that was developed with six- and seven-year-old children. This unit included stories that were read aloud, stories for independent reading, and discussion that focused on the elements of literature.

Stories like *The Crocodile Under Louis Finnebergo's Bed* by Nancy Parker and *The Enormous Crocodile* by Roald Dahl can be used together in a writing unit exploring children's fears. On a lighter note, *Pippin and Pod* by Michelle Cartlidge and *Alexander and the Wind-up Mouse* by Leo Lionni can be used to create a humorous unit about mice or other small animals who do funny things.

During the prewriting period of writing units like the preceding, the teacher should focus on *why* questions. These questions should stress the logical relationship of events. Children can compare characters and settings in various stories they have read as preparation for writing. The discussion questions included in this chapter will help teachers develop prewriting discussions.

Children can list the characters they wish to write about, the setting of the story, the problem to be explored, or a complete story grammar as they prepare to write. After the stories are drafted, revised, and edited, the children may use drawings or photographs to illustrate them.

Jumanji by Van Allsburg was the stimulus for writing instruction in sixth grade (Cowin, 1986). During the prewriting segment of the process, the students discussed their favorite games because this story involves a board game. Then the children described their favorite game and explained how to play it. The next day the children shared what they had written. As one child read, the others listened so they could guess what game the reader was describing. The teacher extended this writing unit by having students write what they thought happened at the end of *Jumanji*. Then the teacher encouraged students to write so that their audience could "see" what happened. The students were paired with other students to revise. The students revised and rewrote. Subsequently, they edited their drafts to a final form, which was mounted and displayed for parents' night.

Discussing literature is an important aspect of the prewriting period, which prepares students to write. During the prewriting discussion, teachers can help students identify structure and organization, as well effective language use. Discussion should stress *why* questions so that children develop a sense of the logical relationship of events. Comparing characters, plots, and settings helps children focus on the elements of literature. Students should learn to help their audience see and experience their writing rather than just telling them about the story.

Writing activities

1. Using the following books as models, have children write their own stories. Remy Charlip, *Fortunately* (New York: Parents Magazine Press, 1964); Joan Lexau, *That's Good, That's Bad* (New York: The Dial Press, 1963).
2. Ask children to write a cumulative folktale based on a model such as *Chicken Little* or *The House That Jack Built*.
3. Write a diary for a literary character.
4. Write a series of questions based on an informational book.
5. Write a one-sentence description of a character or a setting.
6. Write a letter to a character.
7. Write a television commercial for a book.
8. Make a list of the information needed to write a biography.
9. Read part of a story and ask children to write an ending that they think is appropriate.
10. Create a book of unusual words from stories that are read in class.

Drama

Many stories that children read or that their teachers read to them inspire dramatization. Reading poems like "Bam, Bam, Ban" by Eve Merriam or stories like *Stone Soup* by Marcia Brown leads to dramatic responses. Children enjoy dramatizing good stories and poems that capture their imagination. They like literature that is humorous and action packed.

Children should have many opportunities for the spontaneous interpretation of stories. Children enjoy dramatizing story events. Young children often play cowboys and Indians or cops and robbers. "**Creative drama** is a form of pretending. Creative drama is a short, structured dramatic play experience."

Spontaneous

Creative dramatics does not require scripts, memorization, or elaborate staging. Children can dramatize an episode from a story that they particularly enjoyed. Many stories lend themselves to this activity. Folk tales, such as *Stone Soup*, are excellent for dramatization because they are simple and direct stories. Such stories can also involve a number of children in the dramatization. The following are the steps for planning a dramatic production (Chambers, 1970).

1. Select a good story. Read or tell the story to the children.
2. Identify the main events in the story that will provide the basis for dramatization. Sequence these events.
3. Discuss the action in each scene.
4. Identify the setting and props needed. (Keep things simple.)
5. Identify the characters in the story. Discuss the characters' actions, attitudes, and feelings.
6. Assign the roles of these characters to members of the class and confer with them on how they will play their role.
7. Provide the audience with a purpose for watching the play. (For example, ask children to watch for any scenes that do not follow the story line.)
8. Put on the production.
9. Have the class evaluate the play.
10. Put on the play again. The teacher may choose to recast characters this time around so that more children are involved.

Fun

Creative dramatics provide an opportunity for children to express their enthusiasm for literature. It provides an avenue for simply having fun with literature. Dramatization can motivate children to read. It can also enhance their understanding of the stories that are read because they see the action and the characterizations.

Readers' Theater

In readers' theater, two or more students orally interpret a piece of literature before an audience. The staging is merely suggested. Makeup is used more than costumes. Simple props are used. The readers sit on stools and face in different directions. The readers only suggest the action, and they use their voices and facial expressions to create a mood. The story is introduced by a narrator, who speaks directly to the audience. The narrator establishes the background and theme.

Students should prepare a written script for a reader's theater presentation. Children should practice reading to achieve fluency prior to the presentation. The readers must know the meaning of all of the words used in the script. Readers' theater is an effective way for children to enjoy literature.

Art and Music

Children may express their feelings about literature through art and music. Children may draw or paint pictures to illustrate their favorite stories. The following are some suggestions for stimulating artistic responses to literature.

1. Make maps to show the locale of the story action.
2. Using the same media as the book's illustrator, have children create additional illustrations for the story.
3. Create miniatures based upon a story.
4. Make a poster to advertise a book.
5. Draw illustrations that show how a character has undergone a change.
6. Create a mobile of the main characters or the main incidents in a story.
7. Create a new dust jacket for a book.
8. Dress dolls or create life-size models of characters.
9. Create bulletin board displays based on selections that are read.

Many poems and stories have a quality that lends itself to a musical accompaniment. Music may be used to express feelings about literature in the following ways:

1. Select background music to play while a story or poem is being read. For example, the *Grand Canyon Suite* by Grofé can be played for the book *Brighty of the Grand Canyon.*
2. Have children create lyrics to be sung with a familiar melody to express their feelings about a selection.
3. Have children write a song that is related to the title of a book.
4. Children may select music that they think a specific character in a story would enjoy.

Storytelling

Children enjoy listening to stories told well by teachers, parents, and librarians. Listening to stories prepares children for reading stories. Children tend to understand reading content better when they have previously listened to the story read aloud. Listening to stories also exposes children to the sound of English. Teachers should keep several story and poetry anthologies in the class so they will never be at a loss for reading materials.

In order to tell a story, teachers should practice their presentation so that they are comfortable telling the story in front of the class. The storyteller should use a pleasant voice and speak clearly. Pictures are very helpful for the storytelling because they help focus children's attention (Arbuthnot and Sutherland, 1972). Huck suggests making use of real objects and having a "story bag," which contains realia. For example, a story bag for *The Borrowers* might contain postage stamps, bottle caps, thread spools, a letter, and pins. Flannel board figures also help focus children's attention. Puppets can be used to tell or act out stories. The combination of a good storyteller and a few interesting props can create a spellbound audience.

Realia

Time for Reading

Time is an important factor in reading literature. Children need time during the school day to read. Programs like USSR (Uninterrupted Sustained Silent

Reading) give children opportunities to read during the school day. School days are jampacked and children's time at home is often so full that they do not have time to relax and read. In addition, a number of other factors diminish the time allotted for reading.

One problem that teachers often encounter is that children bring books from home and ask the teacher to read these books. Teachers should not waste valuable class time. Children who bring books from home are usually satisfied if the teacher asks them to show their favorite picture to the class or tell what they liked about the book. Children's needs can be met with this approach, without neglecting one's lesson plan.

Time for reading

Children should have time to read books of their own choosing every school day. Children today are very much occupied with such activities as music lessons, scouts, gymnastics, and television, which means that they frequently do not make time to read. When we provide time for reading in class, we are, in effect, showing children that literature is important. Teachers should avoid telling children they can read "when they have all of their work done" because this statement indicates that reading *is not* highly valued by the teacher. Uninterrupted sustained silent reading (see Chapter 7) is an excellent approach to scheduling time for reading. Children can derive much pleasure from "read-in" sessions.

Time should be also provided for children to share their favorite books with their classmates. Children naturally want to share their thoughts and feelings about the books they read with their friends. Written or oral book reports can lose the interest of both reporter and the audience, so these activities should be avoided. A book report tends to be a synopsis of the book and nothing more (Millsap, 1970). These reports often do not require character

Children should be allowed to share their favorite books with their classmates. *(Courtesy Zucker, Stock Boston)*

analysis, personal reaction, or comparison with another book, but rather are viewed as a punishment for reading—because children have the idea of the report in the back of their minds all of the time they are supposed to be reading.

No book reports

Teachers have claimed that they require book reports for the following reasons: to make sure that the pupil has read the book, to make certain that children do read more books, and to make children think about what they have read (Millsap, 1970). Book reports do not achieve these objectives. They certainly do not make children read. Students are very innovative, in fact, in avoiding reading a book for a report. They have been known to take material directly from dust jackets, published reviews, and even the reports of classmates.

Art, music, drama, dance, games, puppets, round-table discussions, and creative writing are good activities for sharing books. Writing is one obvious way in which to express one's reaction to a book and share that reaction with others.

Parents and Literature

Teachers should keep in mind that parents exert a strong influence on children's attitudes toward reading. Hansen (1969) found that children who liked reading had parents with positive attitudes, while children who disliked reading reflected negative parental attitudes. Parents who want their children to exhibit an interest in reading should act as models. Teachers should make parents aware of their important role in their children's reading development. Teachers can also provide parents with lists of books for their children. Some schools send newsletters for parents. Such a newsletter could include information about books the children read in class. This information could be used by parents to discuss reading with their children.

Motivating Children to Read

Some very reluctant readers require motivational strategies to read. Motivation is a very important factor that is directly related to success in reading. Every teacher has seen children who are truly interested read content that was well beyond their so-called reading level. The following are some suggestions for developing the interests of reluctant readers.

1. Choose books that are relevant to children's lives.
2. Use paperback books whenever possible. Children prefer paperback to hardback books.
3. Have children prepare and read a story aloud to younger children in kindergarten and first grade.
4. The teacher can begin reading a book and leave it uncompleted. Children will then have to read the book to find out what happens in the

story. It is wise to have several copies of this book available when you use this strategy.

5. Have children plan a "sales talk" in which they must "sell" the idea of their favorite book to their classmates.
6. Art activities can be related to children's favorite books. Collages, book covers, mobiles, and bulletin-board displays can be designed.
7. The teacher or a group of children can use puppets to present a story.
8. Arrange individual student-teacher conferences to discuss reading.

LITERATURE AND THE CURRICULUM

Literature is important to the elementary curriculum because it stimulates the intellectual development of students, provides models of thinking, and contributes to students' store of knowledge. Both the literature that teachers read to children and the literature they read for themselves contribute to their intellectual growth.

Children's conceptual development is based on their experiences; however, literature contributes extensively to their store of concepts that are used for understanding the world. Books like *Night in the Country* by Cynthia Rylant contribute information and feelings. Readers of this book learn about the nighttime sounds of owls and frogs and of an apple falling from a tree. And the language creates a night mood, the feeling of night in the country for those of us fortunate enough to have experienced this concept. The author says, "There is no night so dark, so black as night in the country." Mary Szilagyi's illustrations join with the author's language to extend our understanding.

An entirely different kind of book, *Nice and Nasty: A Book of Opposites* by Nick Butterworth and Mick Inkpen, develops concepts of another kind. Through illustrating contrasts, the authors develop our understanding of opposites. They introduce concepts like "black and white," "fast and slow," and a roller coaster illustrates "up and down."

These books develop concepts, but they also create models that children can use for writing or telling about concepts that are important to them. After reading books like these, students may create a class book of concepts.

Literature also contributes to developing higher-order thinking skills like problem solving. For instance, Gerald in *The Secret Moose* by Jean Rogers must find a way to keep an injured moose alive. The hero in *My Friend Jacob* wants to help his retarded friend learn to knock on doors. Taro in *The Boy of the Three-Year Nap* by Dianne Snyder develops an ingenious solution to his problem. He is so lazy that he wants to find a way to live without working; he does so and overcomes his nickname, "the boy of the three-year nap."

Literature stimulates the imagination which is so important to thinkers. Books like Ezra Jack Keats', *Regards to the Man in the Moon* and Mercer Mayer's *What Do You Do With a Kangaroo?* help children realize that imagination is a valuable asset. These books illustrate the value of imagination in our lives.

Literature and the Content Areas

Literature can enhance and elaborate the subjects taught in elementary schools. Literature is frequently more interesting than textbooks; and furthermore, trade books are more up to date than are textbooks. Teachers should select literature that will enhance each subject in the curriculum and elaborate on the subject matter in textbooks. Books like these enhance the elementary curriculum.

Literature develops many aspects of the social studies. For example, *Miss Maggie* by Cynthia Rylant makes readers sensitive to the needs of older people and provides insights regarding mountain life. *Three Days On A River In A Red Canoe* by Vera Williams illustrates planning for a trip, maps, and actual travel. The journal style of writing gives children a model they can use in writing about their own travels. *The Great Race of the Birds and Animals* by Paul Goble develops children's understanding of the American Indian. Genevieve Foster's *Year of the Pilgrims* shows the cultural context of a major event.

Multicultural understanding, an important aspect of social studies, is greatly enhanced by literature. Even young children understand what it is to be a refugee when they are read the book *When Hitler Stole Pink Rabbit* by Judith Kerr. *Journey to Topaz* by Yoshika Uchida shows the difficult life that Japanese-Americans experienced in "relocation centers" during World War II. Kathryn Lasky shares her Jewish family history in *The Night Journey,* which helps us understand another culture and to appreciate older members of the family. In *The Road From Home: The Story of an Armenian Girl,* the author tells the story of a family's suffering during the massacre and dispersal of Armenians by the Turks. This book gives readers a glimpse of a culture that is not widely understood in our country. The fact that the author wrote this story about his mother's experiences adds immediacy and reality to this biography.

Children's science background is enhanced by well-researched, accurate books like *101 Questions and Answers about Dangerous Animals, Earth: Our Planet in Space,* and *The Moon* by Seymour Simon. Reading books like *Seeing What Plants Do* and *More About What Plants Do* by Joan Rahn guide children's understanding of the scientific method. They learn to observe, predict, and report their results in these books.

Mathematics understanding is developed in counting books like *Anno's Counting Book* by Mitsumasa Anno. One-to-one correspondence is developed in Eric Carle's *1,2,3 to the Zoo* and Helen Oxenbury's *Numbers of Things.* John Burninghams' *Count-Up* develops basic mathematical concepts. A more sophisticated understanding of one-to-one correspondence is developed in *The Doorbell Rang* by Pat Hutchins.

Books like those discussed in the preceding paragraphs can be read to children and fluent readers can read them for themselves. Whether they read the book or the book is read to them, discussion is an important way to develop children's comprehension and to help them understand that each of us has different experiences and attitudes which influence our understanding of reading selections. The following section presents ideas for developing class or group discussions of literature.

Book Discussions

Book discussions help to develop understanding as well as providing another avenue for responding to literature. When introducing a book that students will discuss, the teacher should read the title and the author's name. In some instances, the teacher makes some introductory remarks to prepare the students for listening to or reading a story. For example, when introducing the book, *The Secret Moose* to a group of third-grade students, the teacher asked if they knew the difference between a pet animal and a wild animal. Then they compared and contrasted pet animals with wild animals, and the teacher told them that the moose in the story was a wild animal with a problem. In the story, Gerald finds a way to help the moose. The teacher suggested that they listen to the story to find out about the problem and how Gerald helped the moose.

When discussing a story with a class or a group of students, questions like the following are useful: Who is the main character? How do you know this person is the main character? How did the author describe this character? Where and when did this story take place? What was the main problem in this story? How was the problem solved? Is this a good solution? Can you think of other solutions?

A discussion designed to develop students' understanding of the story elements (plot, theme, characterization, setting, and style) and the relationships among these elements could be developed with questions like these: What kind of person is the main character? How do you know? How did the main character change during the story? Why did these changes occur? What did the main character learn in this story? What is the setting of this story? Did the setting play an important part in the story? How? Why did the author write this story? Does the title have any special meaning?

When using literature in the curriculum, teachers often find it helpful to encourage children to compare stories or characters in stories. The next section presents this concept.

Comparison Discussions

Books can be examined in comparison discussions. This section will present a comparison of the themes in the books *Where the Wild Things Are* (Sendak, 1953) and *A Very Special House* (Kraus, 1953). These books are based on the theme of escaping from parental discipline through imaginative means. *Where the Wild Things Are* is also based on the theme of the love between parents and children.

Theme

Where the Wild Things Are is the story of Max, who is sent to bed without his dinner. Max escapes in his imagination to be with "wild things" that make

Max the king. Max and his friends have a good time, but Max eventually returns to his room because he smells good things to eat. When he does return, he finds that his supper is waiting for him, and it is still warm. Sendak's illustrations are an important part of this story. The illustrations increase in size as Max's imagination grows. When Max returns to his real life, the illustrations grow smaller again.

Fantasy

A Very Special House portrays a child's fantasy about a remarkable house. In this house, the little boy can do anything he wants. He can walk on the ceiling, put his feet on the table, and bring all sorts of animals inside. The background in the illustrations are simply black and white line drawings, while the little boy is drawn in full color. In this manner, the illustrations themselves suggest that the boy's activities are imaginary. At the end of the book, he does admit that this special house existed only in his mind.

After reading these two stories to children, the following comparison questions could be raised:

1. How are these stories alike?
2. How do these stories differ?
3. How do we know that the stories are imaginary?
4. What is the common theme in these stories?
5. How does the illustrator of each book show that the story is imaginary?
6. Do you ever use your imagination like Max and the little boy?
7. Have you read any other books with this theme? Other books based on this theme that the teacher could have previously read in class include:

> Ben Shector. *Conrad's Castle* (New York: Harper & Row, 1967).
> Maurice Sendak. *In the Night Kitchen* (New York: Harper & Row, 1970).
> Uri Shulevitz. *One Monday Morning* (New York: Scribner's, 1967).

8. Each of these stories has a musical quality. What music could we play as a background for each story? Would the same music be appropriate for both stories?

Suggested materials

When selecting stories for in-depth comparison discussions, teachers should select stories that have strong elements of characterization, style, setting, plot, or theme. The following are some suggested stories for literature instruction.

SETTING:

Esther Hautzig. *The Endless Steppe* (New York: Crowell, 1968).

Jill Paton Walsh. *The Green Book* (New York: Farrar Straus & Giroux, 1982).

Elaine L. Konigsburg. *From the Mixed Up Files of Mrs. Basil E. Frankweiler* (New York: Atheneum, 1967).

CHARACTERIZATION:

Robert Burch. *Two That Were Tough* (New York: Viking, 1976).

Virginia Hamilton. *Arilla Sun Down* (New York: Greenwillow, 1976).

Elaine Konigsburg. *Father's Arcane Daughter* (New York: Atheneum, 1976).

Jean Little. *Mama's Going to Buy You a Mocking Bird* (New York: Viking Kestrel, 1984).

PLOT:

Avi. *Emily Upham's Revenge—or How Deadwood Dick Saved the Banker's Niece, A Massachusetts Adventure* (New York: Pantheon, 1978).

Lloyd Alexander. *The Cat Who Wished to Be a Man* (New York: Dutton Elsevier, 1973).

Christine Nostlinger. *Konrad* (Watts, 1977).

STYLE:

Clyde, Bulla. *Keep Running Allen* (New York: Crowell, 1978).

Rosemary Sutcliff. *Sun Horse, Moon Horse* (New York: Dutton Elsevier, 1978).

Teaching Poetry

Poetry is a special use of language. Good poetry captures the essence of a person, object, experience, or feeling. The ideas expressed in poetry are compressed into fewer words than are used in other forms of literature. "Poetry is compact. It crystallizes an experience and does so succinctly" (Witucke, 1970).

Good poetry for children relates to their world and is easily understandable (Witucke, 1970). Poetry should be read aloud and should be a part of every

Attributes of poetry

school day. Poetry should not be memorized. Children will grow to appreciate the attributes of poetry once they have had several poems read to them. Huck points out that "Too detailed an analysis of every poem is also detrimental to children's enjoyment of poetry" (Huck et al., 1987).

The following poems are suggested for class discussion.

RHYTHM:

Steven Kellogg. *There Was an Old Woman* (New York: Parents Magazine Press, 1974).

Jack Prelutsky. *The Mean Old Mean Hyena* (New York: Greenwillow Books, 1978).

RHYME:

N. M. Bodecker. *It's Raining Said John Twaining* (New York: Atheneum, 1973).

Mary Hoberman. *The Raucous Auk: A Menagerie of Poems* (New York: Viking, 1973).

Jack Prelutsky. *Nightmares: Poems to Trouble Your Sleep* (New York: Greenwillow Books, 1976).

IMAGERY:

Valerie Worth. *Still More Small Poems* (New York: Farrar Straus & Giroux, 1978).

Lillian Morrison. *Who Would Marry a Mineral: Riddles, Runes and Love Tunes* (New York: Lothrop, 1978).

FIGURATIVE LANGUAGE:

Jack Prelutsky. *The Queen of Eene* (New York: Greenwillow Books, 1978).

Teaching Nonfiction

Nonfiction is an extremely important part of the literature program. There is a large amount of excellent nonfiction material that is available for children today. The following are recommended examples of nonfiction.

Byron Barton. *Wheels.* (New York: Crowell, 1979).

Irene Brady. *Wild Mouse* (Scribner, 1976).

Phyllis S. Busch. *Cactus in the Desert* (New York: Crowell, 1979).

Joanna Cole. *A Chick Hatches* (New York: William Morrow, 1976).

Jack and Patricia Demuth. *City Horse* (New York: Dodd, Mead & Co., 1979).

Robin Forbes. *Click: A First Camera Book* (New York: Macmillan, 1979).

Ann McGovern. *Sharks* (New York: Four Winds Press, 1976).

Seymour Simon. *Soap Bubble Magic* (Lothrop, 1985).

Basic types   Nonfiction requires a different approach from teaching fiction. There are two basic types of nonfiction: **exposition** and **argument.** Expository nonfiction explains something to the reader, while argumentive nonfiction attempts to persuade the reader (Felsenthal, 1978). Felsenthal (1978) suggests the use of guiding questions for examining nonfiction. The following questions can be applied to nonfiction discussions.

What is the subject of the book or selection?

What did the author say about this subject? Try to state the author's perspective in 1 or 2 sentences.

Did the author support this point of view or main idea? How?

Identify the author's statements of fact.

Does the author explain causes and effects?

What conclusions and/or generalizations are developed?

What new facts or information did you acquire?

What was the author's purpose for writing this piece?

LITERATURE STUDY

A variety of ideas regarding literature in elementary classrooms have been introduced in this chapter; the goal of this section is to help teachers implement these ideas. This section introduces the idea of webbing and teaching based on a web.

A web is a visual brainstorm that helps teachers generate ideas and link them to a theme or a central focus. Charlotte Huck developed the concept of webbing and introduced it in her book, *Children's Literature in the Elementary School* (1976). Webs are used to begin planning a study of books and to generate the possibilities of a book or books. Developing webs helps teachers become familiar with the content they are planning to introduce and the relevancy of this content to their students' lives and experiences.

Webs are a network of possibilities; they are not followed exactly. In creating a web, teachers explore these ideas: the book or books to be used, ways of initiating study of these materials, building background for the study, discussion questions, and extending literature through the arts. Teachers usually find that discussing these ideas with one another helps in generating and refining them. The webbing process is explained in the next few paragraphs through the actual experiences of two teachers.

Jane Bradley, a first-grade teacher, developed the following web for *Alexander and the Terrible, Horrible, No Good, Very Bad Day* by Judith Viorst. She knew that she wanted to use this book because the children enjoyed it so much that merely reading and discussing it did not adequately develop children's appreciation of it. She started the web by thinking about whether she wanted to develop a web based on one book, one author, a theme, a topic, or a genre. She decided that she wanted to explore this book in depth. Then she thought about ways to introduce the book. She decided to read the book to the children since many of them could not read fluently enough to enjoy it. To introduce the book, she decided to ask the children to think about the worst day of their lives and all of the things that happened on that day. Then she proceeded by telling them that Judith Viorst had written about such a bad day and that she called it a "terrible, horrible, no good, very bad day." Jane decided to show the children the illustrations as she read the text, because the illustrations are so well suited to the author's language. She could have chosen instead to use puppets or a flannel board to introduce the story.

Next, Jane used these references to develop her background and to help in selecting books with similar topics: *Children's Literature in the Elementary School,* 4th ed. by Charlotte S. Huck, et al.; *Choosing Books for Kids* by Joanne Oppenheim, et al.; and *The Read Aloud Handbook* by Jim Trelease.

When she had completed this phase of the web, Jane developed discussion questions that she could use after she read the book to the class. Her discussion questions are shown in the web in Figure 10.1. After composing the questions, she considered ways of extending the book through writing and through art; these ideas are also shown in Figure 10.1. After the web was finished, Jane shared it with several friends who were also teaching first grade. They asked questions and made suggestions which she included in her plans. Jane decided to initiate this web the following week and to spend three days working with it.

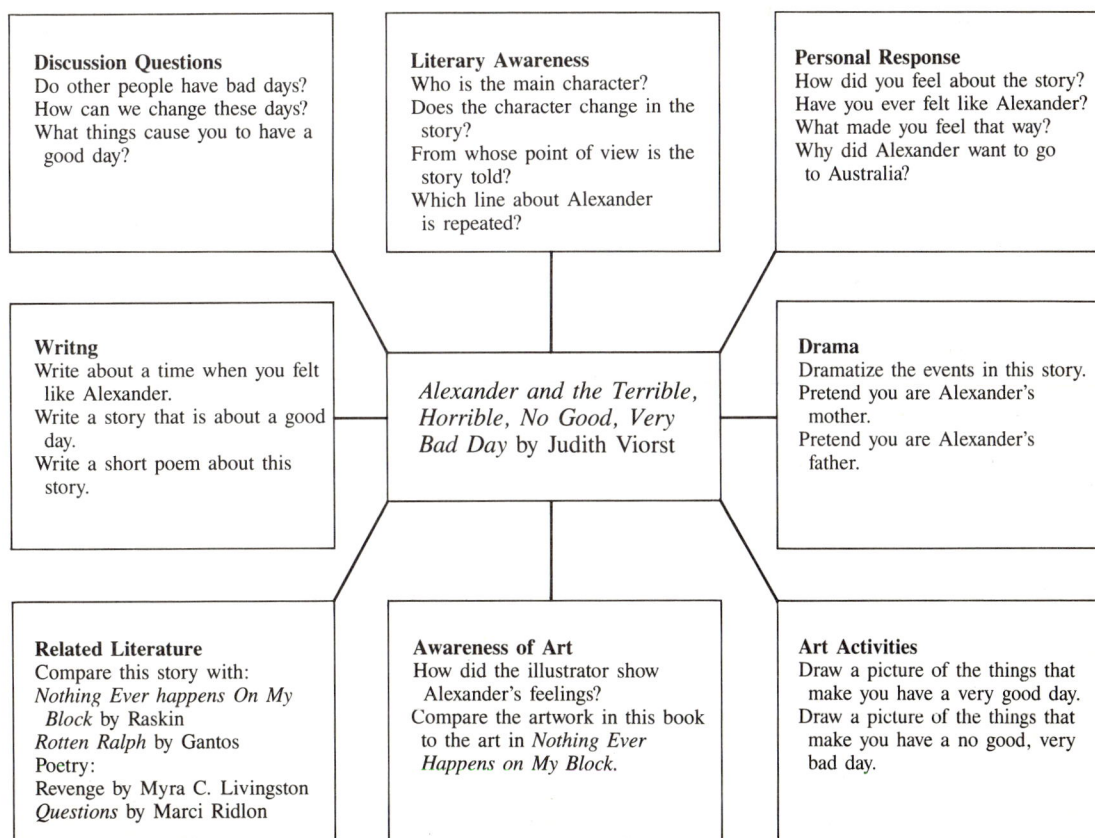

Discussion Questions
Do other people have bad days?
How can we change these days?
What things cause you to have a good day?

Literary Awareness
Who is the main character?
Does the character change in the story?
From whose point of view is the story told?
Which line about Alexander is repeated?

Personal Response
How did you feel about the story?
Have you ever felt like Alexander?
What made you feel that way?
Why did Alexander want to go to Australia?

Writng
Write about a time when you felt like Alexander.
Write a story that is about a good day.
Write a short poem about this story.

Alexander and the Terrible, Horrible, No Good, Very Bad Day by Judith Viorst

Drama
Dramatize the events in this story.
Pretend you are Alexander's mother.
Pretend you are Alexander's father.

Related Literature
Compare this story with:
Nothing Ever happens On My Block by Raskin
Rotten Ralph by Gantos
Poetry:
Revenge by Myra C. Livingston
Questions by Marci Ridlon

Awareness of Art
How did the illustrator show Alexander's feelings?
Compare the artwork in this book to the art in *Nothing Ever Happens on My Block.*

Art Activities
Draw a picture of the things that make you have a very good day.
Draw a picture of the things that make you have a no good, very bad day.

Figure 10.1 A sample in-depth story web.

On Monday, she introduced the story and read it aloud to the class. After oral reading, they discussed the story using the questions she had composed. The discussion focused on the children's feelings and the bad days they had experienced. The children brainstormed words that described terrible days in their lives. They discussed the repeated phrase and its significance. After school, she wrote the words they generated on charts for use the next day. On Tuesday, she used the chart to start them thinking about the book. Then many of the children wrote about their own bad days, although some of them drew pictures about their bad days. After writing or drawing, many of the children read *Nothing Ever Happens on my Block* individually because this book is more suited to individual or small group reading since so much of the action is in the illustrations. Then the children discussed creating illustrations for their stories and poems. Drama was the focus on Wednesday. The children discussed the scenes they wanted to include in the dramatization and planned the characters and action in each scene. After presenting the various scenes, the children had time to revise the writing they had started the preceding day. The children found that acting out the story helped them to visualize what they wanted to write. To close the study, Jane read two poems from her web.

Jane did not use every idea, book, or question developed in her web. She selected those that she thought would be most interesting to the students. After completing this web, she decided to introduce other books by Judith Viorst. Later in the semester she addressed the theme of this book in a different unit of study.

Mary Robbins, a sixth-grade teacher, developed a web for *Julie of the Wolves* by Jean George in much the same way that Jane developed her web. Mary developed the web (Figure 10.2) which she planned to teach over a week and a half. She introduced the book to her class, explaining that Jean George had lived in Alaska for a time in order to develop the background for this story. Then she posed several questions to guide the students as they read the story silently and suggested that they discuss the story in three parts since it was written that way. After introducing the story and showing the students photographs of Alaska, they read silently. The second day, the class discussed the first part of the story focusing on the nature of survival and the meaning of this part of the story. After the discussion the students continued reading the book; as they read they identified colors that reflected Julie's mood and the words that described her feelings. Mary used a poem from her web to open class on the third day. The students discussed solitude in the poem, solitude in the story, and their own experiences with solitude. Their discussion included settings in which solitude could occur, including settings they might use in writing about solitude.

By the fourth day of the web, the students were well into the story and very interested in the character development of Julie. The discussion focused on character development. Mary raised questions about the author's techniques for character development. Then the students used these techniques to write a character sketch. After writing, they continued reading the story silently. On the fifth day, the class discussed the changes in Julie's character as the story unfolded. The students used this material as they revised their character

Related Literature
Poetry:
Solitude by Milne
Journeys:
The White Archer by Houston
Journey Outside by Steele
Courage:
The Boundary Riders by Phipson
One is One by Picard
Survival:
Slake's Limbo by Holman
The Endless Steppe by Hautzig

Plot
Why is the book divided into three
 parts?
What is the meaning of each part
 of the story?
What dangers did Miyax face?
What is the climax of the story?
Is the ending satisfying to you?
 Why or why not?

Discussion Questions
What types of survival are
 discussed in this story?
What are the riches of life for
 Eskimos?
What are considered to be the
 riches of life for our society?
What is solitude? How does Miyax
 deal with it?
How do you cope with solitude?

Julie of the Wolves
by Jean George

Art
Carve a totem of an animal you
 admire
Create a mural of the setting
 Miyax sees when she is living
 near the wolves.
Miyax refers to her memories in
 terms of colors. Choose colors
 that represent your memories
 and paint a picture to illustrate
 one of them.

Characterization
How does Miyax feel about her
 father at the beginning of the
 story?
How does she feel about him by
 the end of the story?
What caused the change in her
 feelings?
How did Miyax feel about the
 wolves?
Did her feelings change? If so,
 how?
Why is the comb so important to
 Miyax?

Drama
Dramatize Miyax's meeting with
 her father.
Dramatize the wolves'
 communication with
 one another.

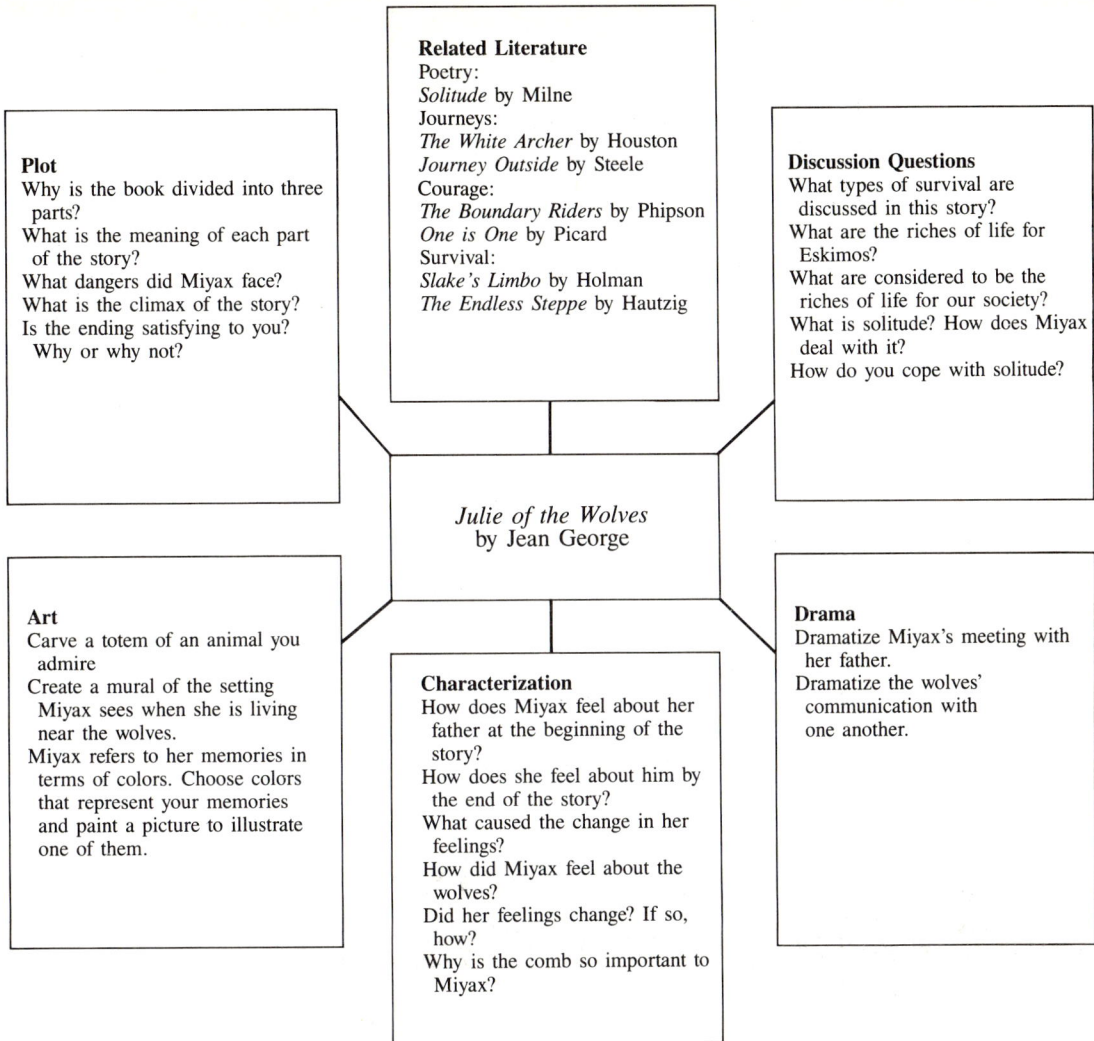

Figure 10.2 A sample in-depth story web.

sketches. Some of the students were especially interested in the wolves and the authenticity of the information about their communication system, so Mary suggested they do some outside reading regarding wolves to check the authenticity of this information.

By the sixth day, most of the students had completed the book so the discussion focused on Julie's feelings about her father, the climax of the story, and the meaning of each part of the story. After the discussion of the book and the character sketches the students had written, they talked about ways of extending this story through art. The students were free to create their own response to the story or to use one suggested in Mary's web. A number of the students were interested in dramatizing the wolves' communication and using their outside research to develop several scenes that expressed what they had learned about wolves' communication. Mary told the students that they should be certain that their art expressed ideas or feelings that were central to their understanding of this story. She also told them that they could share their art, music, drama, or writing two days hence.

On the following day, she had individual conferences with students who needed additional guidance as they worked on their expression of ideas through the arts. Some students had completed their work, and they started reading related books that were identified in the web. At the end of the week, when the students shared their perceptions of the experience, she found that the web was successful, and she thought about the possibilities of moving from this web to one that examined different types of courage.

SUMMARY

The following list summarizes the key points of this chapter.

1. The study of literature is central to the reading curriculum. Good literature stimulates student interest in reading. Literature is important to children for a variety of reasons, but pleasure is the most important of these reasons. Reading literature also develops a sensitivity of language, helps children to understand themselves and others, stimulates the imagination, and develops an appreciation of nature.
2. Reading interests are related to factors of sex, age, literary quality, language, authors, and the reading program itself. Exposing children to literature that is relevant to them attracts their interests. Teachers may use interest inventories to identify children's interests. Reading relevant literature to children also helps build their interest in literature. Children should have opportunities to read during the school day because they may not make time for reading outside of class. Book reports may discourage interest in reading; therefore, other approaches to sharing and discussing what has been read should be employed.
3. The literature program should provide for a broad exposure to literature and in-depth study of books that are read. The elements of literature should be examined in class discussions. Thematic units of study contribute to children's understanding of literature. Fiction, nonfiction, and poetry should be included in the literature program.
4. Children's responses to literature may be expressed through such activities as creative dramatics, readers' theater, art, music, and writing.

SELF-TEST

Check your knowledge of the information presented in this chapter. The answer key is located in Appendix C.

1. What is an "illiterate literate"?
   a. a person who cannot read
   b. a person who reads all of the time

    c. a person who knows how to read, but does not read
    d. a person who is incapable of reading

2. Why are good books better than ditto sheets?
    a. they take less time to complete
    b. books are more interesting
    c. books take up more space
    d. books are easier to read

3. What are some of the values of literature?
    a. language development
    b. developing understanding of oneself and others
    c. stimulating the imagination
    d. all of the above

4. What is the basis for interests?
    a. practice
    b. genetics
    c. experience, curiosity and development
    d. genetics, experience, and practice

5. Which of the following factors influence children's interests?
    a. sex, age, literary quality
    b. compactness, binding, and number of pages
    c. both a and b
    d. neither a nor b

6. Which of the following would be found in a good reading environment?
    a. many books
    b. bulletin board displays and a rocking chair
    c. both a and b
    d. neither a nor b

7. How does the author of this text feel about book reports?
    a. they should be required
    b. children should do both oral and written reports
    c. they are interpreted by children as punishment for reading
    d. they attract children to reading activities

8. What types of literature should be included in the literature program?
    a. comic books and *Mad Magazine*
    b. the basal reader
    c. fiction, nonfiction, and poetry
    d. poetry and fiction

9. Which of the following should be included in the literature program?
    a. authors, types of literature, and elements of literature
    b. reading what critics have said about literature
    c. both a and b
    d. neither a nor b

10. How often should teachers read to children?
    a. once a week
    b. never
    c. every day
    d. on special occasions only

11. What types of instructional strategies might be used in the literature program?
    a. reading to children
    b. creative writing
    c. comparison discussions
    d. all of the above

12. Which of the following statements describes poetry?
    a. it is compact and succinct
    b. it uses more words than fiction
    c. it is unnatural for children
    d. it should be memorized

13. Which of the following are elements of poetry?
    a. memorization
    b. imagery and rhythm
    c. the indentation of lines
    d. the analyzation of words

14. What are the basic types of nonfiction?
    a. poetry
    b. exposition and argument
    c. folktales
    d. anthologies

15. What are the values of reading aloud to children?
    a. motivates students to read
    b. builds comprehension
    c. exposes them to literature they cannot read
    d. all of the above

16. What are the qualities of a good read-aloud story?
    a. slow-moving, detailed
    b. lengthy description
    c. has received awards
    d. none of the above

17. What kinds of literature should be read to children?
    a. poetry
    b. exposition
    c. stories
    d. all of the above

18. How does the literature in the basal reader provide a basis for reading?
    a. it motivates students to read stories by the same author
    b. it motivates students to read stories on the same subject
    c. it can be compared to the original versions
    d. all of the above

19. How is literature related to writing?
    a. it motivates children to write
    b. it gives students a model of writing
    c. both a and b
    d. neither a nor b

20. Why is discussion of literature important in the prewriting period?
    a. it draws students' attention to important aspects of literature
    b. it teaches them to spell words
    c. both a and b
    d. neither a nor b

THOUGHT QUESTIONS

1. Describe the relationship between literature and reading.
2. How is literature related to reading instruction in a basal reading program?
3. Why are good stories important to developing reading comprehension?
4. What is the role of book reports in reading instruction?
5. How are the arts related to literature?
6. Discuss the major values of literature for children.
7. Why is literature the "heart" of the reading program?
8. How are reading and writing related?

ENRICHMENT ACTIVITIES

1. Visit a classroom and read a story to children at various grade levels. Compare the response of different age groups. Tape-recording this experience is helpful.
2. Design a bulletin board display to interest children in literature.
3. Do an in-depth study of authors of children's books. What did you learn about these individuals and their reasons for writing?
4. Plan an in-depth discussion of a book. List the questions you would use to stimulate discussion. If possible, visit a classroom and conduct the discussion.
5. Plan art and music activities to accompany selected books. If possible, visit a classroom and carry out the activities.
6. Construct an interest inventory and administer it to a group of children. What did you learn about their interests?
7. Develop a card file of children's literature. (This will be useful to keep in class when you are teaching.)
8. Using the criteria presented in this chapter, evaluate several new children's books. Which of the books do you like the best? Which do you find poorly written?
9. Develop a web for a children's book. If possible try some aspects of the web with a group of children.
10. Make a display to motivate children to read.

RELATED READINGS

Bauman, M. (January 1987). "Literature, Repetition, and Meaning," *Language Arts,* Vol. 64, No. 1, pp. 610–672.

Benton, M. (March 1984). "The Methodology Vacuum in Teaching Literature," *Language Arts,* Vol. 61, No. 3, pp. 265–277.

Cowin, G. (November 1986). "Implementing the Writing Process with Sixth Graders: Jumanji, A Literature Unit," *The Reading Teacher,* Vol. 40, No. 2, pp. 156–161.

Cullinan, B., Ed. (1987). *Children's Literature in the Reading Program,* Newark, DE: International Reading Association.

D'Angelo, K., S. Korba, and C. Woodworth (March 1981). "Bookmaking: Motivation for Writing," *Language Arts,* Vol. 58, No. 3, pp. 308–315.

Dyson, A. (December 1986). "The Imaginary Worlds of Childhood: A Multimedia Presentation," *Language Arts,* Vol. 63, No. 8, pp. 799–807.

Huck, C., S. Hepler, and J. Hickman (1987). *Children's Literature in the Elementary School,* 4th ed., New York: Holt, Rinehart and Winston.

Larrick, N. (October 1986). "From Tennyson to Silverstein: Poetry for Children," *Language Arts,* Vol. 63, No. 6, pp. 575–585.

Norton, V. (1987). *Through the Eyes of a Child,* 2nd ed., Columbus, OH: Charles Merrill.

Oppenheim, J., B. Brenner, and B. Boegehold (1986). *Choosing Books for Kids,* New York: Ballantine Books.

Sawyer, W. (January 1987). "Literature and Literacy: A Review of Research," *Language Arts,* Vol. 64, No. 1, pp. 33–39.

Squire, J., Ed. (1987). *The Dynamics of Language Learning,* Urbana, IL: National Conference on Research in English.

Trelease, J. (1982). *The Read-Aloud Handbook,* New York: Penguin Books.

Winkeljohann, R. (March 1981) "How Can I Help Children To Enjoy Poetry?" *Language Arts,* Vol. 58, No. 3, 347–352.

REFERENCES

Aaron, I. (1987). "Enriching the Basal Reading Program with Literature," *Children's Literature in the Reading Program,* Newark, DE: International Reading Association, pp. 126–137.

Adelson, L. (1972). *Dandelions Don't Bite,* New York: Pantheon.

Anno, M. (1977). *Anno's Counting Book,* New York: Crowell.

Arbuthnot, M. and Z. Sutherland (1972). *Children and Books,* 4th ed., Glenview, IL: Scott, Foresman.

Belting, N. (1962). *The Sun Is a Golden Earring,* New York: Holt, Rinehart and Winston.

Belting, N. (1965). *The Earth Is on a Fish's Back,* New York: Holt, Rinehart and Winston.

Brewton, S., Blackburn, J., and G. Blackburn (1973). *My Tang's Tungled and Other Situations,* New York: Crowell.

Brown, M. (1947). *Stone Soup,* New York: Scribners.

Burch, R. (1976). *Two That Were Tough,* New York: Viking.

Burningham, J. (1979). *Count Up,* New York: Crowell.

Butterworth, N. and M. Inkpen (1988). *Nice or Nasty: A Book of Opposites,* Boston: Little Brown.

Chambers, D. (1970). *Storytelling and Creative Drama,* Dubuque, IA: William C. Brown.

Cowin, G. (November 1986). "Implementing the Writing Process with Sixth Graders: Jumanji, A Literature Unit," *The Reading Teacher*, Vol. 40, No. 2, pp. 156–161.

Cramer, R. (February 1975). "Reading to Children: Why and How," *The Reading Teacher*, Vol. 28, pp. 460–462.

d'Aulaire, I. and E. d'Aulaire (1976). *The Terrible Troll Bird*, New York: Doubleday.

Dechant, E. and H. Smith (1977). *Psychology in Teaching Reading*, Englewood Cliffs, NJ: Prentice-Hall.

Eldridge, R. (1978). *The Shadow of the Gloom World*, New York: Dutton.

Elkind, D. (January 1978). "Language Arts and the Young Child," *Language Arts*, Vol. 55, pp. 2–3.

Felsenthal, H. (1978). "The Tradebook and an Instructional Tool: Strategies in Approaching Literature," in *Using Literature in the Elementary School*, J. Stewig and S. Sebesta (Eds.), Urbana, IL: National Council of Teachers of English, pp. 21–34.

Goble, P. (1985). *The Great Race of the Birds and Animals*, New York: Bradbury.

Gray, B. (1978). *Manya's Story*, New York: Lerner.

Hansen, H. (1969). "The Impact of the Home Literacy Environment on Reading Attitude," *Elementary English*, Vol. 46, pp. 277–280.

Hanson, J. (1976). *Sound Words*, New York: Lerner.

Henry, M. (1953). *Brighty of Grand Canyon*, New York: Scholastic.

Huck, C. (1971). "Strategies for Improving Interest and Appreciation in Literature," in *Reaching Children and Young People Through Literature*, H. Painter (Ed.), Newark, DE: International Reading Association, pp. 37–45.

——— (1979). "No Wider Than the Heart is Wide," in *Using Literature and Poetry Effectively*, J. Shapiro (Ed.), Newark, DE: International Reading Association, pp. 29–360.

——— (1987). *Children's Literature in the Elementary School*, 4th ed., New York: Holt, Rinehart and Winston.

Hutchins, P. (1986). *The Doorbell Rang*, New York: Greenwillow.

Huus, H. (1975). "Approaches to the Use of Literature in the Reading Program," in *Teachers, Tangibles, Techniques*, B. Schulwitz (Ed.), Newark, DE: International Reading Association, pp. 140–149.

——— (1979). "A New Look at Children's Interests," in *Using Literature and Poetry Effectively*, J. Shapiro (Ed.), Newark, DE: International Reading Association, pp. 27–45.

Kherdian, D. (1979). *The Road From Home: The Story of an Armenian Girl*, New York: Greenwillow.

Kraus R. (1953). *A Very Special House*, New York: Harper & Row.

Lionni, L. (1963). *Swimmy*, New York: Pantheon.

Mayer, M. (1973). *What Do You Do With a Kangaroo?*, New York: Scholastic.

McKenzie, M. (December 1977). "The Beginnings of Literacy," *Theory into Practice*, Vol. 26, pp. 315–324.

Miles, B. (1979). *The Trouble with Thirteen*, New York: Knopf.

Millsap, L. (November 1970). "The Ubiquitous Book Report," *The Reading Teacher*, Vol. 24, pp. 99–105.

Moss, J. (May 1977). "Learning to Write by Listening to Literature," *Language Arts*, Vol. 54, pp. 537–542.

Norton, M. (1953). *The Borrowers*, New York: Harcourt Brace Jovanovich.

Phipson, J. (1976). *The Cats*, New York: Atheneum.

Rahn, J. (1975). *More About What Plants Do*, New York: Atheneum.

——— (1972). *Seeing What Plants Do*, New York: Atheneum.

Raskin, E. (1973). *Who, Said Sue, Said Whoo?,* New York: Atheneum.

Reid, A. (1961). *Ounce, Dice, Trice,* Boston: Little Brown.

Rylant, C. (1986). *Night in the Country,* New York: Bradbury Press.

Sendak, M. (1953). *Where the Wild Things Are,* New York: Harper & Row.

Simon, S. (1985). *101 Questions and Answers About Dangerous Animals,* New York: Macmillan.

——— (1984). *The Moon,* New York: Macmillan.

——— (1983). *Earth: Our Planet in Space,* New York: Macmillan.

Smith, D. (1980). *Salted Lemons,* New York: Four Winds Press.

Squire, J. (1983). "Composing and Comprehending: Two Sides of the Same Basic Process," *Language Arts,* Vol. 60, pp. 581–589.

Steig, W. (1971). *Amos and Boris,* New York: Farrar Straus & Giroux.

——— (1976). *The Amazing Bone,* New York: Farrar Straus & Giroux.

Stanchfield, J. (1971). "Reaction for Improving Interest and Appreciation in Literature," in *Reaching Children and Young People Through Literature,* H. Painter (Ed.), Newark, DE: International Reading Association, pp. 26–29.

Stotsky, S. (1984). "Research on Reading/Writing Relationships: A Synthesis and Suggested Directions," in *Composing and Comprehending,* J. Jensen (Ed.), Urbana, IL: ERIC Clearinghouse on Reading and Communication Skills and NCRE, pp. 7–22.

Taylor, T. (1969). *The Cay,* New York: Doubleday.

Thiele, C. (1978). *The Shadow on the Hills,* New York: Harper & Row.

Vasiliu, M. (1970). *The Most Beautiful Word,* New York: John Day.

Viorst, J. (1972). *Alexander and the Terrible, Horrible, No Good, Very Bad Day,* New York: Atheneum.

Williams, V. (1981). *Three Days on a River in a Red Canoe,* New York: Greenwillow.

Witucke, V. (1970). *Poetry in the Elementary School,* Dubuque, IA: William C. Brown.

CHAPTER 11

Adjusting Reading Instruction to Meet the Needs of Special Students

---

OVERVIEW   Today's teachers teach reading to children with more diverse needs than any previous student population. They regularly teach children who are gifted, educable mentally retarded, sensory handicapped, learning disabled, economically disadvantaged, emotionally disturbed, as well as those students who are learning English as a second language. This chapter explores the characteristics of students with special needs, and the instructional strategies for teaching them in the regular classroom.

Key Vocabulary

As you read this chapter, check your understanding of these terms:

attention-deficit disorder
dialect
economically disadvantaged
educable mentally retarded (EMR)
educational and mentally
   handicapped (EMH)
emotionally disturbed
English as a second language (ESL)

exceptional children
gifted
hyperactive (hyperkinesis)
IEP
learning disabilities (LD)
mainstreaming
sensory (perceptual) handicapped

Focusing Questions

As you read this chapter, think about these questions:

1. How does mainstreaming influence reading instruction?
2. Why do regular classroom teachers teach exceptional children?
3. What are the responsibilities of classroom teachers when special needs students are mainstreamed?

CHILDREN WITH SPECIAL NEEDS

Children with special needs, or **exceptional children,** are youngsters who are special in one or more of the following ways:

mental ability

sensory ability

physical development

social or emotional behavior

communication ability

multiple handicaps

Exceptional children require modification of school practices or special services in order to develop to their full potential. "Almost 7 million school-age Americans (12 percent of the 6 to 19 year-old age group, according to the U.S. Office of Education) are emotionally, physically, or mentally handicapped" (1976). The public schools serve all of these students; therefore, school systems today serve a more diverse student population than ever before.

Individual differences

A variety of factors have led to this diversity of the classroom population. Contemporary social attitudes respect individual differences and there is a strong trend today, as well, toward human rights. Teachers are more aware of individual differences and are accepting the responsibility for teaching *all* children. We also have a greater understanding of the effect of differences on the learning process. In the end, contemporary society appears to have recognized the need to provide an education for all.

Appropriate education

In addition, teachers have a legal responsibility to educate all children. The federal government committed itself to the education of all children in **Public Law 94–142.** This law states that "all children are entitled to an equal education in a form which deviates least from the traditional educational environment" (Harper and Kilarr, 1978). The law mandates that a "free, appropriate public education be made available to all handicapped children." Thus, many exceptional children are being educated in the public school system in America today.

Mainstreaming

Another factor that contributes to the diversity of the school population is **mainstreaming.** Public Law 94–142 does not legislate mainstreaming, but it does specify that children be educated in the "least restrictive" environment, which is usually the regular classroom. "In essence, mainstreaming means moving handicapped children from their segregated status in special education classes and integrating them with 'normal' children in regular classrooms" (Staff Article, 1976).

"The goal of mainstreaming is to provide a favorable learning environment for both handicapped and regular students" (Andelman, 1976). Schools are organized in various ways to meet this goal; as a result, mainstreaming organizations vary from one school system to another. In some schools, handicapped children are in the regular classroom for most of the day and spend a short time with a special education teacher. During this time, the special education teacher works with individuals or small groups, depending on their needs. Other schools are organized so that children spend most of the day with the special education teacher, but join the regular class for specific subjects—such as social studies or reading. The role of a special education teacher varies greatly with the individual school's approach to the mainstreaming situation.

Environment

Mainstreaming has increased the scope of the classroom teacher's responsibility. The teacher must now meet the educational, physical, emotional, and social needs of all children. The children who are mainstreamed through an elementary classroom have a variety of strengths and handicaps. Teachers should keep in mind that all students have "special" needs of one kind or another. When teaching children with such diverse needs, it is necessary to make adjustments in the reading program. The differences between a fast learner and a slow learner are not necessarily related to the kind of learning that takes place, but rather the resulting level of achievement. This chapter is concerned with the programmatic adjustments that will help children achieve their full potential. Note, however, that the teaching suggestions offered

Make adjustments

An individual educational program works well for children with special needs. *(Courtesy Carey/The Image Works)*

throughout this book can be used for exceptional children as well as average children.

Terminology

A number of specialized terms are used in discussing children with special needs. The following is a list of these terms and their respective meanings.

Attention-deficit disorder is a relatively new term used to describe students who were formerly labeled hyperactive. Attention-deficit disorder is considered an appropriate term because the children with this disorder cannot control their attention.

Gifted children are those children who, by virtue of their outstanding abilities, are capable of exceptional achievement.

EMR refers to educable mentally retarded children whose I.Q. is between 50 and 75.

EMH refers to students who are educationally and mentally handicapped.

Learning disabled children are those who have a significant discrepancy between their estimated intellectual potential and their actual level of achievement. This discrepancy is related to disorders in the learning process (Bateman, 1965).

Perceptually or sensory handicapped children have difficulty interpreting the data that are transmitted to the brain by the senses. This handicap is not usually related to the eyes or ears, but rather to the brain's inability to associate meaning with sensory data.

Economically disadvantaged children come from lower socioeconomic status (SES) backgrounds. Socioeconomic status is determined by family income, parental education, and family size (Seitz, 1977).

Hyperactive (hyperkinesis) refers to children who are prone to excessive activity, excessive mobility, or restless behavior. These children cannot control their activity, and their behavior is often described as *driven.*

IEP is an individual educational program that is a plan for educating handicapped children that was developed by parents, teachers, and children working together. Components of this program include goals and objectives, placement and services to be received, and evaluation.

Teachers should keep in mind that the specific definitions of the preceding terms depend somewhat on the region in which one lives. Cruickshank (1967) pointed out that children's disabilities depend on their geography. A child living in Michigan might be declared perceptually disabled, while the same *Classification* child in California would be educationally handicapped or neurologically handicapped. In Bucks County, Pennsylvania, that child would be classified as having a specific language disorder; in New York State, brain injured; and in Montgomery County, Maryland, the classification would simply be for a specific learning disability (Cruickshank, 1967).

The preceding example illustrates the difficulty that arises when one attempts to generalize about exceptional children. The following sections of this chapter will explore the characteristics of exceptional children and reading programs that are designed to meet their needs.

Gifted Children

Attention to the special needs of gifted children waxes and wanes regularly in American education. Presently, gifted children are recognized, due to increased consciousness of the individual needs of all children. Gifted children require educational programs beyond the regular school program in order to realize their full potential. Unfortunately, some gifted children are actually underachievers who have not realized their potential.

Outstanding ability

Gifted children are defined as those children who, by virtue of outstanding abilities, are capable of high performance. School systems use a variety of tests and checklists to identify gifted children; thus it is difficult to generalize about the specific criteria that are used. Terman (1954), who pioneered studies of gifted individuals, stated that children of an I.Q. of 140 or higher are, in general, appreciably superior to other children. Gifted children have a generalized high level of ability in all areas.

Research has shown that we can generalize some characteristics of gifted children, although they are individuals who differ in many ways. Gifted children are characterized by as many individual differences as any other group of children. They demonstrate achievement or potential ability in the following areas, either singly or in combination (Labuda, 1985):

general intellectual ability

specific academic aptitude

creative or productive thinking

leadership ability

visual and performing arts

psychomotor ability

Intellectual stimulation

Gifted children have often been denied intellectual stimulation in our society (Witty, 1951). This has occurred because some educators believed that gifted children would learn on their own; however, intelligence must be directed and developed. Gifted students must be stimulated in order to achieve to their fullest potential and lack of stimulation can lead to irreparable harm. The reading program for gifted children is an excellent vehicle for stimulating the intellectual development of able students.

Reading Strategies for Gifted Children

Reading materials

Many gifted children are precocious readers who learn to read before coming to school. Goertzel (1962) studied gifted people and found that their superiority was most often in the area of reading ability, with many of them reading by the age of four. Clearly, parents are important to the reading development of gifted children. Parents should read to them and take them to the library. Their homes should contain children's magazines, newspapers, story and picture books, and encyclopedias. Gifted children should experience the same kind of environmental stimulation as other children—except that they should be exposed to these opportunities very early in life.

Gifted children who do not read prior to kindergarten can benefit from reading instruction at that level (see Chapter 3). The language-experience approach is an ideal method for gifted children because it encourages creative thinking and reading. Providing opportunities for writing also enhances their reading development. The reading program for gifted children should focus on the thinking and communication aspects of the reading process.

Diagnostic approach

A diagnostic approach is also an important component of the reading program for gifted children. The skills of gifted children should be identified by the use of standardized and informal reading tests. This information will help teachers plan a program of instruction and activities that will be directed toward learning new skills, rather than those that have already been acquired.

Interests play an important role in teaching gifted children. Children's interests can be identified through interest inventories (see Chapter 10) and used to develop enthusiasm for reading. A variety of supplementary reading materials and activities should be available in the classroom to encourage gifted children to pursue their special interests and to expand their present reading interests.

The reading program for gifted children should meet the following criteria:

Stress a creative approach to instruction and learning (Witty, 1985).

Stress convergent thinking (Witty, 1985).

Acquaint students with quality literature (Barbe, 1985).

Teach students how to do library research (Barbe, 1985).

Use reading to pursue special interests (Witty, 1985).

Develop study skills (Wallen, 1985).

Provide guidance when necessary, but allow children to work independently (Shafer, 1985).

Enrichment activities, such as the following, are helpful for teaching gifted children to read.

1. Maintaining a personal journal in which students write each day.
2. Studying the history of the English language.

3. Writing stories, poems, and reports on topics of interest.
4. Illustrating their written compositions with their own art work or photographs.
5. Participation in a literature group. (Children select the books that the group will read and discuss. After reading the selected literature, group discussions are conducted.)
6. Studying their favorite authors in depth by reading their works, finding out about their lives, and even writing letters to them.
7. Writing stories to be dramatized and videotaping or audiotaping these stories.
8. Comparing the illustrations created by various illustrators. (When different versions of the same story are available, these illustrations may be interesting to compare.)
9. Designing new games.
10. Watching the evening news on various television stations and contrasting the commentators' styles and coverage of various topics of current interest.
11. Developing a class newspaper.
12. Expressing one of their stories through the use of art, music, and drama
13. Collecting folklore and investigating the history behind the folklore.
14. Writing an article to persuade classmates to a particular point of view.

EMR and EMH Children

EMR and EMH students exhibit as many individual differences as any other group of children. Thus it is difficult to generalize about these children; however, there is general agreement that EMR children develop one-half to three-fourths slower than average children. This slowed development is reflected in their conceptual and perceptual abilities. The rate of intellectual development is easier to understand if one considers that children with an I.Q. of 75 have a mental age of four and one-half when their chronological age is six (Kaluger and Kolson, 1978). As a result of slowed intellectual development, the academic achievement peaks of EMR and EMH children are at a lower level than average children.

There are no personal or social traits common to all EMR and EMH children, and their interests appear to correspond with those of children of the same mental age. As adults, these persons are capable of doing unskilled or semiskilled work (Smith and Heisworth, 1975). The reading curriculum should build on the interests of EMR and EMH children and provide them with the reading skills that will enable them to function at their highest level of potential.

Reading instruction for EMR and EMH students should be planned according to their learning abilities. These children comprehend well at concrete levels, but abstract ideas appear to cause problems. They are unable to learn *Slower rate* through discovery because they do not understand implied or subtle relationships. The memorization of facts is also very difficult. Instruction should proceed at a very slow rate and frequent repetition should be provided, which will enable these youngsters to achieve success in learning. Success helps build their self-confidence. EMR children should receive immediate feedback about their work, as they will not understand corrections that are given at a later date. Instruction should be focused on realistic objectives, and should focus on only a few objectives at any one time.

Reading instruction for EMR and EMH children should be delayed until they achieve reading readiness skills, which will permit them to have a successful learning experience (see Chapter 4). A long teaching period and focused instruction are necessary for developing readiness skills. Thus a carefully structured reading readiness program is necessary for these youngsters.

A scope and sequence of teaching reading skills to EMR and EMH students is developed below.

I. Reading readiness:
  A. Visual discrimination
  B. Auditory discrimination
  C. Listening comprehension
  D. Following oral directions
  E. Learning the alphabet
  F. Identification of letters
  G. Concept development
  H. Reading simple signs, such as *stop* and *go*
II. Primary level:
  A. Learning high-frequency words by sight
  B. Dictating sentences and simple stories
  C. Reading experience charts
  D. Learning consonant sounds
  E. Learning to read basal reading materials at the first-grade level
  F. Continuing the development of listening comprehension
III. Intermediate level:
  A. Developing knowledge of 220 Dolch sight words
  B. Learning vowel sounds
  C. Developing the ability to use context clues
  D. Developing structural analysis skills
  E. Developing the ability to use phonics to decode new words
  F. Developing the ability to understand at the literal level
  G. Achieving a 2.5 grade level on reading achievement tests (Kolestoe, 1970)
IV. Junior-high-school level:
  A. Using word recognition skills to identify unknown words
  B. Developing skills for reading newspapers
  C. Using the newspaper to obtain information
  D. Reading for pleasure
  E. Developing a more extensive meaning vocabulary
  F. Extending comprehension skills
  G. Reading to obtain information in the following sources:

1. catalogs
2. telephone books
3. dictionaries

Reading Strategies for EMR and EMH Children

EMR and EMH children require more repetition in their instruction than do average children; however, repetition should be interesting and motivating for them. Many of the activities suggested in Chapter 4 can be implemented in the teaching program. Kinesthetic strategies are useful for teaching sight words and sounds. The teacher may use sandpaper letters in the form of the word being taught, or the word may be written in corn meal, grits, or sand. Children should then trace the word five times and say the word aloud as tracing takes place. (They should not, however, spell out the word.) After tracing, students should attempt to write the word without looking at it. Words that are learned should be placed in the child's individual word file for review at a later date.

Tracing

Reading content should include concrete concepts and should be based on the experiences and interests of EMR and EMH children. Instruction should be personalized as much as possible. Children tend to remember words and ideas whose meanings are relevant to them. Write sentences and stories using the children's names. When introducing new vocabulary, compose sentences that relate to children's experiences.

Literature

Literature should not be omitted from the reading program for EMR and EMH children. These children do enjoy literature, and should have opportunities to listen as teachers read stories to them. Literature can motivate these children to read.

The contribution of the reading program to the lives of EMR and EMH children was confirmed by the case of Luther, a young EMR child whom the author of this text taught some years ago. Luther was not only very shy, but he came from a disadvantaged home. Luther spent two unhappy years in first grade prior to entering my first-grade class. He arrived with great reluctance, but our meeting occurred at an opportune time in his life. Luther's chronological age was nine and his mental age had developed to the level of a five-year-old. During that year Luther learned the alphabet, developed a basic sight vocabulary of about 50 words, learned how to write his name, and learned to read at a preprimer level. Luther also learned to count to ten and to recognize the numbers up to ten. Today, Luther is a young man and has a job as an unskilled laborer, which gives him some measure of independence.

Slow-Learning Children

Slow-learning children are not fundamentally different from average children—they simply learn somewhat slower. Children whose I.Q.'s range from 75 to 90 are usually considered slow-learning children. They learn slower than average children, but are not as slow as educable mentally retarded children. Slow-learning children tend to be the "forgotten" children in our schools because they are not slow enough to be in an EMR class and not fast enough to keep pace with the average reading program. They can achieve, however, when given the opportunity to participate in a slower paced reading program in which skills are reinforced.

The following are suggestions for developing a reading program for slow-learning children.

1. Instruction should include more repetition than in the average reading program. There should be repetition of words, sounds, concepts, and even stories. Slow-learning children accept repetition because it gives them a feeling of security.
2. Provide concrete experiences, because these children have difficulty with abstractions.
3. Provide many opportunities for oral reading.
4. Directions should always be clear so that they understand exactly what is expected of them.

Learning-Disabled Children

Learning disabilities may be manifested by difficulties in the following areas:

Academic learning level is one or more years below the child's mental age.

Perceptual-motor skills are weak. The child has poor handwriting and finds directions confusing.

Language and speech problems, which are exhibited as articulation problems, stumbling in oral delivery, or halted or garbled speech.

Thought processes are confused. The child may be easily distracted and thus require additional time in which to complete work. The child may learn something one day and forget it by the next. The child may also work better when the teacher stands nearby. The learning-disabled child may be anxious and lack ego strength (Kaluger and Kolson, 1978).

Learning-disabled children exhibit a wide array of individual differences. The *LD* classification itself provides no specific information about the children's learning disabilities. No one program will be universally effective; thus, individual learning patterns and problems must all be considered in planning the reading program. Frequently, the regular basal reading program is modified for instructing learning-disabled children. The following factors should be considered in planning such a program:

Modifications

1. Since learning-disabled children are distractable, they may need their own private space for reading. A carrel is one solution, or a section of

the classroom may be screened for privacy. Teachers have also been known to use appliance crates or boxes to create "offices" for children.

2. A structured, well-organized environment helps these children succeed in learning.

3. Help children learn to focus their attention on the reading task. Teachers can assist in this area by explaining precisely what is expected of them.

4. Provide immediate reinforcement of appropriate behavior.

5. Give the children short assignments. Several short assignments are easier to work on than a single long one. For example, a workbook page can be folded in half so that children will feel that they can accomplish the assignment that is given.

6. Kaluger and Kolson (1978) suggest that learning-disabled children should be allowed to stand while working because standing eliminates physical stress. They also suggest that some learning-disabled children can work better on a stool without a back.

7. Stress left-to-right scanning of words. The teacher may cover words with a file card and gradually uncover the letters, from left to right.

8. Stress the notion that words represent concepts.

9. Kinesthetic approaches are useful.

10. Teachers should be patient with children who point at and mouth words because this may actually help them to read.

11. Provide quiet opportunities during the school day.

12. Make certain that children experience some feelings of success in reading so they will be motivated to continue reading.

13. Develop alternative approaches for learning-disabled children. For example, they should be permitted to tape-record answers to questions if they have difficulty with writing.

One of the biggest problems facing learning-disabled children is the fact that their handicaps are not readily apparent. The following incident illustrates this point. Sarah was a student in this author's sixth-grade class several years ago. Sarah was an attractive, healthy youngster who had fallen farther and farther behind her classmates in her learning ability each year. Her permanent record showed that her teachers believed her to be lazy, inattentive, and uninterested in learning. Her former teachers agreed that while she was very bright, she was apparently unmotivated. Several teachers suggested that Sarah's parents had contributed to her problems. These teachers believed that Sarah's parents should provide firmer discipline for her.

Fortunately, the school principal had become interested in learning disabilities and recommended that Sarah have a complete physical and neurological examination, and an educational diagnosis. This data revealed that Sarah had petit mal epilepsy, which had interfered with developing the skills and *Cycle of failure* abilities necessary to learn to read successfully. Her failure to learn caused her to lose interest in her studies. Thus, by sixth grade, she was caught up in a cycle of failure. The appropriate medication was recommended for Sarah, as well as placement in a remedial instruction program—in which she began to develop the skills and abilities she lacked in her previous school experience.

Sensory-Impaired Children

Children who have visual and hearing handicaps are sensory impaired. These impairments can lead to reading difficulties and the problems discussed in the following section.

Visually handicapped

Visually handicapped children have incomplete or distorted visual input, which interferes with concept development, with left-to-right orientation on the printed page, and with obtaining a clear visual image of words (Degler and Risko, 1979). These youngsters can be assisted in learning through the use of books with large print. Visually handicapped children should be encouraged to follow the lines of print by pointing to them, thus moving their eyes in a left-to-right fashion. Pictures and objects can be used to develop concepts. Children should also be introduced to stories prior to class readings by discussing the concepts associated with the stories. With some assistance, visually handicapped children can experience success in reading.

Hearing impaired

Hearing-impaired children have not been exposed to the uses of language; thus, they have been deprived of language development. They may have difficulty producing and understanding speech sounds. Structure words are often not heard clearly. This creates a problem in understanding complex sentences and grammar, which in turn interferes with comprehension. They frequently lack understanding of multiple meanings. Since hearing-impaired children do not hear clearly, words that sound alike—such as *toy* and *boy*—merely confuse them.

Hearing-impaired children need opportunities for language development. Earphones are helpful for listening to stories. Teachers should speak loudly and clearly when working with these children. Phonics has little or no value for hearing-impaired children because they cannot discriminate sounds well enough to use phonics as a means of decoding words; therefore, visual approaches to decoding should be stressed.

Emotionally Disturbed Children

Emotions are directly related to learning. Emotions can deter learning. Emotional maladjustment may be expressed through aggression, withdrawal, bizarre behavior, or anxiety.

Hewett (1967) states that **emotionally disturbed** children usually are not ready for instruction in skill mastery. Reading instruction, of course, is aimed at the mastery of various skills. Hewett considers the following five levels of readiness to be prerequisite to skill mastery. Children must be able to:

pay attention to instruction

respond to others in the learning environment

follow directions

meaningfully explore the environment

value social approval and get along with other students (Hewett, 1967)

An emotionally disturbed child who has achieved the preceding levels of readiness is probably ready for instruction.

Teachers can help emotionally disturbed children by implementing the following teaching strategies:

1. *Aggression*
   a. Separate the child from other children when he or she becomes aggressive.
   b. Be very firm with the child.
   c. Be fair in your handling of the situation.
   d. Establish rules for behavior that are enforced in a consistent manner.
   e. Be certain that children understand why their behavior is unacceptable.
   f. Avoid situations that are likely to cause aggressive behavior.
   g. Provide an acceptable outlet for aggression, such as listening to music, playing with punching bags or toys, and doing art work.
2. *Withdrawal*
   a. Help the child establish relationships with other children in the class who have common interests. (For example, both children may own a dog.)
   b. Build self-confidence.
   c. Include both individual and group activities in instruction.
   d. Assign children to groups where they can work effectively during class projects.
3. *Anxiety*
   a. Be supportive of the child but avoid developing dependence on the teacher.
   b. Provide firm, consistent discipline.
   c. Show your sincere interest in children's work and activities.
   d. Provide opportunities for successful reading experiences that develop self-confidence. For example, the child should be capable of reading and interested in reading those materials that are selected. Use the child's strengths to build self-confidence. For example, ask children questions you are certain they can answer.
4. *Bizarre behavior*
   a. Bizarre behavior is very distracting for other members of the class. Teachers should seek outside assistance from professionals (such as the school psychologist) for behavior that is frequently bizarre. Teachers do not have the background to enable them to deal successfully with this type of emotional problem.

Economically Disadvantaged Children

Teachers have long known that minority children have a relatively high failure rate in reading (Ogbu, 1985). Children from low socioeconomic status (SES) backgrounds perform poorly on measures of reading competence when compared with children from economically advantaged homes (Coleman et al., 1966; Jencks et al., 1972; Armor, 1972; Abelson, Zigler, and DeBlasi, 1974). Unfortunately, socioeconomic status is an excellent predictor of reading achievement. Speculation regarding the factors that depress the reading achievement of minority children includes factors such as attitude (Ogbu, 1985), "expectation of success," low level of motivation, limited experiential and conceptual background, and language differences (Hunt et al., 1973; Seitz, 1977).

Ogbu's (1985) research indicates that minority students' problems are not caused by bad teaching or uncooperative/bad students, but is related to the ways minority groups have treated specific minorities. For example, the response of some black students is not to do well in school, for to do so would set them apart from their peer group, which gives them their identity and social support. On the basis of this research, Ogbu suggests that teachers and schools need to develop programs that help minority children learn how *not* to equate mastery of school culture and language with loss of group identity and security, which he calls "accommodation without assimilation." Children from a low socioeconomic status (SES) background perform more poorly on measures of reading competence than children from economically advantaged homes. This section will explore the factors that may contribute to reading problems for this group of children.

The Expectation of Success

Children's expectations of success in school can have a profound impact upon their performance of cognitive tasks (Seitz, 1977). Entwisle and Webster experimented with strategies designed to raise children's expectations of success and found that they could teach children to successfully participate in academic situations. These children became more confident and active in the classroom as a result of these efforts.

Self-concepts

The expectation of success is closely related to self-concept, another important factor in learning (Conn and Kornelly, 1970). Children who have strong self-concepts are more motivated to learn and experience greater success in learning, which in turn motivates them to continue their studies. Thus, improving the self-concepts of disadvantaged children can have a positive impact on their levels of achievement.

The impact of teacher expectations on disadvantaged children's achievement was researched by Rist (1970), who found that teachers' expectations of student success were a powerful influence on achievement. He learned that teachers tended to make judgments about children's educability, and treated them accordingly. Children who were deemed most educable were seated closest to the teacher, while those who were considered unable to learn received more teacher criticism.

Language Differences

Dialect

Language is a sociocultural phenomenon that reflects the speaker's community. Language plays a large role in reading achievement because reading is a language-based skill. Children from economically disadvantaged homes frequently speak a dialectical variant of standard English, which is usually referred to as **nonstandard English.** Nonstandard English is as systematic a language as standard English. Speakers of nonstandard English are actually using a different language system. This is a significant factor because reading materials and instruction are in standard English. Standard and nonstandard English differ in vocabulary (semantics), pronunciation, and grammar. Some examples of these differences are listed below.

1. Pronunciation
   a. Dropping the final sounds in words, for example, pronouncing *told* as *toll* or *past* as *pass.* Another instance might be excessively stressing the first syllable; for example, in *ho*tel and *po*lice (Labor, 1972).
2. Grammatical differences
   a. Perfective construction, as in *I done forgot.*
   b. Absence of the present tense verb, as in *She walk.*
   c. Presence of an invariant *be* category, as in *I be here.*
   d. Extensive use of multiple negation, as in *Nobody don't know nothing* (Shuy, 1973)
3. Vocabulary differences
   a. Examples: *hog* for a *Cadillac, gig* for a *job.*

Dialect is another variation in language, not a language deficiency (Venezky and Chapman, 1973). Language enables us to communicate, and dialect does enable speakers to communicate with one another. Thus, teachers must avoid making value judgments about the dialects their students use.

Dialect does not directly interfere with reading; however, there is an enormous potential for indirect interference. Rupley and Robeck (1978) state that "black dialect has minimal, if any, effects on black children's reading achievement." Seitz (1977) examined the research on dialect interference in learning to read and concludes that speaking a dialect is not a deterrent. Seitz points out that "children who speak dialects other than black English (for example, children who have been raised in south Boston) often learn to read without any apparent difficulty." These youngsters usually speak a regional dialect which is more acceptable than some other dialects. Melmed (1973) studied the role of dialect in reading and found that black students who spoke a dialect were able to comprehend standard English in written form quite well. Thus, there is little evidence to support the notion that speaking a dialect causes reading failure.

Indirect interference of dialect in learning to read can develop from the teacher's lack of understanding of dialect. The teacher is the most important variable in determining whether children who speak nonstandard English will learn to read. "Language is a very personal possession, and when teachers begin to manipulate it in the process of teaching reading, it introduces a threat to the psycho-social stability of those with variant dialects" (Alexander, 1980). Teachers must react to children's language with sensitivity and respect.

They have a responsibility to understand the language of the children they teach.

Experiential Background

Disadvantaged children have vastly different experiential backgrounds from average children. For example, disadvantaged children are usually better acquainted with fire engines because there are more frequent fires in the residential areas where these children live. They do not lack experience and conceptual development in general; however, they do lack the experiences and concepts that are often presented in basal reading materials. Teachers of disadvantaged children must teach the concepts that are taken for granted by average children. Concept development will help disadvantaged children read with greater understanding.

Concepts

Reading Strategies for Speakers of Nonstandard English

Teachers should remember that children from lower socioeconomic status are avid television watchers and are exposed to a variety of dialects. Thus, many of these children can easily understand oral standard English. Classroom activities such as those listed below will help extend the language of children who do not speak standard English.

1. Read literature that reflects different language styles, such as books by Lois Lenski, Gwendolyn Brooks, and Langston Hughes.
2. Discuss the various dialects that are associated with parts of the United States. This discussion may include the reasons that dialects develop, the variations that exist in language, and the need to respect the dialects of others.
3. Role play situations using different dialects.
4. Have children watch television programs and identify the different dialects that are used.
5. Listen to recordings of various speakers, such as the speeches of Dr. Martin Luther King (Rutherford, 1970).

Intelligence Tests

Some authorities believe that traditional tests are culturally biased. These authorities believe that **intelligence tests** accentuate socioeconomic differences because they have a white middle-class orientation; therefore, they penalize disadvantaged children (McNiel, 1975). Intelligence tests rate the average black child 15 points or one standard deviation lower than the average white child (Ornstein, 1976). Ebel (1972) points out that attempts to develop culture-free tests have failed. He further states that these attempts have failed because "testing requires communication and communication is impossible in the absence of culture: its concepts, symbols, and meanings." It may therefore be more realistic to eliminate inequalities through instruction rather than through what appear to be futile attempts to revise intelligence tests.

Parents

Reading model

Parents strongly influence the reading achievement of their children. The home environment and parents' behavior provide early cognitive stimulation for children, a model for reading, and attitudes toward reading materials. "The best way to prepare the very young child for reading is to hold him on your lap and read aloud to him stories he likes—over and over again (Flood, 1977). Some of the following strategies help parents support their children's reading development:

1. Send home packets of children's work to parents. Include experience stories, classroom reading materials, and worksheets for home use (Froclich et al., 1967).
2. Send parents a class calendar that lists the topics studied at school during the course of each week and suggest related book titles that parents could read to their children.
3. Suggest books for parents to obtain from the library to read with their children. Include sample questions for discussion.
4. Make a list of free and inexpensive places in the community that parents could take their children, such as garden shows, history museums, parks, exhibits in shopping centers, and historical sites.
5. Help parents become involved in the child's reading program.
   a. Ask parents to make certain that the child has a quiet place to read.
   b. Ask the parent to check the child's vocabulary from a prepared word list.
   c. Send a book home for the child to read. Attach a sheet to the book that indicates the pages that are to be read and the words that should be reviewed. Parents should sign the sheet and return it to the teacher when the work is completed.

Reading Strategies for Economically Disadvantaged Children

The components of a good reading program for disadvantaged children are essentially the same as the reading program for average children. However, disadvantaged children should have more opportunities for experiences in reading and teachers should recognize that they will need additional time for developing these skills.

1. The reading program should be carefully structured with clearly stated, specific objectives (Grotberg, 1972).
2. The reading program should stress individualized and small group instruction, since children experience greater success in reading in these settings.
3. Suggest activities that enable children to have successful reading expe-

riences. They should receive immediate feedback and encouragement for their work. Develop concrete ways of indicating their progress, such as designing charts and graphs.

4. Expand the experiential and conceptual background of children by looking at pictures, films, television programs, reading literature, and directed classroom discussions.
5. Teach the alphabet and letter-recognition skills (Cohen, 1969).
6. Read to children every day from quality literature. This will help to develop their interest in language and their desire to read (Strickand, 1972; Rystrom, 1973).
7. Provide many opportunities for practicing English as a second language, such as choral reading, creative dramatics, and cloze activities.

English as a Second Language

Educating children whose native language is not English is a major educational concern today; approximately 5 million school-age children in the United States speak languages other than English or live in homes where languages other than English are spoken (Neill, 1979). Sixty percent of these children come from a Spanish-speaking background. Teachers should become familiar with the backgrounds and culture of children who are learning English as a second language in order to teach them to read.

Ideally, students who are learning **English as a second language (ESL)** acquire English while maintaining knowledge of their native language (Kupinsky, 1983). Therefore, children should be exposed to reading material written in both English and their mother tongue. Classroom teachers must understand that students need to learn oral English before they can successfully read it.

Second-language learning through immersion is a current instructional trend (Genesee, 1985). In this approach the second language is not simply taught as another subject in the curriculum, but rather is the medium through which the curriculum itself is taught. For example, in the Canadian immersion programs, all curriculum instruction during the first two, three, or four grades is presented in French; English is used initially to teach English language arts and is subsequently expanded to include other academic subjects. By the end of elementary school, each language is used to teach approximately 50 percent of the curriculum. By using the second language as a major medium of curriculum instruction, immersion programs are designed to create the same kinds of conditions that characterize first-language acquisition. There is an emphasis on creating a desire in the students to learn the second language in order to engage in meaningful and interesting communication (Genesee, 1985).

The following characteristics of ESL students should be considered in planning reading instruction for them:

1. They generally lack the experiences of the dominant culture.
2. They do not have an adequate command of oral English to learn to read, write, and comprehend in English.

3. They often have a low self-esteem due to difficulties in communicating in the school environment.
4. They have great difficulty learning through a phonetic approach because they cannot distinguish many of the sounds of the second language (Modiano, 1973).
5. Learning to read through a knowledge of sight words is difficult because "an individual perceives and remembers only that which has meaning." Bilingual children cannot learn sight words until they learn English.

Diagnosis is the starting point for teaching bilingual children to read. Teachers should assess the following factors through observation and discussion with the child and the parents.

1. What language is spoken in the home?
2. What language or languages does the child speak?
3. Has the child learned to read any language?
4. What does the child know about English?
5. What does the child know about life in the United States?
6. What concepts are familiar to the child?

Reading Strategies for ESL Students

Readiness is another major consideration in teaching reading. The following are the types of readiness objectives for bilingual children.

1. Listening comprehension of English
2. Conversational use of English, including a good vocabulary
3. Awareness of the phonemes of English
4. Knowledge of the alphabet
5. Experiences with the culture and concepts of American English

An aural-oral background in English can be developed by using the following strategies:

1. Provide many opportunities to listen to and speak English. Read to children frequently (Allen, 1979). Some of the following books can be used for this purpose:

   Anno, Mitsumasa. *Anno's Counting Book* (New York: Crowell, 1977).

   Burningham, John. *Seasons* (Indianapolis, IN: Bobbs-Merrill, 1970).

   Hoban, Tana. *Over, Under and Through and Other Spatial Concepts* (New York: Macmillan, 1973).

   Hoban, Tana. *Push, Pull, Empty, Full: A Book of Opposites* (New York: Macmillan, 1976).

   Wildsmith, Brian. *Brian Wildsmith's ABC* (New York: Franklin Watts, 1966).

2. Provide patterned practice with basic sentence patterns (such as those identified by Lefevre that are listed in Chapter 1). Practice with a limited number of sentence patterns at a time, so as not to confuse the child.
3. New sentence patterns should be introduced with familiar vocabulary words.
4. Practice language activities in a natural situation, so that meaning will be reinforced.
5. Never ask children to read or write selections that haven't already been orally discussed (Gamez, 1979).
6. Develop oral language by practicing transformations and expansions of basic sentence patterns. (See Chapter 5 for suggestions.)
7. Children should have opportunities to hear, see, and say the same vocabulary words several times each day—and in two or three different contexts (Feeley, 1977). For example, the teacher could use apples to illustrate concepts in various contexts, such as *apple pie, candy apple,* and even *"the apple of my eye."* Provide as many "firsthand" experiences as possible.
8. Use pictures and picture dictionaries to develop vocabulary and concepts if you are unable to provide firsthand experiences.
9. Plan English language activities based on songs and games so children have opportunities to practice the language patterns they are learning. Games such as "Button-Button," "Simon Says," and "The Whisper Game" are among those that are suggested for this purpose (Minkoff, 1984).

Children who are learning to speak English as a basis for learning to read should be exposed to the concepts of English-speaking peoples because a language reflects the culture of the people who speak it. Firsthand experiences, and watching television and movies, are valuable ways of learning about these cultural concepts.

One of the controversies associated with bilingual education is related to learning to read in the native language prior to learning English. Some professionals believe that initial instruction should be in the native language (Feeley, 1977). Others feel that it is better to teach English before teaching the child to read (Gamez, 1979). This author has found that children who know how to read in their native language have an easier transition to reading English than children who have not previously learned to read. Whatever approach is selected to meet the needs of bilingual children, teachers should keep in mind that they will require special instruction in order to learn to read in the English language.

SUMMARY

All children have special needs of some nature. Their needs must be met if children are to achieve their full potential. The following list summarizes the key points of this chapter.

1. Recent legislation has made schools legally as well as morally responsible for meeting the needs of all children. Teachers today face an enor-

mous challenge in the classroom because they must meet a diverse range of needs. The average teacher may have to teach children who are EMR or EMH, learning-disabled, emotionally handicapped, visually or auditorially handicapped, economically disadvantaged, bilingual, and gifted.

2. Gifted and talented children have a generally high level of ability that must be developed. They learn faster than average children. EMR (or EMH) children tend to learn slower than average children; thus, a longer period of readiness and slower-paced instruction is needed for these children. The achievement levels of learning-disabled children are the average potential for their mental age. Their specific learning disabilities must be identified through diagnosis, since this classification does not specify a specific disability. Sensory-impaired children may have problems in visual or auditory areas, for which teachers must compensate in instruction. Emotionally disabled children may exhibit symptoms of aggression, withdrawal, bizarre behavior, or anxiety. All of these behaviors can interfere with learning to read. Economically disadvantaged children tend to have low achievement levels in school. A number of explanations for this situation have been suggested; however, the issue is not yet fully resolved. Bilingual children come from backgrounds where a language other than English is spoken. These children should have an opportunity to build an aural-oral background in English and to learn about the culture of the United States prior to learning to read.

3. The success of exceptional children in learning to read is directly related to teachers' abilities to meet their individual needs.

SELF-TEST

Check your knowledge of the information presented in this chapter. The answer key is located in Appendix C.

1. Which of the following statements is true about exceptional children?
   a. they are not different from average children
   b. they must be segregated from other children
   c. they require modification of school practices or special services to develop to their full potential
   d. it is impossible for them to develop to their full potential

2. Which of the following factors are related to the current attitudes toward educating exceptional children?
   a. social attitudes
   b. legal responsibility
   c. mainstreaming
   d. all of the above

3. What is mainstreaming?
   a. segregating exceptional children from the mainstream
   b. integrating exceptional children in regular classrooms
   c. both a and b
   d. neither a nor b

4. Which statement is true of hyperkinetic children?
   a. they are extremely calm and quiet
   b. they are prone to sleeping in class
   c. they are prone to excessive activity
   d. none of the above.

5. Why do EMR and/or EMH children progress slower academically than average children?
   a. they are not interested in learning
   b. they develop one-half to three-fourths slower than average children
   c. they have a large number of nonacademic interests
   d. all of the above

6. What kinds of work are EMR or EMH adults capable of doing?
   a. professional work
   b. white-collar jobs
   c. unskilled or semiskilled labor
   d. none of the above

7. Which of the following phrases describes reading instruction for EMR and EMH students?
   a. concrete
   b. slow-paced
   c. provides immediate feedback
   d. all of the above

8. Why are slow-learning children frequently neglected in the classroom?
   a. they are not as slow as EMR and EMH children
   b. they do not learn as fast as average children
   c. both a and b
   d. neither a nor b

9. What kind of reading program probably works best with learning-disabled children?
   a. no reading program, as they do not need instruction
   b. a modified basal reading program
   c. reading machines and computers
   d. a program based on workbooks

10. What impairments do sensory-handicapped children usually experience?
    a. visual and auditory
    b. they have lost a limb
    c. they are orthopedically handicapped
    d. none of the above

11. What kind of reading program meets the needs of auditorially impaired children?
    a. visual
    b. phonics
    c. tachistoscopic
    d. audiometer

12. What are some of the problems of disadvantaged children?
    a. low motivation
    b. lack of experience

c. language differences

d. all of the above

THOUGHT QUESTIONS

1. Explain the role of classroom teachers in teaching mainstreamed children.
2. Discuss the various factors that contribute to the depressed achievement of minority children.
3. Explain strategies that could be used to help minority children achieve without sacrificing group identity.
4. How does the "immersion" approach to second language learning operate?
5. How can teachers meet the reading needs of children who were once classified as "special education" students?
6. Should classroom teachers be expected to meet the needs of exceptional students in their classrooms?
7. Discuss the basic considerations when teaching students to read whose native language is not English.

ENRICHMENT ACTIVITIES

1. Visit an elementary school and interview the principal to find out how many exceptional children are enrolled in the school. Ask whether these children are mainstreamed, and, if so, determine the school's approach to mainstreaming.
2. Interview teachers who teach exceptional children and ask them to discuss the ways in which they meet the special needs of these children.
3. Plan a reading lesson for an educationally handicapped child. What principles must you keep in mind? How have you addressed thse principles?
4. Plan a reading lesson for a gifted child. What factors do you have to keep in mind when teaching gifted children? How have you done this in your lesson plan?
5. Visit a special education classroom and observe the children in the class. Try to identify the special needs of each child.
6. Make a bibliography of reading materials to use for instruction with economically disadvantaged children. Be prepared to explain each selection.
7. Develop a plan for the language development of a child who is new to this country or new to the English language. List activities and literature that could be used.
8. Read journal articles about developing self-concept. Make a list of strategies that you could use to develop the attitudes and self-concepts of economically disadvantaged children.

RELATED READINGS

Abrams, J. (January 1970). "Learning Disabilities—A Complex Phenomenon," *The Reading Teacher*, Vol. 23, pp. 292–303.

Allen, V. (May 1979). "Books to Lead the Non-English Speaking Elementary Student into Literacy," *The Reading Teacher*, Vol. 32, pp. 940–45.

Conley, M. (April 1985). "Promoting Cross Cultural Understanding Through Content Area Reading Strategies," *Journal of Reading*, Vol. 28, pp. 600–606.

Daniell, B. (September 1984). "Rodney and the Teaching of Standard English," *Language Arts*, Vol. 61, pp. 498–509.

Degler, L. and V. Risko. (May 1979). "Teaching Reading to Mainstreamed Sensory Impaired Children," *The Reading Teacher*, Vol. 32, pp. 921–925.

Feitelson, D. Ed., (1979). Mother Tongue or Second Language? Newark, DE: International Reading Association.

Genesee, F. (Winter 1985). "Second Language Learning Through Immersion," *Review of Educational Research*, Vol. 55, pp. 541–662.

Haimowitz, B. (December 1977). "Motivating Reluctant Readers in Inner-City Classes," *Journal of Reading*, Vol. 21, pp. 227–230.

Haynes, M. and J. Jenkins (Summer 1986). "Reading Instruction in Special Education Resource Rooms," *American Educational Research Journal*, Vol. 23, pp. 161–190.

Kupinsky, B. (November 1983). "Bilingual Reading Instruction in Kindergarten," *The Reading Teacher*, Vol. 37, pp. 132–137.

Labuda, M. (1984). *Creative Reading for Gifted Learners: A Design for Excellence*, 2nd ed., Newark, DE: International Reading Association.

Manson, M. (January 1982). "Explorations in Language Arts for Preschoolers (Who Happen to be Deaf)," *Language Arts*, Vol. 59, pp. 33–39.

McCall, C. (January 1987). "Women and Literacy: The Cuban Experience," *Journal of Reading*, Vol. 30, pp. 318–325.

McGee, L. and G. Tomkins (January 1982). "Concepts About Print for the Young Blind Child," *Language Arts*, Vol. 59, pp. 40–45.

Moustafa, M. and J. Penrose (March 1985). "Comprehensible Input Plus the Language Experience Approach: Reading Instruction for the Limited English Speaking Students," *The Reading Teacher*, Vol. 38, pp. 640–647.

Nelson, G. (February 1987). "Culture's Role in Reading Comprehension: A Schema Theoretical Approach," *Journal of Reading*, Vol. 30, pp. 424–429.

Neuman, S. and E. Pitts. (December 1983). "A Review of Current North American Television for Bilingual Children," *The Reading Teacher*, Vol. 37, pp. 254–260.

Raver, S. and R. Dwyer (December 1986). "Teaching Handicapped Preschoolers to Sight Read Using Language Training Procedures," *The Reading Teacher*, Vol. 40, pp. 314–323.

Seitz, V. (1977). *Social Class and Ethnic Group Differences in Learning to Read*, Newark, DE: International Reading Association.

Rouse, M. and J. Ryan. (December 1984). "Teacher's Guide to Vision Problems," *The Reading Teacher*, Vol. 38, pp. 306–317.

Schon, I. and P. Kennedy (November 1983). "Noteworthy Books in Spanish for Children and Young Adults from Spanish-Speaking Countries," *The Reading Teacher*, Vol. 37, pp. 138–143.

Schon, I. (March 1985). "Remarkable Books in Spanish for Young Readers," *The Reading Teacher*, Vol. 38, pp. 668–673.

Smith, R. and Neisworth, J. (1975). *The Exceptional Child*, New York: McGraw-Hill.

Swiss, T. and T. Olsen (January 1976). "Reading and Gifted Children," *The Reading Teacher*, Vol. 29, pp. 428–431.

Thomis, E. (1976). *Literacy for America's Spanish-Speaking Children*, Newark, DE: International Reading Association.

REFERENCES

Abelson, W., E. Zigler, and C. DeBlasi (1974). "Effects of a Four Year Follow Through Program on Economically Disadvantaged Children," *Journal of Educational Psychology*, Vol. 66, pp. 756–771.

Alexander, C. (February 1980). "Black English Dialect and the Classroom Teacher," *The Reading Teacher*, Vol. 33, pp. 571–577.

Allen, V. (May 1979). "Books to Lead the Non-English Speaking Elementary Student into Literacy," *The Reading Teacher*, Vol. 32, pp. 940–946.

Andelman (March–April 1976). "Teachers' Experiences in Massachusetts," *Today's Education*, Vol. 65, pp. 27–33.

Armour, D. (1972). "School and Family Effects on Black and White Achievement," in *On Equality of Educational Opportunity*, J. Coleman, et al., New York: Random House, pp. 65–75.

Barbe, W. (1984). "Ingredients of a Creative Reading Program," in *Creative Reading for Gifted Learners*, M. Labuda (Ed.), Newark, DE: International Reading Association, pp. 25–31.

Bateman, B. (1965). "An Educator's View of A Diagnostic Approach to Learning Disorders," *Learning Disorders*, Vol. 1, pp. 219–239.

Burke, C. (1973). "Dialect and the Reading Process," in *Language Differences: Do They Interfere?* J. Laffey and R. Shuy (Eds.), Newark, DE: International Reading Association, pp. 91–100.

Cohen, A. D. (1975). *A Sociolinguistic Approach to Bilingual Education*, Rowley, MA: Newberry House.

Cohen, S. A. (1969). *Teach Them All To Read*, New York: Random House.

Cohn, M. and D. Kornelly (January 1970). "For Better Reading—A More Positive Self-Image," *The Elementary School Journal*, Vol. 70, pp. 199–201.

Coleman, J., E. Campbell, C. Hobson, J. McPartland, A. Mood, and F. Weinfeld (1966). *Equality of Educational Opportunity*, Washington, D.C.: U.S. Department of Health, Education, and Welfare, U.S. Government Printing Office.

Cruickshank, W. (1967). *The Brain-Injured Child in Home, School, and Community*, Syracuse, NY: Syracuse University Press.

Degler, L. and V. Risko (May 1979). "Teaching Reading to Mainstreamed Sensory Impaired Children," *The Reading Teacher*, Vol. 32, pp. 921–925.

Education of the Gifted and Talented (1972). Report to Congress by the U. S. Commissioner of Education and Background Papers, submitted to the U.S. Office of Education, no. 72-5020, Washington, D.C.: U.S. Government Printing Office.

Ebel, R. (1972). *Essentials of Educational Measurement*, 2nd ed., Englewood Cliffs, NJ: Prentice-Hall.

Entwisle, D. and J. Webster (1972). "Raising Children's Performance Expectations: A Classroom Demonstration," *Social Science Research*, Vol. 1, pp. 147–158.

Feeley, J. (April 1977). "Bilingual Instruction: Puerto Rico and the Mainland," *The Reading Teacher,* Vol. 30, pp. 741–744.

Flood, J. (May 1977). "Parental Styles in Reading Episodes with Young Children," *The Reading Teacher,* Vol. 30, pp. 864–867.

Froelich, M., F. Blitzer, and J. Greenberg (October 1967). "Success for Disadvantaged Children," *The Reading Teacher,* pp. 24–33.

Gamez, G. (March 1979). "Reading in a Second Language: 'Native Language Approach' vs. 'Direct Method,' " *The Reading Teacher,* Vol. 32, pp. 665–669.

Genesee, F. (Winter 1985). "Second Language Learning Through Immersion: A Review of U.S. Programs," *Review of Educational Research,* Vol. 55, pp. 541–561.

Goertzel, V. and M. Goertzel (1962). *Cradles of Eminence,* Boston: Little, Brown.

Green, R. (October 1975). "Tips on Educational Testing: What Teachers Should Know," *Phi Delta Kappan,* Vol. 56, pp. 89–92.

Grotberg, E. (1972). "Implications of Some Current Issues and Practices for the Reading Teacher," in *Better Reading in the Urban School,* J. Figurel (Ed.), Newark: DE International Reading Association, pp. 56–69.

Harper, R. and G. Kilarr (1978). *Reading and the Law,* Newark, DE: International Reading Association.

Hewett, F. (March 1967). "Educational Engineering with Emotionally Disturbed Children," *Exceptional Children,* Vol. 33, pp. 310–318.

Hunt, B., L. Serling, and E. Theriault (October 1973). "Reading in an Innercity School: A Program that Works," *The Reading Teacher,* Vol. 27, pp. 25–28.

Jencks, C., M. Smith, H. Acland, M. Bane, D. Cohen, H. Gintis, B. Heyns, and S. Michelson (1972). *Inequality: A Reassessment of the Effect of Family and Schooling in America,* New York: Basic Books.

Kaluger, G. and C. Kolson (1978). *Reading and Learning Disabilities,* 2nd ed., Columbus, OH: Merrill.

Kolestoe, O. (1970). *Teaching Educable Mentally Retarded Children,* New York: Holt, Rinehart and Winston.

Kupinsky, B. (November 1983). "Bilingual Reading Instruction in Kindergarten," *The Reading Teacher,* Vol. 37, pp. 132–137.

Labov, W. (1972). *Language in the Inner City: Studies in the Black English Vernacular,* Philadelphia: University of Pennsylvania Press.

Labuda, M. (1985). *Creating Reading for Gifted Learners: A Design for Excellence,* 2nd ed., Newark, DE: International Reading Association.

McNiel, N. (November 1975). "I.Q. Tests and the Black Culture," *Phi Delta Kappan,* Vol. 56, pp. 209–210.

Melmed, P. (1973). "Black English Phonology: The Question of Reading Interference," in *Language Differences: Do They Interfere?* J. Laffey and R. Shuy (Eds.), Newark, DE: International Reading Association, pp. 70–85.

Minkoff, D. (October 1984). "Game Activities for Practicing English as a Second Language," *Journal of Reading,* Vol. 28, pp. 40–42.

Modiano, N. (1973). "Jaunito's Reading Problems: Foreign Language Interference and Reading Skill Acquisition," *Language Differences: Do They Interfere?* J. Laffey and R. Shuy (Eds.), Newark, DE: International Reading Association, pp. 31–41.

Neill, G. (November 1979). "Washington Report," *Phi Delta Kappan,* Vol. 61, p. 158.

Ogbu, J. (December 1985). "Research Currents: Cultural-Ecological Influences on Minority School Learning," *Language Arts,* Vol. 62, pp. 860–869.

Ornstein, A. (February 1976). "I.Q. Tests and the Culture Issue," *Phi Delta Kappan,* Vol. 57, pp. 403–404.

Rist, R. (1970). "Student Social Class and Teacher Expectations: The Self-Fulfilling Prophecy in Ghetto Education," *Harvard Educational Review,* Vol. 40, pp. 411–451.

Rupley, W. and C. Robeck (February 1978). "ERIC/RCS: Black Dialect and Reading Achievement," *The Reading Teacher,* Vol. 31, p. 598.

Rutherford, W. (1970). "Teaching Reading to Children with Dialect Differences," in *Reading Goals for the Disadvantaged,* J. Figurel (Ed.), Newark, DE: International Reading Association, pp. 112–123.

Rystrom, R. (1973). "Reading, Language, and Nonstandard Dialect, A Research Report," in *Language Differences: Do They Interfere?* J. Laffey and R. Shuy (Eds.), Newark: DE: International Reading Association, pp. 86–90.

Seitz, V. (1977). *Social Class and Ethnic Group Differences in Learning to Read,* Newark, DE: International Reading Association.

Shuy, R. (1973). "Nonstandard Dialect Problems: An Overview," in *Language Differences: Do They Interfere?* J. Laffey and R. Shuy (Eds.), Newark, DE: International Reading Association, pp. 3–16.

Shafer, R. (1984). "Fostering Creative Reading at the Intermediate Level," in *Creative Reading for Gifted Learners,* M. Labuda (Ed.), Newark, DE: International Reading Association, pp. 80–96.

Smith, R. and J. Neisworth (1975). *The Exceptional Child: A Functional Approach,* New York: McGraw-Hill.

Spolsky, B. and R. Cooper, Eds., *Frontiers of Bilingual Education,* Rowley, MA: Newberry House.

Staff Article (March–April 1976). "What's It All About? Mainstreaming," *Today's Education,* Vol. 65, pp. 18–19.

Strickland, D. (1972). "Expanding the Language Power of Young Black Children, A Literature Approach," in *Better Reading for Urban Schools,* J. Figurel (Ed.), Newark, DE: International Reading Association, pp. 9–17.

Terman, L. (June 1954). "The Discovery and Encouragement of Exceptional Talent," *American Psychologist,* Vol. 9, pp. 556–565.

Wallen, C. (1984). "Fostering Reading Growth for Gifted and Creative Readers at the Primary Level," in *Creative Reading for Gifted Learners,* M. Labuda (Ed.), Newark, DE: International Reading Association, pp. 70–79.

Witty, P. (1951). *The Gifted Child,* Lexington, MA: D.C. Heath.

———. (1984). "Rationale for Fostering Creative Reading in the Gifted and the Creative," in *Creative Reading for Gifted Learners,* 2nd ed., M. Labuda (Ed.), Newark, DE: International Reading Association, pp. 8–23.

Venezky, R. and R. Chapman (1973). "Is Learning to Read Dialect Bound?" in *Language Differences: Do They Interfere?* J. Laffey and R. Shuy (Eds.), Newark, DE: International Reading Association, pp. 62–69.

Sight Word and Phrase Lists

95 NOUNS COMMON TO THE THREE WORD LISTS

apple	duck	milk
baby	egg	money
back	eye	morning
ball	farm	mother
bear	farmer	name
bed	father	nest
bell	feet	night
bird	fire	paper
birthday	fish	party
boat	floor	picture
box	flower	pig
boy	game	rabbit
bread	garden	rain
brother	girl	ring
cake	goodbye	robin
car	grass	Santa Claus
cat	ground	school
chair	hand	seed
chicken	head	sheep
children	hill	shoe
Christmas	home	sister
coat	horse	snow
corn	house	song
cow	kitty	squirrel
day	leg	stock
dog	letter	street
doll	man	sun
door	men	table

Source: "95 Nouns Common to Three Word Lists" by Edward W. Dolch. © 1948 DLM Teaching Resources, Allen, TX 75002. Reprinted with permission.

thing	tree	wind
time	watch	window
top	water	wood
toy	way	

A BASIC SIGHT VOCABULARY OF 220 WORDS

Since these 220 words make up 50 percent to 75 percent of all ordinary reading matter, they should be recognized instantly by sight by all school children.

a	can	get
about	carry	give
after	clean	go
again	cold	goes
all	come	going
always	could	good
am	cut	got
an		green
and	did	grow
any	do	
are	docs	had
around	done	has
as	don't	have
ask	down	he
at	draw	help
ate	drink	her
away		here
	eat	him
be	eight	his
because	every	hold
been		hot
before	fall	how
best	far	hurt
better	fast	
big	find	I
black	first	if
blue	five	in
both	fly	into
bring	for	is
brown	found	it
but	four	its
buy	from	
by	full	jump
	funny	just
call		
came	gave	keep

Source: "A Basic Sight Vocabulary of 220 Words" by Edward W. Dolch. © 1945 DLM Teaching Resources, Allen, TX 75002. Reprinted with permission.

kind
know

laugh
let
light
like
little
live
long
look

made
make
many
may
me
much
must
my
myself

never
new
no
not
now

of
old
on
once
one
only
open
or
our
out
over
own

pick
play
please
pretty

pull
put

ran
read
red
ride
right
round
run

said
saw
say
see
seven
shall
she
show
sing
sit
six
sleep
small
so
some
soon
start
stop

take
tell
ten
thank
that
the
their
them
then
there
these
they
think
this
those

three
to
today
together
too
try
two

under
up
upon
us
use

very

walk
want
warm
was
wash
we
well
went
were
what
when
where
which
white
who
why
will
wish
with
work
would
write

yellow
yes
you
your

SIGHT PHRASE CARDS

These sight phrases are comprised of the 95 most common nouns and the Dolch basic sight word vocabulary of 220 words.

can live	has come back	in the grass
down the hill	as he said	a new book
will walk	the funny rabbit	the red cow
in the barn	at three	the little children
they are	has run away	to stop
if you can	on the chair	when you come
what I say	with mother	the new doll
all day	down there	when I can
some bread	my father	has found
you were	so much	the white duck
to the farm	his brother	is coming
her father	you will do	will go
on the floor	so long	for the girl
from the tree	must be	if I must
was made	will buy	down
at home	some cake	as he did
the black horse	as I said	when I wish
you will like	too soon	the small boy
went away	what I want	it was
in the window	I was	down the street
in the box	at once	the red apple
for him	for them	the little pig
I may go	will think	the little chickens
from home	the black bird	with us
the old men	a new hat	would want
for the baby	about it	all night
the new coat	he is	her mother
a big horse	to go	is going
then he came	we were	it is
by the house	the little dog	will read
the old man	at school	to the school
the small boat	by the tree	they were
I am	up here	he was
a pretty picture	would like	in the garden
as I do	went down	from the farm
he would try	the yellow cat	my brother
we are	up there	your sister
a pretty home	the funny man	too little
must go	I may get	I will come
his sister	if you wish	could make
if I may	can play	I will go
you are	has made	to the barn
did not go	when you know	can fly

Source: "Dolch Sight Phrases" by Edward W. Dolch. © 1949 DLM Teaching Resources, Allen, TX 75002. Reprinted with permission.

a big house
about him
then he said
could eat
to the nest

did not fall
in the water
will look
the yellow ball
was found

your mother
can run
to the house
the white sheep

Graph for Estimating Readability

Average number of syllables per 100 words

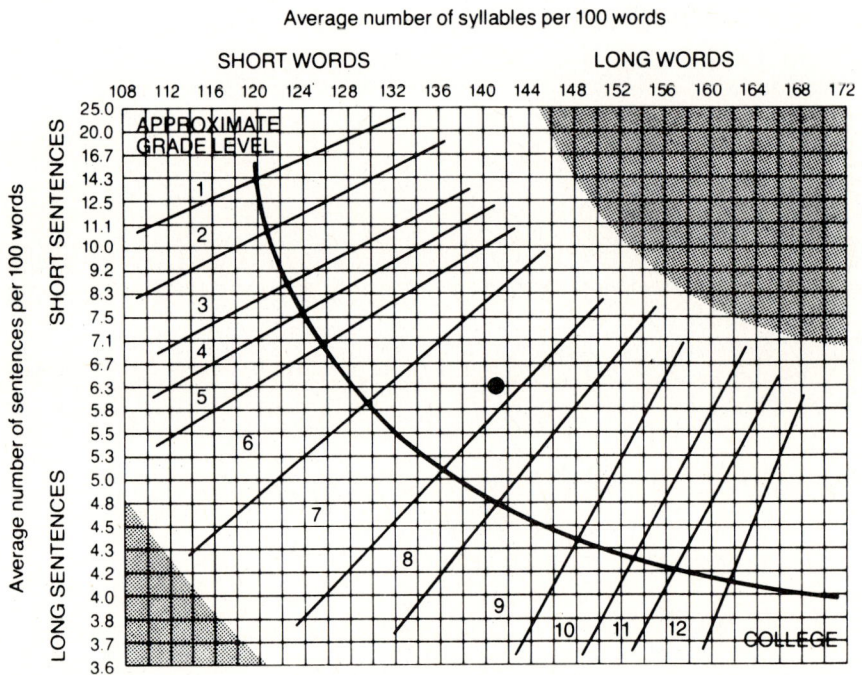

Directions: Randomly select three 100-word passages from a book or an article. Plot the average number of syllables and the average number of sentences per 100 words on the graph to determine the grade level of the material. Choose

Source: Edward Fry, *Journal of Reading,* Vol. 11 (April 1968) and *Reading Teacher* (March 1969). Reprinted with permission.

more passages per book if great variability is observed, and conclude that the book has uneven readability. Few books will fall in the gray area, but when they do, grade-level scores are invalid.

EXAMPLE:

		Syllables	Sentences
1st Hundred Words		124	6.6
2nd Hundred Words		141	5.5
3rd Hundred Words		<u>158</u>	<u>6.8</u>
	Average	141	6.3

Readability 7th Grade (see dot plotted on graph)

APPENDIX C

Answers to Self-Tests

CHAPTER 1
1. c
2. c
3. a
4. c
5. a
6. d
7. a
8. c
9. a
10. a
11. d
12. d
13. b
14. c
15. d
16. a
17. a
18. c
19. d
20. b
21. a
22. d
23. d
24. a

CHAPTER 2
1. d
2. b
3. c
4. a
5. b
6. c
7. b
8. c
9. c

10. b
11. d
12. d
13. d
14. d
15. a
16. a
17. a
18. d
19. d
20. b
21. b
22. d
23. d
24. b
25. d
26. b
27. a
28. b
29. c
30. a

CHAPTER 3
1. d
2. b
3. b
4. d
5. b
6. a
7. d
8. c
9. b
10. a
11. b
12. c
13. a

14. d
15. d
16. a
17. b
18. b
19. a
20. b

CHAPTER 4
1. b
2. c
3. d
4. a
5. b
6. b
7. c
8. a
9. b
10. c
11. a
12. c
13. a
14. b
15. c
16. a
17. c
18. a
19. b
20. c
21. b
22. c
23. a
24. a
25. a
26. b
27. c

28. b
29. a
30. c
31. c

CHAPTER 5
1. b
2. c
3. c
4. c
5. c
6. a
7. b
8. d
9. c
10. d
11. b
12. d
13. a
14. b
15. d
16. b
17. c
18. a
19. a
20. c
21. d
22. a
23. b
24. c
25. b
26. a

CHAPTER 6
1. b
2. a

3. b
4. b
5. d
6. c
7. d
8. a
9. b
10. d
11. b
12. d
13. b
14. d
15. d
16. b
17. c
18. a
19. b
20. c
21. a
22. b
23. a
24. b
25. c

CHAPTER 7
1. c
2. b
3. a
4. d
5. d
6. b
7. c

8. c
9. a
10. c
11. d
12. b
13. a
14. c
15. d
16. a
17. b
18. c
19. c
20. b
21. c
22. a
23. d

CHAPTER 8
1. a
2. c
3. b
4. d
5. d
6. b
7. a
8. b
9. c
10. c
11. c
12. a
13. b
14. d

15. c
16. d
17. d

CHAPTER 9
1. c
2. c
3. c
4. a
5. d
6. c
7. c
8. b
9. b
10. c
11. a
12. c
13. b
14. a
15. c
16. a
17. d
18. b
19. c
20. c
21. c
22. b

CHAPTER 10
1. c
2. b
3. d

4. c
5. a
6. c
7. c
8. c
9. a
10. c
11. d
12. a
13. b
14. b
15. d
16. d
17. d
18. d
19. c
20. a

CHAPTER 11
1. c
2. d
3. b
4. c
5. b
6. c
7. b
8. b
9. b
10. a
11. a
12. d

Glossary

Accent   The amount of stress (force) used to pronounce a syllable. Syllables may have a primary or secondary accent.

Accountability   The responsibility of a school system (and/or teachers) for educating students.

Achievement groups   Grouping students for instruction on the basis of their academic success.

Activating schemata   Recalling schemata that are related to a specific subject and relating these schemata to the content being read.

Analogy decoding   Comparing unknown words with known words or word parts. For example, the word *bluster* could be decoded by comparing *blus* with *blush* and *ter* with the final syllable in *rooster.*

Analytic phonics (intrinsic phonics)   Instruction based on teaching phonemes through known words. New words are decoded through analysis.

Argument   Literature whose purpose it is to persuade the reader.

Attention deficit disorder   Individuals who cannot attend to a task. This term is often used to describe individuals who were formerly labeled hyperactive or hyperkinetic. Some educators believe that attention deficit disorder is a more accurate label, as the learning difficulty stems from students' inability to attend to a task long enough to learn.

Auditory discrimination   The ability to hear likenesses and differences in sounds (phonemes).

Automaticity   Decoding words without conscious effort.

Basal readers   Graded reading textbooks that contain graded reading passages arranged in sequential order. They usually begin with readiness level materials and extend through sixth- or eighth-grade level.

Big books   Enlarged versions of books and stories that children have enjoyed hearing read. The larger size helps children focus on the print as they develop literacy skills.

Bilingual   Students whose mother tongue is not English and who may speak more than one language.

Blend   A cluster of two or three consonants that appear together but each consonant retains its original sound.

Blending   The ability to combine sounds (phonemes) in order to pronounce a word.

Bound morpheme   A morpheme that must be combined with a second morpheme in order to form a word. *Ante* in the word *anteroom* is an example of a bound morpheme.

Chunking The memory system processes chunks of information that may consist of letters or words. A letter and a word are equivalent chunks that require equal amounts of processing in memory.

Cloze A procedure that is based on the systematic deletion of words from a selection (every fifth or tenth word, leaving only the first and last sentences intact). The reader is then instructed to supply the deleted words.

Clustering Grouping related information, ideas, or concepts together to aid recall.

Cognitive psychology theories Learning theories that view human beings as active processors of information and purposeful learners. Learning is considered to be the end result of understanding and experience.

Cognitive skills An individual's thinking skills.

Cohesion The relationship or link between sentences. Sentences that are cohesive are related to one another and are easier to understand. There are five types of cohesion: reference, substitution, ellipsis, conjunction, and lexical.

Competency testing Tests administered to students to determine whether they have achieved the minimum skills specified by the state in which they live. These tests usually assess reading and mathematics skills, and are often used to determine whether a student will be permitted to graduate from high school.

Composing The part of the writing process during which students write their thoughts.

Comprehension The ability to understand written content. Comprehension is based on the student's ability to utilize language, thought, and experience to reconstruct, interpret, and apply written content.

Concept A generalized idea about a category (class) of objects, events, or ideas.

Conceptualizing The process of abstracting the common features and specifying a general category.

Conclusion A statement of a narrow relationship between two concepts; for example, *Jane has lost weight; perhaps she is on a diet.*

Connotation Emotional reactions that are associated with a particular word.

Consonant A sound produced by a flow of air through the mouth that is completely or partially broken by the lips, teeth, and tongue to produce variations in sound. The letters of the alphabet that are not vowels or semivowels are called consonants.

Content materials Textbooks and reference materials used for teaching and learning social studies, science, and mathematics in the elementary school program. Secondary content materials are broader in scope and include such topics as business education and home economics.

Context clues Clues to word recognition that result from word meaning and syntax.

Controlled vocabulary The planned repetition of words, as well as limiting the number of new words introduced at one time.

Creative comprehension Understanding that is based on imaginative, original thinking, which requires the reader to think beyond the lines of print that are being read.

Creative dramatics Informal and often spontaneous interpretation of literature or children's experiences.

Criterion-referenced tests Tests that compare a student's performance to an absolute standard with a specified behavioral performance criterion. (The focus is on what a student can do.)

Critical (evaluative) reading Thinking critically about written content with the aim of evaluating the material. The reader makes judgments about the content and the author's style.

Cultural literacy   World knowledge that enables readers to comprehend text. An example is knowing that the date 1492 refers to the year Columbus discovered America. When readers have this world knowledge, authors do not have to provide a detailed explanation of their reference to that date.

Curriculum   The experiences that develop children's knowledge and skills. The curriculum could be viewed as an intellectual journey that students take in order to become educated.

Curriculum guide   The written reference that identifies a school's philosophy, as well as the scope and sequence of skills to be developed in the various curriculur areas.

DEAR   Drop Everything and Read, which is another acronym for the sustained, silent reading program (SSR and USSR) during which everyone in a classroom or school reads. This is a recreational reading program rather than an instructional program.

Decoding   The skill of recognizing words and associating meaning with a printed word.

Deductive learning   Learning that occurs as a result of being taught specific rules and examples.

Denotation   A formal definition of a word, such as a dictionary definition.

Diacritical marks   Marks used to indicate letter (phoneme) sounds. (For example, the breve [˘] is used to show a short vowel sound.)

Dialect   Language variation that is unique to the various geographic areas of the United States.

Differentiated grouping   Children who are clustered for instruction for specific purposes, such as achievement, skills needs, interests, projects, or friendship.

Digraph   Consonant digraphs are combinations of two consonants that produce a sound that differs from that of the individual letters. The *sh* in *shoe* is a consonant digraph. A vowel digraph is a combination of two letters that represent a single sound. The *oa* in *boat* is a vowel digraph.

Direct instruction   Instruction that occurs when the teacher is interacting with students. During direct instruction, the teacher may define, demonstrate, give examples, model, and guide students' practice.

Directed reading lesson   An instructional plan that includes reading preparation, an introduction of vocabulary and concepts, silent reading, discussion, and extension.

Discourse   Formal speech or writing.

Discourse analysis   Making use of the writing style and organization of the content to aid understanding.

Discussion   Two or more individuals talking and listening as they examine, think about, and share ideas regarding a topic.

D-R-T-A   The Directed-Reading-and-Thinking-Activity.

Eclectic basal reader   Readers that are based on a global approach to reading instruction and that incorporate a combination of word-recognition approaches.

Economically disadvantaged   Individuals from lower socioeconomic backgrounds. Socioeconomic status is determined by family income, parental education, and family size.

Educational Resources Information Center (ERIC)   A nationwide information system. This reading and communication skills center is located at the headquarters of the National Council of Teachers of English at Urbana, Illinois.

Elaboration   Elaboration is embellishing the text. This involves using prior knowledge, inferring, creating mental images, and paraphrasing.

Elementary and Secondary Education Act, Title One   Federal legislation aimed at improving reading ability that provides funds for teachers, in-service education, materials, and equipment.

Emotionally disturbed   Students who are emotionally maladjusted. This may be expressed through aggression, withdrawal, bizarre behavior, or anxiety.

EMR (*or* EMH)   Educable mentally retarded children who exhibit a depression in learning rate and capacity, and whose I.Q. range is 50 to 75.

Encoding   Mentally arranging information for storage in memory.

ESL   English as a second language. ESL students are ones whose native language is not English.

Exceptional children   Children who require modification of school practices or special services in order to develop to their full potential.

Exposition   Content written to impart information.

Extrinsic motivation   Motivation arising from external sources.

Figurative language   A picturesque, expressive, connotative use of language.

Fixation   Periodic stops that the eyes make during reading that last approximately a quarter of a second.

Flexible skill group   Clusters of children that are organized for specific skill instruction. These groups are of short duration and are disbanded when instruction is completed.

Formal assessment   Evaluation based on the use of standardized, norm-referenced, or criterion-referenced tests.

Free morpheme   A morpheme that is used independently; for example, *dog.*

Fry Readability Graph   A graph that makes use of a syllable count and average sentence length to estimate the reading difficulty of content.

Functional literacy   A reading level at which the individual can perform necessary reading tasks.

Functional reading   Reading to acquire information, solve problems, and do research.

Generalization   The statement of a broad relationship between two concepts, such as *all animals require oxygen.*

Generative (transformational) linguistics   The study of the knowledge people use to produce their own language and to understand the language of others.

Gifted   Individuals who are capable of exceptional achievement.

Grapheme   A written phoneme, such as *t.*

Graphic symbols   Written words and letters.

Graphic aids   Maps, charts, graphs, tables, and pictures that are used to aid students' understanding of content.

Gray-Robinson model   A model of the reading process that takes into account perception, comprehension, reaction, assimilation, and rate.

High imagery words   Words the learner can associate with a concrete visual image, such as *cat* and *dog.*

High utility words   Words that occur frequently in written content.

Hyperactive (hyperkinesis)   Students who are prone to excessive activity, excessive mobility, or restless behavior. These children cannot control their own behavior.

IEP   An individual education plan that is mandated by legislation related to students who have special educational needs. An individual educational plan is based on the student's needs, achievement, and potential.

Independent reading level   The level at which a reader can read with 99 percent word recognition and 90 percent or more comprehension.

Independence (in word recognition)   The ability to decode words without assistance.

Index   The section at the end of a book that lists the major topics discussed in the book and the page numbers on which those topics are discussed.

Indirect instruction   Planned learning activities that occur without a teacher's immediate interaction. Completing worksheets or workbooks are usually indirect instructional activities.

Individualized reading   A reading program in which trade books are used rather than basal readers. Children read material they are interested in at their own pace. This approach also involves student-teacher conferences.

Inductive learning   Learning that occurs through experience and that leads the student to generalize concepts.

Informal assessment   Using such materials as checklists, informal inventories, and anecdotal records of observations to assess students.

Informal reading inventory (IRI)   A nonstandardized instrument that can be designed by a teacher to assess reading skills.

Information processing model   A model of the reading process that is based on the assumption that written language is transformed into meaning through a sequence of stages.

Intelligence   The ability to learn and apply knowledge.

Intelligence tests   Instruments used to assess intelligence.

Interclass groups   Clusters of children within a class for instructional purposes.

Interest group   Children who have a common interest and who are grouped together.

Interest inventory   An oral or written instrument designed to identify student's individual propensities. The information derived from interest inventories is used to guide students in selecting reading materials.

Interpretation (inference)   Comprehending meanings that are not directly stated in content by relating facts, generalizations, definitions, values, and skills. The reader must discover the relationships among these elements in order to interpret the passage.

Intraclass grouping   Forming instructional units of students from various classes. These groupings may cross grade lines, so that children from different grade levels work together.

Intrinsic motivation   Motivation that arises from factors within the individual.

IRI   An informal reading inventory that is usually teacher-made.

Instructional reading level   The level at which the reader can read with 95 percent word recognition and 90 percent comprehension.

Job literacy gap   The distance between an individual's reading and writing ability and that ability demanded by jobs available to that individual.

Key words (organic words)   The words an individual selects to learn. These words have emotional impact for the child. Key words are usually associated with the language-experience approach to reading instruction.

Language   A system of arbitrary vocal symbols used for human communication.

Language arts   Speaking, listening, reading, and writing are considered to be the four language arts.

Language-experience approach   An approach to reading instruction that utilizes stories that children dictate to teachers who write them down for students to read. As children learn to read and write more fluently, they write their own reading materials.

Learning   A relatively permanent process that is inferred from performance changes due to practice.

Learning disabled   Children whose academic learning is one or more years below their mental age. Such children may have difficulty in perceptual-motor skills, language and speech, or thought processes.

Learning stations   An individualized approach to instruction that is based on independent learning activities.

Linguistics   The study of language as it is used by speakers of the language.

Listening comprehension (auding)   The level at which children can understand content that is read to them and answer questions based on that content.

Literacy   The reading and skills required by the average person to live a reasonably comfortable life in our society.

Literal comprehension   Understanding ideas that are directly stated in a selection.

Literature   A body of writings that may include fiction, nonfiction and poetry. It is imaginative use of language.

Literature reading   The reading program that develops interest in and appreciation for literature.

Literature web   A plan for teaching literature.

Long-term memory   A relatively permanent memory system with an almost unlimited capacity.

Low imagery words   Words that are difficult to associate with a specific visual image, such as *that* and *way*.

Miscue   Oral reading responses that deviate from the printed text. Miscues result from the use and misuse of available language cues.

Modified alphabet   Alterations made in the alphabet to develop a more consistent sound-symbol relationship than the traditional alphabet permits.

Morphemes   The smallest units of meaning in English. They may occur as free morphemes or bound morphemes.

Morphology   The study of words and word parts.

Motivation   That which activates the learning process and gives direction and intensity to human behavior.

Narrative (story) content   Written materials that tell a story by making use of the elements of plot, theme, characterization, setting, and style.

National Assessment of Educational Progress (NAEP)   A program to assess students' skills in reading and other subject areas. It provides census-like data regarding the educational attainment of American youngsters.

Nonstandard English   A dialectical variation of standard English.

Norm-referenced tests   Tests that compare a child's reading performance with the achievement level of average children at that same grade level.

Norms   Values that describe the performance of various groups on a test or inventory.

Open classroom   A situation where children are free to move around in the classroom as they work with various types of learning materials.

Oral reading   Interpreting literature or reading content aloud.

Paraphrase A restatement of information in an equivalent form.

Peabody Rebus Reading Program A reading program that uses pictures to represent common objects, thereby reducing the number of words the reader must decode.

Perception Associating meaning with information derived from the sense organs. The brain interprets messages from our sensory capacity in the perceptual process.

Phoneme The smallest unit of sound in English, for example, /t/.

Phoneme-grapheme correspondence A letter-sound relationship. For example, the letter *t* represents the sound /t/.

Phonemics The sound system necessary to pronounce the English language.

Phonics The study of the relationship between spoken sounds and written symbols. Phonics involves the analysis of whole words into smaller units.

Phonics skills Decoding skills based on the spelling and sound systems of English.

Phonetics The study and classification of sounds made in speech.

Pitch The height of the voice when pronouncing words.

Poetry A form of literature that involves a special use of language. Poetry is a compact style of writing that attempts to capture the essence of its subject.

Positive reinforcement Pleasant associations with a response that increase the likelihood of the response reoccurring.

Principal An instructional leader of an individual school.

Propaganda A deliberate attempt to influence others.

Psycholinguistics The study of the relationship between language, thought, and the learning process.

Public Law 94–142 The law that insures the right of children to the maximum education from which they can benefit. This law requires that schools document students' educational progress.

Rate adjustment Modifying one's reading rate on the basis of the content, interest, purpose, and familiarity with the material.

Readability The level of difficulty of the content, which is determined by vocabulary, sentence length, sentence complexity, abstractness of concepts, writing style, interest, reader's experiences, and type of print.

Reading The ability to obtain meaning from a written message. A form of communication between reader and writer.

Reading readiness The point at which the individual's skills and the instructional strategies used make it possible for the student to acquire reading ability efficiently.

Reader's theater An oral interpretation of literature by two or more students in front of an audience.

Reciprocal Questioning Procedure (ReQuest) A comprehension strategy that develops active comprehension and questioning skills.

Regressions The eyes return to words that were previously seen on the printed page.

Rehearsal Repeating information (either orally or mentally) to aid retention.

Reinforcers Events that occur close in time to the response. They may have either a positive or negative influence.

Remedial reading Instruction designed to meet the needs of children who fail to progress at a normal rate in the acquisition of reading skills.

Remedial reading teachers The faculty who instruct children who are experiencing difficulty in learning to read.

Retrieval Recalling information stored in memory.

Scanning   Reading rapidly to get an overview of content and to identify main ideas.

Schema   A framework or cognitive pattern.

Schwa   An unstressed vowel that sounds like a short *u,* as in the word *alone.* The diacritical marking is ə.

Self-concept   The set of attitudes and beliefs that one holds about oneself.

Semantic network (map)   A diagram that illustrates the various dimensions of a concept.

Semivowel   A letter that may function as either a vowel or a consonant; for example, *y* and *w.*

Sensory handicap (perceptual)   Individuals who have difficulty interpreting the data that are transmitted to the brain by the senses.

Shared book experience   Using an enlarged book based on a trade book or story that children have enjoyed to develop literacy skills.

Short-term memory   A limited capacity system in which information is retained for only a brief period of time. During this interval, information is either processed into long-term memory or it is lost.

Sight words   Words that are memorized.

Silent reading   Reading that is done mentally and that does not involve oral pronunciation (interpretation) of reading content.

Skills management system   An organizational and monitoring system for reading skills.

Skimming   Reading rapidly to identify specific pieces of information.

Slow learners   Students who learn slower than average children and whose I.Q.'s range from 75 to 90.

Sociolinguistics   The study of language differences that are related to such social contexts as regional differences, educational levels, social class differences, and social setting.

Social reading groups   Units of students based on friendship relationships.

SQ3R   A study method involving the following steps: surveying, questioning, reading, reciting, and rereading.

Standardized tests   Tests that have been standardized by administering them to various sample groups under standardized conditions.

Stimulus-response theories   Learning theory that involves three elements: the stimulus (object or idea), the response (learner's reaction), and the stimulus-response bond (the connection between the stimulus and the response).

Storage   Placing information in memory for later retrieval.

Story grammar   The structure of fiction. Stories are structured through setting, problem, attempts to solve problems, and problem resolution.

Stress   The loudness with which a syllable is pronounced.

Structural analysis   Using root words, prefixes, suffixes, inflectional endings, and contractions as units of meaning to recognize words.

Structural linguistics   A description of oral language that takes into consideration phonemics, morphology, and syntax.

Structured overview   A diagram that shows the relationships among concepts and between concepts and words.

Study reading   A slow style of reading that permits the reader to think as well as make notes.

Subtests   Subgroups of items that are developed to measure specific subareas of a more general ability.

Supervisor   An administrator who is responsible for implementing the reading program for a school system.

Syllable   A basic unit for sounding words. Each syllable must include a vowel sound.

Syntax   Word order or grammar.

Synthetic phonics (explicit phonics)   A phonics program in which the sounds of letters are initially taught first and children later learn how to blend these sounds to build words.

Teacher's aides   Adjunct personnel in the school who help teachers.

Technical vocabulary   Words that represent concepts and have specialized meanings. These words occur frequently in content reading materials.

Test reliability   This term refers to consistency in measurement.

Test validity   The ability of a test to measure what it purports to measure.

Textbook organizer   A written introduction to content that helps students focus on the major ideas and relationships in the text.

Three-level study guide   A written aid to guide study and comprehension that includes questions at the literal, interpretive, and applicative levels.

Time on task   The amount of time spent on a specific assignment or learning activity. For example, the amount of time a student spends actually reading.

USSR (Uninterrupted Sustained Silent Reading)   A recreational reading activity during which everyone in the school or class reads. Such reading activities develop students' reading pleasure, gives them opportunities to practice applying reading skills, and allows them to concentrate on silent reading.

Visual discrimination   The ability to see likenesses and differences in printed words and letters.

Visualizing   Creating mental images of what one is reading. Visualizing is associated with comprehension ability.

Vowel   A sound produced by an unbroken flow of air through the mouth, with variations created by the vocal cords and changing the shape of the mouth cavity. Vowels include *a, e, i, o,* and *u.* Vowels may be long or short, or broad, or have a schwa sound.

Web   A drawing that illustrates the network of relationships among words and related concepts or the relationships within a story or an expository selection.

Whole language   A philosophy of literacy instruction based on the concept that children need to experience language as an integrated whole—to construct a message from print that substantially matches that of the writer. This philosophy focuses on the need for an integrated approach to language arts instruction within a context that is meaningful for students.

Word recognition   Associating pronunciation and meaning with a printed word.

Index